L LOVE ♥ 8-9, 81 (Sexual desire)

Affectionate 34, 36, 44 — why not LOVE? the word?

Princ. of Psyc. 65.

William James

· —— ·

Selected Unpublished Correspondence
1885–1910

William James

· ——— ·

Selected Unpublished Correspondence
1885–1910

Edited by
FREDERICK J. DOWN SCOTT

· ——— ·

Ohio State University Press · Columbus

1986

Library of Congress Cataloguing-in-Publication Data

James, William, 1842–1910.
　William James: selected unpublished correspondence,
1885–1910.

　Bibliography: p.
　Includes index.
　1. James William, 1842–1910—Correspondence.
2. Philosophers—United States—Correspondence.
3. Psychologists—United States—Correspondence.
I. Scott, Frederick J. Down.　II. Title.
B945.J24A4　1986　　191　　86-720
ISBN 0-8142-0379-5

To My Wife

ROSE PAPAC SCOTT

Contents

Preface

THE CORRESPONDENCE HAS BEEN DIVIDED INTO SIX-
teen chapters, each having about an equal number of
letters. It is not surprising that the volume of James's
correspondence increased as he became more famous
and involved in public affairs. A short introduction to
each chapter has been provided to give the reader some
perspective or setting before the details are read.

To preserve the original flavor of James's writing, with
few exceptions an attempt has been made not to alter his
style by modernizing his punctuation, by translating the
foreign words used, by supplying italics for the title of
books and for foreign words, by expanding abbrevia-
tions, or by changing his spelling. With regard to the
latter in particular, the reader should not think that ty-
pographical errors have been allowed to creep into the
text. James used simplified spelling at times in his letters, though seldom in his published works. However,
since he often wrote his letters in great haste, he at times
left out the date of the year. It is hoped that these miss-
ing dates have been accurately supplied. Also, in some
few cases, James assigned the wrong year.

The words James underlined for emphasis will be
shown in italics.

The editor wishes to thank publicly Mr. Alexander R.
James for his kind permission to publish this selection of
letters and Mrs. Catherine Porter Short, James's grand-

daughter, for reading the manuscript and for her ceaseless and indispensable encouragement. The present William James gave crucial support for this publication of his grandfather's letters. Gratitude is also owed to the fifty or more institutions that generously furnished the documents and gave their permission to publish them. Each institution will be named when the source for a given letter is first cited in the notes. Many people, too many to count and name, have graciously replied to my inquiries for information to identify the references made in the letters. I wish to thank the staff of the Ohio State University Press but especially Weldon A. Kefauver for his extraordinary efforts in my behalf. The last to be mentioned but first to be thanked is my wife for her endless hours of assistance.

William James

·———·

Selected Unpublished Correspondence
1885–1910

Introduction

OTHER THAN THE INITIAL PARAGRAPHS, THIS INTRO-
duction is divided into four parts. Part one provides a
brief background of James's life up to the time when the
correspondence begins. Part two traces the development of his writings and the major events in his life after
1885 until his death in 1910. Part three points out some
themes that recur throughout the correspondence and
help to accentuate his character. Part four touches lightly on the relation of the present edition to other publications that deal with James's letters.

Ralph Barton Perry in his Pulitzer Prize-winning
Thought and Character of William James (1935) maintained that in 1885 William James "came of age." That
year has been chosen as the point of departure for this
collection of James's previously unpublished correspondence covering the last twenty-five years of his life. Two
criteria were used for this collection. The first was the
appropriateness of the correspondence to demonstrate
the continuous and harmonious integration of James's
talents, interests, and achievements in the fields of science, psychology, and philosophy. The second was the
appropriateness of the correspondence to portray James
as a pivot around which revolved the lives and works of
so many important women and men. As a result this
edition hopes to furnish the readers with a vivid, de-
tailed, and personal account of a twenty-five year slice of

both American and European intellectual history. The life of James was an important influence on the intellectual character of his times, but also influential were the lives of many of his friends and colleagues, both young and old, with whom he corresponded.

I

William James was born in New York City on 11 January 1842. He was the first of five children born to Henry and Mary R. Walsh James. The others were Henry, Garth Wilkinson, Robertson, and Alice. William's early education was benefitted by two trips to Europe, where his parents took him and his brother Henry. When the family lived in Newport, Rhode Island, James showed an interest in painting. This talent of keen perception and depiction continued to be manifest in his later dealings with people and with intellectual issues. He once remarked, in a perhaps unintentional autobiographical way, "Expertness in philosophy is measured by the definiteness of our summarizing reactions, by the immediate perceptive epithet with which the expert hits such complex objects off."

After much wavering James entered Harvard University's Lawrence Scientific School in 1861; he studied chemistry under Charles W. Eliot and comparative anatomy and physiology under Jeffries Wyman and Louis Agassiz. In 1869 James earned an M.D. degree, also from Harvard, though he never practiced medicine. In that same year, Eliot became president of Harvard. In August of 1872, he appointed James as an instructor in physiology beginning January 1873. In his diary for 10 February, James wrote, "I decide today to stick to biology for a profession in case I am not called to a chair of Philosophy . Philosophy I will nevertheless regard as my vocation." In 1876 he was made an assistant professor of physiology. Though he continued to offer "Natural History 3" on "The Comparative Anatomy and Physiology of Vertebrates" until 1880, in the fall term of 1876 he also offered a course, which was assigned to the philosophy department, using Herbert Spencer's *Principles of Psychology* as a text. Out of it came James's first psychological article, "Remarks on Spencer's Definition of Mind as Correspondence" (1878). James thought, "The conceiving or theorizing faculty . . . functions exclusively for the sake of ends that do not exist in the world of impressions we receive by way of our senses, but are set by our emotional and practical subjectivity altogether." This practical aspect was stressed in his first philosophical paper (written in French in late 1877), "Some considerations on the Subjective Method." Herein James defended the faculties we have to "set ourselves a task in virtue of an act of faith which can be accomplished only by our own effort; and to enter boldly into action in circumstances when success cannot be assured in advance."

James was made an assistant professor of philosophy in 1880. His colleagues in teaching philosophy were Francis Bowen and George Herbert Palmer. With a new sense of academic security and freedom, James expressed his philosophic difference from the imported German type of philosophy, whether the Transcendental Idealism of Immanuel Kant or the Absolute Idealism of G. W. F. Hegel, which was prevalent both inside and outside of Harvard. At Palmer's 1880–81 seminar on Hegel, James read a witty paper, which in April 1882 was published as "On Some Hegelisms." Writing to a friend about the paper, he said, "I think with the summer Concord School of Philosophy and all the rest of you expanding away here and in Great Britain, a little public opposition will be no unhealthy thing." But the real battle began after Josiah Royce from California joined the department in the fall of 1882, when James was on sabbatical leave in Europe. Royce's book, *The Religious Aspect of Philosophy* (1885), defended Absolute Idealism in a way that James for a long time could not refute. James once remarked that he learned more philosophy from Royce than from anybody else. A year previous to Royce's book, James had written an article "Absolutism and Empiricism." In it he wrote, "The question, 'Shall Fact be recognized as an ultimate principle?' is the whole issue between the Rationalists and the Empiricism of vulgar thought." Also, "The one *fundamental* quarrel Empiricism has with Absolutism is over this repudiation by Absolutism of the personal and aesthetic factor in the construction of philosophy."

Though the following quote from James was written in 1900, it is placed here to give the reader a feeling for the philosophic atmosphere in which James worked at Harvard. Hugo Münsterberg and George Santayana were the newer members of the department. Writing to Palmer, James reflected, "If our students now could begin really to understand what Royce means with his voluntaristic-pluralistic monism, what Münsterberg means with his dualistic scientificism and platonism, what Santayana means by his pessimistic platonism, what I mean by my crass pluralism, what you mean by your ethical idealism, that these are so many religions, ways of fronting life, and worth fighting for, we should have a genuine philosophic universe at Harvard. The best condition of it would be an open conflict and rivalry of the diverse systems. . . . The world might ring with the struggle, if we devoted ourselves exclusively to belaboring each other."

Bruce Kuklick, in his book *The Rise of American Philosophy, Cambridge, Massachusetts, 1860–1930* (New Haven, 1977), accurately and fully narrates the interaction of the thoughts of these men. The title suggests the distinction between technical, academic American philosophy, and philosophy in America, which goes back to thinkers as diverse in their occupations as Thomas Jefferson and Jonathan Edwards.

A few notes on the personal side. James married Alice Howe Gibbens in 1878. He once remarked, "I have found in marriage a calm and repose I never knew before." An account of this remarkable woman was privately printed by their son, Henry, in 1938. Their first three children were boys: Henry (b. 1879), William (b. 1882), and Hermann (b. 1884). The family lived at 15 Appian Way in Cambridge, but William was making plans to build a larger new house for his growing family.

II

While James was in England on his sabbatical in 1882, he met Frederic W. H. Myers, Henry Sidgwick, and Edmund Gurney, who were the leading members of the British Society for Psychical Research. James played a major role in the founding of the American Society for Psychical Research in 1884 and contributed to its *Proceedings* through 1889. During this period he also wrote many articles on psychology proper. These and other previous articles were rewritten to constitute a large portion of James's first book, *The Principles of Psychology* (1890), which he had agreed to write twelve years before. It has been noted that the *Principles* employed two methods constituting distinct strands in the psychology: (1) the traditional method of introspection, which, having resulted in the associationist psychology of British empiricism, culminated in James's doctrine of the stream of consciousness, and (2) the newer experimental method which led to the establishment of psychology as a natural science. In the beginning of that year, James's title at Harvard had been appropriately changed to professor of psychology. This is probably also in connection with the fact that, when Bowen retired in 1889, Palmer not James, got the coveted Alford Professorship of Philosophy.

James applied his knowledge of psychology to the field of education, when in 1891 he gave, upon request, a course of lectures on psychological topics of interest to the teachers in Cambridge. He repeated these lectures many times to teachers in their summer schools and institutes. As he said to his friend Théodore Flournoy, the Swiss psychologist, "There is a great fermentation in paedagogy at present in the United States, and my wares come in for their share of patronage."

In 1896 James collected for publication in book form many of his nonpsychological articles, which had been first addressed to various groups on and off campus. They appeared in print early the next year as *The Will to Believe and Other Essays in Popular Philosophy*. These essays illustrated James's philosophic attitude which he called "radical empiricism." The reader should note the different meanings the phrase "radical empiricism" received throughout James's career. In the *Preface* he wrote, "I say 'empiricism', because it is contented to regard its most assured conclusions concerning matters of fact as hypotheses liable to modification in the course of future experience; and I say 'radical', because it treats the doctrine of monism itself as an hypothesis. . . . The difference between monism and pluralism is perhaps the most pregnant of all the differences in philosophy." Since the young German psychologist, Hugo Münsterberg, rejoined the department that year as professor of psychology, James requested that his own title be changed back to professor of philosophy. He was losing his interest in psychology proper and returning to his first love.

The summer of 1898 was the most significant turning point in James's life. Just before he went to California to defend his recent book and to give a lecture at the University of California at Berkeley and to repeat his lecture series to the teachers of California in the adjacent city of Oakland, he overexerted himself in his favorite sport—climbing in the Adirondack Mountains of New York. This brought about a valvular lesion and permanent damage to his heart. His condition was worsened in June of the following year as a result of more "indiscreet" climbing just before leaving to prepare and deliver in January the first series of ten lectures at the University of Edinburgh in Scotland. A few months before sailing, he saw to the publication of his *Talks to Teachers on Psychology and to Students on Some of Life's Ideals.* The three added lectures were delivered at women's colleges. In the *Preface* James again took the occasion to state his "pluralistic or individualistic philosophy according to which truth is too great for any one actual mind, even though that mind be dubbed 'the Absolute', to know the whole of it. The facts and worths of life need many cognizers to take them in. There is no point of view absolutely public and universal. Private and uncommunicable perceptions always remain over." With regard to *Talks to Teachers*, James wrote in October 1902, "To tell the unvarnished truth, this book is better loved by me than any of my other productions, especially the essay 'On A Certain Blindness in Human Beings'." He also said on another occasion that this essay "is really the perception on which my whole individualistic philosophy is based."

After he and Mrs. James arrived in Europe, nervous prostration complicated his heart condition. As a result the lectures had to be postponed until May 1901. Till then James spent the time taking "bath cures" for his heart and seeking suitable climates to rest and write, however little at a time. After a year at home, the second series of lectures (the Gifford Lectures) was delivered in May 1902 and shortly afterwards appeared in print as *The Varieties of Religious Experience: A Study in Human Nature.* This work practically brought into existence the study of religious psychology. James thought that the originality of the work "consists in the suggestion that our official self is continuous with more of us than appears (subliminal self) which accounts for the striking experiences of religious persons; and that this 'more' on the farther side lies open to transempirical realities, and this might allow for the sense of 'union' and other mystical experiences being true."

In August of 1902, James wrote to a friend, "I want now if possible to write something serious, systematic, and syllogistic; I've had enough of the squashy popular-lecture style." He wanted to write a general system of metaphysics. An effort in this direction was the syllabus he wrote for his 1902–1903 course "The Philosophy of Nature" (Philosophy 3). In August of 1903, his ideas were tested on a summer school audience in five lectures entitled "Radical Empiricism as a Philosophy." Between July 1904 and February 1905, he prepared and delivered a new set of lectures, in which he retraced the outline of his system, and which were given in a course on Metaphysics (Philosophy 9). This material found its way into the journals in eight articles that were very technical, abstract, and addressed to fellow philosophers. These articles expressed James's doctrine of "pure experience." The problem he faced was this: "Assuming no duality of material and mental substance, but starting with bits of 'pure experience', syncretically taken, to show how this comes to figure in two ways in conception, once as streams of individual thinking, once as physical permanents, without the *immediately real* ever having been either of these dirempted things, or less than the full concrete experience or phenomenon with its two aspects." James wanted to get this material into book form, but he found it very difficult to get it into shape for any connected exposition and almost impossible to put it into popular form. James believed that "popular statement is the highest form of art."

James taught a general introduction to philosophy course at Stanford University the spring semester of 1906. He used Friedrich Paulsen's *Introduction to Philosophy* as a text. He greatly admired this book and wrote a preface to the English translation edition in 1895. Also, James composed a syllabus to accompany his lectures. The "great earthquake" in April caused all classes to be cancelled. Soon after returning home, James, apparently for the first time, decided to publish *two* books instead of just one. This move is mentioned in a May twenty-first letter to Giovanni Papini: "I expect to publish them [the above-mentioned articles and others] . . . only as a sort of appendix volume containing the *indigestibilities* of my system, after I have published a digestible and popular volume intended as a text-book for students, & sketching the Universe of radical empiricism *à grand traits.*" He never did the former and only half completed the latter.

The textbook was sidetracked by the acceptance of an invitation to deliver another Lowell lecture series in November. James lectured on a topic that went back continuously to the early 70s, when he belonged to the Metaphysical Club in Cambridge, where "Pragmatism" was born. After the series was repeated at Columbia University in early 1907, the lectures were published that year under the title *Pragmatism: A New Name for Old Ways of Thinking.* Not knowing James's more technical writings and desire to write out a "metaphysics," the general public took "Pragmatism" to denote James's over-all philosophy. But the word meant only a *method* (consistent with different philosophies) for determining the *meaning* of our beliefs in terms of their practical consequences. In the book he employed the method to show how some traditional metaphysical disputes could be determined. However, James also veered (perhaps too enthusiastically) in the direction that his two close friends, Dewey and Schiller, were emphasizing, namely, a pragmatic theory of *truth.* James himself spoke of this aspect as pragmatism in "a wider sense." The sixth chapter of the book was entitled "Pragmatism's Conception of Truth." This chapter evoked a storm of protest from his academic readers, who hastened into print to refute his analysis. James replied in print and in private letters to some of his critics through part of 1908.

One of the criticisms was that James maintained a doctrine of Idealism. But he replied that his theory of knowing and truth postulated a realism. He did, however, concede that in his articles on his doctrine of "pure experience," one might find sentences "that squint towards Idealism." One might add that the Idealism was of the Bishop Berkeley type, where to be is to be experienced.

Despite his poor health, James accepted the invitation to give the Hibbert lectures at Manchester College, Oxford, in 1908 because he could not resist the professional challenge. He did, however, regret that the job of writing lectures forced him again "to publish another book written in picturesque and popular style when I was settling down to something whose manner would be more . . . concise, dry, and impersonal." He published the lectures the following year under the title *A Pluralistic Universe,* to which he added two articles from the 1905 period as *Appendixes.* Radical Pluralism was the thesis of the lectures, but the effort was still not the systematic presentation of his doctrine. Thus, on 28 March 1909 he began writing, at long last, his introductory textbook in philosophy for students. "The first eight chapters follow the Stanford syllabus in the order of topics and often verbally" (Perry). But for the next six months he was able to do very little writing due to poor health.

Also in that year, tiring of any hope that any further explanation could clarify his meaning of the word 'truth', James terminated the debate on his part by collecting his writings on this subject into book form. The title of the volume was called *The Meaning of Truth: A Sequel to Pragmatism* (1909).

James, it will be recalled, previously held the pragmatic method to be consistent with different philosophies. But now that "Pragmatism" covered a theory of truth, he wrote in the preface, "It seems to me that the establishment of the pragmatist theory of truth is a step of first-rate importance in making radical empiricism prevail. Radical empiricism consists first of a postulate, next of a statement of fact, and finally of a generalized conclusion. The postulate is that the only things that shall be debatable among philosophers shall be things in terms drawn from experience. The statement of fact is that the relations between things, conjunctive as well as disjunctive, are just as much matters of direct particular experience, neither more so nor less so, than the things themselves. The generalized conclusion is that therefore the parts of experience hold together from next to next by relations that are themselves parts of experience. The directly apprehended universe needs, in short, no extraneous trans-empirical support, but possesses in its own right a concatenated or continuous structure."

James continued to work on his textbook manuscript while in Europe in 1910. But he must have sensed that his extremely poor health would preclude him from finishing it. On 26 July he gave directions for the publication of the manuscript: "Call it 'A beginning of an introduction to philosophy'. Say that I hoped by it to round out my system, which now is too much like an arch built only on one side." He had built a bridge that extended only halfway across the river of experience. He died just a month later. The work was published the next year under the title *Some Problems of Philosophy: A Beginning of an Introduction to Philosophy*. One wonders who was responsible for adding the first part of the title to what James himself said to call the volume? Most likely it was his son, Henry, who wrote in a prefatory note, "For several years before his death Professor William James cherished the purpose of stating his views on certain problems of metaphysics in a book addressed particularly to readers of philosophy."

III

Generosity was one of the aspects of James's character, which appears often in the correspondence. He spent much time and effort in recommending others for teaching positions in the colleges and universities. He was continually giving money of his own or raising money from others to support needy individuals and worthy projects. James spent hours listening to and writing to "cranks"—his way of referring to the eccentric. Many authors profited from his criticisms. He wrote prefaces for the works of five others upon request, which no doubt enhanced the value of the publications.

Another aspect was his role as peacemaker. Just to mention a number of the quarrels he tried to moderate is impressive—between J. M. Baldwin and J. M. Cattell; between H. Münsterberg and D. S. Miller; between E. B. Titchener and E. W. Scripture; between F. C. S. Schiller and Münsterberg; between a whole raft of people involved in a proposed International Congress of Psychology to be held in America—academic politics killed the prospect.

The reader might be surprised to learn that within the twenty-five year period covered by this correspondence, James traveled to Europe eight times. The occasions were various: to attend an International Congress, to visit his sick sister Alice, to spend his sabbatical there with his whole family, to vacation once by himself, and to lecture. Of course, while there he saw much of his brother Henry who lived and wrote in England. Though

James was thoroughly American, he deeply appreciated, and at times envied, European cultures. After he had been in Europe for a while, he was eager to get home. While at home, though of course for longer periods, he could hardly wait to go to Europe. James had many friends in Europe, both personal and professional.

James's long trips were not confined to Europe. In the United States, he went as far south as possible to Florida and as far west as possible to California (twice). Many times he visited Chicago. Once he lectured in Colorado Springs, Colorado. In writing to his hostess, at whose house he stayed while there, he said: "For me change of scenery and life is a vital necessity without which I go out like a fire that isn't poked. I regret it, for if there is anything I *aspire* to, it is to be able to work steadily on day after day with no need of change, but my bad nervous temperament keeps me exiled from that Eden."

A significant confirmation of the integrated interests and talents of James exists in the fact that his peers thought so too by electing him to various organizations. He simultaneously belonged to the National Academy of Sciences, the American Society of Naturalists, the American Association for the Advancement of Science, the American Philosophical Association, and the American Psychological Association.

The only advanced degree James earned was his M.D. degree. But many universities conferred upon him honorary degrees—Padua, both a Ph.D. and a Litt. D. in 1893; Princeton, a LL.D. in 1896; Edinburgh, a LL.D. in 1902; Harvard, a LL.D. in 1903; Durham, a Litt. D. in 1908; Oxford, a Sc.D. in 1908; and Geneva, a Sc. Nat. D. in 1909 *in absentia.*

James's work was honored also by his being elected to many foreign Academies. In 1898 he was elected as a Correspondant de l'Académie des Sciences Morales et Politiques of the Institut de France; in 1900 as a corresponding member of the Royal Prussian Academy of Sciences of Berlin; in 1903 as a member of the Royal Danish Academy of Sciences and also in the same year as a foreign associate of the Accademia Nazionale Dei Lincei of Rome; as a Corresponding Fellow of the British Academy in 1907; and, finally, in 1910 as a full member of the Institut de France, its only foreign philosopher.

IV

James's eldest son, Henry, selected the letters of his father to write what actually is a biography. *The Letters of William James*, in two volumes, appeared in 1920. In his review of the work, Schiller wrote, "There is no noticeable difference between James's books and his letters. Both abound in the same vividness, lucidity, fertility of illustration, and a pure Irish sense of fun, which had no doubt descended to him from an ancestry that came almost entirely from Ulster." And in another writing: "The letters are a complete proof that James could write as well on the spur of the moment as in his most laborious works." The current edition stresses James's professional life, though it also aims to fill in, to some degree, the details of his personal life.

The Thought and Character of William James (1935) by Ralph Barton Perry used about five hundred letters of James to document just what the title states. Perry wove this material into his own account of James's intellectual development and writings. It is not, however, an uninterrupted account. Interspersed are chapters that deal with James's relationship to others, for example, C. S. Peirce, Schiller, Strong, which cover periods of time not related to the book being analyzed. Further, however well Perry fulfilled his task and however indispensable his work has been to subsequent investigators, still it appeared fifty years ago and much James scholarship has intervened and will continue.

Elizabeth Hardwick edited *The Selected Letters of William James* (1961). She drew mainly on the two previous works. However, her edition has eight letters that are not included there but that cover the period of the present edition of the last twenty-five years of James's life.

Robert C. Le Clair edited *The Letters of William James and Théodore Flournoy* (1966). These letters reveal two very like-minded men and scholars. This volume is helpful for our knowledge of philosophy and psychology in Switzerland for the period covered by the correspondence. Flournoy is mentioned often in the present edition, because James spent so much time in Europe and traveled often through Switzerland.

The first full-scale biography of James appeared in 1967 by Gay Wilson Allen. He used for the most part the Henry James edition and *Thought and Character* (Perry). He did have access to some unpublished James family material. As a professor of English and a biographer of Walt Whitman, Allen had the skill and literary experience to portray James with broad, integrated, dramatic, and, at times, imaginative strokes. But, there are far too many factual mistakes, which make his book an unsafe source for the scholar.

Since 1975 there has been in progress a definitive edition of *The Works of William James*. This multivolumed project will include all of James's published and unpublished writing except his letters as such. Citations from such letters, and, more rarely, full letters have been used to document the history of the composition of James's various writings. The present edition may be viewed as a complementary and supplementary work to *The Works*.

A William James Chronology: 1885–1910

1885–1889   Is promoted to professor of philosophy; is
             involved in psychical research; son Her-
             mann dies; daughter Margaret Mary is
             born; G. Stanley Hall starts his journal,
             American Journal of Psychology; oc-
             cupies new summer house and new resi-
             dence in Cambridge; recommends G. H.
             Howison for teaching position; takes brief
             trip to London and Paris

1890–1893   Academic title is changed to professor of
             psychology; writes *The Principles of
             Psychology* and *Psychology: A Briefer
             Course;* takes trip to London to visit sister
             Alice; takes sabbatical leave with family in
             Europe

1894–1895   Makes acquaintance of F. C. S. Schiller;
             is president of the British Society for Psy-
             chical Research; writes articles for the
             new *Psychological Review;* gives presi-
             dential address to the American Psycho-
             logical Association; Münsterberg leaves
             Harvard; James assumes the direction of
             the Harvard psychological laboratory; at-

tends meeting of the Psychological Association in Philadelphia

1896–1897   E. B. Delabarre assumes direction of the psychology laboratory; James lectures extensively in the summer to public audiences; Lowell lectures on "Abnormal Mental States"; *The Will to Believe and Other Essays in Popular Philosophy* is published; academic title is changed to professor of philosophy; Münsterberg returns to Harvard; gives Ingersoll lecture on "Human Immortality"

1898–1899   Stress damages James's heart; takes trip to California; publishes *Talks to Teachers on Psychology and to Students on Some of Life's Ideals*; sails for Europe; takes first series of baths in Bad-Nauheim; in London, nervous prostration complicates heart condition; takes "Nauheim" baths in London; takes trip to West Malvern; postpones Gifford lectures

1900   Josiah Royce visits the Jameses at Rye; James spends nine weeks in southern France; takes second series of baths in Nauheim; travels in Switzerland; takes third series of Nauheim baths; retires to Italy for the winter

1901   James suffers the deaths of several close friends; leaves Rome on 6 March, reaches Rye on 6 April; delivers Gifford lectures at the University of Edinburgh; takes fourth series of Nauheim baths; James's nerves go to "smash" again after reaching home in September; teaches only one course and begins to write second series of Gifford lectures

1902   Tries to get Ingersoll lecture for Schiller; sails for England on 1 April; tours England for a month before lectures begin; lectures from 13 May to 9 June; *The Varieties of Religious Experience* is published in mid-June; tries to secure a grant for C. S. Peirce from Carnegie Foundation; prepares and gives a new course, Philosophy 3 (Philosophy of Nature)

1903   Renews efforts to get a grant for Peirce; distributes syllabus for Philosophy 3 course; does not teach during the spring semester, but takes instead a vacation in North Carolina; welcomes Schiller's *Humanism;* sees a "school" of congenial philosophy developing at the University of Chicago; lectures at "Glenmore" on his philosophy ("radical empiricism"); protests the American government's treatment of the insurrectionists in the Philippine Islands; submits his resignation from teaching to become effective at the beginning of the school year, 1904–1905

1904   Retracts his resignation; visits Florida; tries to keep D. S. Miller from being let go at Harvard; receives foreign visitors to the International Congress of Arts and Sciences in St. Louis; defends Schiller's philosophy against an attack by F. H. Bradley; scolds Baldwin for calling Schiller's style "vulgar"; begins a series of articles on his doctrine of "pure experience"; spends time with his brother Henry; declines offer to lecture at the Sorbonne University in 1905; gives his presidential address to the Psychological Association

1905   James replies to criticism of H. W. B. Joseph; sails alone on 11 March for a three months' vacation in Europe; lectures at the University of Chicago; gives two lectures at "Glenmore"; attends the dedication of Emerson Hall and the annual meeting of the Philosophical Association at Harvard; leaves for California on 28 December

1906   Teaches at Stanford University for four months; writes a syllabus to accompany his "general introduction to philosophy" course; his cousin Henrietta Rodgers dies; submits his resignation from teaching at Harvard; gives another Lowell lecture series; delivers his presidential address, "The Energies of Men," to the members of the Philosophical Association at their annual December meeting

1907   Delivers eight lectures on pragmatism at Columbia University; seeks members for a committee to establish an international language; welcomes Bergson's *L'Evolution Créatrice* and Schiller's *Studies in Humanism;* Horace M. Kallen studies at Oxford; receives Carnegie Foundation retirement allowance; Mrs. Royce translates Papini's article on pragmatism; reviews of *Pragmatism* are critical; is a member of a symposium on truth at the annual meeting of the Philosophical Association

1908   Continues to write on truth; delivers the Hibbert lectures at Oxford University from 4 May to 28 May; visits with friends and tours England; repeats Hibbert lectures at Harvard; declines to give short, after-dinner talk on Darwin

1909   Writes "On a Very Prevalent Abuse of Abstraction" and "Report on Mrs. Piper's Hodgson-Control"; resigns membership in the National Academy of Sciences; receives honorary degree from the University of Geneva; his books *A Pluralistic Universe* and *The Meaning of Truth* are published; visits Clark University; Eusapia Palladino visits America; writes "Confidences of a Psychical Researcher" and "The Moral Equivalent of War"

1910   Writes article "Bradley or Bergson"; his portrait is presented at a dinner; is elected to the *Institut de France;* Schiller fails to win the Waynflete professorship of philosophy; an attempt fails to hold an International Congress of Psychology in America; travels to England to visit his brother Henry; takes another trip to Nauheim via a week in Paris; returns to "Chocorua"; dies on 26 August

I

1885–1889

PART OF THE MEANING OF JAMES "COMING OF AGE" IN 1885 was his promotion to the rank of professor of philosophy. In that same year, his colleague in the department, Josiah Royce, published *The Religious Aspect of Philosophy*. This book provided a challenge to James's philosophic talents because it defended a position that James found difficult to refute for many years.

The subject of psychical research is prominent in the letters of this chapter. James was instrumental in founding the American Society for Psychical Research, which held its first formal meeting in Boston on 18 December 1884. James thought that the election of the mathematician-astronomer Simon Newcomb as the first president of the Society was an "uncommon hit" because of his stature in the scientific community. Many people were chary of this kind of investigation. In fact, James and Newcomb engaged in a brief controversy over the interpretation of some automatic drawings in 1886. When the psychologist G. Stanley Hall of the Johns Hopkins University started his *American Journal of Psychology* (1887), he devoted a long review to the work of the English Society for Psychical Research. His colleague at Johns Hopkins, Christine Ladd-Franklin, won James's praise for her article in this first issue of the journal. She too showed some interest in the field of psychical research. James did not feel that he was the right person to review Hall's new journal for the *Nation*.

Another topic of this chapter, which recurs throughout the correspondence, is James's generous efforts to help others, especially to secure teaching positions for them in the colleges and universities. One of these was George H. Howison, who was a long-standing and cherished friend for life. Howison had begun to teach philosophy at the University of California in 1884, but was for awhile a bit dissatisfied there.

Since James taught a course in ethics for the first time in 1888, it is not surprising that he showed interest in the people who were working in this area of philosophy.

On the personal side, William and Alice James lost their eighteen-month-old son, Hermann, on 9 July 1885. Their next child was a girl, Margaret Mary ("Peggy"), who was born on 24 March 1887. At the end of that summer, the family first used their new summer home "Chocorua," which was near the town of Tamworth Iron Works in New Hampshire. At the end of the 1889 summer, they moved into their almost completely finished home at 95 Irving Street, Cambridge. Shortly before that William had returned from a two month's visit to see his brother Henry and sister Alice in England and to attend an International Congress of Physiological Psychology in Paris from August 5th to the 10th.

Cambridge
March 19 [1885]

My dear Hall,

I rec'd your letter some time since, and am glad of the prospect of seeing you. Interested also in the Ashfield house you announce. Who ought I to write to about it? Is there any land? Is drainage good, etc? Water? etc.?

My wife has had scarlet fever for three weeks—none of the children. We don't want to take them back into the Appian Way house this spring, and must look for quarters for May and June. I suppose the Spring is pretty late in Ashfield. I am either incubating the fever myself or having a masked attack; Have been feeling excessively sick & queer for 4 or 5 days. Curious to hear what you are doing in Hypnotism. Psychic research very stagnant hereabouts.

Always yrs.

Wm James

You ask about Palmer. He would assuredly make you a good speech. But I fear he would decline.[1]

· *To Helen Bigelow Merriman* ·

95 Irving St.
March 21. [1885]

My dear Mrs. Merriman

I have at last read your beautiful article. I don't know how transparent it will be to the common herd—it is too original to be very popular, I am afraid. Indeed I think that the title shows a certain inaptitude on the author's part for making herself exactly popular—too much inside of her subject to feel how it looks and sounds from the outside, for who of the Andover Review's readers ever heard of "*the school of 1830*" by that name? *I* never did! But you are most originally and deeply inside of your subject, and see it out of your own living eyes, giving the reader the sense of new ways of getting at deep mysteries. The analogy, however, which lights up so much for you because you have lived so intimately with it, may not be so immediately clear to every one else. Of one thing I am sure, however, and that is that the article will be read over many times by those whom it strikes. There is a mysterious pithiness and pregnancy about these things which are written from original intuition, which makes one feel that he has not exhausted their significance; so one puts them carefully aside and after an interval reads them again. I have a number of articles which I treat in this way, and I know that such will be the fate of this. Not so much with me perhaps, for I think it is all tolerably clear to me, but with others.

Pray continue!

With warm regards to both of you, believe me always cordially yours

Wm James[2]

Cambridge, Mass.
April 23. 85

Dear Sir,

I don't know what your power is, unless it is ordinary mesmerism or hypnotism. I wish you would describe exactly the process. Do the persons know you are intending to operate on them? Is the power "not always with" you, even for the same persons under the same conditions? I can put certain "subjects" to sleep even without waving my hands, but I don't regard it as any peculiar power in me, it is merely that they fall into that condition in presence of anyone who will see that they relax their muscles, empty their minds and wait a few minutes.

If your "power" is anything different from this, I should be much interested to hear some details.

Very truly yours,

Wm James[3]

Chas. Marseilles Esq.

· To Charles Marseilles ·

Cambridge
Apr. 26 [1885]

Dear Sir,

Nothing in your letter proves to me that your power is anything different from ordinary mesmerism, animal magnetism, or whatever you call it. It is still a mooted question among the learned in such matters whether some individuals really have a native "power" that way, or whether their greater success is due to collateral circumstances, as awakening more expectation from the "subjects" etc. If you ever come this way I wish you would let me know of it in advance. I might be able to test this power in you. You make no allusions to the literature of the subject, which is very large, especially in the french tongue. I advise you to read what Carpenter says in his "Mental Physiology." As to the differences found in his patients by your "rubber" friend, I have no opinion to offer. The whole matter of personal healing powers is beyond my understanding at present.

Very truly yours,

Wm James[4]

· 30 ·

Cambridge
April 30 [1885]

Dear Sir,

Nobody understands Mesmerism. Dr. Carpenter's book will not *explain* it, only describe it. Not in one case in a million has it the slightest connexion with will power in the operator. It is merely a peculiar condition into which the subject is liable to lapse and in which he will obey the suggestions of persons with much weaker will than himself. Whether the millionth case is different, is a mooted question about which the best authorities disagree.

Hastely Yours,

Wm James

· *To Alexander Graham Bell* ·

Cambridge, Mass
May 8, 85

A. Graham Bell Esq.

Dear Sir,

I hope that my scientific purpose will excuse the liberty I take in invading your precious time with a question. I imagine you are better able to answer it than anyone in the country and it has important theoretic connexions in my mind.

Are you acquainted with any cases or records of cases, in which a *normal* child has been bro't up to the age of four or afterwards without being taught to speak? The only likely way of its happening would be in the case of a hearing child brought up in a deaf and dumb family without neighbors. Are there any such cases known? I want to discover how easy or how difficult speech is to learn when the natural age for learning it is past. The Indian wolf-children are the only examples I can find, but they are too dubious and excentric to set any store by. Hoping a reply may not inconvenience you too much,

I am very truly yours,

Wm James[5]

· *To Katharine James Prince* ·

Cambr.
June 1. 85

Dearest Kitty,

The lectures are over, the examinations begun, the quarter's salary paid! Would it were bigger. I'm going to see a materializing medium to night,—the most promising we've yet got hold of—in the Institute of Technology. Don't you think it is a harmonious locality? Alice goes with me—the first enjoyment we have had in common for a long time,—barring the Julius Caesar. . . .

Good night.

yrs ever affect.ly

W. J.[6]

· *To Katharine James Prince* ·

Cambridge
July 1. 85

My dear Kitty,

Your letter came yesterday morning, with its precious and munificent clinching of the invitation to Amherst,— I had to laugh at the six dollars—the "Daily Strength etc" and the two lovely bookmarks which we shall both use till they are worn out. The Daily Strength shall also be tried by us both faithfully. Many thanks for all, and especially for the good news you give of yourself.

I got home the day before yesterday. Our poor little baby is in a very critical condition, and we are prepared to have him called away. It is too bad, for he is the flower of the flock—but we can simply be expectant, never knowing in these matters what is best. Alice bears her broken rest wonderfully and her goodness of character is a lesson. The thing will probably be decided in another 48 hours, and whatever comes we shall cheerfully accept. If he goes it will make the others more precious. I will write to you again soon. I hope to get to Amherst before September, but can make no definite plans just now. I am not sure yet what disposition to make of the six dollars—the journey being so far ahead, and I so rich! I am going to wait for light! Meanwhile I am very sensible of your delicate generosity. Pray continue well, and believe me ever affectionately yours,

Wm James[7]

· *To G. Stanley Hall* ·

18 Garden St.
Cambridge
Nov 25th [1885]

My dear Hall,

I ought to have written you long since to explain the pleasure with which I read your *Sensations of Motion* paper in *Mind*. It is a wonderfully thorough piece of work—and as far as my knowledge goes nothing like it has yet been produced out of Germany. I hope you will go on in the same line.

Can you tell me the name of any work on General Pedagogy from which one may get hints of real practical value to be woven into psychological lectures. Pedagogic literature seems to contain such vast quantities of chaff that one hardly knows where to seek for the grain.

As usual I can make no report of progress myself. I have been working so hard that I am already much fagged, but it is all over teaching and *Bekanntes Zeug*. I have 120 men to teach in Logic and Psychology, 6 in advanced Psychology.

I suppose you have heard of Jim Putnam's engagement to Miss Marian Cabot. With best wishes

Ever yours

Wm James[8]

· *To Katharine James Prince* ·

New York
Dec 25. 85

My dearest Kitty,

A Merry Christmas to you from this merry place, where I arrived a few hours since, to smooth the way for the coming of Mrs. Gibbens and her daughter Margaret, who sail tomorrow A. M. from Jersey City. I have been to see the steamer, which is a fine one, and find they can spend the night on board. I have also made arrangements for taking their baggage across the city with no loss of time, when they arrive to night. I feel almost tempted to elope with them, the weather is so perfect and the boat looked so good. I hope my dear Mother in law will enjoy it when once she is on the other side. I don't think she carries a very light heart away. It will be a great separation for Alice. But the years fly rapidly by now, and she won't spend more than two of them abroad.

I spent yesterday & last night at Kitty Temple's at Pelham. I never saw anything more salubrious & robustious and physically and morally sound than her brood of six—and Kitty is a worthy mother of them—

very stout & buxom. They were at their Christmas revelries nearly all night.

Mrs. G's departure leaves us with a house with a spare room in it, which some time you must come and occupy. I shall return by way of Newport & the Tweedies. I've been working pretty continuously and feel entitled to a little holiday. Alice & the children are well. I hope your condition keeps on a good level. Your dayspring arrived & will doubtless ere this have given great pleasure. I left home on Wednesday. I hope all goes well with the Seelyes with a happy New Year for them, my remembrances to Mr & Mrs Scott, and a warm embrace to your self. I am ever your affectionate

Wm. J[9]

· *To Simon Newcomb* ·

Cambr.
Feb. 12. 86

My dear Mr. Newcomb,

I have just read your reply in Science of today's date. I suppose it's no use troubling the public with any more talk. But I immediately took my pencil and with tight-shut eyes scrawled the figures I enclose. The effect of the short practice is well shown by the difference between the [drawing] in the sheet marked *1st*, and in the sheet marked *2nd. attempt*. I admit entirely that the figures in the "Proceedings" are remarkably good for closed eyes. All I contend for is that they are not so far out of the *range* of ordinary work of that sort as to brand the whole observation to which they belong as probably spurious. The boy who drew them is said to be a mesmeric subject. Such subjects occasionally have a fabulously accurate use, in *writing*, of the muscular sense. It *may* be that his concentration of mind in guessing these figures gave him something of this power. It may be that he has had much practice; it may be that he is naturally a very accurate draughtsman. With these possibilities open, it seems to me, to say the least, as wise to accept the testimony of the Committee as to his being able to draw such figures blindfold, as by the impossibility that *other* individuals should draw them, to conclude that he must have "peeped."

As regards the general question, notwithstanding all that you & Preyer say, it seems to me that the presumption, after the english testimony, is against such a *mass* of it being all explicable by mystification, conscious or unconscious, on the part of the actors. But of course that presumption, so long as *possibilities* of deception remain, is any thing but proof. The lesson of the recent controversy to my mind is simple—find out more apparent cases—and hunt them down. *Conviction* either way now can only come from a much larger mass of fact observed.

Very truly yours

Wm James[10]

Cambridge
April 14 [1886]

My dear Hall,

Here are the 11 dollars, with many thanks. New England air makes one feel like a man again. The most impressive of all my experiences during the week away—more so even than the sight of the tomb of Washington—was the sight of you at your work. Hitherto I have seen you at ease, or working for yourself alone. Now I have an image of you as master, with your burden of responsibility, and I assure you without flattery that it is a truly august figure which remains on my mind's eye. Only you are worked down to the bone, and *must* take things more easily.

Ever yours

W. J.

· *To G. Stanley Hall* ·

Cambridge
April 22 [1886]

My dear Hall,

I am told by Mr. Hiram M. Stanley of his intention to apply for a philosophical fellowship with you, and have promised him to send you a recommendation. He is a stubby little fellow with no manners or social gifts, but with genuine grit and power of productive work in a rare degree. His printed things will speak for themselves. I have seen a manuscript essay of his which showed an unusual mastery of Hegelian thought—without belief in it—and I *expect* a very good Ph.D. degree from him this year. He is modest, self respecting, but very reticent & hard to get at personally. He missed our Walker travelling fellowship in Philosophy last year by a close shave, being considered an exceptionally strong candidate intellectually.

As between him and Strong I should find it very hard to decide. Strong is the more complete man all round, and *much* the more polished one. Whether he has as much native vigour & originality as Stanley remains to be seen. Stanley turns all his work to account—can show something definite for it—a very rare thing. He is older & needier than Strong. On the whole I might think it my duty to appoint him. Both are unusually strong men. Either would be a good appointment. Stanley, if made a fellow, would probably keep much to himself. Strong would circulate more.

(Have you rec'd the eleven dollars I returned to you in a registered letter? My wife just tells me that P.O. receipt for it has arrived.)

One word about the comparative amount of your *chemical* work & hours. I happened to quote what you told me Professor Remsen had said concerning publications in his chemical journal to Prof Jackson here, who told it to Hill, who denies it *in toto*. He told me yesterday he had gone over all the numbers but the last, says the relative number of *pages* is 100 for Harvard to 62 for the J.H.U., of *titles* 100 for H. to 75 for J.H.U. Harvard has given as many titles as J.H.U. & Yale put together. Of quality he says nothing—leaving that to other judges but hopeful of their verdict. I wish you would quote this to Remsen, and I think Hill & Jackson wish it too. In haste,

Yrs. ever

W. J.[11]

· *To Simon Newcomb* ·

Cambridge
July 7th [1886]

My dear Mr. Newcomb,

I took pains à propos of our little correspondence about the diagrams, to lay the matter before Edmund Gurney, two communications from whom I enclose, as is but right, since my own superior skill (!) in blindfold drawing made you drop your original objection and the drawings herewith enclosed are of a nature decidedly to strengthen it, in your eyes. You will observe that Gurney admits this himself.

The problem suggested is interesting. I feel as if the evidence for thought-transference were very good, and I must say that the a priori arguments of your presidential address were far from shaking the effect upon me of the whole body of concrete experience in favor of some thing of the kind. The moment a context is found to make it continuous with other phenomena, I shall be much surprised if it does not become an orthodox scientific fact, realized like many other facts, in individuals of a certain idiosyncracy. I am very much disposed to doubt your suspicions in this case. Possibly Smith, like many hypnotic subjects, may have had a temporarily exalted sureness of hand when doing these experiments. But obviously your objection is a pertinent one, and it will be much for Gurney's interest to clear it up by further observations upon Smith.

Very truly yours

Wm. James[12]

· *To John Forrester Andrew* ·

18 Garden St
Cambridge
Jan 13. 87

My dear Forester,

Let me still call you by the name under which you were known to me ere you were old enough to "run" for governor. You probably know that you were elected into the Society for Psychical Research the other night. It has languished in the midst (as I believe) of plenty of material for study, simply because none of its members seem to have time or inclination to work. The enclosed circular explains the plan for remedy. I don't know how much either you or Mrs Andrew cares for the objects of the Society, or how much you could spare from other needs for it, if you did care. I write this only to say that in my opinion this plan merits help. Mr. Richard Hodgson, one of the Council of the English Society—the same whose report fatal to Madame Blavatsky made so much noise,—will come and give us all his time and the benefit of his experience for one year for 1500 dollars.

If you feel like subscribing to the fund proposed, you will gratify no one more than yours always truly

Wm James

P.S. We trust to vote you into the State House yet.[13]

· *To Katharine James Prince* ·

Cambridge
Feb. 3. 87

My dear Kitty,

It is long since I have written—my life has been so chopped up with multifarious things. I got your last letter duly, with the extracts from the sacred anthology and the almanac. The extracts I enjoyed, though, as you well know, I have not the power you have, of nourishing myself on *scraps*—I need something with a good long rhythm and context, to produce a very strong effect. As for the Almanac, I smiled, as I thought of your experience with Howard jr. To tell the truth, I haven't in years missed so many afternoon naps as since the year began. Or to put it better, I haven't taken so few—I cannot count more than three. One reason is that I have had late morning sleeps (after a vigil between 3 & 6 A.M.) & they always make the afternoon nap impossible. Another reason is that I have made 10 visits to a mind-cure-doctress, at either four or five P.M., and postponed my doze till I should be seated beside her. Another is social or other duties which invaded the hour. I think I am getting into a state where loss of sleep doesn't affect me as much as heretofore—a consummation devoutely to be wished, for the P.M. nap, *as a regular obligation,* is an excessively inconvenient feature in the economy of my life. I cannot see that the mind cure has done me any positive good, though I shall go twice more, having resolved to give the good woman at least a dozen sittings, for fair trial's sake. She has done wonders for some of my friends.

I am just back from a day at Lake Chocorua, N.H. talking with a carpenter about what can be done to make the buildings on my new estate habitable for the summer. The day, Tuesday, was one of the most crystalline purity; I don't think I ever saw such blinding light as was made by the sky & the snow together, and the mountains looked most exquisite. In doors, too, the finest wood fires I ever saw in a hearth. But wood fires and pure snow, however dazzling, are a lean diet for the soul for 4 months without a break, and I believe the countries where the earth is bare and wet, with occasional snows in winter, are the richest environment for a human being.

Alice is well. She expects her confinement about the first of April, and it is astonishing to see how busy she keeps notwithstanding, looking after the children and other duties. Little Billy has grown asthmatic, and, as his grandmother wishes an excuse to go south herself, she has agreed to take him for 2 or 3 months, probably to Aiken, S.C., though we are not yet sure. Harry is very well and a model of schoolboy vigor. We are plying him with such books as Pilgrim's Progress, and the Iliad & Odyssey, which he enjoys hugely now, read aloud, because we feel sure that when he once begins the more highly seasoned contemporaneous literature for boys, and is able to read to himself, these simpler things will seem insipid.

My bro. Harry is still on the Continent. Sister Alice is in his London rooms, rather poorly again, I fear.

I hope & trust you are doing well, and long to hear of your housekeeping possibilities. Write when you can, to yours ever affectionately

Wm James[14]

·

· *To Eliza Putnam and Margaret Merrill Gibbens* ·

18 Garden St.
March 24. 87
9.30 A.M.

Dearest Mother in law & Belle-Soeur!

This morning with the *Frühroth* came a *daughter*—the living image of her Mar. I kept talking of it as *he* & *him*, from force of custom. Alice was in pain only about 2 hours and a half. Everything promises well. She took hardly any ether. Dr. Call has left, and will be back this evening. The whole thing was so quiet and Miss Lespierre has foreseen all contingencies so neatly that one would hardly notice that such a thing was going on. I will send you daily bulletins. We are having a cold snap. Ground hard frozen up again—but the sun shines bright today. Love to both of you. Margaret mustn't trifle with the New Yorker's affections!

In haste
yrs. ever

Wm.J.

The child was born just before the Doctress arrived—
tho the latter got here in an hour and a half from the time
I left the house to go to the stable.[15]

· *To G. Stanley Hall* ·

Tamworth Iron Works, N.H.
Aug. 1. [1887]

My dear Hall,

I write this to the accompaniment of the carpenters'
hammers, which are nailing together the boards of my
Château. I never felt so oppressed by the weight and
value of my material possessions, and for the past 24
hours have felt like setting fire to the whole concern, so
as to own nothing any more and be free.

As for going to Ashfield I fear it is more impossible
than ever. I've been there twice. You must come here. It
is on the White Mountains division of the Eastern R.R.
17 miles south of N. Conway. The Station is West Os-
sipee. I thought the place a great bargain when I bought
it, but the unforeseen expenses are going to ruin me. We
shall probably be in a fit state for guests in September,
and you must then come.

As for your Journal, it is the greatest confidence game
in N. America. Collecting subscriptions a year nearly
before its appearance! It must be good, when it does
appear. I do hope & trust you'll publish it on date like
Mind, or else not date the numbers like Pflüger's Archiv
etc.

I do nothing but manual work. My eyes have had a
bad period for the past three months, & are apparently

no better. I have no chance to try them, however, at present, and they may respond when I do. But my inability to study fills me with despair.

In the matter of Palmer, he ought to be President of Wellesley. I fear the trustees don't know what a prize they would gain in him. I long to see you & talk over the prospects of Psychology.

Yrs ever

W. J.[16]

· *To Jacob Gould Schurman* ·

Cambridge, Mass.
Oct. 30, 1887

My dear Schurman,

I have to thank you for your charming little book on Ethics, which I duly received, and should have acknowledged earlier. But I waited to read it, and even to obey the "Nation," by scribbling a notice of it, which I have just put into an envelope to mail. You certainly write most charmingly. I myself kept wishing as I read for some more radical carving, but after all there is no public of readers with just my wants. I imagine that you will clear up the ideas of the clergy very much in both ways. I profited most by Chapters V and VI. I did not know how weak Darwin's derivation of conscience was until I read Chapter V. And, (altho I speak as one ignorant of these matters), your demolition of McLennan & Co. seems quite conclusive.

I trust that you enjoy things at Cornell. Pray give my regards to Strong when you see him. I hope he takes hold easily.

I send you herewith reprints of the last three numbers of my paper on Space in Mind. I sent you Part I when it appeared.

Thanks again, from

Yours always truly

Wm James[17]

· *To G. Stanley Hall* ·

18 Garden St.
Cambridge
Nov. 5th '87

My dear Hall,
Is Kandinsky's thing a book or an article? Can you without trouble send me date and place of publication?

Your letter about the *Nation* notice, I confess embarrasses me a little. Garrison wrote to me enclosing a torn-off bit of your letter and asking me to write a "longish notice" which would have been sent before your note came had not an attack of stiff neck stopped my writing.

I think I will now withhold my hand till I hear from you again. You implore me so vehemently to pay it no general compliments that for fear of displeasing you I am quite paralyzed, and think that possibly Jastrow or some one else whom the *Nation* will doubtless accept at your suggestion, might write something that would please you better.

It would be quite unprecedented for the *Nation* to devote a special article to a number of a Review as technical and esoteric as this, nor should I think, bearing its readers in mind, that it would be proper to go at all minutely into any of the articles. What I proposed doing was to state the results of the four principle ones (with a cry of admiration at Mrs Christine Franklin) quote some passages from your Psychic Research article, and then make some general compliments of the sort that you say you don't want on the probable great utility of the Magazine, and the devotion of its Editor. You see, my dear fellow, one can't deal with a multifarious aggregate like a periodical except in a "general" way.

If this programme suits you, let me know and I will proceed. If not, I shall not feel at all put out if you get Garrison to confide the job to some one else.

Your Ladd article I think admirable in every respect, and fully agree with each word of it. About the Psychic Research criticism I could say much if I had time. The gist of it all would be that, to take sides as positively as you do now, and on general philosophic grounds, seems to me a very dangerous and unscientific attitude. Where observations are in process of accumulation, and one doubts them, the best thing is to wait. There never could be an observation so minutely recorded that a critic bent on proving the observers dupes, might not find such possible reasons for his faith as you bring forward in the omissions of the record. Nevertheless, if the observations multiply, all such objections fall to the ground. The history of Hypnotism is most instructive in this respect. Now what these English fellows are doing is to try to multiply observations. And that seems to me the only healthy thing. The fact that no more new cases are found is, to me, far more damaging to the existing cases than any number of cavils about the record of the latter, could possibly be. *Any how* the non-appearance of new cases is puzzling. Fraud and hyperaesthesia ought to be recurring causes as much as "thought-transference." I cannot but regret that you should try to pin the latter upon Gurney & Co. in the form of a spiritualistic theory. Gurney has no positive theory whatever as to what the thing is, and has repeatedly said that he uses the word merely to cover some agency outside of the common channels of sense. You ought not, by the way, to quote Ochorowicz as an opponent of thought-transference. Ochorowicz, if I understand his position, though I confess I have not read the whole of his book carefully, believes there are cases which neither fraud nor hyperaesthesia can explain. The only really important things in your notice as it seems to me, were your accounts of the sniffing and toe cases, (I wish you had explained the latter more fully)—those were positive hypotheses to account for the kind of results recorded, and not mere general suspicions of dupery. And why do all the critics spend so much time over the Creery children when all the really important evidence lies in the later cases? Hodgson tells me that Gurney and Mrs. Sidgwick have had the Creerys again and caught them cheating and will soon publish a full account of it. But hold! I am giving you a deluge. I should express the difference between our two positions in the matter, by calling mine a baldly empirical one, and yours, one due to a general theoretic creed. The Gurneys, Sidgwicks are baldly empirical. I don't think it exactly fair to make the issue what you make it—one between science and superstition.

Always truly yours

Wm James[18]

· 49 ·

Cambridge
Nov 10. 87

My dear Hall,

I have been trying to write the notice of the Journal for an hour or more, but find that all spontaneity has left me for the purpose, and that between my conscience towards the Nation, towards you, and towards myself, I feel so paralyzed that to copy the prospectus and table of contents is all I'm good for. It doesn't do to have a slight job made formidable. I read in your letter of yesterday "I *desire* most of all such a notice as Science gave to the J. of Morphology." My wife took the letter & read "*dread*"!!

I will write a line to Garrison saying "I am so occupied that it is impossible for me to write the notice," and you may, if you like, simultaneously tip him a hint as to who might do it easily.

Pray don't think me "put out" in the least. I started to write with the heartiest good will to the job, but found myself so subtley inhibited that it would not go. Tameness incarnate became the only possible line—and that wd. please you as little as it pleases me.

I have relished your three reviews—McCosh, Dewey, Bowne amazingly. There is a palpitating and unexpected quality in your style which makes it recognizable anywhere. Beware however of Germanisms, and sentences with too many coordinate & subordinate clauses, parentheses and adjectives—I fear they are growing on you! Need "protocol" be used instead of "record" or "notes?" I find the fine print a little too small. It does for a lot of short notices, but articles of such importance as your long reviews and Charles Peirce's are hard to read by such eyes as mine. On the other hand, the large type is perhaps unnecessarily luxurious.

Robertson wrote me last Spring asking if an agent for *Mind* mightn't be found. After being rebuffed by a couple of publishers I went lately to Heath, who said he must consult you. Yesterday he writes, enclosing your note, and saying he should like to hear from Wms. & Norgate. So I've sent his letter to Robertson. In the end, however it might be in a year or two, these Journals must help each other, and prepare readers for each other.

Thanks for your offer to send Kandinsky. The title was all I wished—I have just ordered the book. Always truly yours

Wm James[19]

· *To Felix Adler* ·

Harvard University
Cambridge, Mass.
Jan. 11. 88

My dear Adler,

There seems but one impression of your lecture, which is that it is the greatest address ever delivered in that theatre, except perhaps the extraordinary oration of Wendell Philipps (sic) 9 or 10 years ago. Our fortune was great in "securing" you! The impression will be lasting. I found myself the next day addressing my students in a strain of impassioned eloquence to which they were altogether unused. I hope I didn't even imitate the sound of your voice—the source of my inspiration would have been too obvious then. Meeting Frank Peabody the following morning, the first words he uttered were: "It's lucky that that man has no religion. If he can do so much without one, he'd smash everything if he had one." He then gravely allowed that you had a religion without knowing it; and I agreed with him that if you try to base such a moral idealism as yours theoretically (*i.e.* save it from being an individual caprice) you are led to a superhuman mind as its ground. However, no theories now. This is merely to thank you once again, and to say that, with warmest regards to Mrs. Adler from both of us, I am always yours

Wm James

P.S. We were mortified at not having provided a carriage for you to come—and especially to go. I don't see how it came not to be thought of by any of the cooks that had care of the broth. It was quite inexcusable, but the less said about it now the better.[20]

· To David Jayne Hill ·

Cambridge Mass
Jan 21. 88

President D. J. Hill

Dear Sir,

I have to thank you for the gift of your Elements of Psychology, which came to me a couple of days ago.
    I myself believe it more intellectually profitable for

the student to go more minutely over a more limited field, if he has not time to master a larger book than yours. But I cannot but admire the skill with which you have kept things short, and yet at the same time supplied so much information about recent psychologic work.

Thanking you again, I am very truly yours

Wm James[21]

· *To Christine Ladd-Franklin* ·

Cambridge
April 12 [1888]

Dear Mrs. Franklin,

Your letter interests me very much, because the account you give is similar to accounts which I have heard from others of the influence upon them of the hand of a certain Mrs. Wetherbee who is a "magnetic healer" here, and who, on members of my wife's family, has certainly "charmed away pain" in a most surprising manner. I know Dr. Crockett also, and like him. I have had hitherto only his own accounts of his performances, not knowing any of his patients but one, on whom he failed.

But I am very dubious of the poor little Soc. for Psych. Re. accomplishing much by seeking to "investigate" these things. Of all earthly things, therapeutic effects are the hardest to run to ground, and convince a skeptic of. There will always be a dozen loopholes of escape from any conclusion about therapeutics, and the mind will take which ever one it prefers. I think the history of opinion about homeopathy (or about the single drug alcohol) is enough to make anyone hopeless of making therapeutic evidence satisfactory to *all*. Money was offered to the Society for the purpose of investigating the "mind-cure." It was (as I thought, rightly) refused. Practical physicians are the only ones who can say an influential word in these matters; and they must have already made themselves influential in *other* matters, or they will simply discredit themselves by speaking of such things as those of which you write. A Charcot can afford to risk his reputation in this way; a common practitioner cannot. Meanwhile such experiences as yours, mentioned by such a person as yourself, will accrete with others and little by little invite the attention of the competent.

I think the "Journal" of the Society, which we are seeking money to get published for circulation among members, would be a very good place to receive such contributions, if their authors were willing to have them appear.

I came very near noticing Hall's Journal of Psych. for the Nation. Had I done so, I should have burst into loud cries of admiration over your horopter article, which seemed to me by far the best thing in the number. To discover a new optical illusion is already a great feat. To explain it, and to use it for another purpose, as you have done, is simply, what,—delicious! Excuse my enthusiasm, and believe the admiration and respect with which I subscribe myself

Very sincerely yours

Wm James

P.S. There is a great bulk of printable matter already on hand; but no money to print or to edit. Hodgson is an admirable fellow, but one man can't do everything, and he is well nigh single-handed in the matter of investigation, every one else being either busy, lazy, or incompetent.[22]

· *To Charles Marseilles* ·

Cambridge
April 14 [1888]

Dear Sir,

Of the effects of oil on waves I know nothing, except that there was in the weekly "Science" during many numbers last year a discussion of the theory and a recital of facts.

Of the quotation's original I know nothing, nor, I am sorry to say, do I know anything of Meuzel who wrote "Christian Symbolism." I never heard of the book.

Regretting to return you so ignorant a reply, I am very truly yours

Wm James[23]

Cambridge
Feb 28. 89

Dear Mrs. Franklin,

I am highly pleased at having converted you so easily. As for your own interpretation of the putty experiment, I don't see why it won't do perfectly well. I like hugely your general formula that what we are conscious of is what *precedes* the innervation, and that when this is *usually* followed by a movement we assume invariably that it must be so followed even when the movement fails to occur. I had never expressed the law in that general and radical way, though if you turn to pp. 255–6 of No 3 of the Proceedings of the American Society for Psychical Research you will see that I came very near to it.

Your observations on pressing the eyeballs are highly curious. On what the structures revealed may be, I will not risk an opinion, tho' your description is very suggestive. Many years ago I used to indulge in the pastime and got entirely different symptoms. I have refrained from repeating the experiment since reading in Helmholtz, I think, that it was quite dangerous and might lead to detachment of the retina, or something equally formidable. Thanking you very much

I am faithfully yours

Wm James[24]

Cambridge
March 22. 89

Dear Miss Thomas,

I learn from Mr. Mead that he is unable to leave his present work.

Meanwhile there is Santayana, whose romantic fascinations I couldn't help smiling at to myself after you were gone—I had so emphatically dwelt on them. I think it most likely that if you saw him you would not find them to exist, and would wonder what I could have meant. They consist mainly in *youth*. As I said, he is the best *intellect* we have turned out here in many a year, and if you are aiming this year at a *pro tem* appointment on a low salary, I should think it might be very wise to try him.

I ought to say that it is possible that Santayana may be asked to give some instruction here next year at a still lower salary. If so, he may conclude to stay rather than change his abode.

Very truly yours

Wm James

P. S. Many thanks for your Program and the XIXth Century. As I have already read Miss Smith's article and have the magazine, I send back this copy, that you may "place it where it'll do most good."[25]

34 De Vere Gardens, W. London
July 26. [1889]

Hon. Geo. W. Ross
Toronto

Dear Sir

I am asked by *two* friends Professor Howison of California, and Mr. James G. Hume of Toronto for recommendations for the vacant professorship of Logic and Metaphysics in the University of Toronto.

Howison is a well known man, an admirable lecturer and writer (tho for some reason unknown to me he writes but little) and very learned in the metaphysical field. Personally also he is agreeable, and his moral character is spotless. Of his actual success as a teacher you will doubtless learn through some ancient colleagues at the Technological Institute in Boston, and directly from California. I have no observation on that point. I can only say that I regard Mr. Howison as one of the ablest philosophical minds in our country.

Mr. Hume is, of course, more of an unknown quantity. He is one of the 2 or 3 most promising students of philosophy whom I have had in 15 years experience at Harvard College, and I hope and expect a brilliant future for him, especially in the way of *writing*. Of his other qualifications & attributes you can judge from nearer witnesses than I.

Believe me with high respect

Yours very truly

Wm James (Prof. of Philosophy
Harvard University)[26]

34, De Vere Gardens. W
July 27. 89

My dear Howison,

Delighted to see your handwriting again, and well
pleased to think that you may be coming East, though I
supposed you were happy in California, and that it was a
better Professorship than the Toronto one.

As for the latter I wrote *immediately* (2 days ago) on
the receipt of your letter, to the Minister of Instruction.
Strangely enough I received by the same mail a letter
from a student who was with us last year, reminding me
of my promise to recommend *him.* There was no comparison possible, as he is (although a very strong man I
think) all *in posse*, whereas you are an accomplished fact
as well as an accomplished philosopher. I wrote about
both of you, saying as much.

Hume was the favorite pupil of the former incumbent,
Prof. Young; he seems to have warm personal friends in
the University, and he is now in Toronto. I know not
what other candidates there may be.

I am, as you see, in London, taking an heroic vacation,
and bound for an "International Congress of Physiological Psychology" in Paris Aug 5. I shall be back home by
Sept 1, I trust. The necessity of these expensive vaca-
tions is one that I hardly enjoy, but only on such conditions does life seem to go on. I am just packing for
France, which makes me brief.

Yours ever

Wm James[27]

Cambridge
Oct. 31. 89

My dear Howison,

I regret to inform you—though I suppose you know it already, and can hardly regret it very much yourself— that the Toronto vacancy has been filled by *two* men Baldwin of Lake Forest, who recently pub'd the Psychology and Hume a recent Toronto graduate who studied here last year and has one of our fellowships. The campaign appears to have been most singular. Baldwin was the candidate of the clerical party, Hume that of the recent graduates who were anti-clerical and devoted to the memory of Prof. Young whose favorite pupil Hume had been. Baldwin was pushed by McCosh, Patton & Co. The city newspapers took up the fight, Hume being a Toronto boy. The minister of education seems to have feared to offend either side, and so made a new professorship. Both are good men. Hume full of strength & promise—but the *place* must be very crude and the climate harsh enough. Bowen resigned here last month and the President told me yesterday that the Corporation had voted the place to Palmer. Confirmation by the overseers is, I suppose, a matter of course. Royce is working like 3 men, and thinking like 100. I slug along, much kept down by a constant deficit of sleep.

Pray write and give me a hint as to why you are anxious to leave Berkeley. It has been a great surprise to me. Of course I have mentioned it to no one. Your young friend Mezes has presented himself but not yet given me your letter. He looks promising. Please give my regards to your new Classic colleague Richardson and believe me with respect to Mrs. H. & best wishes

Yours ever,

Wm James[28]

II

1890–1893

ON 8 JANUARY 1890, JAMES'S ACADEMIC TITLE WAS changed to professor of psychology. This was a more appropriate title due to the nature of his teaching and writing since 1885. He had agreed in 1878 to write a textbook in psychology for the Henry Holt Publishing Company. He finally finished writing the book in early 1890 and spent the summer in proofreading. It appeared in September in two huge volumes as *The Principles of Psychology*. This work was too large to serve as a textbook, so the publisher asked for a smaller version for such a purpose. James worked on this project in 1891. The book appeared in 1892 as *Psychology: A Briefer Course*. In the preface he wrote that he regretted not being able to supply a chapter on pleasure and pain. Interest in this topic led him to enter into a long correspondence with Henry R. Marshall, a New York City architect, whose articles on this topic had begun to appear in the English journal *Mind* in 1889. Also in 1891 James was asked by the Harvard Corporation to give a series of lectures on psychology to the Cambridge teachers. This series was begun in the late part of the fall semester after James had returned from a ten day visit to England to see his sister Alice, who was failing rapidly in health. It was also in this year that James began an intimate correspondence with the Swiss psychologist, Théodore Flournoy, which lasted to James's death.

After all this exhausting work, James welcomed the chance to take a year's sabbatical leave from teaching. Reminiscent of his father's earlier venturousness, William took his whole family with him, which had been increased in size by one. Alexander Robertson had been born on 22 December 1890. The family sailed for Antwerp, Holland on 25 May 1892. They stayed in Germany most of June. About two and a half months were spent in Switzerland. While there, James contacted the young German psychologist, Hugo Münsterberg, who was about to begin teaching at Harvard. They then moved on to the more moderate climate of Florence, Italy, for the fall and winter months. In early December James was honored with degrees of both Doctor of Philosophy and Doctor of Letters by the University of Padua.

Though on sabbatical James continued to write for the newly founded *Philosophical Review.* In 1893 he also engaged in a controversy with F. H. Bradley, the English philosopher, in the journal *Mind.* G. F. Stout had become the new editor in 1892 after the death of G. C. Robertson. With the coming of spring the family moved back to Switzerland. Mr. and Mrs. James took off by themselves for London in the months of June and July for some type of respite. After returning to get the children, they sailed from England on 25 August.

James found it difficult to get back to teaching again after so long a time away. In fact, he became a little melancholic. However, he was enthusiastic in obtaining subscribers for the new *Psychological Review* (1894–), of which J. M. Baldwin and J. M. Cattell were co-owners and coeditors. James attended the second annual meeting of the American Psychological Association at Columbia University, 27 and 28 December.

· *To Christine Ladd-Franklin* ·

Cambridge
April 29 [1890]

Dear Mrs. Franklin,

Do you happen by any accident, still to have a letter
which I wrote you last year (or possibly earlier) about the
illusions of motion, and the primitive condition of our
sensation of motion being that of the relative motion of
background and moving body. I happen to be writing on
the subject again, and feel as if what I then said might
help me. But it is hardly possible that you should have
kept the letter.

Sincerely yours

Wm James

· *To G. Stanley Hall* ·

95 Irving St.
May 16. 1890

My dear Hall,

I am shocked to hear of the stunning blow that has fallen
on you, & must send you a word of sympathy. Yet, death
for death, who could wish a better one? I hardly know
whether the little girl going too makes it worse or better.

That such big things can happen so easily gives one a strange suspicion that our instinctive ways of feeling about things are wrong and that if we knew reality even this might seem light and benign. But I can express nothing but my heartfelt pity, my dear old friend, and pray that ere long you will find yourself again *zurecht*. I am sorry that I can never see her again.

Bless you!

Wm James[1]

· *To Christine Ladd-Franklin* ·

Cambridge
May 19 [1890]

Dear Mrs. Franklin,

Here is your document at last, since you wish it back. It is simpler than I tho't and I need not have sent for it.

Congratulate me! I have this day finished the manuscript of a "Principles of Psychology" which ought to be out in September, and which has been sticking to me like an old man of the sea for the last 8 or 9 years. I feel like a barrel with its hoops gone! and shall grow young again.

As for your logical papers you can perhaps now understand why I have not read them. I have not passed 5 minutes since last August which was not in some way connected with that infernal manuscript. I mean now to begin to read something, but am quite brain fagged at present, and am anyhow absolutely non-mathematical and non-higher-logical, so I'd better wait for a more propitious moment for your articles. I have found some of the C. L. F. abstracts in Hall's Journal very good.

Poor Hall! what a blow! A friend who was at the funeral tells me that he bears up very well.

With respects to your husband, believe me

ever truly yours

Wm James

· *To G. Stanley Hall* ·

Tamworth Iron Works, N. H.
June 20. 90

My dear Hall,

I am most happy to hear from you directly again. Your trial will still be a heavy one, no doubt, but there is a momentum in the lives of us individuals which makes its way through everything, and you will find yourself in equilibrium again in spite of the tremendous shock. Your boy's face is a most noble one; and he will be a comfort.

I wish that I might get to Ashfield; but I sent off my big Psychology MS. to Holt a month ago and expect to be confined here all summer with the proofs. I may be obliged to break away for a change in September and then if ever would be the time. But can't you come up here for a week, almost at any time you may find convenient, the sooner the better. I should like to show you my little place, and we have lots of Psychology arrears to make up in the way of talk.

Let me hear from you as soon as possible.

Yours most affectionately

Wm James

· *To Katharine Peabody Loring* ·

95 Irving St.
Aug. 13. 1890

Dear Katharine,

This is only to bid you a hearty god-speed. Both Alice and I have racked our brains to think of some token to send Alice, or of something to give you for the voyage— but see what a sterile thing is a critical intelligence— nothing that is imagine[d] will stand the test—so nothing goes. We have both written notes to poor Alice. And I do hope you won't have too bad a time.

You're a blessing, as perhaps you yourself know.

Affectionately yours

Wm James[2]

· *To Kenneth Mackenzie* ·

Tamworth Iron Works, N. H.
Sept 22. 90

Dear Dr. Mackenzie,

I feel much touched by your thoughtful regard for me,
and shall be much interested in reading the little book
you have sent. I don't know whether, if unconverted, I
can give you a very articulate account of the reasons why
not, but we shall see. These things are always excessively complex. I confess that in my own case it has so far
been the Bible itself, both old Testament and New,
which has seemed to me the document most fatal to the
claims of the traditional christian theology. All changes
in theology have had their source and authority in ways
of reading the Bible. The merely humanistic way which
comes so natural to men of this generation hangs together with a way of looking at things with which the
christian scheme of salvation is (I may say almost invincibly) incongruous. And the Bible-text lends itself so un-
constrainedly to the humanistic interpretation, that anything beyond that seems artificial. I am of course a most
convinced *Theist*, as you know.
Thanking you again, I am always,

Yours

Wm James[3]

· 68 ·

95 Irving St.
Cambridge, Mass.
[October 16, 1890]

Dear Mrs. Franklin,

I thank you for your most appreciative note. My book is too long for any one to read, but if you read anything I wish it might be last Chapter of all. It needed re-writing, but I had no time. I should like to know, however, from you particularly, whether it seems to you that I have given any sort of pitch forward in that Chapter to the old quarrel over the existence of a priori propositions and necessary truth.

I had read the two reviews you sent me from the Nation, and suspected their authorship. Your reviews are really useful. Did you also write the review of M. Ch. Henry's work in last week's number?

Always sincerely yours

Wm James[4]

95 Irving St.
Cambridge, Mass
Oct 22. 90

Dear Prof. Newcomb

Thanks for your note. It is flattering to have anyone *react* on one's book, especially when the reacter is a man like you. I have never seen your articles in the Independent, nor can I get them here. But I agree with you that a lot of the discussion that goes on is logomachy from not defining terms. I think that "materialism" is very well kept with the vague meaning (said to be ascribed to it by Comte) of "the explanation of the higher by the lower." But of course one may define it as one will; and I, so far as I can remember, have abstained from using the term at all in my book. I think the word "freedom" is deplorable from its ambiguity. Once you speak of "indeterminism" you have a clear objective issue before you, about which it seems to me that there is the most serious issue that philosophy contains, no less than that between monism and pluralism überhaupt. I stand out for pluralism against the whole line.

As for mental states that are not states of consciousness, I don't know what can be meant by them. Brain-states I know, and states of consciousness I know, but something that is more than a brain-state yet less than a state of consciousness I know nothing about, nor do I see the use of discussing its existence. I am sick of the subject of psychology for a while and shall lie fallow for a year.

Yours always truly

Wm James[5]

95 Irving St.
Cambridge, Mass.
Dec. 7. '90

Dear Mr. Baldwin,

I am afraid that the readers of Science may not be as deeply interested in our dispute as we are, so I send you my remarks on your last letter in the shape of a private communication. And to save trouble I will paste your text in, and say what I have to say in the shape of notes thereupon. I confess that I find a certain difficulty in being sure that I catch your reasoning. To me the alternative is this: Are certain sorts of stimuli (objects at a certain distance felt by the eye) natively correlated with paths leading to the right hand? or are the paths *natively* indifferent, and is the choice of the right hand for response to such stimuli due to reminiscences (explicit or implicit) of former experiences in which the right hand showed itself most fit to react upon them? If the latter view be adopted, then another alternative comes up, thus: Are the reminiscences those of "afferent" or "efferent" experiences?

The fact that all movement was inhibited when the stimulus was too far away, looks as if reminiscence had something to do with it, for I *suppose* (and you will know whether I am right) that *originally* the child would have been excited to grasping movements of both hands, by objects presented beyond reaching distance. He has now learned the uselessness of this, we will suppose; and similarly must have learned for a certain range of distance the superior usefulness of the right hand, we will say. In your words: "The new element must represent the influence of former experience. I see no way to avoid this alternative. This is what I meant by 'memories,' merely some kind of a conscious modification which alters future re-actions. A purely physical modification would not suffice, for it would have its full force also in cases which involved no effort. Now, we may hold that such 'memories' are exclusively of afferent nerve processes, or that they involve also a conscious modification due to efferent nerve processes. If the former, we may attribute them to the greater 'promptitude, security, and ease' of right-handed movements, as Professor James suggests, or to former movements of the eyes, involved in the visual estimation of distance (which I am astonished he does not suggest). [James: Of course the present eye adaptation must be the cue which calls up the memories of the arm movement whichever they be.] The first alternative which Professor James asks my ground for rejecting, is inadequate for the following reasons. If such memories of afferent processes be of movements with effort, they are already right-handed, and the question is only thrown farther back."

I don't see the force of this objection. The right hand we must admit to be natively the cleverer. Grant that both hands set in movement by a stimulus so far away that it is reached with difficulty, and it will inevitably happen that in continuing the movements the child will feel its right hand *succeeding* oftener than the left. This "success" is unquestionably realized in various pleasant afferent feelings and the absence of unpleasant ones, sympathetic contraction elsewhere etc (whether efferent feelings be present or no). It seems to me that *some* sort of right-handed achievement "already," is an essential element in every *possible* explanation by reminiscence, of the facts observed. You continue: "but, if they be of effortless movements, then their motor influences would be perfectly indifferent, as I said in my former letter."

For effortless read "easy," and I suppose it can be

admitted that either hand reaching the goal promptly, no discriminative memories of the right hand's superiority would be stored up, and both hands might continue to be used.

[Baldwin] "My experiments show this. If there had been differences in 'promptitude,' etc., the child certainly would have shown preferences for the right hand in effortless [James: not so for the reason just given] movements during the latter six months of the first year. But, on the contrary, it was only when making violent effort that there was any preference at all. [James: because only then had the right hand's native superiority manifested itself in former trials.] Even after she developed such preference in cases of effort, the use of her hands when no effort was required continued to be quite indifferent. Does not this indicate that the traces left by former afferent processes of the same sense are not sufficient?" [James: not sufficient, merely, for choice of right hand where either hand had previously done the work with success.]

[Baldwin] "Moreover, in the absence of all feeling of the efferent movement, what could sensations of 'promptitude,' etc., be but the consciousness of better adaptation and co-ordination of movements? But at this stage of life all the child's movements are so ataxic that there seems to be no practical difference between two hands in regard to the lack of the tactile delicacy in which pathological cases show motor ataxy to consist."

My view is just this, that the right hand is natively less "ataxic" than the left, and, having proved itself so, is thereafter chosen more than the left. The ataxia is originally not a fact of sensibility, but of motor coordination. The experiences of "failure," however, of retarded reaching the goal and groping, and continued contractions, which lead to the left hand being inhibited when the eyes see an object 14 inches off, are sensible experiences.

[Baldwin] "If we seek the needed "memory" among the sensations of eye-movements in the case where the stimulus is weaker (more distant), it is possible that we may find an afferent element which brings up the intensity of the hand memories to the necessary pitch. There may be a connection between the centres for feelings of eye-movement and feelings of hand-movement, so that their united "dynamogenic" influence is the same as the high intensity of the color stimulus."

It would not have occurred to me that the stimulus needed to be *more intense*, for the right hand to be chosen. It happened, indeed, to be so in your observations with the colours, and I noticed it as a remarkable fact. A certain sort of stimulus produces a certain sort of reaction, there is a specialized native adaptation of movement to visual sensation—that was what the observations on colours seemed to me to show. By analogy there *might* be a similar native specialized adaptation of right-handed movement to a certain range of accommodation and convergence, whether more or less intense. It actually is *less* intense in the case we deal with. [Baldwin] "But, while freely admitting such a possibility, it only pushes the question farther back again; for how do we know that these eye-memories do not involve consciousness of the efferent process which innervates the eye-centre? And, besides this, there is another element in the hypothesis that afferent elements from other senses may furnish the "kinaesthetic co-efficient" for a given voluntary movement, namely, that such activities of the other senses invoked took place along with movements of the attention, which might, and probably do, contribute an efferent element to consciousness. This possibility I have never seen anywhere recognized."

All this seems over subtle and *I* don't need it. You have been misled by my quoting the bright colours into supposing that I required an *intenser* stimulus every-where, for the discharge of the right hand.

[Baldwin] "But in this case my experiments show con-clusively that eye-movement memories did not re-en-force the intensity of the arm-movement memories; for, when the distance was more than fourteen inches, the re-action was inhibited altogether. The distance of the stimulus as apprehended by the eye, therefore, instead of giving the increased motor excitement which we re-quire, rather diminishes it, and makes the need for some other explanation all the more imperative.

It appears, therefore, that the element needed in con-sciousness to explain the facts cited in my former letter is some kind of a difference in sensation corresponding to the outgo of the nervous current into the right arm, be it as vague, subconscious, and unworthy of the name of "memory" as you please, that is, I still think that my experiments support the traditional doctrine. On any other theory, right-handedness would have been devel-oped independently of effort." J. Mark Baldwin, Toron-to, Ont., Nov. 18.

Not so, as I think you must admit, if by effort be meant retardation & difficulty of execution owing to an original ataxy which is least in the right arm!

Admitting the experience hypothesis, (which I adopt from you now, since I have made no observations and your sense of what is likely in this regard seems to me to have great weight) the way I represent the matter to myself is this: the child originally responds to *all* optical excitements which strike his attention by bounding up & down and moving both arms. Erelong the movement becomes one of grasping with both. Some graspings prove easy, and the original bilateral mechanism con-tinues for a while associated with these. Others are pro-tracted, and the superior native efficiency of the right hand in reaching the goal here, acts so as to inhibit the left hand altogether when the stimulus suggests a case of this kind. Others again never succeed, the object being beyond range altogether, & all movements are inhibited for these at last.

Although I have made every possible concession to the experience theory, as adopted by you, I must say that the notion of a specialized native impulsiveness for the right hand when certain distances appeal to the eye lingers in my mind as that of a natural possibility. Surely the similar native impulsiveness when bright colours appeal is a suggestive analogy. In neither case however, should it ever have occurred to me to resort to *efferent* "memories." They seem quite superfluous; nor do I understand why *you* should so cling to things confessedly impossible to isolate by introspection, devoid of significance in speculative regard, and apparently only tending uselessly to increase, if they should exist, the complication of our machinery.

I am taking a terrible vengeance on you by sending you this long letter. But you began! I will promise to make no reply if you write.[6]

[unsigned]

95 Irving St.
Cambridge, Mass.
Jan 3, 1891

Dear Professor Langley,

I am sorry to say, in response to your inquiry, that I know of no such article on hypnotism as you describe. Everything that I am acquainted with is either too long or too insignificant. I am, however, a poor person to apply to, for I don't follow the more popular magazines, & there might be lots of things in the Revue des deux Mondes, or the Deutsche Rundschau, etc., which never would come to my knowledge. Hodgson tells me of an article by one Herter in the Pop. Sci. M. 1887 or '8, but I don't know it. I am very sorry not to be more helpful.

The S. P. R. fund doesn't mount up brilliantly. Even your letter wouldn't draw anything from Mr. Forbes. But we will enter upon our first half year of 1891 and trust to Providence to pull us through.

Very truly yours

Wm James[7]

95 Irving St.
Cambridge, Mass.
March 23. 1891

Dear Thos.

I have read every word in your book about the Greek
philosophers, and can't refrain from expressing my high
satisfaction with the manner in which 'tis done. It
couldn't be better for the purpose, Plato especially.
Readable, light, varied, and full of accurate information.
Many of your sentences I have used in my lectures. It
was a good test for I read half a dozen other accounts
simultaneously, always with an eye to practical use, and
yours had no appearance of insolidity, altho so much
lighter and more agreeable to read than the more technical accounts. Keep on! One thing has struck me about
your book. When a thing is as big as that it takes a rather
heroic reader to go at it at all. Does not *such* a reader
want the originals? In other words, is there need of
"popular" books on that scale? Make your roman literature short & bright.

Yrs ever

W. J.[8]

95 Irving St.
Cambridge
Nov 18. 91

Dear Mr. Marshall,

I got your reprints of Pleasure & Pain etc duly, but not before I had cracked my brains over the articles in Mind's own pages. You have certainly come to closer quarters with the question than any previous analyst, and your scheme seems to cover more facts than any other—in fact there is no other which seems to have been framed under such a pressure, from all sides, of the facts which it was bound to keep account of. Other writers give far more the impression of starting off "at a tangent." One thing occurred to me as an objection of a rather radical sort when I was reading, but I didn't note it down, and it doesn't come back to me now as I write. It doubtless will ere long. The great trouble with the theory is its extremely abstract character. One doesn't represent to one's self at all just what is meant by your two energies and their relation. The formula *has*, however, to be ultra-vague—the "energy of the stimulus" especially must be kept vague. You can't mean a real numerical $\geqq$ relation, for the stimulus, numerically taken, may be vastly less than the reaction, & probably yet give pain. In the case of muscular reaction Matteucci found the relation to be 27.000 over 1 when the stimulus was a galvanic current applied to the motor nerve. What your formula means is evidently $\geqq$ than the normal ratio, which normal ratio must differ from one organ to another, and from one person to another of different habitual experience. Nevertheless the formula expresses a *real*, as distinguished from a merely *ideal* relation.

I regard it as one of those things which one must keep & use before one can know how much or how little there is in it. So far I can truly say that it is the deepest thing I know on the subject—the most scientific. It is hard reading—so very deficient in concrete illustrations.

One of my students offers a report of it to our "Seminary" next Wednesday evening. Others have been reading it, and I wish that you might come to the discussion. Can you? I can put you up, and you might find it a lark—though I can't offer to "pay your travelling expenses."

If you can't *come*, can you at least let me have before next Wednesday evening an elucidation of a point which I have found obscure? From the passage on p. 352 it would seem that the pains of obstruction are *vascular* pains. Do you mean anything more definite by this than appears? It appears somewhat like an hypothesis because there *must be one*—a stop-gap to round out the form of the scheme. It is not fair to judge your theory definitely till one sees what it will do in the sphere of aesthetics proper. You apply it now only to simple pleasures & pains. The pleasures & pains that come from mutual futherance & hinderance of processes might be conceived as pleasures of enhanced reactive energy and as pains of obstruction. Do you carry the thing all the way through on the same lines?

I hope I am not troubling you. The upshot of my reading this fall is to make me realize how few *ideas* there are in the literature of this subject, and how we still wait for an entrance to the method of treatment which is to prove really scientific. So far I confess you are ahead of anyone.

I do hope that you may come.

Very truly yours

Wm James[9]

· *To Henry Rutgers Marshall* ·

Cambridge, Mass.
Jan 31. 92

My dear Marshall,

I have read your reply to Sidgwick with interest, though it seems to me that the case is insoluble in general terms and without making discriminations which (as you say) language has not provided for. I found Sidgwick's article instructive, and as I use the words "desire" and "painful" have felt like subscribing to it. Most desires, like most volitions, lead immediately to action and even incipient gratification seems to neutralize effectively whatever may be unpleasant in the desire, just as the sensations of an accomplished muscular contraction eclipses instantly the image which defined it to the mind as an object of volition. If the action is thwarted, we have an "uneasiness" which leads to "pain" if the thwarting becomes strong or prolonged. But whenever there is a crescendo in the direction of prompt satisfaction, to my consciousness, its pleasure is much stronger than the potential pain of the desire, in ordinary cases.

Delboeuf some where asks whether the beginnings of sexual desire are not pleasant. I suppose most men would say yes. Only after considerable thwarting will "pain" come in.

That is all I can say of the matter just now.

I thank you for your invitation to the Century. I can't tell now how many hours I can spend in N. Y., but I will let you know in time.

Yours very truly

Wm James

Of course *send your rejoinder!*[10]

· 81 ·

95 Irving St.
Cambridge, Mass.
March 3. 92

Dear Mrs. Franklin,

It gives me great pleasure to receive your letter which in business like and expeditious manner, I must answer point by point. I had no idea you were abroad and on the whole congratulate you on the opportunity. I am myself to have my "sabbatical" next year, and take the family in July to Germany. Possibly you and Professor Franklin will still be there.

Thank you for your continued indulgence as to the Psychology. The last chapter however is the one for which I mainly craved your approval as a logician & mathematician, and now it turns out to be the one which you chiefly disapprove! The unfathomable ways of woman! If I ever do revise the book you shall go in with the horopter. I didn't mention that because it seemed to me to have much more mathematical than psychological interest—in fact hardly any of the latter except what your illusion gave it.

I have a sort of terror of Müller as of all mathematically minded geniuses including yourself. But I'm glad you & he are such good friends—of course we are going to have women in Harvard soon—Göttingen mustn't be allowed to get ahead there. But which theory of Hering's do you mean—he has so many? Is it colour, space, contrast, what? I rather admire Hering all round. Helmholtz of course is much the greater man, and yet he probably has made more mistakes. I shall be greatly interested in your article, whenever it appears.

I shall be delighted to read your Intuition and Reason in the MS., and to do what I can to recommend it. Don't you want the Pop. Sci. M.?

Always faithfully yours

Wm James[11]

· *To Hugo Münsterberg* ·

Vers chez les Blanc, sur Lausanne
9. 8. 92

My dear Münsterberg

I have but just received your letter from Freiburg of the 2nd August. I am *excessively* grieved to hear of your illness. That it should have come at just this particular moment is indeed a most unhappy stroke of fortune, for the visit to the London Congress would have been not only a most agreeable but also a most instructive experience for you, and the assembled psychologists ought certainly to have had the advantage of seeing the face and hearing the voice of one whose works have excited so much of their attention in recent years! You speak of a gastric fever—an acute gastritis is a pretty serious thing, and I hope it is not that from which you have suffered. But since you speak of being already convalescent, and of travelling away again soon, I assume that all cause for anxiety must be over, and I only hope that you may never have a relapse.

I am using certain scraps of paper which are all that I can lay my hands on. I only arrived here last night, and my wife who has the paper supply locked up is gone off on a walk. It would appear from your letter that two of our epistles have gone astray. I never received the letter you say you wrote me from Berlin, the last letter I had from you being at Lucerne, on the eve. of your departure from Freiburg. You on the other hand appear never to have got a letter I wrote you from Lucerne (about the 8th of July?) in which I advised you to telegraph to Mrs. Gibbens to take the rooms in Sumner Street for you. I did this in consequence of a letter from her, and am glad to hear that Royce has already taken them. I sent my letter to the care of your brother Otto in Danzig.

I hope you have already received the $600 for travelling expenses concerning which I wrote to President Eliot. A letter from him of July 20th says "There will of course be no difficulty in M's getting the $600."

As for ourselves, we are both feeling well, and I have had a certain amount of walking in these beautiful mountains, though less than I could wish. I am just back from a flight of 8 days to the Engadin and Italian lakes, *solus.* "The educational problem" is still *infernal!* Our boys are at present in the families of 2 pastors, one at Lausanne, one near Vevey, learning french, and I think that in no case shall we go to Paris. It looks as if we might stay hereabouts. But I hanker after Germany; and having just heard of the Realgymnasium at Stuttgart with Willman at its head, I am turning over the whole question again, and *may,* in a few days, run off to Stuttgart to see whether the place looks tempting for a winter abode. Had I forseen this trouble, I should not have brought the children, nor taken my year of absence but simply given myself a long vacation of 4 months, bringing Mrs. James for perhaps two months, and gone back to work in Cambridge next year. At present I envy you your prospect. I hear nothing from Nichols and shall be sorry if he goes away to Cornell, for you will find him very useful if he stays. If he does go, I should think that Mr. J. R.

Angell would be the best man to appoint in his place. Angell is young, but *exceedingly* clear headed and practical, and made a more favorable impression on me last year than any student I have ever had, from the experimental point of view. As this is only a one year's appointment, we can hardly secure a better-known man. But I must leave that whole question to Royce, Nichols, you, and the President.

I hope that Mrs. Münsterberg is refreshed by her "Kur," that you will have no sea sickness, and that after the first shock of our American butter, bread, street pavements and various other things, you will begin to like the new life very well. You had better address me in case you write again before you leave (but I hardly think you will do so) Pension Cruchon, Vers chez les Blanc, sur Lausanne, Schweitz.

Always heartily yours

Wm James[12]

· *To James Mark Baldwin* ·

Pension Cruchon
à Vers-chez-les-Blanc (sur Lausanne)
Switzerland
9. 8. 92

Dear Baldwin,

On returning from a 10-day trip *solus* to the Engadin, I find your letter of Aug 5 relative to an "extraordinary Congress in America next year," and containing the flattering suggestion that I should be its president.

You ask for an immediate reply. I confess this gives me some embarrassment, for I do not yet fully understand the plan. Still, whatever it be, I don't see how I can possibly be "President" next year. All my plans are at present laid to continue in Europe with my family until the very last day of the vacation next summer and I am by nature so little of a man for Societies, organizations, secretaryships, presidencies, powers, principalities, & politics (even the politics of Science) that I can't bring myself to change them. So that to that part of your letter I must return a regretful but decided "no." Either you or Stanley Hall would be a vastly more *efficient* president than I, even were I to be on the ground.

Next, as to the existence and organization of the proposed reunion. *Prima facie*, I can't say that it seems to me desirable to have the "International Congress" diminish the emphasis of its great meetings by intercalating extra meetings any where, though you who have been on the ground this summer may have seen reason to believe in good effects from more continuous intercourse. As a member of the *International Congress*, I should be rather opposed to this irregular offshoot. If, on the contrary, it is to be considered as a purely American affair, I think it ought to be referred to the newly constituted American Club of Psychologists of which you have doubtless received notice from Jastrow. My own sentiment (which may, I confess, be entirely subjective) is that we Americans should do better to aim at the 1904 meeting. By that time, the beginnings which are so promising now with us will, I trust, have borne some rather solid fruit, and we might well expect to produce a somewhat startling impression of our activity on the foreigners who might come over. Just now we are hardly mature enough to offer them any very striking results. *I* say, therefore, *bide our time* and *claim* the 1904 meeting! I see no great use in the meeting you propose for next year, which will be neither genuinely American nor genuinely international. Aim at an American Club pure & simple, and get all its members interested in working towards a great success at a meeting of the International Congress in America twelve years hence! Psychology, I opine, is at present hardly a massive enough subject to bear too frequent international assemblages. Hoping that this churlish sort of a response will not displease you too much, and feeling sure that my humble opinion will have very little practical effect on you more active men, I am ever faithfully yours,

Wm James

P.S. I have my boys in pastors' families near here learning french, but the winter abode is still unsettled. You tell me nothing of the Congress, but I expect to hear all about it from the Myerses who are to arrive here tomorrow. I hope it was a great success. Poor M'berg writes me from Freiburg that he is down there with "gastric fever." I am sorry.[13]

· *To Jacob Gould Schurman* ·

I hope you ordered the fee for the article in Nov. No. about deaf-mute sent to the d'Estrella California Institution for Deaf & Dumb, Berkeley, Cal., as I asked you in the Spring. It reads delectably, I think. My fees might be sent in checks payable to order of Mrs. Eliza P. Gibbens (Irving St., Cambridge, Mass) until my return. I suppose or [sic] ought to review for you Fouillée's 3

· 87 ·

Idée-force volumes, when the two latter ones appear. I
think the review keeps up well.

Wm James

16 P.ᵃ dell' Indipendenza
Florence
Nov 21. 92[14]

· *To Carlo Francesco Ferraris* ·

16 P.ᵃ dell' Indipendenza
Florence
Dec. 12. '92

My dear Sir,

Back at home again, after the festivities of last week, I
must write a word to express to you my appreciation for
the great courtesy which was shown to me in common
with all the delegates, and my admiration of the beautiful and admirable manner in which the ceremony was
carried out. To you especially our thanks are due for
your indefatigable attention to every detail. I should
think you would need a month's vacation to recover from
the fatigue!

Long live the University of Padua and its present in-
domitable rector!

Believe me always admiringly & respectfully yours,

Wm James

Professor Ferraris
Rector of the University
Padua.[15]

16 Piazza Indipendenza
Florence
April 9 [1893]

Dear Mr. Stout,

I send a reply (which I wish were more short and less arid) to "E. Ford's" criticism in the current Mind. Why will people not write their names in full? I don't know whether Ford is he, she, or it, Mr., Mrs., or Miss. I suspect "Miss," I know not wherefore; but I have left blanks in the text, for you to fill out with the proper sexual titles & pronouns, and have put "carets" in the margin to guide your eyes to them. I dare say that Ward will also have replied, in which case there may be too much of the matter.

I have been much interested in Bradley's article this time. He has taken pains to make his meaning clear, and succeeded perfectly.

I shall leave florence in less than a week and make my way gradually North.

The best address to send proof to will be 34 De Vere Gardens, London West, where I may arrive in a fort-night. If not, things will be forwarded to me on the Continent.

Yours sincerely

Wm James[16]

I hope (not doubting) that your fellowship was duly renewed!

Pension Gottlieben
Meggen bei Luzern
May 24. [1893]

My dear Katherine

Your pleasant words and pretty good night were duly received, and should have been responded to long since. But I hoped from day to day to be able to tell you something more definite about our own plans, and indeed even to be able to propose to you to come to the Verschez-les-Blanc pension above Lausanne (of which I spoke to you) and help beguile *our* time there, for we have been playing fast and loose with the notion of going there ourselves. Now, at last, we have finally written them that we don't come—so *that* dream also fades. My wife, mean while, who has been to Munich for a week by herself (her first absence from the marital roof since our marriage) enjoyed it so much that she meditates a visit to Vevey and Geneva next week, when our little nurse-maid (now on a visit to her folks at Aigle) shall have returned, and will do herself the honour of waiting upon you. I hope that she will find you at least as comfortable as I did, and at most infinitely more so. Life must be pretty monotonous for you both. We have been quietly breathing the air and absorbing the view here ever since I left you. Two sisters from Boston are with us, one an invalid, and Harry came down from Paris and stayed ten days in Luzern, finishing some work and walking, sailing or driving to us every afternoon. He said he hadn't had so soothing a time in many a year. His life seems to condemn him to cities. Alice sends you her most sympathetic greetings, and I my love.

Yours (both of you) affectionately

W. J.[17]

· *To George Frederick Stout* ·

Vers-chez-les-Blanc
Switzerland
June 5, [1893]

Dear Mr. Stout,

I am too happy to lift up my feeble voice in your favor, and I hope you will get the place, for among the younger men in your Island I am acquainted with none more able.

July will be early enough for me to receive my quietus from Bradley. I hope to be in England in a week's time, shall soon make my appearance in Cambridge, and trust then to be able to see you face to face.

Truly yours

Wm James

P.S. On proceeding to write a few lines (*re* your appointment) to whom it may concern, I suddenly find myself embarrassed by the miserable character of my memory which loses every detail of anything it may read, and retains only a sort of generic wraith of its quality. Your Herbart articles I remember well enough; but of two other articles of psychological analyses by you, I have forgotten even the titles and subjects, and can only recall the impression of their thorough and acute texture. Five minutes glance at a file of Mind would bring the whole thing back to me. I read these articles last year when I was in a state of bad brain-fog, and I am appalled at the vacancy of my mind now in respect of all work done at that time. Perhaps I had better postpone my testimonial till I reach 34 De Vere Gardens London W, and if you could meanwhile send thither reprints of these articles (Ob. & Subject in Cognition?—or is that *Shand?*) together with the name of the body whom I ought to address, that will perhaps be best.

W. J.[18]

· *To George Frederick Stout* ·

34 De Vere Gardens, W.
June 16 [1893]

My dear Stout

(Isn't it time to begin to stop *betitling* each other?) I got here last night and began feasting on your articles at 1/2 past 6 this A.M. At half past 8 your note of yesterday arrives (the one sent to Switzerland has not yet come), and finds me primed for my testimonial. Your achievements are certainly far in advance of those of any possible other of the younger candidates. The Apperception and the Tho't and Language I had not read. The other two articles revived as soon as I saw them. I got behind hand with my reading through getting my books published. The year 1891–2 was one of such bad brain-fog that I was obliged for reasons of safety to stop work and come abroad for the year. I am all right now; and mention this merely that you should see that the reasons for my vagueness concerning articles as important as yours are physical rather than moral.

I enclose the word to the judges or whatever they are, and hope you will get the place.

What is the matter with Adamson?

Very truly yours

Wm James[19]

· *To the Council, Owens College* ·

34 De Vere Gardens, W.
June 16 [1893]

To the Council
Owens College, Manchester

Dear Sirs,

Hearing from Mr. G. F. Stout that he is a candidate for the Professorship lately held by Prof. Adamson, I desire to add my humble word to the testimonials that you will already have received in his favor.

I know Mr. Stout only as Editor of Mind and as contributor to its pages. His Editorship is admirable, and his articles on various psychological and philosophical subjects are of an importance which entitle him to a place amongst the three or four first English writers on Psychology. I can hardly imagine that you should have a candidate whose scholarship, clearness and originality were equal to those of Mr. Stout.

Believe me, with great respect, yours very truly,

Wm James[20]

(Professor of Psychology
Harvard University
Cambridge, U. S.)

· *To James Bryce* ·

34 De Vere Gardens, W.
July 8, 1983

My dear Bryce,

The American Academy, etc. is one of the oldest and most respectable learned bodies in the United States, and contains all the wisdom of our "section of the country" in its sheltering folds. The only trouble about it is that it is rather too respectable and its meetings too slow. It has lost importance as a publishing body now, on account of the rise of so many special Journals. But it is really an honor to be elected by it, and you need not hesitate to accept. Cooke & Jackson are Harvard Professors of Chemistry. The Academy has also a section for historical and philological science.

I echo your wish about London. To lie on one's back under a tree on the mountains, early in vacation time is the only *satisfactory* position for human intercourse, in my opinion. Then what people have in them *comes out*—doesn't have to be pumped out or drawn out etc.

May a kind Providence some day provide that mode of coming together for you and me and several of "we-uns", is the wish of

Ever yours

Wm James[21]

· *To Jacob Gould Schurman* ·

London
July 17. 93

Dear Schurman,

Another book-review—would I could make them shorter, but my pen will run away.

My disciple Miller sent me a letter from you in re an article of his of whose editorial treatment he had complained. It was very good reading, and the aforesaid Miller seems to have enjoyed it hugely, in spite of the fact that you had chewed him up so. He said it gave him a great appetite for your acquaintance, although he could not agree in your doctrine of editorial duties towards articles that were signed. It gave me no envy of your editorial tasks! He is a delectable young fellow, of whom the world will doubtless hear more.

I return home, a some what saddened and impoverished man, on August 24th, and on the whole shall be glad to be in harness again—even as a tub may be glad to feel the hoops driven on tight.

I write by lamp light at midday, a classical green London fog having descended on the town!

Best wishes and greetings, from Yours ever,

W. J.[22]

· *To Parke Godwin* ·

95 Irving St.
Cambridge, Mass.
Sept. 4. 1893

Dear Mr. Godwin,

I have just got back from Europe to find a mass of reading "matter" on my table waiting for me, and amongst it your address on poor Geo. Curtis, which has caught my eye and compelled perusal to the end. It is extraordinary that at your age you should have written a thing so full of fire & literary vitality. Of course the subject was one that appealed to your heart, but the result is of the happiest, and worthy of the admirable man and citizen who is gone.

I stayed a couple of days in Paris with the good Pillons—the best of human beings both of them, but with that curious french timidity about the outer world which made me think of two mice living in a hollow cheese. It would never enter their conceptions of possibility to take, *e.g.* a journey to England, seven hours away. Pillon told me that you had ordered his photograph, and seemed to wonder greatly at this inscrutable unknown American who followed his career with such sympathy. Have you, by the way, read Renouvier's paper on Schopenhauer in the last Année Philosophique? R. is 80 and almost deaf, but he never wrote anything more vigorous or deep-cutting, and the *form* of this paper makes it one of his best works.

And now comes something which I tremble to write, and which I might best have begun by. I am about to *beg*, and I never should have tho't of begging of *you* if you hadn't sent me the oration, and if the matter of Pillon's photograph hadn't reminded me of your paying for the index to the Critique Philosophique many years ago. This made me think that you might wish to waste money on philosophy or psychology, and might help me out of my present scrape, which is briefly this.

We are starting, that is Baldwin of Princeton, Cattell of Columbia, and practically all the good psychologists of the country with two exceptions, a new psychological Journal. We have vainly tried to get Hall of Clark University whose American Journal of Psychology is considered by all to be carried on in too narrow a way, to consent to enlarge it and better it, and are determined now to have a thoroughly broad and worthy thing which will cover the whole field. There are enough trained men in the country now to make the journal a success as regards quality, but we need to guarantee the finances to the publisher for the first couple of years. The publisher will be Macmillan, probably, and the first number appear Jan'y 1st. I have undertaken to raise a few hundred dollars. Are you willing to contribute one hundred (or more if you wish) to such a cause? It may all come back to you in a couple of years.

An early answer will oblige and put me out of my misery. If negative *just write "No" on a post card* and I will understand.

Remember that you have brought this on your self! and believe me your once young and now senescent friend

Wm James[23]

· *To James McKeen Cattell* ·

Cambridge
Dec 30. 93

Dear Cattell,

I hope that after life's fitful fever you sleep well. I think that the whole thing was a success, and that *you* distinguished yourself by your tact, good humor and flexibility of intellect! I am only sorry that poor Baldwin had to absent himself the second day.

I enclose a check for 100 dollars towards the expenses of the review, being 2/5 of the 250 which Münsterberg & I promised to raise. You may perceive that it is from that veteran man of letters Parke Godwin and not from Harvard University, which had a big deficit last year and is lying low at present. Knowing Godwin's weakness for philosophy, I successfully applied a stimulus calculated to elicit this generous reaction—I imagine that even Scripture would not despise the operation because the time was not accurately measured. The remaining $150.00 will be supplied whenever you notify us that they are needed. If you endorse this check to Macmillan's order it will be a voucher to the good Godwin that the money has found its destination. *He ought also to be added to the free subscription list.* I have lost his N. Y. address which will be in the Directory.

Happy New Year

W. J.

I suggest that copies of No 1 be sent also to Henry Holt, Thos. W. Ward, and Gouverneur M. Carnochan in N.Y. (Address in Directory) and to George B. Dorr, of 18 Commonwealth Avenue, Boston. They may be tempted to subscribe. Also to Dr. W. S. Bigelow, 70 Beacon St., Boston.

Happy New Year,

W. J.[24]

· *To James Mark Baldwin* ·

Cambr.
Dec. 30. 93

Dear Baldwin,

Life was such a fitful fever on Thursday and Friday A. M. (I having made an appointment to visit the Wards Island Asylum) that I had no chance to look you up and see how you were. I hope your ailment was a brief one. You were missed at the various meetings and at poor Alexander's dinner, which went off very pleasantly, and I dare say that you yourself lost a little of that curious solidification of one's sense of what the concrete psychological Treiben and industry is in our country, which I gained from hearing the other men talk on the second day. I think Cattell appeared to great advantage all through, and I received from Ladd a curious impression of a consciousness in him of his own commanding position. With best wishes for your health and happiness next year, yours and all of yours, I am ever cordially

Wm James[25]

III

1894–1895

FERDINAND CANNING SCOTT SCHILLER OF ENGLAND
merits a special introduction because he was to become
one of James's closest friends, a disciple and helper.
Through James's many letters to him, we learn much
about James's European friends, trips abroad, and the
development of the English philosophic scene. Schiller
came to Cornell University in the fall of 1893 to teach
philosophy there and to work toward a doctoral degree
in the subject, though a doctorate was not a common
possession of English philosophers. In fact, Schiller, to
the surprise of every one, did not obtain the degree. In
1897 he went back to England to teach philosophy at
Corpus Christi College, Oxford University.

During the years 1894–95, James was president of the
British Society for Psychical Research. The American
Society had disbanded in 1889 and formed Branches of
the British Society in Boston, New York, and Philadelphia.

During the early years of the new *Psychological Review*, James contributed very many review articles. In
its pages he also engaged in controversy with G. T. Ladd
on whether psychology was a science and with others
who disputed his theory of emotions. He was persuaded
by Baldwin to submit two entries to a revised edition of
Johnson's Universal Cyclopedia.

A young psychologist named George T. Stratton from the University of California, with his new wife, stayed in James's Cambridge house during the summer of 1894. He was attending the Harvard Summer School in preparation for studies in psychology in Germany. The letters that James wrote to him from Chocorua reveal a very human and humorous side of James's personality.

In late December of 1894, James gave his president's address to the members of the American Psychological Association at their third annual convention at Princeton University. The title of his address was "The Knowing of Things Together." He and Mrs. James stayed in the home of the Baldwins.

Since 1892 James had repeated his series of lectures on psychological topics of interest to teachers in many of their summer schools and institutes. In August of 1895, he traveled as far as Colorado Springs, Colorado, to participate in one such school. He stayed in the house of Mrs. Elizabeth Cass Goddard, who was also a friend of Henry Marshall. In fact, James had met another friend of Marshall, Rudyard Kipling, in the early part of the year.

Just before James left for Colorado, Münsterberg left Harvard to return to Germany. This left the psychological laboratory at Harvard under James's care. James did not particularly like such minute investigations. However, he did have some able young assistants. One instructor, Herbert Nichols, is an example of James's fairness, honesty, and generosity in helping disadvantaged people.

The fourth annual meeting of the Psychological Association was held in Philadelphia in late December. As a member of the Council James was expected to help arbitrate a dispute between E. B. Titchener and E. W. Scripture. James suggested that they fight a psychological duel!

95 Irving St.
Cambridge
[January 1, 1894]

Dear Mr. Schiller,

I was much mortified to fail to appear at Hodgson's dinner last night, but in the afternoon tonsillitis with a high fever began, and I had no choice.

It seems to have been an unlucky Christmas time in many social ways, and I especially regret not meeting you.

We had a good Psychological Association Meeting in New York and wondered why some of you Cornell people didn't come.

Hoping to see you somewhere before 1894 is over, I am, with a happy New Year to you,

Very truly yours,

Wm James[1]

95 Irving St.
Jan 22. '94

My dear Cattell,

I send you my review of Janet, to which I have appended two other notices of works of similar import. They ought to be printed consecutively as they stand, and the matter seems to me so important, both from a psychological and from a practical point of view, that I hope the available space will not be overrun.—Will you please send me *two* proofs—I should like to give one to a medical friend.

Yours always

Wm James

P.S. Thanks for Ladd's formidable looking book about wh. I fear I shall have to hasten slowly. He has sent me no copy, possibly because he knew I should get my copy from you.[2]

· *To James McKeen Cattell* ·

Cambridge
Jan 26. 1894

Bradley is an important book, but *I* can't review him, as earlier in the season I thought I might, for I don't get time to read him. Royce has been vainly trying to review him for I forget what review. If you like, I will try to get him briefly but well reviewed by someone. I don't think the thing very urgent.

I think it would be well to make the correction in the Philos. Rev.

W. J.[3]

· *To James McKeen Cattell* ·

Cambridge
Jan 28. 94

Nichols is quite cut up about the probable expense, etc. You can count me in for 10 dollars towards it, if it is decided to go ahead.—I told him that one *specimen* of the tables in full ought to be enough to print, and that the *results* of other tables similar in principle would do. He disagreed & said that Münsterberg also tho't these tables should go in in full. What do you think? I know nothing of the details of the investigation, but some of the results seemed to me quite startling.

W. J.

95 Irving St.
Cambridge
Feb. 18. [1894]

My dear Cattell,

1) Here is some stuff for the P. R. 2) If you can send me two extra copies of the March No. it will be even better than revises of my notice of Janet's book. 3) Don't you think it will improve the table of contents on the cover to have the pages given? I always curse a magazine that makes you grope after your article. 4) I suggest that you might send Marshall's new book on Aesthetics to my colleague Santayana who is giving here a very successful course on that subject, and is an exquisite critic and writer—Dr. Geo. Santayana, Stoughton Hall, Cambridge. 5) I thank you for proof of Fullerton. I won't make any direct reply to it, for I hope to cover the whole ground it touches on in a general theoretic article, which Deo volente I will write next summer.

Yours ever truly

Wm James[4]

· To John White Chadwick ·

95 Irving St.
Cambridge, Mass
Feb. 23, 93 [1894]

Dear Mr. Chadwick,

I am amused at your assumption that I may be a stranger to you, I who have followed your career with admiring eyes since those old divinity school days when I used to hear poor old C. C. Salter and May talk so incessantly about you.

Well you've given a fine puff to my book, and I hope will have no reason to repent it. It's a fine sermon. Only I am not so sure about "our *whole* self acting spontaneously" etc. It is a deeper stratum of our self which kills the rest, and I don't wonder at the traditional interpretation of it as miraculous grace acting in us.

My wife begs her remembrances, and I am always sincerely yours

Wm James[5]

95 Irving St.
March 1. [1894]

My dear Cattell,

1) I will see to Bradley. 2) I return note to Creighton, which I think good, 3) I return the Nichols correspondence. Of course he made no *complaint* of you; but felt cast down, being so poor, at the probable size of the bill. I will try to induce him to abridge the paper. 4) Thank you! I don't care to see MS. of Association report. Enough reading on hand now with exams., students' theses, Ladd, and Paulhan, and the entire subject of Cosmology now being lectured on by me for the first time!

Yours as ever

W. J.[6]

94 Irving St.
Cambridge, Mass.
May 27. [1894]

Dear Baldwin,

Here is my photog. and much may it decorate the collection!

Only two more lectures this year Gottlob! How is it with you?

How glad I am that Binet will review Paulhan's "Caractères"!

The occasional "lack of perspective" which I complain of in your style "crops out" on this card. I cannot gather the meaning of "I sent you a letter through the Johnson Cyclop. people."—At any rate I have received none whether "through," from, or to, them.

Yours always

Wm James[7]

Cambridge
May 30. 94

Dear Baldwin,

Your note received, and I congratulate you on being so
early "through."

"Personality" and "telepathy" I'll attend to, if the re-
muneration tempts. But spiritualism is too much for me.
I recommend Hodgson as the best man extant for the
purpose, if he will do the job: R. H., 5 Boylston Place,
Boston.

I am trying to get down to N. Carolina, leaving before
the end of next week, to see the forest and the mountains. Could you be one of a party of 4 or 6 to spend a
fortnight at most? If so, reply to

Yours always

Wm James

I'm not sure that I can go myself, but want to make an
hypothetical arrangement first.[8]

June 6th. [1894]

My dear Baldwin,

Could you send me by return mail, any old examination paper that you may have on your own book? I have "a mid-year make-up" for one man on your book, and naturally wish to lighten my labor, by finding a ready made paper if possible.

Yours

Wm James

Hodgson is *the* man for your article "Spiritualism." He seems willing to do it if he need not put it in till the autumn.[9]

· *To James Mark Baldwin* ·

Cambr.
June 8. [1894]

Dear Baldwin,

I am most *heartily* sorry. I had hoped for this best of all opportunities to become intimately acquainted with your personal moral and social virtues, as I already am in a measure with those of your intellect. Perhaps you may join me down there later, as it is *if* I still go. I will keep in communication with you.

Thanks for the exam papers which I return. I enclose my own midyear one on your two vols. Don't return it.

Yours sorrowfully,

W. J.

· *To George Herbert Howison* ·

Newport, R. I.
June 11, 1894

My dear Howison,

I got duly your letter of the 25th, but tho't that I would see Stratton before replying. Everything will go on now as if nothing had happened. Münsterberg took Stratton's visit too seriously and you took Münsterberg's letter too seriously—hence your fears. Münsterberg is sensitive by nature and has smarted under the ferocious enmity which he has aroused in some of his colleagues in Germany, one of the ugliest incidents in the academic life of that country that I know. You have no conception of the hideous virulence of some of it. Well, knowing that they will disdain to discriminate between a vacation course at Harvard and a regular academic course, he felt that if Stratton should go to Leipzig with only his summer course to brag about, they would rejoice in hearing that that was all that the great Münsterberg could do, and spread the news of his superficiality. Moreover, he thought that after the correspondence, etc., Mr. Stratton might expect more, whilst he, Münsterberg, couldn't physically give more than the one hour a day to the whole class. Thus between his reputation abroad, his desire to do much for Stratton, and his inability thereto, he felt "bad" and wrote you the letter of which you send me a copy.

Stratton seems perfectly to see into the situation, and if he only insists on making it clear in Leipzig that what he took with Münsterberg was a vacation demonstration course for ordinary teachers, and not one for professionals, all will go smoothly, and you need not fret any more.

My work, Gottlob! is over, and I am on my way for a fortnight in the N. Carolina Mts. to "recuperate" withal. Warm regards to you both, from

Yours always

Wm James[10]

· *To James Mark Baldwin* ·

Cambridge
June 25. 94

My poor Baldwin,

I am *very* sorry; but the hopelessness and springlessness of early convalescence is well known, and in the twinkling of an eye all will be changed a little later on.

My wife and I may possibly pay a visit at Bar Harbor in August. If we do I shall go over to S. W. H. to see you.

Cattell has sent me proof of Ladd's retort, which I

have enjoyed for its literary cleverness—Ladd is certainly a growing man in this respect,—but I have felt rather badly because I seem to discern an undertone of personal irritation which perhaps is justified by what I wrote of the youths & maidens etc. It makes me wish never to write a review again! I respect and admire Ladd's capacity very much, and this particular "Galileo" and "Lavoisier" discussion we have stumbled into is about as profitless a thing as one can conceive.

Sursum cor—my dear Baldwin. The sun will shine on you yet.

Yours always

Wm James[11]

· *To James McKeen Cattell* ·

Cambridge
June 26. 94

Dear Cattell,

Hyatt says he cannot review Bateson. As it is a book I have been desirous of reading carefully, and as only the more psychological parts of it (if there be any) are desirable for the Review, I should be glad to try my hand at it briefly myself, *if you can't get a really competent biologist*. Mail it to me at *Chocorua, N. H.* if you so decide.

Ladd's article rather fills me with sadness for I fear he is personally hurt. The literary cleverness of the reply must however be some consolation to him! It is great. Of course I can make no retort, for I am on the barren heath of mere subjective peevishness and dissatisfaction, so long as no real theory of body and mind exists. I refuse however to believe that there *is* no matter for theory hidden away in the facts, or that the human mind will forever be without one. I am sorry (or half-sorry) that I let out my feelings as I did, in my review.

Yours truly

Wm James[12]

· *To George Malcolm Stratton* ·

Chocorua, N. H.
July 5, 1894

Dear Stratton,

It is convenient to have a tenant to whom one can confide philosophical as well as practical chores. Will you do for me one of each?

You will find an interleaved copy of my psychology in 4 bound volumes in the shelves at the left of my big writing table. In (I think) the 3rd vol. is the chapter on Emotions. Either near its beginning or end is a leaf with a manuscript reference or quotation from Dr. W. L. Worcester and another medical man, about anaesthetic patients in whom all the emotions seemed preserved. Will you kindly notice the reference (possibly elsewhere) to a number of the Open Court in wh. Dr. W. has made these statements, either 1892 or 1893. If not in the larger Psychol., it may possibly be found in the smaller one (Chap. on Emotions) which is on the west wall of the library about level with your eyes. Or you might, by looking over the numbers of the Open Court behind the leather sofa in the library, discover Dr. W's article itself. *Pray send it to me* by mail. There is wrapping paper in the compartment at the base of the bookcase behind the Japanese Screen, and some five cent stamps in the little Japanese metal box on the library table.

Secondly will you take *all the shoestrings* from the middle drawer on the left hand side of the smaller library table, and send them to me in an envelop?

By doing these things you will eternally advise

Yours very truly

Wm James

I hope you enjoy your peaceful solitude, and (now) a little cool weather. I suppose Münsterberg's lectures begin today, and I am rather curious to know how many students have come.[13]

· *To Henry Rutgers Marshall* ·

Chocorua, N. H.
July 5. '94

My dear Marshall,

I have at last read your book and sent off a review to the Nation. I feel as if I owed you contrite apologies for the delay. You may remember that I gave you warning; but I didn't think myself that the procrastination would extend so far. I was sick in bed for five weeks in the spring, and my miserable head made it impossible to do any reading beyond what was necessary for my College tasks. The book is a robust one, easier to feel vaguely dissatisfied with than to correct. But my candid opinion is that it will remain as one of the landmarks in the history of the subject. I wish it might have been a little less drily written!

It seems to me more and more as if pain proper were a specific sensation, and that you are wrong in lumping it with all the other displeasures. One verbal point: why, when in common speech *pleasant* is a sufficiently good word, should writers on ethics and aesthetics think it necessary always to employ the barbarous form *pleasurable*?

I hope that you are well, and having, or being-about-to-have, a good wholesome vacation. After such a book, you'll have to turn to writing another one to make you feel happy. Why not take up special effects in aesthetics? Not much hope?

I was gloating lately over some specimens of the new blown glass vessels etc. which Mr. Tiffany has been making, and which surpass anything Venetian. Many of them very dull and dingy in tone, with such effects as any candy window or heap of rotting vegetables will present. Yet they seemed so unspeakably *precious*. Why so? It may be that your formula, of mutual reinforcement of elements by contrast, etc. will cover the case. But this ought to be shown in detail. Why not take up these glasses as a specific problem?

The best thing about your aesthetics is its empiricism, and subjectivism.

Yours always faithfully

Wm James[14]

· 117 ·

Chocorua, N. H.
July 6, 1894

Dear Stratton,

Two more chores, if you can stand it! Perhaps the fair fingers of Mrs. Stratton will wrap up the book?

It is Lehmann's Hauptgesetze des Gerfühlslebens, which I find I need. It *ought* to be in the region of bookshelves just above the leather sofa. It is a rather slim octavo, bound in darkish cloth (brown or maroon). If you don't find it thereabouts, don't waste time in looking for it, but let me know, and I will send for the library copy. My own copy has notes in it, which I can use.

2. Will you kindly step into the Charles river bank, and grab a dozen or so of the "tickets" for entering deposits of money, which you will find alongside of the blank checks on the desks, and send them to me?

I too am engaged in agriculture. Yesterday and today all hands are haying. Glorious weather. Greetings to the bride!

W. J.[15]

Chocorua, N. H.
July 14. '94

Dear Baldwin,

Cattell writes me that he is now going to visit you, so I address my contribution to the September P. R. direct to you, though I suppose it is still poor C's duty to look after it. I hope that it is not too unconsciously long, and that if you deign to read it, it may end by converting you to the truth! Of course it goes in as 'Discussion,' in the finer print.

Herbert Nichols is staying with me for a few days. He is about as big a fellow in all manly moral qualities (as pluck, magnanimity, sympathy etc) as I ever knew, and that is saying a good deal. Fate seems unaccountably against him in the way of an *Anstellung*, though he richly deserves one.

Proof should be addressed to me here. Best regards to Mrs. Baldwin, Cattell and all your circle.

Always yours,

Wm James[16]

Chocorua
August 6th. [1894]

I am reminded that I should probably have mentioned Münsterberg in my article on Emotions in the *note* in wh. I mentioned Miller & Nichols as believing pain proper to be a matter of reflex intolerability. In his 4th Beiträge, if I recollect rightly, he expressly says this. Do you or Baldwin remember ought of this? And if I be not certainly incorrect, & if it be not too late, can you *by any modification whatever* in the note, lug in his name? I am sorry to trouble you, but such an omission might seem queer in me to Münsterberg & I haven't his Beiträge here.

Wm James[17]

· *To James McKeen Cattell* ·

Chocorua, N. H.
Aug 11. 94

Dear Cattell,

Here is my review of Bateson, an interesting book. I will send a notice of Galton as soon as I get at my number of Mind, probably early in September.

I hope that S. W. H. is lovely and that you and Baldwin do not quarrel.

Yours sincerely

Wm James[18]

· *To George Malcolm Stratton* ·

Chocorua, N. H.
August 14th, [1894]

My dear Strattons,

I am almost afraid that this note of good bye will reach you too late. I hope that things have continued to go well, and that you have gained a good smattering of phenomena & instruments from the Summer School. Now your real fun is to begin, and I trust it will be "fast & furious." Write about Christmas time what your impressions of "abroad" are. I will send you a note to Stumpf when you write me that you are going to Berlin. See that the house is well fastened (cellar door locked, etc.), leave the key at Miss Norton's, and believe us both your friends & well wishers,

Wm James (and wife!)[19]

Chocorua, N. H.
Aug. 25. 94

My dear Baldwin,

Your hospitality and friendliness are worthy of the golden age. We have had so many friends with us this summer—four of them at this moment—that other things have languished and what can be done in September will depend on what is done between now and then, the ups and downs of my constitution being always a Hauptmoment which can't be exactly foreseen, since the tide of well being, when it comes, has to be taken at the flood to do a little work in, and when it ebbs is a good time to get away for a change, and the ebb and flow are rather capricious. At any rate my *wife* can't get away from house keeping, so with heartiest thanks to Mrs. Baldwin and yourself she begs you, with much regret, to count her out.

I will let you know at the earliest possible moment just what the possibilities are. I should like extremely to be with you. Please say to Jastrow how sorry I am that his letter reached me so late, and that he couldn't stop here. Possibly he may do so on the way down or may meet me in Cambridge on Tuesday or Wednesday of the 1st week in September. I have to go there for two days then. I suppose the letter I sent him at Phila. was forwarded to S. W. H.

I am at present trying to dig some rational truth out of myself for a future number of the Psych. Rev., but it comes hard and has to be blasted, and I fear will result in shapeless debris.—By the way, how Titchener seems to have taken upon himself the office of sole protector, defender and guardian of Wundt. Yesterday came his Brain-review of W. & Külpe. His loyalty is commendable, but he rather overdoes the business in my opinion and his luminousness is less than his zeal. But he's an amazing fellow for getting up details. Warm regards to both yourself & Mrs. B. Also to Cattell & Jastrow.

W. J.[20]

· *To James Mark Baldwin* ·

94 Irving St.
Cambridge, Mass.
Sept. 26. [1894]

Dear Baldwin,

I hope you all got prosperously home. I am just back (finding your letter about Cyclopedia etc., already answered verbally) after a glorious day yesterday—steam launch to Seal Harbor then over Sargent's Mountain home. I never saw so much *character* in so few miles. I bethought me after leaving you that I hadn't paid my telephone to B. H. and that you probably had. Keep the enclosed dollar bill, please, as a fractional reimbursement of all the various payments you have had to make on my account.

Good luck and thanks to you both for your kindness, and may the Princeton year run merrily to its close.

Yours always truly

Wm James

Cambr.
Oct. 24. [1894]

Dear Baldwin,

Here goes a rather stout Hallucination report—but the subject is so important if the english Committee's conclusions are true, that the thing had to be done carefully and well. I wish it might get into the Jan No. But you know what is best. . . .

Tout à toi

W. J.[21]

· *To James Mark Baldwin* ·

Nov. 19. 94

Dear Baldwin,

Please thank Mrs. Baldwin ever so much & say that my wife and I will be too delighted to be her guests and yours during the famous Association meeting, and shall duly appear on the 26th.

Yours always,

Wm James

P. S. Is any one noticing Hirsch's Genie u. Entartung for the review? If not, I will do so briefly.[22]

· *To Martha Carey Thomas* ·

95 Irving St.
Cambridge
Feb 12. 1895

Dear Miss Thomas,

I know Hodder intimately, and for intellectual capacity he is one amongst a million, I was going to say; combining in a very high degree both philosophical and literary taste and ability. His learning too is varied and miscellaneous. His style is remarkable for rhythm and musical quality—also for classic simplicity in matters of philosophy. His only "out" is a certain *insouciance* of character; but he has no crotchets or angles, and is perfectly amiable. I should think him a prize for you (or for us) degree or no degree, and I find it hard to believe that you stick at such pedantries, at Bryn Mawr.

I can't answer the question you ask about our giving him a Ph. D. degree. The committee would have to meet and consider an application eventually made by him. I imagine it might be done.

I am glad you like Miller who is certainly great, and ever growing greater. A *satisfactory* creature to have dealings with!

Sincerely yours

Wm James[23]

Cambridge
March 20. [1895]

Dear Professor Creighton,

The Am. Psych. Assn. voted at Princeton to give its report to any journal that cared to print it. The Secretary Dr. Sanford, of Clark U., has the matter in his charge. If you wish to print, not the entire report, but only some papers, I am sure you are welcome to my summary of mine, as far as I am concerned, and as far also as the Association is concerned, for the larger permission covers the lesser one.

I regret to say that I am too balled up with work to review Baldwin's new book, even for your review. Believe me,

Truly yours

Wm James[24]

· *To George Malcolm Stratton* ·

Cambridge, Mass.
April 12, 1895

My dear Stratton,

I am a sinful creature to have left you all winter without a line either of friendliness or of introduction to Stumpf, in spite too of your charming epistle of Jan 13th. duly received from Leipzig. I can give no excuse but invincible *eboulia* in the matter of letter-writing, and I suggest to you as an interesting theme for a psychological essay the question why it is that a letter not answered immediately, once postponed, inevitably becomes one impossible to answer at all. I have had the liveliest *regungen* towards you, and seen your letter weekly, but no go! I couldn't write to you till tonight. I suppose that by this time you are beyond the need of any introduction to Stumpf, to whom I nevertheless send you a brief line of recommendation. I am sorry to hear so many Americans write of his lectures as very dry. But he is clear and a born analyst, and a true hearted man. I hope you may have met our men Bakewell and Pierce in Berlin— Bakewell has an especially fine intellect. The year is speeding away here—next week being Easter holiday, and then only 5 weeks more of lecturing, Gottlob! Münsterberg will already have written you of his plans. The laboratory-work seems to have gone on exceedingly well this year—there are Wednesday evening meetings now with reports of work, and I get the highest impression of the vitality of the whole affair, and most devoutly wish that Münsterberg were not going or only going for one year. His health has been fairly good, but his poor wife you know has had to have an operation for appendicitis, from which she has now made complete recovery. I am well enough, and next year must take entire charge of psychology save that the experimental work that Münsterberg has under way will be subject to his epistolary guidance. I hope that Mrs. Stratton is as enthusiastic and cheerful about Germany as she was about Cambridge. More so, I have no doubt, even though that was the honeymoon. Let me know dear Stratton what your future plans are, & believe me always sincerely yours—and hers

Wm James[25]

· To Martha Carey Thomas ·

95 Irving St.
Cambridge
May 17th 1895

Dear Miss Thomas,

Some time ago our friend Hodder told me that he should consider himself in duty bound to resign his recent appointment at Bryn Mawr in case he failed to get the Doctorate the possession of which had practically been made one of its conditions.

Well, the committee on Philosophy decided yesterday that his thesis was not of the proper sort for the degree, and as one of that committee I wish to say to you on my own account that this does not in the least carry with it the consequence that Hodder is not a Ph.D. man. He most emphatically is so in the opinion of all of us, but the circumstances under which he came up this year, the short time, the aloofness from philosophy of the past two years, the literary and unpedantic form itself of the thesis itself made it not quite substantial enough in bulk and detail for our standard, and we have done what we often have to do, remitted it to the candidate for more elaboration. I hope sincerely that he will not come up again and that you will not accept his resignation. I expressed to you at the time my own opinion of the vanity of the Ph.D.–bauble where there was independent proof of the man's power, and it would be sheer injury to Hodder and his work with you to have his attention and strength turned from literary matters to the refitting himself for this examination next year.

The worst punishment I can wish to you, dear Miss

Thomas, for driving Hodder into this degree-business, is that by his failure you may lose his services!

Pray excuse the impertinence of this epistle, and believe me most sincerely yours,

Wm James[26]

· *To Paul Carus* ·

95 Irving St.
Cambridge, Mass
June 6. 1895

Dear Dr. Carus,

Mr. Albert Gehring of our graduate school has written an essay which I have advised him to brave your editorial terrors with. It goes with this, and I bespeak for it your editorial attention, for it seems to me both solid and interesting, though in case you accept it, you may have certain suggestions of improvement to make.

The Monist holds its own well, and I hope will maintain its speciality of what may be called cosmological as distinguished from psychological and metaphysical articles.

With cordial greeting, I am truly yours

Wm James[27]

Chocorua, N. H.
July 9 [1895]

Dear Baldwin,

Your card received: thanks.

I send you my only contribution to the next number—
in two envelopes, since I have no large ones. I have been
taking a month of mental vacuity, and find it a very
natural condition to remain in. In a few days I shall
attack Sergi on pleasure and pain for you; and then *your*
Mental Development—you see how slowly I get round.
Keep well at South West Harbor, and give most cordial
regards to Mrs. Baldwin. I start next Monday on a summer school lecturing job which will last a month and take
me by August as far as Colorado.

Yours as ever

W. J.[28]

· *To Edward Bradford Titchener* ·

Cambridge
Aug. 20. 95

Dear Dr. Titchener,

Can you tell me with any approach to exactitude when your translation of Külpe's Psychology is likely to see the light, and oblige

Yours sincerely,

Wm James[29]

· *To Henry Rutgers Marshall* ·

95 Irving St.
Cambridge, Mass.
Sept 29. 95

My dear Marshall,

My "seminary" is going to tackle pleasure-pain again for the first half year. The laboratory library is always a beggar. Could you endow it with your egregious little book, seeing as how it will be much needed? The bigger book is there.

Fie on a beggar!

Someone told me that you had seen and approved my very brief notice of the worklet which I do indeed think important.

Has business revived? Or has the philosophic character blasted your worldly fortunes forever? I hope not.

I have had a fine vacation with no head work, and feel very well. Family ditto. I stayed at Col. Springs in the charming house of the charming Mrs. Goddard—a house which you know.

Yours always

Wm James[30]

· *To Charles William Eliot* ·

95 Irving St.
Cambridge
Oct 22. '95

Dear President,

I have just sent my check for $350 to the Treasurer, the sum having been raised from friends for the improvement of the laboratory.

I have also asked him for $150 appropriation for current expenses. There is a falling off of graduates for psycho-physical work this year, only two having presented themselves who wish to spend a large amount of time thereat. There are two others who give afternoon hours to investigations in which they are interested, and Royce, Singer and Lough are continuing the researches they left unfinished last year. I am certain of the occasional help of a few other graduates and many undergraduates, and although things will go slower than under

Münsterberg, I doubt not we shall get out a number of results, large or small.

My seminary has 19 students, 4 undergraduates having been admitted. It promises well, & I am confident of doing a good deal of experimental work in connexion with that.

Very truly yours

Wm James

P.S. You may remember subsidizing the Psychological Review which prints our laboratory Contributions. The editors assess me for $150. I have vainly tried to raise it from a gentleman in N. Y. and now have recourse to you again. I believe it was charged to "Advertizing" before; and the Review will probably make that title more substantial hereafter by printing accounts of the Courses given in the Universities that subscribe. I trust it will erelong pay its expenses.

W. J.[31]

· *To Henry Rutgers Marshall* ·

[October 24, 1895]

incomplete

me now, as my only escape from this inner torture, if you deem it *safe* for me to pay the Macmillans, as that is *what I should like to do*—safe from the point of view of *your* interests. I believe the MacM's [sic] to be villains anyhow.

We had a symposium over your book last night and your letter with its formula of S $\pm$ n written on the blackboard made it very clear that the absolute value of A had nothing to do with the matter. At the same time I think it makes still more clear the provisional character of your formula from a *physiological* point of view. The term S is not a *present*, but an absent or ideal fact, and you seem to require some observer to notice the relation to it of the present S $\pm$ n that replaced it. This *altered relation* to be physiologically effective ought to be expressible in terms of an actual *physical* process. It probably can be so expressed, but as yet it has not been so expressed. Another grave shortcoming of your theory is that it is dumb as to the opposite *motor* results of S + n A & S − n A. These seem so intimately bound up with pleasant *a* and painful *a* that a definitive theory must surely include and explain them. Meanwhile I fancy that the whole class agreed with me that your theory took more elements of the problem into consideration than any other, and is the most successful attempt yet made to unify the matter.

I think that your quarrel with Nichols about specific nerves could very well be vacated if you would admit that pain-proper (localized skin or tissue skin-pain) might have them, and he that nothing else need have them. Your formula would then cover the *unpleasantness* of pain-proper but not its specific sensation-quality, which it seems to me has nothing in common with other unpleasantnesses. Eliminating it from the aesthetic series leave the latter much more manageable.

I remember the Kipling visit with delight, & hope that business is better than then.

Tell me about the MacMillans!

Yours ever

Wm James[32]

Cambridge
Nov. 6. 95

Dear President Gilman,

Will you allow me to add one word to my recent letter
about Herbert Nichols? He writes me that you received
him very kindly, and that your last words were "President Eliot is to be here in a few days and of course I shall
ask him about you." "This," adds Nichols "will of course
settle Hopkins for me, as it has other places."

All I wish to add is in justice to N. himself of whom
President Eliot has seen little but what may be called the
seamy side. I know all sides of N. and the seamy one is
strong, but the others are *very* strong too, and in some
respects he is one of the very finest human beings I
know. Take therefore *along with what* Eliot says, also
what I and others say about him!

His trouble is misunderstanding others. He got into
an almost insane misunderstanding with Münsterberg,
which however *started* with false facts, for which he was
not responsible. In an *autonomous* place, where he
should not have to square himself daily with someone
else about every detail of work, knowing both sides of
him as I do, *I should nevertheless appoint him, and be
sure of solid and brilliant service.* Of course with rival
candidates, I should weigh them carefully. Pardon my
prolixity, and believe me always sincerely yours

Wm James[33]

Cambr.
Dec. 21. [1895]

Dear Baldwin,

What's up now betw. the belligerent Tit. and Scripture?
I can't act as appeaser till I know s'thing of the quarrel.

What with Armenia and Cleveland, Olney and our
savage-idiotic fellow countrymen, we are surely bur-
dened enough with war without having a Scripture-
Titchener issue to complicate the state of the world.

Let them fight a duel at Phila. next week!

W. J.

Must our Council apologize to Titchener generally or for
some specific offense? Gad! I begin to bethink me. Is it
the plagiarism in S's Seeing & Thinking? Does T. demand S's expulsion by the Council, or what?[34]

IV

1896–1897

THE ABSENCE OF MÜNSTERBERG COMPLICATED THE
promotion of Santayana and also necessitated hiring E.
B. Delabarre of Brown University to direct the psychological laboratory for the academic year 1896–97. There
was some rumor that Baldwin would take Münsterberg's
place. In June of 1896, Schiller began to express his
desire to leave Cornell. James wrote testimonials in his
behalf to secure a teaching position at other institutions.
Because of Schiller's publications, James saw in him an
ally in his own attack on the established philosophical
position called "Monistic Idealism."

James agreed to contribute some articles to Baldwin's
proposed *Dictionary of Philosophy and Psychology*. One
of his pleasures from summer reading was Santayana's
new book, *The Sense of Beauty*. But most of his extra
time was spent in lecturing. At the end of August, he
traveled even to Chicago to repeat his "talks to teachers." Soon after school started, James received from
Princeton University on October 22 an honorary degree
of Doctor of Laws. This rash of activity was topped off by
the Lowell Institute lectures in Boston on "Abnormal
Mental States" in October and November. It was about
this time that a change in James's interests was taking
place. He wrote to a friend, "I feel as if I had bought the

right to say good-bye to psychology for the present, and turn myself to more speculative directions."

Since the fifth annual meeting of the American Psychological Association was to take place in Boston, James invited Baldwin and Schiller to stay with him. Afterwards he wrote to a friend about Schiller: "I find him a most peculiarly delightful fellow. His philosophy and mine run abreast in an altogether gratifying way to me."

James's first book in philosophy proper: *The Will to Believe and Other Essays in Popular Philosophy* was published in February 1897. In the preface he wrote that the philosophical attitude which the essays express could be called "radical empiricism." When it became clear that Münsterberg would return to Harvard as professor of psychology. James expressed his preference that his title in the department revert to professor of philosophy. This title change became effective on 31 October 1897. In this capacity he gave the second Ingersoll lecture, "On two supposed objections to the doctrine of a future life," in the Fogg Museum at Harvard on 10 November.

Instead of attending the sixth annual meeting of the American Psychological Association in late December at Cornell University, James went to Chicago and Buffalo to lecture.

95 Irving St.
Cambridge
Jan. 9, 1896

Dear Mr. Schiller,

Many thanks for your Riddles which I shall, I know devour with voracity, though probably not with promptitude for reasons connected with the course of life, that you probably know as much about as I do.

It seems a swindle that my remark should have made you give me the book. I shall certainly give you my next one if such a thing exists. I was just thinking of ordering your volume when it arrived.

Many thanks once more!

Yours sincerely

Wm James[1]

Harvard University
Cambridge, Mass.
Jan. 24. 1896

Dear President,

Royce informs me of his talk with you about Santayana, and says that you may settle the matter on Monday. As I can not see you between now and then, I venture to write my own opinion, which is briefly this.

S. is a very honest and unworldly character, a spectator rather than an actor by temperament, but apart from that element of weakness, a man (as I see him) of thoroughly wholesome mental atmosphere. He is both a "gentleman" and a "scholar" in the real sense of the words, an exquisite writer and a finished speaker. Those qualities ought to weigh, when one considers the personal crudity of so many of our candidates.

We sorely need a Greek-philosophy specialist. It seemed to me a ray of light when S. expressed his desire to be that, for in that field his merits would count for more than his defects would be noticed. Moreover he is the only man who knows something of scholasticism, & we oughtn't to let a man with such a point as that slip lightly away.

I know of no available man to teach Greek philosophy who would be as safe as S. Bakewell *might* develop into something even better, or we might send abroad—but there is the possibility of disappointment later, and here we know the worst. I therefore advise keeping Santayana.

But I see the pecuniary difficulty which may occur if Münsterberg returns. Would this be possible?—To let

S. go next year on the understanding that he returns *promoted* in case the psychology business can be more cheaply arranged, but with as early promotion as possible in case a new full-salaried psychologist has to be paid. I think that *no* pledge of promotion at all would be taken (as it seems to me rightly taken) by him as notice to quit.

All these points I think should be considered in your decision.

Very truly yours

Wm James

· *To James Mark Baldwin* ·

Jan 29. [1896]

Dear Baldwin,

I forgot yesterday to notice your demand as to my remarks in the discussion on Weismannism.

The Secretary has also asked me for them, but has seemed quite satisfied with my answer that there was nothing in them fit to print, and that the best service one can do the race in this overprinted age is to print nothing when one has nothing to say.

Pray accept this answer also for the Review.

W. J.[2]

95 Irving St.
Cambridge
Feb. 22. [1896]

Dear President,

I hope that you will be able on Monday if possible to settle the question of Delabarre being invited to direct the laboratory next year and give the course in Physiological psychology which is almost exclusively practical. He says he can make arrangements to come from Brown University 3 days in the week, but appears impatient to know his fate, and we too must make our announcement soon.

He is the best man for the purpose any of us can think of—very solid, already with a good reputation, and pupil both of Münsterberg and of myself.

I can make myself useful enough outside of the laboratory. What is proposed by me so far for next year is the psychology-part of Phil. I, a 1/2 course in English Philosophy, the "Philosophy of Nature" course, and a seminary in Kant's Philosophy.

Very truly yours

Wm James[3]

March 9. 96

Dear Baldwin,

How absurdly rumors fly round! Of course *I* call Harvard a promotion, but Harvard itself would be promoted in turn by having you here. I still hope however for Münsterberg the great and glorious in spite of his finite mortality. Allin visited us t'other day, and we may get him for a "fellow" next year. Our graduate students are at a low ebb *this* year. Singer on the other hand is proving stronger and stronger, an *absolutely* satisfactory man.

We found the Pension Gottlieben at Hinterweggen near Luzern a delicious place in May and early June. Frau Tschopf the landlady an excellent woman. Rooms with balcony overlooking the lake. Vers chez les Blanc is too retired for you, but just the place for the children.

Yours always

W. J.[4]

· To David Peck Todd ·

Cambridge
March 28th. [1896]

Dear Sir,

I thank you for the volumes of the Columbian Knowledge Series, and your flattering invitation. To the latter I
have to return a sorrowful negative. It will be quite
impossible for me to write such a book or booklet as you
propose. Apart from the labor—I write with incredible
slowness and difficulty—I cannot express myself on
these old subjects in new ways, and should have simply
to copy my own "psychology." Moreover I am deep in
arrears of other work long since pledged and overdue.
Regretting to be so disobliging I am truly yours

Wm James

Professor Todd
Amherst[5]

· To F. C. S. Schiller ·

Chocorua, N. H.
June 9, 1896

My dear Schiller,

(I propose that we cease Mister-ing each other). I should
in any case have written to you today even had I not
received your letter, simply to express the pleasure with

which I have just read your article on Lotze in the last Philosophical Review. You carry me with you in all your positions. I have always been a special enemy of the principle that the alternative: absolute unity or absolute disconnectedness between things, is exhaustive and you have put the matter splendidly. What I admire as much as the matter of your article is its classical simplicity and directness of style and arrangement. I feel a little more tender towards Lotze's Idealism than you seem to. If I remember rightly, he first establishes his *One* to account for interaction, without specifying its Nature and then he hypothetically gives it the thinking nature since in our own thought we have the sole example known to us of manyness in oneness. The argument for the One is the weak thing. The idealistic hypothesis can stand on its own legs and need not be that of an *absolute* Thought in any case.

I am profoundly sorry, now that your request comes, that I haven't yet looked into the Riddles of the Sphinx. Not a moment of time. But it was laid out to be my first philosophical reading of the vacation and would undoubtedly have been begun next week. I am brain jaded now and have bro't up here nothing but some novels to recuperate upon. I go back to Cambridge on Saturday. I am sorry you want to leave America but on the whole am not indignant. Here is my humble word of praise for you. I would apologize for the paper but believe the original is not to be seen.

Wishing you success—though as an American I hate to lose you, I am always,

Truly yours

Wm James[6]

· *To James Mark Baldwin* ·

North Elba, N. Y.
Aug. 25 [1896]

Dear Baldwin,

Replying to yours of date Munich 10th inst. wd. say
"Barkis is willing, but damns you all the same."

I envy you your glorious tour. I have had a somewhat
unwholesome but instructive summer lecturing and gab-
bling with strangers. Only 8 days now of real vacation,
up here. Off to Chicago tonight to lecture again.

I wish that you had gossiped more about the Congress
and less about the dictionary! I tho't I had answered your
M–g letter—possibly I didn't because you sailed so
quick thereupon. I haven't your fears. The talk about his
insulting his assistants all comes from one [Mr. X] of
Philadelphia who was his assistant, and is I think practically insane. M. is idolized as a lab. chieftain by every
one else. M. has his weaknesses "as who has not?"—but
take the algebraic plus & minus, and it gives a strong
sum to the good. I don't fear him at all in the University—quite the contrary, although personally we are so
bad a conversational blend. He follows his inner destiny
as a psychologist unmodified by the communications of
others—and for the matter of that we all do, more or
less.

As for your neurologist conundrum, how about Herrick, editor of the J. of Comp. Neurol.? Why can't you
duplicate a university, though? If you can, there's Donaldson of Chicago, and Parker of Harvard. Good luck to
you!—and to Mrs. B.

Sincerely yours

Wm James[7]

· To Wincenty Lutoslawski ·

Chicago
September 2nd, 1896

Dear Professor

Your card from Lomza reached me the second of June and I am much to be reprobated for having left it so long unnoticed but I have been overworked and traveling and interrupted by all sorts of experiences, so that my correspondence in general has been neglected and I am only now beginning to catch up. It flatters me that you should express a desire to hear of my news. I have read your two articles in the Monist with much interest and I was particularly interested in the anonymous paper on Polish Individualism in the Geneva periodical. It inspired me with a lively desire to read Polish history, which I hardly need say, has been followed by no active results. I am growing, myself, more and more pluralistic and individualistic in my general views of things; and I think that against the monism which dominates everywhere the philosophic mind, men are needed to stand stoutly up for that opposite view. Probably the rest of my life will be devoted to defending it more and more.

You do not say why you left Kazan or whether political unpleasantnesses had anything to do with it. As you are fond of going to congresses I daresay you may have been at the Munich Congress. Unfortunately l could not go.

I shall be much interested in seeing your work on Plato when it appears, although as you probably know, Greek philosophy is not my forte.

Thanking you for remembering us and with cordial greetings I am

Always truly yours

Wm James

P.S. Are you going to remain permanently in Spain, or is this an interlude to be followed by university work somewhere else? Does the diet of nuts still "obtain?"[8]

· *To F. C. S. Schiller* ·

Beede's, N. Y.
Sept. 15, 1896

My dear Schiller,

I have at last read your Riddles and though you are probably out of the country and very likely have shaken off its dust forever, (I have learned nothing of the success of your candidacy), I must sit down whilst the warm fit is on me and express my very great delight. How strange that a book so capitally written, so "live," so original, so bold, should be so little known! That I myself who am so exceptionally in accord with its fundamental positions, should until now have ignored its contents! But don't fear! It will be known and little by little quoted and then some fortune will be made. It is too rich as it now stands. It is a young man's work—he puts in at once all his system. When you dole out hereafter the small change of many of your chapters more technically and formally, attention will be drawn to the whole thing. The speculations of the last chapter are foreign to my range—I am too timid—but they have struck me very much. I only mean this for a general hurrah, so I go into no detail. I can foresee a more or less systematic siege of monism and absolutism on my own part for the rest of my days (so far as I may retain ability to do anything) and it cheers and enlivens me immensely to find a gleichgesinnten Menschen of such superior power to follow. I hope you will come back to this country, which after all has its good "p'ints." E.g. the political campaign is really inspiring and ennobling. Such admirable documents! even on both sides.

Fraternally yours,

Wm James[9]

· *To James Mark Baldwin* ·

Cambridge, Mass.
Oct. 9, 1896

Dear Baldwin,

Poor Nichols! Why does the Creator make men with such brilliant qualities and deny them the gift of seeing things in their right perspective? I haven't read his American Naturalist yet; Cattell wrote that it was off the mark.

Santayana is your best aesthetic man, but he is traveling in Europe, and probably is unavailable. The next best I know is Benjamin I. Gilman, of the Boston Art Museum, a thorough scholar and an extremely conscientious man, but he may be too hard pressed to do your job.

I am sorry, but I cannot do Head. Too fearfully busy with my new courses. I hear that Münsterberg has been called to Zurich. I am eager to see you on the 21st.

Always yours

Wm James

P. S. No! I can't add anything to my review of Hirsch.[10]

· *To F. C. S. Schiller* ·

Cambridge
Oct. 17, 1896

Dear Schiller,

I trust you are going to the Psychology Association next Christmas, which you will observe meets in Boston. I write you thus early to bespeak you as our guest while it lasts. The Baldwins, I hope, will also be here, so do not refuse. Your letter received ten or more days ago gave me great pleasure, as I hardly need say.

Always truly yours,

W. J.[11]

· *To James Mark Baldwin* ·

Cambridge, Mass.
Feb. 9, 1897

Dear Baldwin,

The editor in you is decidedly getting the upper hand of the philosopher and friend of the human race. I am excessively sorry that you should have spent so much precious time in writing arguments to me by which I cannot be convinced—with your own hand too, instead of by stenographic aid, which in your position you ought to employ for all correspondence. I say I am not convinced because, although trash may have sometimes to be uttered under the spur of official duty or what not, to put one's self down in print is a deliberate act for which one is held accountable. And as I really have nothing to say on this subject, I respectfully decline to spend any time in trying to make it look like something. Very sorry to disoblige you, but you see what I am gaining already by having my name left off the title page.

Always affectionately yours,

Wm James

· *To Charles William Eliot* ·

95 Irving St.
Feb. 21. [1897]

Dear Mr. Eliot

In re Münsterberg I feel like making a few comments additional to what Prof. Royce informs me he wrote you.

I believe that M. is far and away, all things considered, the best man in the field.

Baldwin, all things considered again, is a close second. He hasn't anything like M's experimental fertility & originality, but he is full of ideas otherwise, and tremendously energetic. He will write many books. He is one of the founders of the Psychological Review; editor of a great philosophical dictionary, soon to appear; a gentleman; and a most agreeable man socially with no angles or anafractuosities in his moral character that one has to make allowance for. If invited here, they will no doubt make every effort to keep him in Princeton, and may succeed.

The alternatives come in *longo intervallo,* none of them promising to be men of the "size" that we should like to have permanent figure heads in our philosophical department. The most important are

Delabarre;

Sanford, now at Clark, a good & careful, but not original experimentalist;

Witmer of Pennsylvania U., energetic, intelligent, but not heavy weight;

Titchener of Cornell, very energetic and reputed a great success as a teacher, but apparently not original in the way of ideas, and (although from Oxford) quite a barbarian in his scientific and literary manners, and quarrelsome in the extreme;

Jastrow of Wisconsin, perhaps the most deserving of American psychologists after Cattell for his experimental work, but a narrowish intellect, I am afraid, and (possibly) with uncomfortable peculiarities of character;

Scripture of Yale, energetic but shallow, and a complete barbarian;

Finally Jim *Angell* of Chicago, a fine mind & character, but too young to have shown his hand much yet.

I don't mention *Cattell* of Columbia, who is very strong in all ways, because he is getting involved in editorial work which will more and more arrest his laboratory activity. Besides he probably would not leave his very peculiarly arranged berth at Columbia.

These are the only obvious names, and that of Delabarre seems to be the one with fewest *minuses,* though I fear he will be inferior in point of productive energy to some of the others.

If I myself had the responsibility of the decision, I should prefer half a year of M–g with the chance of his perpetuity, to an irrevocable arrangement with any of these men, beginning next year.

M. will probably come for the whole year anyhow if you insist, but if he should not, I don't regard the half year arrangement as being quite as fatal as do Royce and Palmer. It is more a matter of appearance and advertisement than of reality, though of course I admit some grave objections.

My own strong conviction is that the Harvard policy ought to be that of always striking for the most *distinguished* man in the market when we have a vacancy. This means a mature man with a good salary elsewhere. But we can economize then in the grade and rapid rotation of our assistants. This is why I go in for Münsterberg or Baldwin, altho' I fear that neither of them can be counted on for more than 5 or 6 years longer to pay very assiduous personal attention to the laboratory work. But Assistants will long after that work well under their inspiration, and they will never fail to be leaders in *some* way, and men whose names will be an honour to us, whereas your conscientious mediocrity with no marked agressiveness [sic] or originality becomes only a wheel in the machine, which the machine then has to be trusted to keep running.

I hope you are getting well fast, and though I send this in today, I trust you won't read it till you're better. Of course you will make no reply. Nor does the hurry of a decision now seem as great. The department can reserve 5 hours of Psychology for the incumbent whoever he be, and arrange the announcement of its other courses without delay.

Sincerely yours

Wm James[12]

Cambridge, Mass.
March 6, 1897

My dear Schiller,

I am shocked and outraged at what you tell me of Cornell no longer requiring your services. Their finances must be very much straitened indeed to make them confront such a decision. If only we might get you here! You and I could then found a regular school of pluralism and sweep the country. But the devil of it is that there is absolutely no place here for anyone new but an experimental psychologist who, we hope, will be [Hugo] Münsterberg. But the money question as regards him is an excessively difficult one to solve and of course a man of your type (unless I should die or resign to make room for you) is out of the question. It cannot be that you will lack employment for long and I will write you testimonials by the yard, whenever you apply to me for such a thing. You are certainly one of the two or three constructive philosophers in the country. I don't include Silberstein among the sacred number. The story of that book is a long one and I am glad that Seth has noticed it at all, for I suppose that Silberstein would rather be sunk by the shots of an enemy than let the waters of Lethe close over him with no human being becoming aware of the fact. Believe me,

Always truly yours,

Wm James[13]

Cambr.
Mch. 23 [1897]

Dear Doctor,

If I had the thing written out, I should give it to you, but as matters stand with me, it is quite impossible to write Deg. & Gen. out for an indefinite period.

Yours always truly,

Wm James LL.D.

(verso)

Dear Gilder,

Here, just recovered, is the note to you (in reply to your request for my lecture on Genius for the Century Magazine) which swapt envelopes with the letter you kindly sent back to me.

Forgive yours truly,

Wm James

Cambr.
March 29 [1897][14]

· *To F. C. S. Schiller* ·

Keene Valley, N. Y.
April 22, 1897

Dear Schiller,

I have just got yours of the 16th. forwarded from Cambridge. I write by the same mail to the "President" of Corpus [Christi,] though that seems to me an incredible title.

Second thoughts—I will put "Head" on the outside and apologize inside for my ignorance. I shall wait to be asked before writing to London. I recommended you last week to Professor King of Oberlin (who had written for advice) as the best man I know who was out of place. He replied that he had his eye on you already. Oberlin would be a good sociological study, though I fear you are not gospel-hardened enough to stand such an environment.

I am up here for the holiday week; thermometer 6° yester morn and I with "pink-eye"—so no more.

Yours ever

Wm James[15]

Cambridge
June 5, 1897

Dear Marshall:

Since your letter reached me with the reprints I have
been so miscellaneously, not to say tumultuously, occupied, that I have not had an instant to cast my eye
upon the Religious Instinct. It will give you an idea of
my busy life when I tell you that perhaps the thing that I
have wanted most to do in the way of reading this year
has been Santayana's book; but although I have had it by
my bedside, in view daily, I have only found an opportunity as yet to read about fifty pages of it. But the
college year is hastening to its close for me, and I am
hoping to clear out to the country in a very few days. You
speak of coming on here before the 12th. Would it be
possible for you at that time to take a trip, with two or
three boon companions of the higher sort, to the Adirondacks or to Nova Scotia? I am wavering between a trip of
that kind, to start in about a week, and going straight to
my own place at Chocorua, and cannot decide for a few
days. Let me know promptly what your possibilities are,
and we will take the Religious Instinct along and jabber
about it on the way.

Always truly yours,

Wm James

H. R. Marshall, Esq.[16]

· To F. C. S. Schiller ·

Cambridge, Mass.
June 5, 1897

Dear Schiller,

I heartily congratulate you on the appointment, though I am very sorry indeed that we are to lose you. I was always hoping that you might become an inveterate yankee. There is nothing I should like better than to have a long talk with you before you go, but I can make no appointment for a few days, since my own plans are uncertain. I am rather used up with the year's work and find that the best thing is to clear out of Cambridge at the first possible moment, for the doorbell rings all day and admits cranks and bores of every description to devour one's time and life and the month of June seems to be their flowering season. I am trying to get off early next week, but whether it be to my own place in New Hampshire or for a trip with some friends to Nova Scotia I do not know. What is your earliest possible date of arrival?

Always truly yours,

W. J.[17]

Cambr.
June 8. 97

Dear Baldwin,

I have received a paper by Bastian from you for notice. I will look it over and see what I can do—possibly get it done by some one else.

I return the pamphlets you sent me last fall, sorry to have been unable to touch them. My powers are too slight!

What are your summer plans? I suppose you go to Toronto, being a man of affairs. I don't! I shall stay at Chocorua, bating 10 days here at summer School, until Sept. when to Keene Valley.

Best regards to you both

In haste

W. J.[18]

· *To Charles William Eliot* ·

Cambridge
June 9. 1897

Dear President,

If you are making re-appointments etc. just now, I send you a word in writing about my *title*.

If Prof. Münsterberg be called by my present title

"Professor of Psychology" it will (first) surely please him, and (second) make him exclusively responsible for a department which he is better fitted to swing than I now am or for the matter of that ever was. All which does not mean that I shall not be willing to give help in the psychology teaching whenever it seems objectively best. For instance I am down for the Seminary next year.

The title I should prefer would be "Professor of Philosophy." Royce also prefers this. Palmer is quite willing, though he says that his preference would be for "Professor of the Philosophy of Nature," on account of the principle of specification which he believes in.

I should rather have either than my present title, and leave it entirely to the Corporation.

Sincerely yours

Wm James

P. S. A rumor reaches me that you are still somewhat unsettled as to the usefulness of J. J. Hayes, Instructor in Elocution. Fresh from a great debt to him, I feel like expressing my gratitude. A week before my "effort" in Music Hall I suddenly bethought me that I should need some advice from Hayes. He tried me in the Sanders theatre, with the result of revealing an awful vice of intonation, from which in two more lessons he entirely freed me. I should in many ways have been lamentably bad if I had simply followed my instincts. I consider Hayes an admirably sensible critic & skilful teacher.[19]

· *To Charles William Eliot* ·

June 10. 97

Dear Mr. Eliot,

It just occurs to me that before 1890, when I became "Prof. of Psychology," I was called "Prof. of Philosophy" pure and simple. What more natural, in giving place now to Münsterberg, than to resume my former title? Psychology is not a big enough subject to be represented in the titles of two full professorships.

Truly yours
Wm James

· *To James Edwin Creighton* ·

Chocorua, N. H.
Aug 19. 1897

Dear Professor Creighton,

You will have received a Ms. on Hume by a friend of mine, J. B. Peterson, for which I should like to venture to bespeak a more favorably careful examination than usual, on account of the circumstances of the writer. You will see immediately how clear and euphonious his style is, and note that his criticisms are just. Whether at this date so minute a criticism of Hume is called for is for you to decide.

Peterson is a self taught man, unable to do anything

but philosophize, and consequently in the direst poverty, since the book-notices on which he lives bring in so
little. If you print this, it will make him think his life less
of a failure. If you decline, it will be rather a stab; so do
all you can conscientiously. The odd thing about P. is
that he is just the reverse of a crank, having no hobbies,
but a fair open aired mind of common sense conservative
type.

Sincerely yours

Wm James[20]

· *To James Mark Baldwin* ·

Cambr.
Oct. 9. 1897

Dear Baldwin,

The Harvard Nat. Hist. Soc. is an undergraduate &
graduate student affair, to be associated with which is,
an und für sich, neither glorious nor wealth giving. All
these societies give *themselves* glory occasionally by inviting lecturers. Much as I should like you to come here
(staying with us) I advise you under the circumstances
not to do so, for your own sake. It is very hard to get out
a really big audience for any of these extra evening lectures—we have too many. On the other hand the audiences being select, are more specially interested than
in smaller places when they are general.

I got your card a week ago, and am very sorry to hear
of your breakdown. Too much *editing*? dictionary etc?

Too much ambition? disinclination to say no? pride? spirit? etc. I fear so. Go slow, my dear friend and all will be right again. Never lecture for less than $100, & they'll let you alone.

I got a letter from Fullerton about your successor at Ithaca. I cd. only think of Hyslop, who is rather deadly; and, among the younger men of J. R. Angell. But I had no list, and have been expecting to hear something from Cattell, whose proposal would probably be judicious. Of course Münsterberg would make the best speech of anyone of the remnant, but he may be better to keep for another year. What do you think? Who is your candidate? *I* shall not go to Ithaca at all.

I had a shining month in Keene Valley—3 weeks rather, but was wakeful all the time. The rest of the summer very well (but doing no work) at Chocorua. We are all now well here, and the first week of the College year gone by with very little of the usual *Pech*. I do hope that with prudence you will soon recover. You do work enough for 3 ordinary men.

Best regards from us both to Mrs. B. & you

W. J.[21]

· *To Frank Thilly* ·

Cambridge
Nov 24. 97

Dear Prof. Thilly,

I am ashamed to say that my acquaintance with Paulsen's Ethics is limited to 2 or 3 chapters from the middle of the book. One lives on an inclined plane of hopes as regards *reading,* on which like the snail of mental arithmetic one slips back more in 24 hours than one gains. I can therefore give you no opinion of the sort you ask for; but I will send your letter to my colleague Palmer, the Moralist, and possibly he may have something to write you.

Our colleague Wiener read me the other day (confidentially) some passages from a letter of yours in which you alluded to certain trouble which the bigots of your environment were giving you. You have my heartiest sympathy. Stand firm! If you should lose that place you surely after a year could get a better one. Our country is pretty barbarous, there is no doubt about it; and we in Cambridge, in the midst of our freedom, don't sufficiently realize the fact.

> Believe me sincerely yours
> Wm James[22]

· *To Charles William Eliot* ·

> 95 Irving St.
> Dec. 2 1897

Dear President,

I was most agreeably surprised yesterday by the check from the Treasurer, showing an increase instead of the diminution of salary for which my mind was prepared. I cannot help expressing to you my thanks, and my resolve to "deserve" the confidence shown.

And whilst I am writing this, let me ask one more question about what the Ingersoll lecture requires. The New World (and later the Atlantic) has begged me for it.

Does the Ingersoll printing preclude other printing, or not? I care nothing for the matter myself, one way or the other, but Prof. C. C. Everett is pressing me for a definite reply.

Always truly yours

Wm James[23]

V

1898–1899

UPON JAMES'S RECOMMENDATION SANTAYANA WAS promoted to assistant professor in 1898. James himself was honored by being elected a corresponding member of the Academy of Moral and Political Sciences at the *Institut de France* in February. However, this year was a turning point in James's life and career. He loved to hike through the Adirondack Mountains in New York. That summer he overexerted himself while hiking and developed an enlarged heart together with chest pains. The significance of this did not become apparent till later. It certainly did not stop him from taking a long trip to California in August and September, where he lectured at the University of California and repeated his lectures to teachers in nearby Oakland. James's lecture, "Theoretical Conceptions and Practical Results," made more broadly known Charles S. Peirce's "Principle of pragmatism," which James applied to certain topics. This visit included a camping trip to Yosemite National Park in the Sierra Mountains with Charles M. Bakewell, a former student, who was teaching at the University. Shortly after his return to Cambridge, James's Ingersoll lecture was published as *Human Immortality: Two Supposed Objections to the Doctrine.*

From December of 1898 through May of 1899 James engaged in a controversy about "involuntary whisperings" with E. B. Titchener both through private letters and letters to the journal *Science*. Also, he was a bit upset by D. S. Miller's article on his Will to Believe doctrine. Münsterberg's criticism of psychical research in his article "Mysticism and Psychology" was characterized by James as "a monumental exhibition of asininity." Tired of repeating the lectures to teachers, James had them published in April along with three other lectures as: *Talks to Teachers on Psychology and to Students on Some of Life's Ideals*. Later in 1902 he remarked, "To tell the unvarnished truth, this book is better loved by me than any of my other productions, especially the essay on a certain blindness in human beings." In June he aggravated his heart condition by, as he himself put it, some "indiscreet climbing" again. This is when he became conscious of the seriousness of his heart disease.

With his wife and daughter, James sailed for Europe on July 15 to prepare and give the Gifford lectures at the University of Edinburgh, Scotland. The first lecture was scheduled for 15 January 1900. They landed in Hamburg, Germany, so that James could go immediately to Bad-Nauheim, Germany, to take a series of baths for his heart trouble during the month of August and most of September. He and Mrs. James afterwards headed via Switzerland for his brother Henry's country home (Lamb House) in Rye, England, for a short, one week visit, arriving on 3 October.

In order to rest and write his Gifford lectures, they then occupied Henry's London apartment on De Vere Gardens. However, James's heart condition became complicated by nervous prostration. A series of "Nauheim" baths were undertaken in London, during which he was forced to decline visits from his friends. He was especially upset by Schiller's review in *Mind* of Münsterberg's book *Psychology and Life*. A doctor recommended that James spend some time in the supposed more favorable climate of West Malvern, northwest of London. Since this venture also failed, the Jameses returned to Rye on about 15 December to stay for about a month. James's condition was so bad that he had to postpone the lectures for another year and ask for a second year of absence from Harvard.

· To Charles William Eliot ·

95 Irving St.
Jan. 24. 98

Dear President,

I learn from Prof. Royce that the Corporation is making up its mind about the question of Santayana's promotion.

I wish to say that I am distinctly in favor of it. He has fairly earned it, to begin with. And whatever shortcomings may go with the type of mind of which he is a representative, I think it must be admitted to be a rare and precious type, of which Harvard University may well keep a specimen to enrich her concert withal. We shall always have "hustlers" enough—but we shall not often have a chance at a Santayana, with his style, his subtlety of perception, & his cool-blooded truthfulness. He is so modest that I dare say he never sent you a lecture to the Ladies Club at Buffalo, which they printed, so I send it with this.

It seems to me that when we possess a fellow of that *quality* it is a pity to lose him.

Sincerely yours,

Wm James[1]

Cambridge (Mass.) U.S.
le 17 Mars. 1898

My dear Sir,

Wishing to send to the Académie des Sciences M. et P. copies of the few books which I have written or edited, and not knowing whether the Institut has a common Library or whether the libraries of the several Academies are distinct, I take the liberty of addressing the volumes to your care, and of begging you to transmit them to the proper official.

I consider this election even more as a compliment to my University than as an honour to myself. In both respects it is most gratifying.

I trust that in some future visit to Paris, I may have the opportunity of enjoying some of the privileges which this new confrérie offers, and of making the acquaintance of some of my illustrious colleagues, especially, my dear Sir, of yourself.

Believe me, with the highest respect, very sincerely yours,

Wm James

Monsieur Georges Picot
Secrétaire perpetual.[2]

[May 18, 1898]

Dear Howison,

Palmer tells me that Bakewell is going to Bryn Mawr—
why, I can't imagine, for I should myself hate to be
under that petticoat regime—and that he, P., has recommended Montague to you as his successor. Lovejoy,
who has already been recommended by our department
for our Walker travelling fellowship, reports that he is
applying also for Bakewell's place.

Lovejoy deserves all praise, and both personally and
intellectually is first class, but Montague wishes to get at
teaching immediately and has applied for no fellowship.
Why not put in Montague for a year and try him, free to
try L. when he returns from Europe?

Montague does a heap of work, and for originality and
genuine *metaphysical* ability, goes ahead of anyone we
have ever had as a student in my time. He is also a most
modest tractable creature, with agreeable voice, and
clear powers of statement, who, if he once found himself
speaking *ex cathedra* would develop an ease and authority, I should think, which would make him a highly successful teacher, from the students point of view. We all
believe him to have a great philosophic future. Try him!

Yours in haste

W. J.[3]

· To James Mark Baldwin ·

Cambridge, Mass.
Oct. 11. 98

Dear Baldwin,

I am delighted to get your letter, particularly since it seems to show you to be in such good shape. Your activity of mind and body are both alike admirable, and only matched by your extraordinary social activity.

As regards your two queries: My instinct would be to leave out contemporary names, if for no other reason, for the reason that it is so hard to know when to draw the line among them.

As regards Royce's article. I confess I find it difficult to give a decided opinion, being completely ignorant as I am, both of it, and of the other articles of its class which you have. On general principles I believe that books of reference should have very short, concentrated articles, bristling with *points* of information, and referring to places where more extended treatment could be found. I do not believe in essays or explanations in a dictionary like this. Following these general principles I should incline to rule Royce's article out. I suppose it would be impossible to abridge it, and I suppose the "Philosophical Review" or "Mind" would gladly publish it in its present form, so his labor would not be lost. At the same time these opinions of mine are not decided, for the reasons above given. I shall not mention this matter to him.

I went for a couple of months to California this summer, and enjoyed it greatly, and am now hard at work, with all of our philosophy courses bigger than they ever were before.

From yours very truly,
Wm James

Warmest regards from us both to Mrs. B., as well as to yourself.[4]

· *To Wincenty Lutoslawski* ·

Cambridge
Nov. 4. 98

My dear Lutoslawski,

Your 3 post-cards, one from Lomza, 2 from Helsingfors, have duly come, along with the Individualism pamphlets. I answered the Lomza card some 3 weeks ago, and I am afraid sent my reply to Lomza instead of to Berlin Poste restante, in which case I much fear you will have missed it. You see how incorrigibly careless I am! My letter explained, without excusing me, how your inquiry of last Spring came to be left unanswered. I will not *infandum renovare dolorem* by repeating here what I said in explanation, or how I went on to tell you that there was no chance of the authorities here inviting you to come over from Europe. Only the greatest *sommités* & celebrities can be so invited, and though you are sure to become one, you are not one yet.

Can't you come at your own risk. You might then, with your great versatility and facility, get a number of paying lectures at different places. But at the moment you are known only as a some what excentric genius of whom people will be afraid. One of our greek professors told me he distinctly did not wish his students to be put to such unintellectual work as counting Plato's words etc.

I have to confess to my shame that I have not read your Plato, although you sent it to me. A genius of our own who was staying with me shortly after the book arrived fell upon it and devoured it, and so I gave it to him, as he said he wished to write a notice of it for the Nation. Neither notice nor book have I seen, and being driven to death for the next 2 years on absolutely incongruous lines, I fear it will be long ere I get back to it. The moderate tone of your reply to Shorey is very pleasing.

I have read your individualistic pamphlet with *extreme* satisfaction, and can easily place a dozen more copies where they will do good, if you should care to send them. It is exceedingly clear and complete, and altogether has struck me as the type of a new sort of philosophic statement, affirmative rather than polemic, yet clearly setting forth the contrasts with other theories. I can't write letters, or express myself on paper without an almost deadly effort, so I make no criticisms and express no doubts. On the whole your philosophy is also my ideal. It must be worked out into clearness. At the same time the monistic or universalistic view seems to have an *authority* that altogether goes beyond reason. No monist can ever be converted—you get no "purchase" on him at all, you don't *start* him. An unsatisfactory state of things!

Forgive! forgive! forgive! my delay, and believe me, with cordialest sympathy your colleague

W. J.[5]

95 Irving St.
Cambridge
Dec. 22. 1898

Dear Mrs. Merriman,

Did you think you were never to see your precious MS.
again? At last, le voici! The secret of its over long deten-
tion is a long story. I was about 1/2 way through it some
4 weeks ago, but a sudden wave of desperation came
over me, at the fact that for nearly two months that the
term had lasted I had hardly put in *one hour* of work on
my own task the Gifford lectures, and I resolved that
instead of trying to do other business first so as to clear
the way for that—and *never* clear it, I would do no other
business on any day till I had put in at least one hour on
that. Since then I have been happy; but many letters
have had to wait, many requests to be declined, and
some manuscripts returned without reading. But I have
actually done some of my work, though the daily hour
was often not given, and I have now read with great
interest the whole of the Religio pictoris. Strange that I
should live to 56 before finding out that one must do
one's work *first*, or never do it.

Now for the MS. Last summer I was with Prof.
Howison in California and asked him why he wrote so
little seeing he brandished so fine a style. "Ah!" he said
"that is what I like to hear. Nobody talks to me like that.
James, what we philosophers need is *praise*. I perfectly
crave it and never get it. Harris (to wit the Philosopher
W. T. H., of the Journ. of Spec. Phil.) calls it *recognition*—I've known people to call it *criticism*, critical

notice, but it is *praise, praise,* that we need." Now you, my dear Madam, have expressly asked for cold "criticism." But, being a true philosopher, I am sure that you must conform to the type of the genus, and in your heart of hearts also desire a touch, *tant soit peu,* of praise. So I will say that the essay seems to me an extraordinarily distinguished piece of work, from the point of view of its harmonious inner beauty and cleanness of style. Not a slouchy sentence anywhere; everything precise, varied, effortless, and concrete, as from a copious yet easy pressure of thought. The analogies from painting form an extraordinary happy feature, and the illustrations from a high-born lady's housekeeping problems are no less felicitous, and both give a great air of sincerity & reality to the performance.

And when I come to supply the 'criticism' which you also want, I find myself very hard put to it, because it seems to me that the thing must be taken as a whole or left—to that degree has it unity. The part up to p. 84 seems to me well nigh perfect—not a jot or a tittle can be altered. After that the composition strikes me as a little looser, and I am not sure that it would not gain by abridgment between, say, pp. 110 & the "Conclusion." At any rate this part was what bit into me least in the reading. Your own sense for compactness will be the best guide as to this; I can make no suggestions in detail. Altogether, I am the worst possible critic for such a piece of work. There is no use in crowding foreign categories upon a work like this. Unless the critic works out from the author's point of view and simply suggests ways of making the author's work more of an harmonious whole, he does harm, not good. And, as I have often explained to you, my point of view is exactly opposite to yours. The master of Baliol [sic] would be your man, for he would *develope* you. I would only impede you, were I to try to ameliorate your thought after my own fashion. You regard the whole as secure, and a point of departure to return to. I as an ideal to be creatively achieved. To me, such terms as "whole," "the law of the whole," "relations" etc, are merely formal and empty when taken abstractly. I ask, *which* of the many possible wholes, laws, relations, etc. And I still ask which, in spite of your fine pages about monist & pluralist, etc. in the beginning of your "Conclusion." It is as good as Emerson in its way, but not sufficient for the technical philosopher d–n him! But to you this requires no farther analogies, for these terms already indicate the deity, are deified. But would I have you go beyond this wholeness of your own thought, resting in these its categories? Never! for that would break a beautiful vessel from which the ointment would be spilled, and nothing integral gathered up out of the ruins. The *form* of your thought, being integral, is vastly superior to that of any possible analytic attempt to define the *matter* farther; and my whole effort is to do that, with complete disregard of "form" of any kind. I am sure that you will find a large & appreciative audience of persons who are hungering for just what you give them, and who will miss nothing of the diseased technical side which I care for so exclusively. Write for *them, affirmatively*. The beauty of your thing is largely due to the serenity of it. It is not querying & wrangling, but *round*. Leave it so. Care nothing for more "analytic" minds. You are analytic to fine effect, *within* your circle.

When I see the enormous circulation of so many of these works from what I call the mind-cure side, I realize the immense demand there is for religious philosophy that is both unconventional and untechnical, and your treatise is so superior in every point, style, illustration, reasoning, etc, that I shouldn't wonder if it had quite a surprising success. The only practical suggestion I can make then is that you should *consider* a little the question of condensation, in the 3rd quarter of the work.—See how useless I am!—Tell your husband that I rec'd his Philippine sermon with hearty sympathy and approval. Results show that youth and barbarism still rule the world.

Merry Christmas to you both.

Affectionately,

Wm James[6]

· *To Elizabeth Glendower Evans* ·

95 Irving St.
Jan. 13. 99

Dear Elizabeth,

Many thanks to Mrs. Hill, and still more to you.

I have given P. 25 of your 50 dollars, and shall give him the rest next month. Mrs. Hill's the month after.

He sent me last week a paper criticizing certain of the traditional views of the syllogism—perfectly sound and good—I should be proud had I been able to write it myself. I sent it to the Philos. Review, whose editor Creighton, in acknowledging reception, and promising reading, adds: "Peterson's style is certainly charming, and reminds one, I think, of the older english philosophers." I can't imagine a greater compliment.

Yours til deth

W. J.[7]

· *To James McKeen Cattell* ·

Cambridge, Mass.
Jan. 18, 1898 [1899]

Dear Cattell,

I am horrified at your idea of returning me the 100 dollars—which belongs to the Review. I refuse to take it back; it was a free & willing gift which I am very glad to have been able to make.

I thank you for the Psych. Rev. for Nov. 1897. I never dreamed of your having to send it yourself.

I note with exquisite gratification your benignant words towards psychical research. Continue along that line and you will be saved, will very likely after "passing away" become a "cabinet control" and instruct the younger generation in spiritual things.

"Yours for the truth"—(as *we* always subscribe ourselves when writing to each other)

Wm James

When I asked Münsterberg to come to Mrs. P., he said: "I am hypnotizable, and if I got such results as you relate, I should simply conclude that I had been hypnotized." I said: "then bring your wife and sit by, & see what *she* gets." "Oh no! I should never suffer my wife to go to such a place." I call that real sportsmanlike keenness for new phenomena! However, it is what Titchener calls the "straight scientific path!"[8]

Cambridge
Jan 29. 99

Dear Dr. Jacobi,

I ought long since to have thanked you for your criticism
of Flechsig, which I confess opened my eyes to much in
his system that I had not realized in my hasty reading to
be there, and much more (the order of development etc)
which I did not know to be still contradicted by his own
earlier observations and by others. You took him seriously all through and squeezed him hard. His intellectual centres for example I took in the roughest desig-
native way as places where association fibres met and
crossed with certain relays. But I see that your reading of
him is altogether the proper one, and I am glad he has
been so thoroughly criticized. I have always felt a lamen-
table want of general culture and philosophic intelligence in F. Your scientific barbarian is a bad kind because he is always so arrogant.
  Believe me, with best regards, sincerely yours,

Wm James[9]

95 Irving St.
Cambridge, Mass.
Feb. 2. '99

Dear Meyer,

I only learned quite recently that you were back at Worcester, entirely well, and doing your old work. Pray believe that this news gave me profound pleasure. I only wish that I had heard it directly from yourself.

Can't you spend "next Sunday week," the 12th, with us? I say Sunday meaning to include Saturday, Monday, and as much margin, anterior and posterior, as you can put in. I think it very likely that Dickinson Miller of Philadelphia may be here at that time—a charming fellow—and you and he ought to be acquainted.

Very truly yours

Wm James[10]

Cambridge
March 3. 99

Dear Howison,

We have been asked to nominate a philosophy instructor
at Adelbert College, Cleveland, and have written in
favor of a man named Buck, altho' if we had thought
Montague's chance with you were *nil*, we should have
put *him* forward, as the Cleveland place is a good one,
and M. is the more powerful man. But we hope still for
Berkeley for him, as being the more important place.
Palmer said lately to me: "If Howison only had Montague for a year near him, he would end by perfectly
adoring him"—and I fancy he was perfectly right.

The moment you are sure you *don't* want him, let us
know and we'll try to get him into something else. But
take your time, otherwise. Far be it from me to wish to
force your hand!

Warmest regards and good wishes to you both from
yours affectionately

Wm James

I enclose another copy of my Philippine letter. Give it to
somebody. Our nation is in a bad plight with that mis-
managed job. A delicate psychological problem settled
by the simple method of Huns or Tartars![11]

95 Irving St.
Cambridge, Mass.
March 24. 1899

Messrs. Henry Holt & Co.

Dear Sirs,

I have yours of the 23rd., and am glad your estimate of the advertizing expenses is so low. You might fill in fifty dollars; or leave the pencilled emendation which I marginally suggest. The latter would seem better to cover all eventually [sic] possibilities.

I see that your right to sell signifies more than I supposed, though I should imagine this particular contract not to have any great market value. So I agree to it.

The terminability of the contract seems to me however an absolutely fair mutual provision; and I hope you will agree to it—six months notice being given by either of us to the other.

No matter for the voucher clause since the advertizing is so inconsiderable. The commission notion was my own idea, which I discussed as a possible alternative.

I corrected the last page proofs to day, and the plates will soon be all cast.

On Monday I will send you the "talks to students" part. It has a somewhat different character from the teachers part, and might possibly justify a slightly different advertizing. The book will cost me, bound, 56 cents per copy at the present estimate, and contain 317 pp. all told. How many copies ought I to give away for publicity? And can you judge of the right price from these facts? or must you have the book in your hands? I will send you dummies of binding as soon as they are got out.

Truly yours

Wm James

P.S. I send the last pp. *now* instead of Monday.[12]

· *To Henry Rutgers Marshall* ·

95 Irving St.
March 31. 1899

Dear Marshall,

I do so hate discussion and explication of differences of opinion, that I owe you a perfectly colossal debt of gratitude for publicly defending me so completely and successfully against D. S. M.'s curiously irrelevant paper. You have written a beautiful article—in point of style more graceful and persuasive, I think, than anything that ever came from your pen. And you have made a contribution to the philosophy of the subject that will be of lasting value.

I wish I could agree more completely with your view of the ancestral experience derivation of so many of our religious tendencies. It seems to me a fact that one can hold with the same passionate persuasion with which "conservative" opinions are held, great novelties in the way of morals and religion. The "subliminal" roots of these things are hard to lay bare. You and Caldwell are here on identical ground, though I must say that C's paper seems so carelessly and obscurely written that yours is to it as Hyperion to a Satyr.

I think I shall leave Miller in your 4 hands, & not make any reply myself.

Always faithfully and gratefully yours,

Wm James[13]

· *To Edward Bradford Titchener* ·

Cambridge, Mass.
May 6, 1899

Dear Professor Titchener,

A letter to Science *re* our late little "scrap" over Lehmann's "unwillkürliches Flüstern" etc., has just been published, and I venture to call your attention to it, if it has escaped your notice. You will, I am sure, take no umbrage at the "gentle irony" with which I express myself. Psychical research in these days of scant justice from the scientists, has to avail herself of every possible weapon by which to score a point.

It is but fair that you should see Lehmann's original letter, which I enclose, begging you to make return. You will observe that he absolutely succumbs to Sidgwick's and my contention as to the indemonstrative character of his own experiments, and that he adopts Sidgwick's hypothesis that the coincidence between his errors and Sidgwick's was probably in large part due to the accidental coincidence of similar number-habits in the experimenters.

On the main point, of "telepathy" being established,

he doesn't give in. That was hardly to be expected of him. As between you and myself, however, the only point under discussion was whether Lehmann had experimentally refuted Sidgwick. I think, if you will re-read Sidgwick's criticism, you will now agree with Lehmann.

Sincerely yours

Wm James

P.S. Unfortunately "fortgesetzte Versuche" are incapable of settling this particular question, for the Sidgwick's own experiments were only about 1300 in number, and that I judge from my own results to be much too small a term of comparison.[14]

· *To F. C. S. Schiller* ·

Cambridge
May 19, 1899

My dear Schiller,

Your review of Münsterberg's unimaginable asinine rot is the sweetest thing in that line I ever read. I believe no more classic model of that kind of composition was ever written, with its humor, irony and logic all *durcheinander*. You are in sooth an almost Godlike being. The trouble is, I fear, that poor M. himself won't feel hurt. Not that he has no sensibility to irony, humor, and logic as formal modes of thought, but that he is so fatuously stuck in his silly metaphysics as to be beyond the reach of any rational effect from them in this case. Real life excludes psychical research, because it offers phenomena in time and the real life is timeless. Science excludes them, because they are mystical. So there is no place for them in God's great universe at all. Happy M. to be the owner of so convenient a philosophy!

And now my dear Schiller, I am going to run the risk of taking a certain liberty with you, which I hope you will condone and at any time take your *revanche*, if it should turn out to subject you to any inconvenience. Some friends of mine in New York, the Goldmark girls, are about to start for a summer abroad with one or two feminine companions and should be at Oxford for a day or two about the middle of June or a little later. They are friendless and inexperienced and when Miss Pauline G. was at my house the other day, I told her that I would write to you and you might possibly put her and her sister in the way of seeing something at Oxford that otherwise she might miss. She will, in consequence, probably make bold to send you a card or a note when she arrives. If you have no time to call, all you need do is to write and excuse yourself. They absolutely expect no entertainment or hospitality—just a word of advice. She and her sister Susan (who is lame) are Bryn Mawr graduates and great friends of Miller. Pauline is a biologist, has done practical philanthropy work among the poor in N. Y., is athletic, a tramper and camper, and lover of nature such as one rarely meets, and withal a perfectly simple, good girl, with a beautiful face—and I fairly dote upon her, and were I younger and "unattached" should probably be deep in love. Be friendly if you can, to however slight a degree, and I will in turn send letters, to precede your arrival, to the presiding dignitaries in the realm of the blest—with whom my influence is peculiarly great.

So be a good boy, and thank me for throwing so charming an acquaintance in your way. Would I could be there myself, simultaneous!

My own plans are hardly settled. I shall leave probably about the middle of July and go with my wife for six weeks to some German *Bad-ort*. After that, whether England or Germany, I know not. I must write two courses of Gifford lectures within the year (have done practically nothing as yet on that job and am now in my spring condition of brain tire) so I feel as if I must place myself in good condition for work and stay there.

Always affectionately yours

Wm James

I am writing a word about the girls to both Merriman and Dyer, but have said nothing to Pauline about it. Will you therefore notify their arrival to them, leaving them thus free to see the girls or not?[15]

· *To Edward Bradford Titchener* ·

Cambridge, Mass.
May 21, 1899

Dear Professor Titchener,

I got your letter of the 8th duly, and postponed answering till I should have seen your letter to Science. Being in New Hampshire during the past days, I have only just found it on my return.

I must say that in my humble opinion you don't seem

to reinstate the value of Lehmann's paper very effectively, and I have said as much in a still later letter to Science. This, however, I fear Cattell will not print, leaving you in the public eye with the unanswerable word.

I seem myself telepathically to discern that, like all Scientists, you felt so absolutely sure that any criticism of telepathy must be essentially sound, that you didn't read the talk the other way with sufficient care. If you didn't think that Lehmann had successfully interpreted Sidgwick's results as whispering, what *had* he done that made him worth quoting at all? Surely his general remarks about telepathic evidence don't exhaust the subject.

Of course he disclaims an *exacter Beweis*. The nature of things excludes that; but he does claim to have made the alternative explanation, whispering, overwhelmingly probable. He has failed to make it *probable*. Therefore he has failed altogether *in re* Sidgwick, as he admits himself.

I think myself that the *experimental* evidence for "thought transference" is lamentably poor in amount, and for the most part in quality, to serve as basis for admitting a phenomenon so subversive of our scientific beliefs. I think the Sidgwick series, however, an excellent model of research; and I hardly see what any one can do, but "hang it up" as something unexplained. That seems to me the attitude of the truly "scientific psychology"—"facts," however anomalous, are worth more than all our theories, however many *other* facts the latter may explain.

I candidly admit that what has made me hospitable to telepathy in general, is the particular case of Mrs. Piper, who so far outdoes these experimental things, and to me is absolutely inexplicable today. Such investigations are fearfully tedious and in all sorts of ways uncontrollable, but they awaken conviction if one works at first hand, without prejudice and gives time. My colleagues for the most part, when invited, have simply refused to see Mrs. Piper. Royce, e.g., who had only to step from the next door but one into my house. Münsterberg said it was no use; if he got such results, he would know himself to have been hypnotized. I said "bring your wife, sit in the corner and observe and see if your accounts agree." He replied "I should never allow my wife to visit such a performance." I call that real sportsmanlike keenness for new facts!

No matter! truth will prevail.

I echo your wish that we might meet. I heard of your being lately here, but you didn't look any of us up, and I was sorry. I am to leave Cambridge for almost the entire month of June, and to sail to Europe the middle of July—to be gone throughout next year. That looks like a meeting long postponed! I hear splendid things of your success as professor at Cornell, and of your admirably systematized methods in the laboratory.

I take the liberty of sending you a little volume of mine, just out, light stuff enough!

Very truly yours

Wm James[16]

· *To Edward Bradford Titchener* ·

My dear Titchener,

I am much pleased with the tone of your letter and I feel as if the episode had on the whole tended to promote understanding rather than to increase misunderstanding.

I gave a false impression if I suggested in any way that psychical researchers were suffering from martyrdom. I don't think that I myself have sacrificed anything by having my name associated with the cause. The only feeling I carry into the matter is one of irritation that in a subject, which to my mind, is one altogether of empirical details, in which no general philosophic tendencies have as yet begun to reveal themselves, so many of my colleagues should keep in the attitude of "authoritative aloofness."

You deserve credit for your small departure from this attitude; Lehmann still more credit for his large departure, but you must admit that there was a certain insolence, and an insolence that felt itself secure from impunity, in the last paragraph of your original article, where you almost apologized for condescending to touch the details of such a subject. I see from what you now say that you were thinking of the whole Lehmann-Sidgwick controversy in a more superficial way than it deserved, and I do hope that hereafter you may keep on the deeper level. The stuff is fearfully dry and its personal aspects are very repugnant to me, but I believe it is a genuine "find," and I *do* think that those who won't come to close quarters with it in detail, ought not to pronounce *ex cathedra* judgments.

I, for example, decline to discuss Münsterberg's article with him. I have served my time with *a priori* arguments, and henceforward will only listen to those who bring definite talk about particular facts.

You say that you have a right to fight for your side as I have a right to fight for mine. What I deny is that at the stage at which things now are, anybody has the right to fight for either side by abstract generalities.

Of what you call "the wretched Schiller business" I know nothing, except the bare fact that he lost his degree. Nutt has done nothing but praise your laboratory methods; Cogswell I have not seen, so pray don't think that any bill is rolling up in this quarter against Cornell.

After this correspondence, dear Titchener, we shall meet somewhat as old friends. I wish that it were not likely to be at so remote a date. If you should pass through Boston any time before the 15th of July, you must not fail to look me up. Believe me,

Always sincerely yours,

Wm James[17]

Westport, N. Y.
June 10 [1899]

Let me know (Adirondack Lodge, North Elba, Essex
Co., N. Y.) when you expect to be up here and what
your Lake address is. I hate to go off without seeing you
again. If you could come up to the Lodge which is one of
the most wonderful forest sanctuaries in creation, we
could have some fine days together. Miller will be thar.
Let me know. I shall be at least a fortnight between
there and Keene Valley.

Wm James[18]

· *To Katherine Rodgers* ·

Villa Luise, Linden St., 1
Bad-Nauheim
Aug 5. 99

Dear Katie,

You don't know how pleasant it was to receive your letter, forwarded by Harry, on my arrival at this place five
days ago. I had wondered before leaving home how long
it would be ere we establisht communications through J.
S. Morgan & Co., and here they are already establisht,
telepathically apparently, for I don't know how you
heard of my intention. I am here with Alice, all the boys

· 193 ·

being at home, and the girl at the Ceresoles above Vevey. My particular trouble is a dilation of the heart (d–n it), for which these baths etc. are supposed to do wonders, and here we must stay for 6 or 7 weeks probably, leading that vile, inert, cowardly professional–invalid life, with which you girls are by this time grown so familiar, probably, as to have forgotten that there is any other. I envy you your Swiss outlook and air. I fear I am cut off from the mountains forevermore; for the chief part of my trouble is due to indiscreet mountain climbing, and I dare not trust my self to the presence of temptation. "This losing is true dying, this is lordly man's downlying, etc."

You poor children, entirely made over again into a new order of creature by your well nigh 10 years in Europe. How I should like to see you! But I fear I may not now. I am booked to give 10 lectures in Edinburgh, beginning Jan. 15, only one of which is written, and that in the roughest draft. So I cannot lose a single day, and as work will probably be impossible under these bath conditions, I shall have to shoot straight to Rye, and settle down in the country near there and write for dear life, as soon as I get released from this purgatory. I am glad of the good news you give me of your own and Henrietta's condition. Pray write more at length, telling me of your peregrinations. Where do you feel most *at home* now? My wife sends her love, and so do I, to you both.

Your ever affectionate

Wm James

Villa Luise
Bad:Nauheim
28. 8. 1899

Dear Lutoslawski,

I received your letter of the 23rd. the day before yesterday, and yesterday I completed my "preface," such as it
is. I didn't send it immediately, or write, because you
spoke of a supplement to your letter, to be written the
next day, and I wished to reply to every thing together.
But since the supplement does not come, I write
immediately.

First, as to the preface. In finishing the reading of the
book it seemed to me aesthetically absurd that so original and vital a production should be *"introduced"* by any
third person. It is like a candle introducing an electric
light, or some little schoolmaster introducing the book of
revelations. Then it seemed out of place that *I* should
write the introduction, because you splash round in the
full deep ocean with your faiths and thoughts, whilst I
wet my toes in the surf, and am entirely given over to all
sorts of technical scruples and objections, which come
up incessantly, apropos of the detail of what you say. It is
ridiculous. Life needs no introduction from half-life.
Nevertheless, I fulfilled my purpose in the only way in
which I could fulfill it—disengaging my responsibility
for detail, and applauding the general spirit as I could
sincerely and admiringly do. The result will seem, I fear,
a little patronizing to you, and the compte-rendu one-
sided. Therefore I simply say to you—do what you like
with it. Don't print it, if you have the slightest feeling
that you would rather appear in your own stark naked

person. Max Müller published his "centennial" translation of Kant's K. d. r. V., in two volumes, of which the first consisted of an Essay by his friend Herr Ludwig Noiré. This always seemed to me a reduplication of the famous entrance of Pontius Pilate into the creed. Now my preface has a similar impertinence. So I sincerely beg you to use it or throw it into your waste-paper basket, as you prefer. Or rather, if you don't use it, send it back to me, and when the book does come out, I can let most of it appear as a review, somewhere. I suppose that from the publisher's market point of view, such a preface will be all right.

I am exceedingly sorry for your poor condition of nerves. No matter! It is probably very transient. When you get students again, it will in large part disappear. As for your visit, I shall be too happy; and can see you every day from 5 to 8 o'clock P.M. My case is not so very bad. But, before proposing any thing practical, I want to hear from you again.

My wife sends her best regards to you both; and I beg you to thank her for her kind autograph message.

Always truly yours

Wm James[19]

· *To Katherine Rodgers* ·

Hotel St. Gotthardt
Luzern
Sept. 23, 1899

We got here, after two days of intoxication (moral) (produced by being discharged from the "Kur" and by the advent of beautiful weather) last night; and the first thing I did this A.M. was to telephone to Sonnenberg to see if you still were there. Alas no!—But we shall turn up at Geneva within 10 days, and of course proceed for your sweet sakes to the Hotel de la Paix.—No more then at present except that I hope we shall find you well, from

W. J.[20]

· *To F. C. S. Schiller* ·

De Vere Gardens, W
October 11, 1899

Dear Schiller,

Your letter and we arrive here almost at the same time and after its round about journey it deserves an immediate reply.

Your Oxford cordiality delights my soul as an abstract principle of my being, but in the concrete it makes me crouch and wince. The truth is that I am in no very good ways as to the health, and the delays have been such that only today has it come about that I have been able to take out some paper and give two hours of serious labor to the Gifford job. I composed this morning an introduction to the first lecture, advertized to be given at 4 P. M. of Monday January 15th., with 9 others to follow. You see what a spurt I must make, the which, with sleep bad, eyes bad, brain bad, heart bad, no excitement, fast walking, sudden movements or energy of any sort allowed (I must return again to Nauheim in April) doesn't dispose me to play the part of a lion of however small a size. Therefore don't expect me at Oxford at present! Having come to this rest, I must stay here, with my wife, the world forgetting, by the world forgot, *incognito*, buried, and see if strict hygiene, early hours, plain diet, omnibus rides for recreation, etc. will pull me through. A year hence (*Deo Volente*) after two more Nauheim courses, I have hopes. I look well enough, but have had very disagreeable chest symptoms since leaving Nauheim. Today, however, they are slight; and I imagine that they are matters of mere innervation that needn't make me anxious.

I am glad you have pitched into Münsterberg's philosophy too. It seems to me awful trash. Have you kept, and can you send me Hodgson's accounts of his plaints? He certainly ought not to be allowed to see Mrs. Piper. He will be hypnotized, if he gets anything—if not, he will have exploded the phenomenon. It is too late!

Item, have you a reprint of your paper in *Mind*? My *Mind* goes to America and is not reforwarded hither.

Pauline Goldmark wrote me of the extreme kindness you had shown them at Oxford, and of her gratitude. Accept mine once more, and draw on me ad libitum for corresponding *gracieusetés* to any friends of yours who may come to Cambridge, Mass. If you knew the above Pauline Goldmark as well as I do, you would have fallen in love with her. She has the best working qualities, and will make the best wife of any girl I know. Probably you saw her too short a time, and not in the mountains, etc. Anyhow, receive my eternal thanks.

A pleasant letter from Miller today, who to my great delight is letting my eldest boy Henry chum with him.

Affectionately yours

Wm James

We are here indefinitely and you mustn't fail to come in, if you ever come to town. I certainly meant to send you my address before: c/o Brown Shipley & Co, London and now superseded by De V. G. Yes! Ward's Gifford lectures are good and, in the actual state of thought, important.[21]

· *To Henry Havelock Ellis* ·

34 De Vere Gardns, W.
Oct. 17. [1899]

Dear Mr. Ellis,

Here goes the preface: valeat quantum!

My illness and hardpressed condition prevent me from copying it out. But I fancy that this pencil draft will be legible both to you and the printers. I should be thankful for any suggested amendments to the proof; and I still feel that a preface from me is rather impertinent.

Sincerely yours

Wm James[22]

De Vere Gardens, W.
October 19, 1899

Dear Schiller,

I ought to have sent these things back earlier. I am much obliged to you for sending them. Also for the Educational Review. How playfully you *can* write!—it seems as 'twere easily too, but it may not come so easy. The Educational Review article gives me a much better insight than I have possessed into your Oxford system. A priori it seems to me vicious, as regards the relation of the teachers to the examinations—but the abstract worst is often the concrete best—and one must live in a system to judge it. You don't get "production" on a scale commensurate with our education; but from the point of view of the wider philanthropy, I am not sure that the frustration of much writing is not genuinely the good to be aimed at. I suppose it may be safe to say that the indispensable genius will be irrepressible and that their truths will leak out. On the other hand a lively debate-publicity seems to be a great raiser of the general level of discussion—which in Germany *is* high. I think you might easily with a page or two more have made your article on Münsterberg in Mind more effective. You treat his absurd a priori dogmatism of Science too much as a separate doctrine. It hangs together with the others; and all are about equally vulnerable. He would be more sensitive himself to an attack along the whole front, than on the one position. I am grievously disappointed in the sort of philosophic rubbish he is hatching out, though like much of his psychologic work it may prove valuable by being *anregend,* and discussable. I think your tone in the Mind article *tant soit peu* reprehensible for its patronizing quality. Only the Mysticism article deserved that tone. No more at present, from,

Yours ever

W. J.

Oh! I ought to acknowledge gratefully your puff of my Oxford reputation. But how comes it that Caird has never let Royce's Spirit of Modern Philosophy afloat there? Royce is so unscholastic in his form, that I hate to hear of his lack of world fame—that seems to me such a transcendent merit. Also re the Goldmarks: I hope you don't think I introduced her as a candidate for Corpus Fellow's fiancée! Never! I used the words in general praise of her exalted character to which I feared you might be lacking in sensitiveness. She isn't *brilliant* unfortunately. Surely Münsterberg chose a queer form in which to incorporate his polemic against my emotional metaphysics! His own real life also is *all* emotion.[23]

· *To Macmillan and Co.* ·

34 De Vere Gardens
Nov. 7. '99

Messrs. Macmillan & Co.

Dear Sirs,

I regret to say that I must make the same reply to your note of the 6th which I made to your inquiry of a year ago.

For many reasons I should like to publish under your auspices, and your offer is a liberal one, but unexpected illness has obliged me to postpone the date of my Gifford lectures, the writing of which is hardly yet begun. Until I possess the manuscript complete I prefer to postpone the question of a publisher.

I will keep note of your proposal, and very possibly communicate with you again before the year is out.

Thanking you for your interest in my work I am

Sincerely yours

Wm James[24]

· *To George Herbert Howison* ·

34 De Vere Gardens
London W.
Nov. 9, 1899

My dear Howison,

Baldwin was here on Wednesday and reported having seen you only once, adding that you seemed to go about but little, and that he had not seen Mrs. Howison. I fancy that you feel in Oxford, as I do in every foreign country, very shy of intruding upon the natives, shy both personally and naturally. But it doesn't do to carry this too far—on natural grounds I should not like to think of Mrs. Howison not becoming widely known.

I myself have been here for a month unfortunately with a bad organic heart trouble of which I can't cypher out the issue. Only 6 pages of Gifford lectures are written out and for a month to come at least I am forbidden to make any exertion, physical, social or intellectual. Yesterday the doctor forbade me absolutely to receive any more visits—so I must postpone my meeting with you until a brighter day. I hope that you are profiting by Oxford and enjoying it and getting on with your written work. Pray drop me a line and tell me how things are. I live on letters just now and the thought of old friends. With warmest regards to Mrs. Howison who, I hope is well and happy, and the same to yourself. My wife joining too

Always affectionately yours

Wm James (by A. H. J.)[25]

· *To George Frederick Stout* ·

34 De Vere Gardens, W.
Nov. 11, 1899

My dear Stout (can't we drop the handles to our names?)

I am pained beyond expression to have to write such a reply to your so friendly note, but the Doctor has just given me imperative orders not to see *anyone* whilst the Nauheim baths are going on. Every visit I have had so far has produced disagreeable cardiac symptoms, and although I have been slow in coming to it, I now see that I must for the present forego all society save my wife's. Fortunately we are on good terms. I *must* see you some time. I found your Analytic Psychology a most genuine and vital performance which I could understand and enter into. Your presidential address the other night is from the same tap, and interests me much. I have had no chance at your new book yet,—Sully praised it to me highly. I trust that in the matter of us four meeting, *aufgeschoben* is not *aufgehoben,* and I will write to you again.

Sincerely yours

Wm James[26]

· *To George Frederick Stout* ·

34 De Vere Gardens, W.
Nov. 17, 1899

My dear Stout,

I have just received two letters from Harvard, written by Münsterberg and Palmer, our professor of Ethics, respectively, and both in a state of furious indignation over Schiller's animadversions on M's English in the October *Mind.* I myself deeply regret these animadversions, for M's *style* (in the larger sense of the word as distinguished from grammar) is excellent, and his English, however uncouth, highly creditable for a foreigner. He says himself rather pathetically "I find I am whipped and not welcomed in the house where I came as a guest."

Both these friends seem to expect me to do something about the matter. Münsterberg says that he must now confine himself to the German language in all future writing, which would be a pity.

I am advising them to write directly to you, for I can in

no way take a hand in such a quarrel. I wouldn't, even if my cardiac condition permitted any controversy, which it does not. Pray show this to Schiller. I think it my duty to warn you of the storm which is about to burst upon your heads.

Very truly yours

Wm James[27]

· *To F. C. S. Schiller* ·

34 De Vere Gardens, W.
November 17, 1899

My dear Schiller,

Just one word! I have written to Stout a letter I want you to see. I do regret your criticisms of Münsterberg's English.

As regards the Proceedings article I hope that you have prepared a postscript for the *next* Proceedings, printing the full context of the "undignified" quotation and expressing regret. Hyslop made the same omission in the Psychological Review and Münsterberg has the strategical cleverness to fall back on this misquotation as his sole reply to both of you. It is a pity to leave him in possession of so labour-saving a coign of vantage.

Heart has been very bad, but begins to show some signs of mending. As ever,

Yours

Wm James (by A. H. J.)[28]

· *To Hugo Münsterberg* ·

34 De Vere Gardens
London W.
Nov. 17, 1899

My dear Münsterberg,

Your and Palmer's letters both received. Hurrah for the laboratory and Seminary!

As regards the Schiller matter I can myself do nothing. You and Palmer must write direct to Stout. My cardiac condition absolutely forbids work and a fortiori getting mixed in controversial matter.

I deeply deplore Schiller's remarks on your English which is wonderful for a *foreigner,* and Schiller should have been more courteous. But don't take it too seriously, and for Heaven's sake don't carry out your threat of confining your printed utterances to German hereafter.

I wrote to Schiller as soon as I saw his notice protesting against his tone, and I have just written briefly to Stout, a private letter about your and Palmer's state of mind saying I sympathize with it, but I can absolutely do no more.

As regards Schiller's other article I think you have no just cause of complaint. Your mysticism article, to speak with perfect candour, seems to me a monumentally foolish performance. The time is passed for metaphysical dogmatism about natural phenomena and I think it was a great compliment that he should have discussed your paper at all. If discussed, how could it be discussed but in a comic vein? Pardon these sentiments, my dear colleague, you can easily understand them; brevity forces me to be blunt.

And for Heaven's sake, don't stop writing in English. Your *style*, in the large sense of the word style, is admirable.

We both hope that the Münsterberg household is well. Only illness has prevented my writing to express my admiration of your article on Germany and America.

Always truly yours

Wm James

Private post-script
Dear Mr. Münsterberg,

Mr. James is very ill, and every excitement affects his heart unfavorably, so pray, if you write again, avoid controversial subjects. These two letters about Schiller have quite upset him, so I am constrained to sound a note of warning.

Very truly yours

Alice H. James

· To Charles William Eliot ·

Lamb House
Rye, Sussex
Dec. 20th '99

Dear President,

The enclosed petition to the Corporation will acquaint you with the scrape in which I find myself, if you have not already learnt it from other quarters.

Dr. Bezly Thorne, the first English heart-specialist, thinks I ought, with repeated Nauheim baths, to get into working shape again. Meanwhile, so far, the progress has been down hill and it is impossible to foretell how the balance will ultimately incline. If favorably, I hope to be able, by remaining in Europe, to give next year that first course of Gifford lectures from which I have had this year to withdraw. My second Gifford Course would then be indefinitely post-poned.

Should I be able to resume my duties at Harvard in 1901, it seems certain that they would have to be in diminished amount, probably reduced to one full course or its equivalent, with proportionate decrease in pay. I should greatly deplore having to resign entirely from the College, for I feel as if my philosophical out-put might, at last, begin to be important. My project of staying here next year rather than returning to Cambridge, is determined by the practical necessity of being near Nauheim. If I don't get better by mid-summer, having taken my Spring Course there, I shall return home and make the best of things as I may.

I am ordered by the New Year to proceed to a more out-of-door climate, probably Hyères or thereabouts.

It is particularly painful to me to ask for this favor for a year when Royce was planning to take his first Sabbatical. Nothing but absolute necessity could bring me to do it. With Miller already in training perhaps Royce can get off. Miller's intellect and character are both of distinguished quality, and Palmer writes that his teaching is a success. If you need a second man, I should like to urgently recommend Ralph B. Perry, a Ph.D. of last year, now filling Professor Russell's place *ad interim* at Williams. I have the very highest opinion of his talents and character and I am sure of his successful development.

I hear splendid things from Palmer and Münsterberg

about our department, things which make me glad and homesick.

We both hope that you and Mrs. Eliot are well and I hope the Faculty meetings have not yet made you curse God and die.

What a squalid thing is this Boer war! But the sobriety of temper of the papers and people seems beyond all praise.

Believe me, with profound regret for the contents of this letter.

Faithfully yours

Wm James[29]

VI

1900

Royce visited the Jameses at Rye on 4 January. He was about to give the second series of his own Gifford lectures at the University of Aberdeen.

The Jameses left England on 13 January to accept an invitation from professor Charles Richet to spend a little over nine weeks (22 January to 2 April) at his Château de Carqueiranne in the southern part of France along the Mediterranean coast (Costebelle-Hyères). Richet and his family had moved to Paris. Before moving into the château, the Jameses stayed in the Hotel d'Albion for a week. Frederic Myers and his family shared the château with them for awhile. A bit of comfort was the news that James had been elected a corresponding member of the Royal Prussian Academy of Sciences of Berlin. Furthermore, his health improved by the very favorable climate and rest to the point that he was able to do some work on the postponed first series of lectures. The letters of this chapter and the next record the stages of their composition, little by little.

He wrote to a friend, "The problem I have set myself is a hard one: *first*, to defend (against all the prejudices of my 'class') 'experience' against 'philosophy' as being the real backbone of the world's religious life—I mean prayer, guidance, and all that sort of thing immediately and privately felt, as against high and noble general views of our destiny and the world's meaning; and *second*, to make the hearer or reader believe, what I myself invincibly do believe, that, although all the special manifestations of religion may have been absurd (I mean its creeds and theories), yet the life of it as a whole is mankind's most important function."

After leaving the château, the Jameses stayed on in this lovely area at the Hotel Costebelle until 23 April. J. M. Baldwin and his family visited them here from 8 April to 10 April. James also offered some advice to the young R. B. Perry about his academic future.

The Jameses headed for Nauheim again by way of Geneva to see the Flournoys. Also Mrs. James needed more clothes made, now that they were staying away longer than expected. The second Nauheim visit lasted through the month of May. This series of baths hurt James more than they helped him. Afterwards they spent the summer vacationing in Montreux, Ouchy, Geneva, Luzern, Paris, and Ostend, where they met Schiller. It is surprising that James returned to Nauheim for a third time (24 August—7 October) after the disastrous second visit and his protest against medical advice. After this "cure" the plan to return to Rye was dropped, and instead they went south to the more moderate climate of Rome via Switzerland, spending twelve days in Geneva again. They arrived in Rome on November 1. They lived in the Hotel Hassler until 6 December, when they moved to the Hotel Primavera on the Via Veneto. Although there was some thought to leave Rome at the end of the year, they actually stayed on until 6 March 1901.

Lamb House
Rye
1 January 1900

Dear Lutoslawski,

Your postal card the other day took a great load off my mind. I had been aiming for a couple of weeks at a letter to you but owing to my weakness had not been able to accomplish it; and I had begun to think from your long-continued silence, so unusual in a man of your uncontrollable epistolarity, that you had fallen seriously ill, or even had committed suicide, and would be heard from no more. I see now that it was nothing but the hard work at the University that had kept you from writing. My prediction is that you will gradually outgrow these fits of prostration and resume your old vigorous habit of body and mind.

Let me tell you about myself. I went through my course of Nauheim baths in London and found myself in a most exhausted state at the end. The doctor sent me to the tonic air of West Malvern to recover strength. I had a bad breakdown there and for three weeks have been at my brother's here, but am still unable to make the slightest effort. Even dictating a letter *greift mich an* considerably, so I must be very short with this one. By the ninth or tenth of the month we expect to depart for Costebelle near Hyères in France, to get the benefit of an open-air life which in the English winter it is impossible to enjoy unless one be exercising. I will report from thence how things go.

The Towianski book arrived duly and is an extremely interesting document. His intellectual content seems to have been of the simplest, but as a saintly character he was evidently among the first of men. There are some splendid personal anecdotes in the book.

I made return by sending you a little volume to which I also wrote a preface at Nauheim. I think it an extremely instructive work. The author is my former student. From Blackwood's long retention of your manuscripts I should tend to draw a favourable augury.

I have seen neither of the Sidgwick's; nor have I seen any other English friend for more than a few minutes, having been so ill that conversation upset me. With best regards and good wishes from both of us to your household.

Believe me always affectionately yours,

Wm James[1]

· *To Ralph Barton Perry* ·

Lamb House
Rye, England
2 January, 1900

Dear Perry,

I was delighted, about a month ago, to receive your good letter. I had been trying to bring myself to the point of writing to you for some time previous for news of yourself, but this answered my immediate need. I am exceedingly glad to learn that the work and you suit each other so well, doubly glad that you had so good a time at the Putnams' and fell in love with Keene Valley. Did you

make Adler's acquaintance there? I hope from now on-
wards that you will get a few weeks there every summer.
I love it like a person; and if Calais was engraved on the
heart of Mary Tudor, surely Keene Valley will be engraved on mine when I die.

I heard of you at Bryn Mawr the other day indirectly,
but am unable to report authentically the impression you
made. I got Royce's book this morning and am expecting
to have an interview with him in a couple of days. Isn't
he a strong man rejoicing to run a race?

I regret to say that I myself seem about withdrawing
from the career. I have had to resign my Gifford job on
account of heart trouble, which has been developing
rapidly in the last six months, and have applied for a
second year of absence from Harvard, which will of
course be granted. I can at present do no work whatever,
and cannot tell how long it will last. This makes an opening into which, my dear Perry, I devoutly hope you will
be thrust. This will be a blank sight better than Bryn
Mawr, of which I therefore say nothing. Miller of course
is sure of another year of it—I hear that his work has
been very satisfactory; but if Royce comes abroad next
year there will be plenty of stopgaps needed and, knowing you as I do, I shall use all my efforts to get a berth for
you in the hope that you may grow up as one of our
permanent and most illustrious features. Of course it will
mean pure philosophising; and this, after all, may seem
to you the more insipid part; but I am more and more
convinced that pluralism and radical empiricism need a
prophet and that, if one springs into being, he will not
preach to altogether deaf ears, *par le temps qui court.*

Streams of consciousness are going on inside of me
which make me feel that if the working power were
allowed, I might really now begin to publish something
worth while—something, at any rate, much more connected in form and fundamental in content than I have
hitherto allowed myself to touch. The doctors take a not

unfavorable view of my case, and we will hope for the best. But I doubt whether lecturing will ever agree with me again unless possibly on a *very* restricted scale.

A good deal of this is rather confidential: you will of course judge how much to keep to yourself.

Good-bye, dear old boy, and a happy new year to you. Keep your health, your spirits and your faith; and believe me always affectionately yours,

Wm James

Tell me how it goes with Prof. Russell. Has he too broken down in health? and with what ailment? and where is he?[2]

· *To Katherine and Henrietta Rodgers* ·

Lamb House
Rye
5 January, 1900

Dear "Girls,"

You must have wondered what had become of us. The truth is that in October I sent a post card to the Hotel Moser, Vevey, thinking you had gone there. As no intimation of reception came I gave you up, not remembering who your bankers were until the other day, when it occurred to me that Morgan was the place. I wrote, and they told me you were at Ouchy; but I send this to their care—it seems to me likely that you may already be in Florence.

I hope things have gone well with Henrietta and that

her malady is by this time cured. If it isn't she will not be pleased with this message, as I find by my own case that people who are ill don't thoroughly enjoy hearty messages from home deigning to deal with them only on the basis of their supposed recovery. Pray write soon, addressing Brown, Shipley & Co., and telling us just how it goes with you.

We have been for three weeks here—at Henry's in this charming abode, with its walled garden, in a little town all composed of tiny old brick houses with innumerable chimneypots and nooks and corners between them,—trying to gather strength for a journey to the south of France, whither I am ordered for my unfortunate heart, which gets worse instead of better and which, it is hoped, will improve if I can keep more in the open air. It is, of course, a terrible disappointment to me to have run down hill so far; but there is no thorn without a rose, and it brings out in brilliant display the angelic qualities of my wife who seems really enthusiastic now that she can hold me completely under her thumb and treat me like a baby once more.

H. J. seems in complete agreement with his environment—middle-aged, calm and industrious and eager to know, when we came back, whether we had seen you and all about you.

I must be brief in my letters nowadays, and this is mainly meant to get one from you in return. So believe me, with most affectionate regards and wishes for a happy new year for both of you,

always your faithful cousin,

Wm James

· *To F. C. S. Schiller* ·

Lamb House
January 9, 1900

Dear Schiller,

My trip to West Malvern, whither I was ordered after
my course of baths, proved rather disastrous than otherwise, and I have been for three weeks recuperating here
at my brother's. I am still weak and unable to make the
slightest effort without cardiac symptoms. I am going to
the south of France in a few days to get the benefits of
more life in the open air. The doctors take a hopeful view
of my case, but it needs a lot of passivity on my part to
win through, if I ever do so.

I need not say how extremely sorry I have been to
spend all these weeks in England and see nobody. Peculiarly sensible have I been to this privation in your case.
Of course I have sent in my resignation from the Gifford
Lectures, and my only hope is that the Committee will
let me postpone them indefinitely. Good-bye, dear
Schiller. If I get sensibly better, be assured that I will let
you know.

Yours most truly and affectionately,

Wm James

Thanks for your jolly good letter from Gersau, which
came after this was dictated. I will order a photo sent you
from Cambridge—enjoyed your squibs—hope to live to
enjoy your essay, and your future book. Have you seen
Royce's Gifford course? Also [Théodore] Flournoy's admirable monographic study of a medium? Des Indes à la

Planète Mars (Alcan, 1900). It ought to make Münsterberg feel ashamed. My address is always c/o Brown,
Shipley.[3]

· *To Ralph Barton Perry* ·

Dover
Jan 13. 1900

I forgot the other day to speak of your literary plan. *No
use dealing with a publisher beforehand!* But by all
means write!—whatever comes of it, it will be good for
you to be getting at work done with the intention of
production, and your scheme of an "Introduction" seems
to me capital. We are off in an hour for Hyères, on the
Mediterranean.

Wm James[4]

· *To Josiah Royce* ·

Carqueiranne (Var)
Feb. 8. 1900

Dear R.

I hope the lectures are reeling off to your best heart's
desire and that you feel like a regular Aberdonian towns-
man by this time. What will the title of the 2nd. volume

be?—I am now in my 4th week here. The climate is magnificent, but my condition doesn't improve as fast as it promised to in the first week or 10 days.—We are trying co-operative housekeeping with the Myerses and it works very well, M. revealing an exceedingly gentle and patient side of his character. Your book is the heaviest reading I've done, and we live mostly on home letters. I still can't get to writing. It would be too careless on the part of the Absolute to leave your lectures undestroyed by mine but it looks as if the old sinner might be going to do it. Write us a line ere you return.

Affectionately

W. J.[5]

· *To Henry Rutgers Marshall* ·

Carqueiranne (Var)
Feb. 18. 1899 [1900]

Dear M.

Your letter of Jan 25th (which came duly) was a kind act. Now that I am knocked out, I am learning from many quarters how much friendliness and sympathy exists in the world, and *your* demonstration is one for which I am most grateful since I am peculiarly sensible of your existence as one of the valuable features in the frame of things. You tell me nothing of your own history, health or fortune, so I can merely hope that all goes well. My nervous condition, quite prostrate since the middle of Nov., took a sharp turn upwards 10 days ago, and tho the heart is no better, I began yesterday to work for an hour on Gifford lectures, & hope to continue daily. But I must limit correspondence to post cards. We are enjoying Charles Richet's château here in company with Fred Myers and family.

Wm James

· *To Arthur Auwers* ·

Carqueiranne (Var), France
March 1st. 1900

My dear Sir

Of course I am immensely pleased at your letter addressed to London, and informing me of my election as corresponding member of the Academy of Sciences of Berlin. Your letter sent to America has not yet arrived, but I shall doubtless receive it duly.

I accept the honour most gladly, although I well know how little worthy of it I am.

I deeply regret to say that the bad state of my health at present will make it entirely impossible for me to go to Berlin to take part in the solemnity. I am recovering very slowly from a bad attack of nervous prostration consequent upon heart disease, and am unable to bear the slightest excitement or muscular exertion. It is a great pity to be forced to absent ones self from an occasion so brilliant and interesting, in which one has been invited to take part.

My permanent address is Cambridge, Mass., U. S. of

A., whither Sitzungsberichte and other printed matter should be sent.

I beg you to send the *Program* of the ceremony and whatever other official communications to me there may be, to the care of Brown, Shipley and Co., Bankers, London, E. C. I shall probably not remain in this part of the "Riviera" very much longer.

With thanks to all to whom I owe this honour, and most respectful greetings to yourself, I am always sincerely and faithfully yours,

Wm. James

Herrn A. Auwers
vorsitz. Secretar der Kgl. Akademie d. Wissenschaften
Berlin[6]

· *To F. C. S. Schiller* ·

Carqueiranne (Var)
Richet's Château
March 6, 1900

It is high time after all your epistolary favors to me, that I should send you a word of our news. We are now in our eighth week in this region, 6 having been passed with the Myers in this once stately but now somewhat neglected house. The climate is simply glorious and my nervous system, which had become acutely "prostrated" in London, and stayed so for two months, is rallying, though less fast than I should like it. The heart symptoms proper remain stationary so far as my feelings go and I must await the Nauheim doctor's verdict a couple of months hence to know how that objectively is. Meanwhile I have had at last to give up the attempt to walk at all, so certain is even *crawling* for 1/4 of an hour to bring on protracted distress. I am at last able to write in bed an hour or more each morning, and the Gifford work is begun, which is of priceless value to my spirits. Have you read Flournoy's admirable book? I think your apology to Münsterberg in the Proceedings left *him* rather worse off and wish you had left out the joke about his presenting variety shows. Myers' medium is very extraordinary.

Yours,

Wm James[7]

· *To F. C. S. Schiller* ·

Carqueiranne
March 15, 1900

Dear Schiller,

Your jolly letters in return for my post cards are an exchange of gold for copper, but so be it for the present, if you are willing. Your photo came duly; refreshed one's memories, and kept alive one's belief in the existence of beauty being still possible in this senescent and ugly growing world! Mine should already have reached you. I wrote to my son to send you one from Cambridge. I really *exalt* over your ghost house, and hope and trust it can be published in extenso in the *Proceedings*. How's this? Why on evolutionary principles may not all these phenomena be residues of the chaos out of which our official universe extricated itself in such solidly organized shape? Parts imperfectly connected with the rest yet connected enough still to hang on and break in occasionally and not entirely disappear like the earlier portions of the disorder which are so discontinuous as to be absolutely beyond reach?

W. J.

· To F. C. S. Schiller ·

Carqueiranne
March 30, [1900]

I believe I altogether forget to acknowledge and praise your paper from the Proceedings on the Logic, etc. I think it *admirable* and calculated to clear the atmosphere. I am worse again, after being better—one must expect ups and downs.

We leave this hospitable roof on the 2nd. for the Hotel Costebelle, Costebelle-D'Hyères (Var), France, to be there a fortnight. Thence to Geneva, and by May 1st. at Nauheim again.

W. J.[8]

Hotel Costebelle, Var.
April 6, 1900

Dear Schiller,

As usual, I reply to your magnificent letter by a postcard, having to economize my stock of literary energy for the great Gifford effort, page 15 of Lecture 3 completed today. I am glad you are reviewing Flournoy whose medium I may not see. I will read him your private remarks on his book. I don't see why some things should not permanently be only half way in the cosmos. This is a purely abstract proposition. It is absolutely incredible to me that Hyslop should officially suffer for what he has done, tho' such a lying rumor may well arise.

Wm James[9]

· *To Josiah Royce* ·

Costebelle
April 9, 1900

Dear Royce,

Perry asks for my endorsement *re* Walker fellowship. It is of course unnecessary, since the department knows him so well. I regard him as one of the most unexceptionable candidates for that fellowship that we have ever had, and expect the best things from him.

Yours ever

Wm James

Dear Royce—Just one word ere the mail goes. I hope you bear the Spring work well. I should think there'd be a little collapse after all your tension. Baldwin & family arrived at this hotel (for a day or two) last night. He seems in good order, and the sight of him makes me feel rather "old." I am able to dawdle through the days, & am on my 3rd lecture—but I fear it is poor stuff, written with so little grip on any thing. In a week we go to Geneva, thence early in May to Nauheim.

I enclose a notice lately received from Sorley—the last page may please Mrs. Royce. Don't return it. I suppose your 2nd course will now be rushed through the press. What have you decided, or shall you decide, about your own Sabbatical?

Always affectionately yours

Wm James[10]

· *To Ralph Barton Perry* ·

Dear Perry,

I have written to Royce to *appuyer votre candidature* for the Walker fellowship on the Committee. But I am sure that my voice is not required. In a week we leave for Geneva where we hope to meet the Russells. I am relatively comfortable now, but progress is disappointingly slow, and it may be only superficial. I can't tell till my thorax is again percussed and ausculted at Nauheim in May, just where I am.

I hope you *will* get the Walker F–p. A year abroad will be just the thing for you at this stage. Most of it in Germany, I suppose, but I can't advise as to where. If you do come I hope that we may drift together. I should give a great deal to see you over here. My own plans are entirely contingent on the Medical Advice I shall get in 3 or 4 weeks, so I can predict nothing as to where I shall be at all after it. I can write, but only a *very* little, and the two and two-thirds lectures already accomplished are, I fear, rather inferior stuff.

Let me know of whatever your prospects are.

Yrs. in haste

Wm James

Costebelle-Hyères
April 20. [1900]

We leave next Monday night for Geneva, where we are
to finish the week at Prof. Flournoy's, 9, Florissant. We
may have to stay on longer at some pension or hotel, in
order for Alice to finish some dress making.—Pray send
a line to tell us where you are, so that a meeting may
take place if possible. We were very thankful for your
last letter of information, but you see the season proved
so cold everywhere, that we did best to stay in this
sunshine. I hope that you have both got safely through
and especially that H. is cured of the trouble. Hoping
soon to see you, I am always affectionately

W. J.

· *To Charles William Eliot* ·

Geneva
Apl. 30. [1900]

I have just received a diploma making me a corresponding member of the Berlin Acad. of Sciences. As this is a
compliment to the University as much as an honour to
me, I think I should let you know. There seem to have
been 51 similar appointments, of whom Willard Gibbs
and Rowland were Americans. Only 3 of them were philosophers, the other 2 being Wundt & Heinze of

Leipzig, so I am the only foreign philosopher. The vanity (in both senses of the word) is the greater; for if one philosopher was to be taken, the frenchman Renouvier was absolutely the one indicated—I say nothing of lesser rivals!—Don't think of writing to congratulate! I am in the main better, and shall soon have the doctors at me again.

Wm James[11]

· *To Ralph Barton Perry* ·

Villa Luise, Nauheim
May 16, 1900

Dear Perry,

Your note of May 5th has just arrived and I reply immediately.

The ideally best thing for you would no doubt have been the Walker fellowship abroad. As between next year at Harvard and a probably permanent place at Amherst, it seems to me that the balance is in favor of Harvard.

If you take Amherst now, you are stuck for many years in a community with almost no philosophic companionship. Russell has recently been complaining bitterly to me of what he considers the bad effect on him of his long isolation at Williams. No one but beginners; and you are too young yet to live entirely on your own stores.

True you would have Garman, but he is so terribly peculiar and autocratic (this between ourselves) that his presence might be a positive objection to the place. He is good for students, but not for colleagues—at least so I fear.

Of course life at Amherst would have many ideal features, but at Harvard you would have at least one year more of strong philosophic stimulation, with possibly another chance as good as this Amherst one at the end of it. My condition of health makes the state of the philosophic department year after next an open question. I shall certainly never take up more than one course again, if that; so there will be both work and money for an additional man, and to be on the spot is an advantage. Miller is already on the spot, with greater claims than you and I should myself hate to be forced to choose between you. You are both such tip-top A. 1 fellows for elevation of character. Miller is a perfect hero for magnanimity of disposition, that you ought to be bosom friends, and I hate to think of your being rivals, for there probably would not be room for both of you so soon. But objectively considered such rivalry is a good condition of things, so that should not deter you.

I am ignorant of the pecuniary importance of the choice, as you are situated, but apart from that it seems to me that sticking to Harvard is playing the game of your life in the bolder and larger way; risking more for greater possibilities.

I saw your Chieftain Russell a good deal during the first week in May. He has had a rather doleful winter, but seems pretty well and will probably do his work all right, if they don't kill him with Faculty meetings.

I have at last settled down to my 3rd Nauheim cure, so called, and begin bathing tomorrow. I will let you know the results later on. What will be your address through the summer? I do hope that you will get to Keene Valley again. I wish that I might believe that I should.

In any case, Perry, it seems to me that you are a lucky boy to have no worse dilemma than this to trouble you at the end of your first year.

With warm regards from us both, I am

Ever truly yours

Wm James

P.S. Fool that I am! I hastily read Amherst instead
Smith, misled doubtless by my old associations with the
name of Seelye. Gardiner is, I imagine, a man easy to
live with—but on the whole, I give the same advice! You
will probably have made up your mind long ere this
reaches you. [12]

· *To Ralph Barton Perry* ·

Hotel Beau-Rivage
Ouchy. Lausanne
17 June 1900

Dear Perry,

Yours of the 4th. came yesterday. I am sorry you shd.
have had a bad 1/4 of an hour over my contrary advice. I
dare say that Palmer's was better; and in any case, if the
Harvard chance had not simultaneously offered, you
would have been esteeming yourself the happiest dog in
the world to get so promptly into such a first class berth
as Smith. I am impressed by it as much the best of the
women's colleges. But can your susceptible heart, at so
inflammable an age, stand the exposure? Won't your
intellectual life, properly so called, be sadly interfered
with? By way of derivative, I am giving you a note of
introduction to Mrs. Goldmark, Adler's mother in law,

who lives next to him in Keene Valley. She has 3 very nice daughters, Bryn Mawr girls, "Pauline" being on the whole the finest girl I know, for general character. I also enclose a note of introduction to Adler, whom you must cultivate. He is one of our first Americans.

Has Smith left Smith College (if so, whither?), and does Pierce step into his place. I think you'll have first rate company there now, for Pierce is very nice, and Gardiner is a first class judicious philosopher, and very agreeable man. Moreover the place and region are exquisite.

My 3rd Nauheim exp. has left me worse than ever. I wish I had never known the name of the accursed place. I just vegetate here, but have hopes of getting on to some sort of a working level yet.

Write to me again when you get to Keene Valley.

Yours ever,

Wm James[13]

· *To James Mark Baldwin* ·

Geneva
June 19. [1900]

Dear Baldwin,

This is news indeed, and I hope, for the honour of the flag, and the general spread of international relations, that you will both decide to be a candidate and get the place. You are already identified enough with America for us to keep the *credit* of having produced you.

No other candidate can point to an *output* like yours, unless Bosanquet should apply—or Shadworth Hodgson—but he, I suppose, never would.

I can't in my present state, write a separate and variant letter to all those names you give me. Those at Oxford know you: which of the outsiders are most important? Wire me *whether*, & to whom to write—here, Hotel Metropole, Geneva.

I can't reconcile myself to the Sidgwick tragedy. I fear he will go with the chief fruits of his philosophic reflection unuttered. I can't express my estimate of the loss to clear philosophic thought which this may mean.

Nauheim knocked me flat, again, after only 5 baths! I have but just recovered the ground lost, nervously. Morally, I have gained emancipation from specialistic advice. Henceforward James M. D. is my only doctor—at least the only one from whom I shall receive *orders;* and, he helping, I expect to get on to some sort of a working level. I should certainly have been a better man today, had I never left home, but simply rested, with a little advice from my good practical Cambridge Dr. Driver.

Yours, with best hopes,

W. J.[14]

Luzern
June 28, 1900

Dear Howison,

Your letter from Basel, which I got at Geneva, 3 or 4 days ago, was a most agreeable surprise. I had been wondering about you, knowing that the time for your return was drawing nigh, yet unable to communicate, for I had lost the Rothschild address you gave me in America, and you sent me no address when you last wrote—I sent a post card or two addressed simply "Oxford"—I doubt whether they were forwarded. On the whole with Oxford and Italy, and one volume ready for the press, your year seems to have fulfilled its purpose pretty well, though all such years are apt to be a disappointment. Mine has been a fearful one. Encouraged by 4 doctors (!) I tried Nauheim again last month—with disastrous results. But I was prudent enough to back out before grave damage had been done (the doctor loudly protesting against such blaspheming) and by this time I have got back and more than back to where I was at the end of April. I forswear *all* specialists henceforward, and mean to take care of *myself.* My heart is organically in no such bad shape, and many a man of my age lives long enough with arteries like mine, and I mean and fully expect to have some working life yet. But d–n the doctors! I believe that Nauheim has done me pure harm, and that I should have been comparatively well had I just stayed at home & rested. I haven't written a line for 3 months, but mean in a week to recommence. The Gifford & Harvard authorities have vied with each other in indulgence, so I shall pull through, somehow.

I see Baldwin has the first Oxford honorary doctorate of Science. No doubt it pleases him. I hope you liked him as much as he seems to have liked you. We had 2 very pleasant days with them at Hyères.

I am glad you find Lorenz's translation good. I confess to my shame that I cdn't bring myself to read a word of it. It is bad enough to see ones self in English!

We shall spend a month in this region, and (probably) go to my brother's in England in the fall. I am extremely sorry that the Howisons & Jameses haven't met—especially the *Missuses,* but still more especially *Mr.* James & *Mrs.* Howison. Shall we ever meet again? I think, on the whole, that that California trip was the high water-mark of my existence. I trust that work won't seem too onerous on your return, that you'll like your new president, Montague, Bakewell's wife, and all. You'll doubtless miss McGilvary. Be sure and vote for Bryan! I should were I at home.

Yours ever

Wm James[15]

· *To F. C. S. Schiller* ·

Paris
July 28, [1900]

Your letter arrived this A. M., and I wrote a card to welcome you on Tuesday next. But I am a football in the hands of higher powers, and an hour ago it became necessary to repair to Ostend tonight, where I shall be at least a week, and miss you unless you go that way.

W. J.[16]

Bad-Nauheim
September 30, 1900

Dear Schiller,

Your letter makes me think you never received a post card of mine sent to Oxford about a week or two ago.

I am still here, but about to get off in a few days for Luzern, then Varese, and mean to reach Rome about November 1st. and see how much of the winter there will suit. My nerves are better, but I'm otherwise non valid, yet I don't give up hope of improvement, for the most promising therapeutic card is yet to play.

D. S. Miller is gone home, pronounced "cured" as to the heart, by Schott, but very sensitive, and I tremble to confess I think it possible his case may follow my example—I mean in being incurable by Nauheim.

Hurrah for the Axioms as Postulates! Do you contributors dedicate your several essays? If so, I shall be too proud! I have become a mere clothes-horse on which to hang literary distinctions. "La renommée vient à ceux qui ont la patience d'attendre, et s'accroît à raison de leur imbécillité!"

Münsterberg's book is announced to be out in a few days. It will probably be better than the rude rehearsal in English. Anyhow, the dedication saves it! Think kindly of him hereafter, yoked together in a common personal devotion! He has his faults, as who has not, but he is not as bad as you think him, and may yet be a ministering angel when you lie howling.

I wish you could give me *offhand and without taking trouble,* one or two short quotations to illustrate the fundamental Trostlosigkeit of the outlook on life of the early Greeks—the ultimate unintelligibility and cruelty.

One passage from a dramatist, one from the greek anthology perhaps—*not* in the original! The "joyous" greeks forsooth! If you can't do it offhand, don't think of doing it at all. I can get it when I return to England. I hope the College year looks rosy! Warm regards from both of us!

Yours affectionately

Wm James[17]

· *To James Rowland Angell* ·

Nauheim
Oct. 4. 1900

Dear Angell,

Your jolly good letter of Sept 22. finds me here where I am just finishing a third "cure"—so-called—of baths for my sick heart and aorta. It is good to hear from you, and to see that your animal (or intellectual?) "spirits" are unabated. How many years is it since we have met? By this time you are one of the veterans, as I am one of the fossils!

I didn't know that Salter was going to run a muck among the Xian Scientists, and on . . . sorry. It is a religious movement essentially, and is based and propagated largely on personal experience. Against such things attacks from *outsiders* are as nothing. They only confirm the other outsiders in their contempt; and what is gained by that? The thing must be reformed from within, or by the other schools of healing. Have you seen

H. W. Dresser's "Philosophy of Mental Healing"? (N. Y., Putnam). An *admirable* work, as is also his little "Living by the Spirit." *That* is the kind of criticism that Christian Scientists can be moved by, but hardly by anything from Universities, or psychological Laboratories. Still, follow your own impulses. You may partly educate the public. A couple of months ago, I succeeded in writing a Gifford lecture, only the 4th of a course of 10 for which I have contracted, entitled (not the course, but this lecture) the religion of healthy-mindedness, in which I treat the entire mind-cure movement with great respect. I think it deserves it, as a bit of religious experience, though of course the Eddy school are intellectually absurd.

I have to stay a second year away from home, and mean to attack Rome for the winter. I can make no *efforts* whatever, and my working power is reduced to a mere trickle. I ought *eigentlich* to write no letters, so I will stop this one.

With warmest regards from both of us, and thanks to you for writing, and with profoundest respects to Mrs. Angell and the baby, I am ever truly yours,

Wm James[18]

Nauheim
October 6, 1900

Dear Schiller,

You are a trump, and act more poetry than your illustrious namesake Friedrich ever wrote. I refer of
course to your new and unheard-of-nominations of me,
which, the world being all prose, it is impossible for me
to think of for a moment. *Va pour* the Romanes Lecture,
were I *imstande,* but I am leading, and shall probably be
condemned to lead until I shuffle off, an almost vege-
tative existence. I have resigned from my second Gifford
course, and should do so from my first one, save for the
already written contract. No new lectures or honors are
possible. If I do any work hereafter, it must be with the
pen only. As for the Electorship etc., though I don't just
know what sort of a Kurfürst it may be, it is safe to give
an absolute no to that also. *Duties* I can't perform, and
sinecures I disapprove of in my own person. So take my
thanks for your unending kindness, and let the President
R. I. P. ! I wish they would name *you* for the Romanes
Lecture—I am sure that you could write a good one for
the times we live in.

Poor Lutoslawski! He is going greatly to alter his text,
I believe, and I wish that some one would lend a touch to
the proofs. I might undertake half of them, if you would
do the other half.

As for the Greek texts, you are a regular fundgrube of
ready erudition. I ask you for a tuppence and you give
me a sovereign! It shows that the higher learning—
which in this case I showed myself to possess—consists
chiefly in knowing to whom to apply for information. I

have a great mind to impress my readers with all your raw Greek in my footnotes. Alas! I cannot read it, having both begun and abandoned the study in my 14th year and knowing now barely how to look up a word in the lexicon. Five or six of your citations will suit my purpose admirably, in English, and save me a lot of *pech* in turning books over when I come near a library. Thank you everlastingly.

We leave tomorrow for Switzerland. The weather still is heavenly and beats our much boasted American autumnal article.

I enclose some scraps towards your Immortality collection. They are from a fine old Russian epicurean, Baron Ostensacken, dipterologist and ex-consul general, in New York, one of the happiest men in *this* existence whom I've ever known, but wütend against the other. Keep or destroy them as you see fit.

Yours ever

Wm James

I am forgetting to re-applaud the Proceedings review of Münsterberg. It is grossartig.[19]

Geneva
Oct 21. 1900

Dear Grace,

Your good and delightful letter of July 29th. reached me
duly and I have just read it again. It brings you vividly
"home" to the imagination, in your quiet house, with
your books and your interests not bounded by the village. Boerdom, China, and the Philippines are still unsettled, though the summer has given way to the Fall.
To day is a bleak low-clouded cold-winded forerunner of
winter, but it is the first. We brag too much in America
about everything, and I have been inwardly celebrating
to myself our impassioned American climate ever since I
have been abroad until within the past six weeks, when
there developed itself here a run, seven weeks long
without a break, of weather of our best late September
type, warm, & golden, or pearly, & misty as the days fill
out, but exquisite and good to live through. You can
imagine how favorable it was to the Nauheim patients,
and how by me in particular it was enjoyed. It is probably over now for good, but in the 12 days in which we
have been here, I have spent six entire ones on the lake
steamboats taking an air– and sun-cure, and found it
delightful. We are here to get some dresses made for
Alice—Geneva seems an admirable place for "retail
trade"—and the day after tomorrow we hope to leave via
the St. Gotthardt for Rome. Since being here I have
found myself surprisingly well, it seems certain that my
nervous prostration is in full retreat, and as for the
organs of circulation, I took a walk an hour ago, longer
than any I have taken within twelve months, and *no*
symptoms of distress! Hurrah! hurrah! It takes my breath

away!—or rather it doesn't!—or rather it does so morally but not physically as heretofore. I enjoy greatly feeling myself in Switzerland. Surely S. *is* 'the' pays modèle, and its civilization the best "out." The natural beauty, the civic order, the good health and good manners, the intelligence and thrift, the immense trade prosperity, the low taxes, the church without snobbery, and the army without militarism, the democracy, the laboriousness, the cheerful tone, the freedom from the corruption that every "great" country shows, all make me wish to be a Swiss, were I not a citizen of Massachusetts. In fact it *is* a glorified Massachusetts erected into an independent State. I believe in it & love it, and but for climatic reasons would never go to Italy. To tell the truth, I rather shrink now from the Italienische Reise. It is a sad thing that what under one set of conditions is the rarest treat (as a short legitimately earned vacation, for example) under other conditions becomes a weariness to the flesh. If you knew how weary we both are of dragging out this hotel to hotel existence! The narrow bedrooms, the society of chambermaids and waiters, the absence of any books save those immediately in use, no hooks, no decent table, never a shelf to put a book on, oh! it is dreary in the extreme, and in Rome at present what I foresee is only its continuation. One does depend, as one grows older, especially if one has to be as inactive as I am, on "things," on one's *own* things. To live in a room with a book case, & writing table, and large enough to walk about in, seems to me by this time to be all alone enough to make a man happy. But the months will speed away: The Gifford people have very obligingly put off my course till May or June, so I shall have *plenty* of time to write, now that I am so distinctly better, my last 5 1/2 unwritten lectures. And then hey for home.

You speak of several books you have been reading. I know Veblen's & Maeterlinck's, the first awfully jolly in spots, & telling much truth, the latter much other truth, and very *distangy* all over—a little too sweetish for my taste. But surely an original force in french style. I am deep in Münsterberg's last volume. I wholly fail to assimilate its chief theses, but it is a prodigious example of audacious and clever system-making and for mere talent displayed, both in ingenuity of ideas and clearness of exposition, keeps him at the very head of German psychological writing. *Fundamentally* rotten, all the same, though, in my humble opinion. So *systematically* rotten, that I shouldn't at all wonder if he became the leader of a great German school of thought. That seems the essential requisite in Germany. Don't publish this opinion miscellaneously till I publish it myself!

How delicious it is to think of all you Irving St. people beginning the cheerful College year together! We hope soon to see Richard with his full $100,000 in hand. I congratulate W. Bullard on his marriage and hope you will all be enriched by having the bride in the family. I trust that all are well at Shady Hill and especially that Lily's summer has been free from the ancient trouble. Tell her I owe her still two letters, and her father one. I tho't his address at Ashfield, which I read in the admirable Springfield Republican, most wonderfully well put. I don't think he ever did anything better either for *fond* or *forme*. Good bye, dear friend! Keep well and going till we return. We both send love, to you and all the Nortons in sight.

Affectionately yours,

Wm James[20]

· *To F. C. S. Schiller* ·

Albergo Primavera, Rome
December 28, 1900

Yours of the 22nd. very welcome indeed. I can only
reply by post-card, "nerves" which in October seemed
to be mending very nicely having lately gone to utter
smash and smithereens. 'Tis very disheartening indeed,
and I don't understand it at all. I hope the immortality
circular will be disseminated in America. Haven't yet
read your unmoved mover article—it got mislaid in our
various moves and packings and hasn't yet turned up.
Münsterberg's book a monstrously able performance,
which I have actually read through, on account of the
dedication. But to my mind it doesn't *essentially* mend
matters over the *Psychology and Life* book. We must
leave Rome. Do you recommend *Gersau* after the new
year to one who can't stand cold? It has been strongly
urged upon us by Mrs. Frazer. Can one have an open
fire in Gersau? To me the air tight German stoves and
unventilated rooms are an abomination.

W. J.[21]

VII

1901

FREDERIC MYERS DIED ON 17 JANUARY 1901 IN THE same hotel in which the Jameses were staying. Myers's illness and death took a lot out of James, who paid his tribute by writing a memorial paper on Myers's services to psychology. Besides Myers, other close friends of James had recently died—Henry Sidgwick, Charles Carroll Everett of Harvard, and his old friend Thomas Davidson, whom he missed most of all. The stay in Rome was conducive enough for James to finish writing the first series of lectures. They left Rome on 6 March.

On their way to Rye, the Jameses stopped off at Perugia, Assisi, and Florence in Italy; Luzern, Montreux, and Geneva in Switzerland. They arrived at Rye about 7 April. While there James expressed enthusiasm for but declined to participate in Schiller's scheme to publish a comic treatment of some philosophers and the journal *Mind*. But, James did comment on Schiller's "Platonic Dialogue on Pragmatism," disclaiming the credit for being the originator of both the name and doctrine called "Pragmatism." The stay at Rye was interrupted by a week's visit to London (29 April—6 May) and terminated on 13 May when they left for Edinburgh by way of London again.

The Gifford lectures at the University of Edinburgh began on 16 May and ended on 17 June. They were a great success, and James felt a great sense of relief that they were over. Two of their children, Margaret Mary ("Peggy") and Henry ("Harry"), were there too. The family did some sight-seeing before returning to Rye for a brief visit. At the end of the month, they traveled to Nauheim for a fourth series of baths, which extended to the middle of August.

Afterwards they tried unsuccessfully to stay in the Vosges area, but did visit Paris briefly, Rye again, and London for a day. They sailed for home on 31 August from the port of Liverpool.

After James returned home, his nerves went to "smash" again. He received some relief from injections of the Roberts-Hawley-Lymph-Compound, to which Dr. William W. Baldwin introduced him while James was in Rome. This was a sterilized preparation of goat's lymph. James took these injections for many years. It is not surprising that after such a long absence, a great deal of mail to him had accumulated. It took some time to reply to those correspondents whose letters had not been forwarded. His teaching schedule for the fall semester was light enough to be able to complete the second course of Gifford lectures. Appropriately enough, he taught Everett's old course, the philosophy of religion.

Hotel Primavera
Rome
Jan 18, 1901

Dear Mr. Andersen,

Our friend, F. W. H. Myers died yesterday, and the circumstances so filled the day for us that I was not able to write you a line of thanks for the photographs which you so kindly give me.

The figures are really glorious, ideally significant of human nature before its eating of the fruit of the fatal tree. They step with the "frohlocken" of the heroic age and I find them strangely fascinating. They form, moreover, a singularly interesting matter for comparison between the male and female type. Work so elevated and strong makes me greatly desire to see photographs of your other productions. Have you no views which we might see of these figures in profile or part profile?

I won't appoint an evening *yet*, to ask you to come and dine with us and bring us as many photographs as you can, because of the Myerses and other immediate complications, but after a couple of days please expect to hear from us.

Believe me, with hearty thanks and admiration,

Yours very truly

Wm James[1]

Rome
Feb. 5. 1901

Dear Mrs. Whitman,

Owen Wister's *Grantlet* came duly as a characteristic reminder of you. Characteristic in that you are always mediating between people, and characteristic in that you are always pouncing on individualizations of *quality*, and picking them out under every disguise. This little tome was really colossal, and gave me a new idea of the way in which it is possible to write history. I didn't know, having hardly ever dipt into his romances, that O. W. was so great a man! The book will probably inspire other men and other books to tell the truth straight as from one gentleman to another, whatever be the subject (though of course a biographic subject is easiest) and to slough off circumlocution. And how instantly one sees a subject like Grant growing vital, the moment one orders the whole with reference to the *moral* centre, as Wister does so quickly. Upon my word, the booklet is *refreshing*! I passed it along to Jos. Thacher Clarke who was here a few days ago.

I wrote to you in rather gloomy mood a few weeks ago. Since then much Tiber has flowed under the bridges, and I have been up & down, up when I do nothing, down when I do anything, but on the whole I believe that the bigger tidal movement is upwards, and now that the year has turned distinctly Springward, I feel a brighter spirit. Poor Myers died here a month ago, as you doubtless know by the papers. He suffered horribly from his breathing, but so absorbed was his mind in wider matters and so intense his intellectual activity (having essays & editorials read to him only a couple of hours before the death-rattle, etc.) that he was a sublime spectacle, and much impressed his doctors. It shows also what a real *belief* in immortality can do in the way of making a man indifferent to temporal vicissitudes. The whole thing, which lasted 4 weeks, took it out of me very much, but Myers remains an elevated image! Everett, Davidson, Sidgwick, Myers! One's philosophic circle groweth smaller. The one I miss most is Davidson. I didn't realize, till the blow fell, how much his existence there in Keene Valley had been meaning to me in these later years. He was a free man, "without a collar," and with a genius for being genuinely the friend of very disparate people. I think of him as the very incarnation of friendly delight in human individuals. And in that deepest of function all minor angularities like his melt into insignificance.

I hope your winter is passing actively and cheerfully away. I wish you'd give my fond regards to Pauline Smith when you see her—I cannot write—when I take the pen little tends to come but querulous sentences, so I leave her epistles unanswered, and in general confine myself to post cards.

I'm safe now for Edinburgh, having blackened enough paper to last through 10 hours of reading in May—and that is a great point "off one's mind." Continue, dear Friend, your life of energetic well-thinking and doing until we get home again and never wander more!

Ever your affectionate

Wm James[2]

· To Ralph Barton Perry ·

Rome
Feb. 5. 1901

Your letter of Jan 6 was most welcome. I had longed for
news of you and you send me good ones, which your
President Seelye, whom I met a couple of days ago in a
Church here, corroborates. Truly you are leading a "full
life" with 120 fair penitents in a course on ethics—I
wonder how your sentimental architecture stands the
strain at all. I haven't yet read your Kant—which I rejoice to see; but will read it now in a couple of days. Like
"Science" in Locksley Hall, I move slowly creeping on
from point to point. I feel very hopeful though just now;
have already enough written for May at Edinburgh, and
have ventured to offer Phil 6 (Everett's old course: Philosophy of Religion) at Harvard for next year, hoping I
may come up to the scratch. It does my old bones good
to hear you write of your great programs of work. But
don't get feverish over it!

Wm James[3]

· *To F. C. S. Schiller* ·

Rome
March 3, 1901

I have sent off a 1/2 hour paper on Myers' services to psychology, to be read, if time allows, at the memorial meeting at Westminister Town Hall on the 8th. I don't suppose you'll go. If you do, you will see that the theoretic part of it consists almost wholly in your own thunder, stolen by me with no acknowledgement. It seems pedantic in such a paper to bring in a literary reference, but those who have read will understand. My stuff will of course appear in the Proceedings. We go northwards in 3 days, but probably won't stay at Gersau. We expect to be at Rye by the first of April.

Best wishes!

Wm James[4]

· *To F. C. S. Schiller* ·

Rome
March 6, [1901]

I quite forgot, in writing to you yesterday, to thank you for the second copy of "Energeia akinesias," which I read "enthralled," for it is a notion so far reaching in consequences for the pragmatic-pluralistic philosophy that it starts one dreaming. In fact a new program to be worked up to, and needing subsidiary bulwarks in all directions. You only begin to indicate them. Rarely have so few pp. been so pregnant, or put a big thing so briefly. The equilibrium of contrary impulses is the immediate case that suggests itself. But how charmingly the Hegelians will (and can) work it. Not no-motion in abstracto, but contradictory motions preserved in the concrete highest synthesis which is truth. Keep on!

W. J.

· *To Ralph Barton Perry* ·

Montreux
Apl. 2. 1901

I should long ago have "reacted" upon your article on Kant which I read with both admiration and interest. It puts you amongst the foremost K.–philologians! I imagine that K. would not have felt comfortable under your interpretation, but what involved and convoluted phrases of rejoinder he would have made I cannot divine, and for myself, if one is perforce to make a consistent outcome of his thought (which always seems to me *fundamentally* confused and 1/2 extricated from its diversity of premises and interests), I am well contented with yours. But it's a strait-jacket for the poor man, all the same. Pray contribute no farther (having hereby proved your capacity) to philosophy's prison-discipline of dragging K. around like a cannon ball tied to its ankle. I am lunching off a ham omelet in sight of the full beauty of the upper end of Lake Leman! But under the conditions, I but 1/2 enjoy it, being hardly better than I was last fall in the same locality, and on my way to Rye till May 16 when I appear in Edinburgh. I long for Keene Valley more than for anything else.

Warmest good wishes

W. J.

· *To F. C. S. Schiller* ·

Geneva
April 5, [1901]

Your letters are always a blessing; they seem to come from a quarter of Being where energizing is easy— *akinetic* in fact. But whom do you ask to contribute to a comic Mind? If there ever was any comedy in me, it's now extinct. I ought to be saying my prayers, and not going to face my Maker with lewd jests upon my tongue. No! Count me out. I wish I *could* write a parody on Kant! Your dialogues are charmingly pretty and good as parodies, and so refined! There is no hurry about the thing. Keep it mulling and possibly matter will accrete. Royce might contribute. Miller might. It oughtn't to be of one school. We leave tonight for Lamb House, Rye, Sussex. Thank God!

W. J.[5]

Lamb House
Rye, Sussex
April 11. 1901

Alice got her dresses & hats satisfactorily sent home a quarter of an hour before we took the train at Geneva. The journey went off well; smooth crossing; I came here straight from Dover; Alice went to Harrow, but has now been here two days, with Peg. The house is extremely comfortable, the liberty of it and its walled garden make it possible for me to stay with perfect content within its bounds, and not to go out into the town, as I had to in Geneva, to my detriment. The english richness and *colour* do beat the world, and the english people inspite of all the talk about their contempt of the intellectual, their bad army organization etc., still strike one as potentially the *strongest* of all races. I hope, K., that you are well again, or at least up to the normal usual level. Pray drop a card ere long. We have had poor weather, mostly, ever since we left florence, and I for some unexplained reason have continued to "run down." But I am "liable" to run up again, so don't be scared. Much love, also from H. J. who asks to have the epithet "tender" attached.

W. J.

Lamb House
Rye
April 27, 1901

Dear Schiller,

I have been off my feed (scriptorially) for a week—hence my abominable delay in answering yours of the 16th. and in sending back Hugh Leigh's eloquence, which I find tip top as such, though I am not sure I like the name of the critter—*is* it an improvement on the raw Greek? It contains no joke in English. Your fecundity in the way of "Limerick" is portentous. Keep them and polish them. Alas! that I can't contribute something! Once I had animal spirits in me, now I am a vegetable vegetating "and nothing more."

Oxford, I regret to say is *impossible,* I fear so in June also. I go to London on Monday to get some clothes, etc. and expect to stay at the Charing Cross Hotel there for a week. I feel reasonably certain of reading my lectures myself at Edinburgh now and hope there'll be no backsliding.

Pray send me your dialogue on Pragmatism to the C. X. Hotel, provided it be in type. Otherwise I wouldn't run the risk and had rather wait. I re-enclose *Hooley*—why not that name rather than Hugh Leigh?—he speaks "bottom truth."

Back here again May 4th. or 6th. to wait till we start for Edinburgh by the 14th or 15th.

Affectionately yours

W. J.[6]

· To F. C. S. Schiller ·

Dear Schiller,

Back here alive and stood London better than I feared! One grows too pusillanimous leading the life I've been confined to.

I return your circular and a couple of others by inferior organisms, as Hodgson would say. If you will send me some others, I will try to get them filled at Edinburgh.

I saw Piddington and Shadworth Hodgson in London—the latter somewhat in the sere and yellow leaf, poor fellow. He gets no appreciation and seems to have no social compensations for it. As Howison once said to me "What we philosophers crave, James, is *praise*, real flat footed praise. W. T. Harris called it "recognition," but it's *praise*." Where should I be, spiritually, if you hadn't praised me in Mind? Piddington showed me some Myers and Henry Sidgwick communications through Mrs. T. The Myers part poor enough, the Sidgwick part more suggestive of reality. Her husband almost immediately forbade more sittings and there probably will be no more for a year.

Thank you for your message about my boy. It is Henry, the eldest, a level headed youth, of whom I'm not ashamed. He must go to Edinburgh with his daddy. After which he will doubtless go to Oxford for a few days and any kindness which you can show him will increase my "praise" of you as a philosopher when you write your next book. Best regards!

Yours ever

W. J.[7]

· *To F. C. S. Schiller* ·

Rye

May 10, 1901

Dear Schiller,

I return the dialogue, which is *delectabilissimus (–a – um)*. I have only three remarks to make:

1) I think that if pub'd it should be pub'd simultaneously with a fuller account of the principle it announces. Lacking that help, it is too brief to be effective. But it whets curiosity for that.

2) It ought to have more of a sting in its tail-end. I don't know what to suggest, but it needs an epigram, anecdote, or brief stocking illustration of the pragmatic principle in action. This you can invent, in time.

3) as to W. J. Your calling him a god begins to satisfy even *Mrs.* W. J.'s philosophic desire for "praise." She sees herself a goddess already. But you will please remember that it is C. S. Peirce, who invented both the thing and the word pragmatism, therefore, if divine honours go with it, he is the candidate for apotheosis. The poor fellow needs it, too, more than I.

Ever thine

W. J.[8]

· *To Ralph Barton Perry* ·

Dear Perry,

Yours of May 20th was welcome the other day. I'm glad
you've got through this arduous & exciting year in such
good shape, and glad you're re-appointed. At Harvard
you observe they've made no changes, of which on the
whole I feel glad.

I am getting through the lecture strain famously. After
the 4th. I thought I might go under, but I lie very low
between whiles, and had a first rate day yesterday after
the seventh, so I now feel absolutely certain of fulfilling
the contract and earning my salt again. It is a delightful
feeling. Edinb. is a strong, proud, severe place, full of
theology & theological interest, and my lecture room
which seats three hundred is as crowded as on the first
day. I succeed in puzzling them!—and that keeps up the
interest.

I am exceedingly glad to hear that you are going again
to the Putnams. I don't know the young people of your
party but the moral atmosphere and tradition of the
whole place is fine, and there are always some individuals worth knowing. I look forward to it as an important bit of the education of my younger three. It is very
engrossing, but I hope you'll get some chance to slink
away to Adler's and the Goldmark's—the former you
know, and the latter are such fine unworldly people.
Pauline is quite my ideal. Also by all means visit
Bakewell's school at East Hill, up the Valley—successor
to Davidson's. Poor T. D.! I miss him tremendously

from this upper world. Our date of return is still uncertain—I fear not till September.

Yours ever

Wm James[9]

· *To Katherine and Henrietta Rodgers* ·

Edinb.
June 18th. [1901]

Veni, vidi, vici! You will be pleased to hear that the awful lectures are over, and over most successfully, to judge by the audiences and the general interest aroused. "The bloody dog is dead!" And the bloody puppy who writes (you will also be glad to learn) is much tougher than when he came here, which shows that invalidical life was making him soft, and that what he needs is to work a little harder and be made to sweat—no bad thing for any of us. The weather has been abominable—cold & cloudy. But today bright sunshine, and Alice & the 2 kids have gone to the Trossacks, leaving me alone. We go to Nauheim next week, and [sail for ho]me Aug. 31st.

W. J.

· *To F. C. S. Schiller* ·

Rye
June 29, 1901

Dear Schiller,

I should have written to you long since, not only "in reply" but to thank you for what you do to my Harry and to tell you of the happy completion of my Edinburgh trials and of my speedy departure for Nauheim, where we shall probably stay till about August 20th. and then sail from Liverpool on August 31st.

The Edinburgh experience has put a new sort of aggressive tone on me. I look to the future with *designs*— and though far from being as can'n balistic as you are even when you are asleep, I may mean mischief to the enemies of the truth yet.

You are awfully good in your desire to have me go to Oxford. I went for one day to Cambridge, in obedience to a promise made to Mrs. Myers at Rome. But I was too tired to do a thing more and could not even call on the 3 or 4 friends whom in London I wished much to see. I am essentially better than I have been, notwithstanding, and if the same rate of improvement I have felt for 2 and 1/2 months past keeps up, I shall get into s'thing like an active life again.

What are your vacation plans? Do they bring you anywhere near Nauheim? Write and let a fellow know.

Ever truly yours

Wm James[10]

· To Charles Montague Bakewell ·

Bad-Nauheim
July 14. 1901

I have to thank you for your good long satisfactory letter of many weeks ago, and I suppose now for the international J. of E. with your splendid and really worthy article on T. D. It makes him look as big as he was, and the extracts are very characteristic—showing too, I think, the excess of heat over light. I think your description of him hurrying down hill with hand extended particularly felicitous—how the *trait vif* lights up literature! But why did you say nothing of his unfinished *magnum opus?* Of all the roll of deaths of my friends in the last 2 years none leaves for me as big a hole as T. D.—a result that a little surprises me, for I consciously antagonized T. D. so much when alive.—I am intensely curious to know how the summer at Glenmore is speeding. I hope it isn't giving *you* too much *Pech.* A letter from Howison grieves me by obscure references to broken health. His book makes a fine impression on me of elevation. The style is most distinguished, I think.—My lectures were a success, and I the better for giving them. We sail on Aug. 31st.

Best wishes

Wm James[11]

Nauheim
August 12. 1901

Dear Lutoslawski,

We leave Nauheim tomorrow and it is high time that you & I should have some communication. How has Rajecifürdö treated you? Well, I hope?

Nauheim this time has treated me very well. I am fearfully weak with the bathing, but the pectoral condition is distinctly better, and having learned prudence, I am in no danger of falling into the frightful nervous prostration which overtook me a couple of months after your departure in 1899. I began to mend nervously four months ago, and with that amendment the cardio-aortic symptoms have troubled me much less. The amendment continues steadily, and has evidently not yet reached its term, so I feel hopeful.

I made the acquaintance recently of a young french philosopher, F. Abauzit, of the Lycée at Pont-à Mousson (Marne et Moselle). His bride (of a year) is a granddaughter of Old Herzen, daughter of Prof. A. H. in Lausanne. Ab. is devoted to Plato and has the liveliest admiration of your L. of P. We talked much about you. He is a free man mentally, a protestant, full of ideality, but (as usual!) not strong in health.

I leave for a *nachcur* in the Vosges, my wife will (I think) go straight to England, where in a week I shall rejoin her. We sail on August 31st., and am happy enough over the prospect. I have just read a very good, tho' very prolix work of Eucken's der Wahrheitsgehalt der Religion, from which I have received encouragement and instruction. I am now in the middle of

"Wirklichkeiten" by K. Lasswitz, 1900, in which that most accomplished thinker and writer sets down his formulation of the intricate relations of World, Brain, & Tho't, Feeling, Science, Religion, etc., helping along a little the result, but on the whole much hampered in my opinion by his fidelity to the terms of Kant's system.

Let me know at Lamb House, Rye, Sussex, how it goes with you. I hope well, but I am always anxious. We both send our love.

Yours ever,

W. J.[12]

· *To Paul Carus* ·

Rye
August 19. 1901

Dear Dr. Carus,

I wish to bespeak your special attention for an article by Mrs. George Boole (widow of the logician) which I have read and advised her to send to you as the least convention-bound of Editors.

It is a little excentric, and probably needs pruning, but it is full of most suggestive matter and moves amongst the concrete facts of human nature in what to my mind is a refreshing way. Moreover its English is first rate. If you reject it, pray do not think you must give *me* any explanation. I know an editor's troubles!

My Edinburgh lectures went off well, and I made Forlong's acquaintance. A fine old fellow, not well adapted, I should suppose, to his *milieu*. I am better, but still far from well, & return (with great joy) on August 31st.

Hoping that you & yours are well, I am always, truly yours

Wm James

I have just read with great profit & admiration (tho' I am no such Kantian) Lasswitz's "Wirklichkeiten." What an accomplished & gentlemanly mind; and what a respectable synthesis to live by![13]

· *To Katherine and Henrietta Rodgers* ·

Intervale, N. H.
Sept 30. 1901

Dear Girls,

3 weeks in America to day. Good journey, no one sick but Peg, whose state may best be imagined by a remark of the stewardess to me: "Yes sir, she do seem to have a great deal of bile for such a young woman." Drop the veil. Our weather was splendid on arriving and our "home" looked sweet & harmonious. But I was in bad plight (nerves!) and came straight up to the Salter's at Chocorua & go back in half an hour, after a 3 days visit at some friend's here, much recuperated by the conditions—living level with the ground & communing with a nature but slightly humanized as yet, and less so than it was two generations ago. But we had stayed away too long! All America seemed strange & remote, and the effect on my spirits has been bad. The douche of snarling

catarrhal nasality of speech which struck us on the steamer was awful, and the general penury and poverty stricken appearance of the woods, the roads and the habitations here in N. H., is something of a shock. But the weather, light, & colour are superb in their intensity and spirituality, and I shall soon bridge over the chasm of years and work back to the old sentiment of intimacy. But I advise you to make the best of it where you are— *being* there. The *bad* thing is to oscillate! Alice is struggling with servants. She writes me that she & her mother spent an hour the previous day at an intelligence office, crowded with *maîtresses de maison,* eager to commend themselves to the few haughty domestics who were there. Not one of them would look at Alice. She says it was a humiliation. I give a lecture tomorrow— God help me! Bill ought to have returned yesterday from the Hawaiian Islands, so we shall be *au complet* tonight. Delightful thought. This will find you on the Avenue Eglantine. I hope in a good state of repose, especially dear you, Katie, since Henrietta is, I fully believe, out of the woods. You do well to keep to Switzerland & Italy. Were I to settle in Europe, I should hover between the two. Much love, dear girls both, and do you Katie occasionally drop one of your incomparable postcards.

Affectionately yours

Wm James

· To Mary Whiton Calkins ·

Dear Miss Calkins,

A pleasant surprise—your masterly book, "Chère et illustre maître." I have just spent a couple of hours fumbling over it. It covers the ground wonderfully, and is real, sincere, and full of fact & truth. Likewise of noble independence. I must thank you for puffing me by such reiterated use of my poor name. The only thing I doubt is whether *for the needs of the market* you may not have covered the ground too fully. However judicious, too many opinions & points of view, indigest the student who begins—but as you suggest skipping is within the reach of the humblest. It will run my book hard, and I hope that you will make a good income from it. If I'm spared to write more, I think I can easily remedy the "oscillation without explanation" of which you complain on p. 445. Since my return, I've gone to *smash!—absolute* nerve prostration! Good bye, have a good year and grow in grace, wisdom & "culture."

Ever your friend

Wm James[14]

· *To Ernest Howard Crosby* ·

95 Irving St.
Cambridge
Oct 23. 1901

Dear Mr. Crosby,

I reached home six weeks ago, after two years spent in Europe, & found half a room full of "printed matter" that had accumulated in my absence. Not much of it needed acknowledgment, but your volume of verses cannot be put away in silence. I find them exceedingly pure and dignified in form, and usually very telling. With their spirit I feel the strongest sympathy, even when it is denunciatory, for I believe in Tolstoi-anism (so to call it for short) as the best life, yet lie myself in the bonds of mammon, and think some denunciation called for. Yet after all I like the positive evangelic pieces better, and ask myself whether, in so inveighing against the competitive and capitalistic social system at large, you don't take a target both too big and too invulnerable. It is the result of ineradicable instincts, and harbors most of the good we actually know of. The same instincts are rampant both in the "ins" and the "outs," and with *any* system the "Uebermenchen" would be ingenious enough to get on top and *exploiter* mankind in the interests of their egoism. And so long as *freedom* remains, isn't the way for the lovers of the ideal to found smaller communities which should show a pattern? That they can't be founded more successfully shows the strength of the anti-brotherly leaven, *everywhere.* Nevertheless through small systems, kept pure, lies one most promising line of betterment and salvation. Why won't some anarchists get together and try it. I am too ill (and too old!) or I might chip in myself.

I enjoyed greatly meeting a sister of yours in florence last May.

Believe me, with thanks and admiration,

Yours sincerely,

Wm James[15]

· *To Pauline Goldmark* ·

95 Irving St
Nov. 8, 1901

My dear Pauline,

I have just read Miss Wyatt's book, letting it solace me in the dead watches of the night, and I find it hard to express my opinion of it without foolish extravagance. Why did you, in mentioning it, brag of it so little? To think of my having spent more than 24 full hours close to that paragon of genius, and never divined her, and done nothing but speak impudently to her! I am ashamed! The book is simple perfection in its kind. The good humor, philanthropy, observation, humorousness, the admirable style, modesty, etc., etc., etc. make it as good as any thing can possibly be in the compass which she sets herself to fill; and with such a sense of limits, & such a feeling for human nature and such powers of writing English, I don't see what she may not do if she tries more ambitious canvasses. But where did she learn so much of life? Pray send her my blessing and prayer for forgiveness, & receive, yourself, my gratitude for the book.

With her and the girls who illustrated your Almanac, Bryn Mawr may well be proud.

It will please you to learn that a fortnight ago I began to rise from the trough of the sea in which I was wallowing when you were here, and that my progress since then has been surprisingly rapid. I hope to be a well man yet. I am glad you liked the photocroms, & didn't already have them. They seem to me a most wonderful reduction of space to a small compass. Pray thank your sister Susan for her letter. I earnestly hope that she is improving as fast as I am now. These nervous attacks do end!

Ever affectionately yours,

Wm James[16]

· *To Ernest Howard Crosby* ·

95 Irving Street
Cambridge
November 8, 1901

Dear Mr. Crosby,

Thanks for your extremely friendly letter. I didn't express my thought fully about anarchists founding communities—I knew these latter invariably to fail, and my thought was, "When men are so essentially repellent of one another, even under the easiest conditions of brotherhood (small numbers and common beliefs), isn't it unreasonable to blame the *forms* of the larger society for evils, when it is after all the human substance that is to blame?"

Man's instincts are rapacious, and under any social arrangement, the *raptores* will find a way to prey.

Thank you for the paper on Edward Carpenter. His *Towards Democracy*, which I only became acquainted with a year ago, is one of my favorite books.

Sincerely yours

Wm. James[17]

· *To Adolf Meyer* ·

95 Irving St.
Cambridge
Nov. 28, 1901

Dear Meyer,

I hear with pleasure that you are to be head of the N. Y. Pathological Institute. I hope it will now get out of hot water. I know nothing of Dr. Peterson, but have just received two letters, one from Sidis, the other from Hyslop, who consider his clean sweep of the old Institute, in asking for everybody's resignation, an unjust proceeding. Sidis doesn't say what his own prospects or aims now are. I consider him, although somewhat cranky in intellect, *a splendid fellow* on the whole; and the easiest man in the world to get along with, if you don't *directly* oppose him, when he becomes tediously argumentative. He will yield easily to flank movements. I wish you could see your way to re-appointing him, for he has really fruitful ideas, & tireless energy, and someone, it seems to me, of his general sort, ought to utilize the State material for psychology. Of course I write in ignorance of what the precise complaints against him are. He has ideal qualities.

I went to pieces nervously on first returning home, but am improving and better now than for 2 years. Activity much reduced, though, still.

I hope that you are well.

Faithfully yours

Wm James[18]

· *To Ralph Barton Perry* ·

95 Irving St.
Cambridge, Mass.
Dec. 3. [1901]

Delighted at the prospect. Of course we hope you will come to stay with us. Say yes. I am *much* better. Have just read Royce's new vol. & think it a beautiful piece of thinking.

W. J.[19]

VIII

1902

JAMES TRIED A NUMBER OF TIMES TO OBTAIN THE INgersoll lectureship for Schiller but to no avail. But he was successful in having Perry hired for the next academic year on a one year basis as a sabbatical replacement. The proofs of the printing of James's Gifford lectures were corrected and sent to the printer before he and Mrs. James sailed for England on 1 April. Before sailing James also arranged to see Oliver Lodge, while in England, on matters pertaining to the Society for Psychical Research.

The first lecture was scheduled to be delivered on 13 May. But before that they toured England for a month. First, James received an honorary degree of Doctor of Laws from Edinburgh University on 11 April. Then, in turn, they visited Oliver Lodge in Birmingham, Edward L. Godkin for a week at Torquay, James Bryce in London, Henry James in Rye for another week, and Schiller at Oxford on 9 and 10 May. Then they headed north to Edinburgh.

James's last lecture was delivered on 9 June. They sailed for home on the next day, cutting short their previous plans to stay longer. James was quite exhausted by the traveling and the lecturing. His book, *The Varieties of Religious Experience: A Study In Human Nature*, appeared shortly after the lectures ended. About the lectures he said that they "are all facts and no philosophy." He didn't have the physical strength to keep his original plan for the second course "to defend *radical* pluralism and tychism." James received many letters of praise from all quarters for this very popular writing.

On their return home, the Jameses retreated to their summer home in New Hampshire. The vacation was interrupted by his return to Cambridge in July to give two lectures in the Harvard Summer School of Theology. While at Chocorua he continued his efforts to secure a grant of money from the Carnegie Foundation of Washington for C. S. Peirce. He also tried to secure a teaching post at Harvard for his wife's brother-in-law, Leigh Gregor.

Now that the "religious psychology phase of [his] existence was wound up," James's new philosophic interest was the preparation and presentation of a new course, Philosophy 3 (Philosophy of Nature), for the fall semester. It was the first time in his life that he gave systematic lectures without using someone else's text as a basis. He was very enthusiastic about this endeavor. In this course he tried to construct before the students a sort of elementary description of the constitution of the world as built up of "pure experiences." His readings were mainly along this line, e.g., McTaggart's *Studies in the Hegelian Cosmology*, Wilhelm Ostwald's *Vorlesungen über Naturphilosophie* and Henri Bergson's two books *Essai sur les donnés immédiates de la conscience* and *Matière et mémoire*. To concentrate on this course, James had to decline many invitations to give lectures and to write books. This course extended over into February 1903.

Jan. 7. 02

Dear President,

You may remember my suggesting to you the name of
Canning Schiller, of Corpus College, Oxford, as the next
Ingersoll lecturer.

I mentioned to him the fact in a recent letter. He says
in reply: "I should be glad of such a good excuse to
renew my acquaintance with the Great Republic and
observe the improvements. Besides, I really want to
lecture on the *questionnaire* material, which I am sure
will make up into something interesting. Moreover I
want to boom the inquest a bit, and get more answers, so
that the book will be not merely stimulative but
important."

The "questionnaire" is a circular regarding peoples'
feelings (as distinguished from their beliefs). Schiller
suspects that the majority don't care for immortality. I
know of no one whose lecture could give new material
except Schiller.

Faithfully yours

Wm James

· *To Mrs. Thompson* ·

95 Irving St. Cambridge
March 3. 1902

Dear Mrs. Thompson,

I send you the end of lecture XX and of the book, though I may conclude to add an Appendix to this lecture in a few days. I send back some additional corrections—you will be able to manage the galley part—I have lent the corresponding proofs in page. I shall not change the end of Chapter XVII, so you may proceed to the casting as soon as you like.

Sincerely yours

Wm. James[1]

· *To Ralph Barton Perry* ·

Cambridge
March 7th [1902]

Dear Perry,

At our committee meeting this A.M. things jumped in an unexpected way. We decided to take no decisive measures for another year, but to ask you as a stop-gap, Palmer & Royce intending each to take a 1/2 year's leave of absence, and one man's work, including some part of the big Phil. 1. to be given by you if you come. Münsterberg our chairman was to communicate with our president as soon as he could get him, and you will probably get an official letter soon.

You should distinctly understand that the appointment is for but one year, and that we are committed to absolutely no renewal of it. You have therefore to give up a highly desireable permanent place for a possibility. If you ask my advice I say "come!" nevertheless, for there will undoubtedly be a good many openings erelong, and this is a good place to start from if one can't stay here.

Personally, my dear fellow, I am delighted at the turn which things have taken.

Hastily and heartily yours,

Wm James[2]

· *To Oliver Lodge* ·

Cambridge (Mass.)
March 23. 1902

Dear Dr. Lodge,

I am going to sail, with my wife, on April 1st for Liverpool. I have my Gifford lectures to give, and we wish to spend a few weeks with my brother at Rye. I ought to have, and should like to have, some little conversation with you about S. P. R. affairs, and if that time suited you, the surest and most expeditious way to meet you would I suppose be immediately, on my way from Liverpool to London. We ought to be arriving on the 8th or

9th. Will you kindly have a letter awaiting me in charge of the Cunard Steamship Company, indicating me as a passenger arriving on "Ivernia," and telling me inside whether this is a convenient time for you to see us if we stop at Birmingham. I do no psychical research work whatever now, nor have I for several years done any, but in a general way I follow Hodgson's work, and wish to talk to you about it. Mrs Myers is here, returned from California, & about to sail for home in the Oceanic, April 2nd. She read me yesterday reports of 2 1/2 sittings with Mrs. Piper. Myers came very poorly in the first one; but I confess that the dramatic impression which I received from the later two was favorable as regards sincerity of effort to communicate. The turn which the Myers communications here have lately taken improves in my estimation the probability that they may be real. But these are matter of "impression," and it is hard to give articulate grounds. I hope to bring you a batch of recent reports of Mrs. P.

I got the proof of your presidential address and admired the clearness and frankness of it.

Believe me, dear Dr. Lodge, yours ever truly,

Wm James[3]

· *To F. C. S. Schiller* ·

95 Irving St.
Cambridge, Mass.
March 24, 1902

Dear Schiller,

I hope that all goes well wi'ye. I am flourishing like a green bay tree—corrected last page of proof of last lecture yesterday and leave on April 1st. for your Island to deliver the 2nd. course of Ingersoll [sic] lectures. Enclosure explains itself!

Ever truly yours,
W. J.[4]

· *To F. C. S. Schiller* ·

Charing Cross Hotel
April 18, 1902

Dear Schiller,

Your warm hearted welcome has but just come into my hands, we arriving only last night from Edinburgh whither we were whisked straight on landing (to get a LL. D.), thence to Birmingham for a day with Lodge to talk over the American Branch's affairs (He seems to me a very big man—"presidential size," etc. His 15 children a mere *nebenwirkung*), thence to Stratford for my poor wife's sake, though the country awfully pretty and now here for two days of shopping, etc., on Saturday to Torquay to spend a week with the Godkins and see a little of Devonshire (unknown to either of us), then to my brother's at Rye after a couple more days at London and to begin to lecture again at Edinburgh on May 13th.

You see that Oxford can't well come in till after Edinburgh. Between June 24th., where I am D. C. L.'d at Durham, and July 5th. when we sail, there may be a chance. I should like to know Stout, but I confess that I am growing more and more shy of seeing strangers generally, however good and great, for a soul meets some so little! You I should be greatly disappointed not to see, but it ought to be Switzerland and mountain sides together. In case Oxford is unfeasible, could you possibly come up here for a day some 10 days hence?

Write me at "Hatley St. George, Lower Lincombe, Torquay, and I will keep you informed. Yes! Rhodes' will makes him loom large!

Yours ever

Wm James[5]

· *To James Bryce* ·

Hatley St. George, Torquay
April 23, 1902

Dear Bryce,

Our two last letters crossed, and it touches me profoundly that a man on whom the future of an Empire depends should spend so much time over so unworthy a pair of "trippers" as ourselves. I couldn't write to you this morning because it was impossible before hearing from another quarter fully to determine our dates. It is now certain that on Wednesday the 30th and Thursday the 1st of May we shall be in London, and if you & Mrs. Bryce have a free hour on either of those days, we should be delighted to come to Portland Place—lunch, "tea," but not dinner, unless there be no other chance!

Godkin's good spirits and his wife's efficiency are spectacles for the Gods. I find him in better shape than I anticipated, both mentally and physically—but Heavens! if I were as reduced as he is from my natural estate, I should shrink from "society." It shows a much robuster grip on existence in his case.

With warm regards to both of you, from each of us, I am,

Ever truly yours,

Wm James

· *To F. C. S. Schiller* ·

Hatley St. George, Torquay
April 24, 1902

Dear Schiller,

I have read your Essay but once as yet, and am about to proceed to read it again, pencil in hand. It is a supersplendent thing, a big synthetic program for endless filling in and a genuinely vital piece of philosophizing, which ought to insure your recognition as a leader of thought. It inspires me greatly and I should like to spend the rest of my life building it out. Thank you for mentioning me so often. I will soon write again or rather, since I hate to write, I will talk with you of it in more detail when we meet. In case we should stop at Oxford on our way North say May 10th. (or 9th. and 10th.) should you be there and disengaged? We have also to see the Diceys (Albert) and Louis Dyer. Address B. S. & Co.

Yours "for the truth"

Wm James[6]

· *To F. C. S. Schiller* ·

Hatley St. George, Torquay
April 24, 1902

Dear Schiller,

You are a good letter writer! I am always surprised at your prompt returns. Pray let the degree rest—those vanities and humbugs literally turn my stomach. Now for your questions. You and I are so well understood now to be of the same gang and you praised my *Will to Believe* so inordinately in *Mind*, that I should think it might be better if Ward were to notice this new book of mine. Its only originality consists in the suggestion (*very* brief) that our official self is continuous with more of us than appears (subliminal self) which accounts for the "striking" experiences of religious persons; and that this "more" on the farther side lies open to transempirical realities, and this might allow for the sense of "union" and other mystical experiences being true. Ninety nine one hundredths or more of the book is descriptive and documentary and the constructive part is a mere indication. I confess that I should rather, for my own curiosity, hear how Ward takes this than how you take it, for of your hospitable reception I am assured in advance. I engage you for my next book which will be philosophical and constructive! How *is* Ward? He looked terribly when I saw him last August.

2) I will review your essays for *Mind* with the greatest alacrity and glad of the opportunity. It rejoices me that they should be out so soon. This is another reason against your reviewing me, it would look too much like log-rolling.

Didn't I write to you that Eliot—no, I remember that I only wrote anent *this year!* Well the man is an ass in this respect—he not only said he couldn't appoint you, but actually wrote a note explaining how foolish it was for a man to hope to gain anything of value by such a circular. This attitude of his leaves, I fancy, little to be hoped for the future. I will nevertheless go at him again. Why will people be *omniscient* asses when they are asses? Eliot is no ass in practical affairs, but the habit of authority infects the mind. As for Stout's Essay, I will wait for the book.

Yours ever

W. J.

If you *meet* Dicey (not otherwise) you might mention our probable advent. To what Hotel should one go?[7]

· *To Martha Carey Thomas* ·

April 29. 1902

Dear Miss Thomas,

Professor Leuba writes to me that you are in need of some testimony as to the value of his "original work."

I am acquainted with nothing but his articles on Religious Psychology in several Reviews. He suggests that I should send you my opinion of them. I have been steeped in literature relating to that subject during the past three years, but have read almost nothing as instructive as his contributions. In this field he is certainly one of the most important living writers.

Sincerely yours

Wm James[8]

· *To F. C. S. Schiller* ·

Lamb House
Rye
May 2, [1902]

Dear Schiller,

Your daily letter never fails—nor mine! You scare me by the awful amount of sociability in prospect. How can you and I innocently philosophize at all? And how can my jaded nerves recuperate? But since *le vin est versé, il faut le boire.*

I accept your Saturday dinner and Sunday lunch. I really don't think I can stand the President's breakfast too, unless it be short and simple. But I'll wait till he asks me. How, by the way, *heist er?* I'm ashamed of my ignorance and of my general rusticity of nature towards "mixed company," loving only as a rule sweet dalliance with friends.

Sunday night there must be no dinner engagement, as the [train] for Edinburgh leaves London at 10 A. M. and I have to guard against fatigue pretty carefully still.

Ever yours

W. J.

Thank you for the "Useless Knowledge" which I shall gladly re-read. Of course I gladly accept the lodging you so kindly offer me. *Das versteht sich von selbst.*

· *To F. C. S. Schiller* ·

27 Alva Street, Edinburgh
May 17, [1902]

Dear Schiller,

I return herewith your MS which alleviated my journey North very much. It is in your best vein as regards "atticism" and persiflage. You seem to me quite unique at that. As for the practical scheme, altho' I think it well worth ventilating, for the reason that all such ventilation awakens the public conscience on the general interest involved, I have such a noted aversion to examination rule and rulers überhaupt and the priggish element involved is so strong that I don't feel like hurrah-ing immediately. I hark back to Galton's suggestion of dowries for girls coming from numerous families (if I remember aright) as better. The whole business of sex relations and breeding is so awfully complexly conditioned, I fear the effects of rationalism on the result and when I think of the probable composition of any jury who should try to mould it, I should rather trust to the chances of individual choice, with all their danger.

I have given 2 lectures and feel like a humdrum citizen. Excitement never strikes twice in the same place and I am low-spirited, neurally tired, and long for the job to be done, so that I can at last recuperate with fair play in my own native conditions in New Hampshire. It isn't exactly fair play now.

We move on Wednesday to 5 Athol Crescent, whither anything had better be addressed. I enjoyed amazingly my day of dissipation at Oxford, especially the Stout part of it (after the Schiller part, of course). We are about to go out to Hawthornden for lunch and a 4 hours conversation (no shorter train interval) with the good Campbell Fraser and his family. Too long!

Yours ever

W. J.[9]

5 Atholl Crescent
Edinburgh
May 30th [1902]

My dear Reid,

Let us drop titles of dignity & honour!

Here I am, you see, finishing up my Gifford Lectures, and your letter has been forwarded to me. Many thanks for Wells's book, which I do not own, but which I recently read with the utmost avidity and shall make my boys read out of your copy. He is eminently a "growing man," and destined through the type of his imagination to exert an influence on the rising generation. I cannot but believe that many a young man, who will have to be counted on in our future social evolution, is now having the type of his character and aspirations fixed by that and other writings of Wells's. He makes a sudden daylight break through innumerable old blankets of prejudice. But, in my opinion, with his belief in the "efficient" and "functional" type exclusively, he leaves out too much of human nature, which, if the past is any indication, will always continue to set as much store by the aesthetic and useless as by the practically needful. When I think who, of my acquaintance, who be on the High Commission of the Intellectual élite who should castrate or behead the rest of us in their wisdom, I shudder, and would rather take my chances on the old fashioned basis. I could write long on W.'s book, but am too tired just now. Thank you again.

I give my last lecture next Monday and sail from L'pool on Tuesday. You will receive the volume of them next week some time. If you deign to read them, you will see why I am not out and out with Wells, though I have relished him so amazingly & think his way of hitting the nail on the head and his impatience with conservative stupidity perfectly *köstlich*.

I wish you would write s'thing purely psychological. It couldn't fail to be important.

Thank you—I am vastly better than last year, only I find that the past month has consumed my "margin" rather faster than I like.

Yours very truly

Wm James[10]

· *To F. C. S. Schiller* ·

Edinburgh
June 8, [1902]

Dear Schiller,

You by this time have got my volume and I trust that I shall not be long at home without receiving yours.

I sail on Tuesday, quite used up in "nerves" (damn 'em) by the escapade abroad. But once on my native ground in New Hampshire the interrupted process of "recovery" which went on so well last winter will resume its reign. I pant for simplification of life and am now in the midst of terrible confusion.

Yours ever fondly

Wm James

June 9th. Just home from my last lecture, thank God!

Audience very cordial, but end of lecture flat—composed by mind debilitated by fatigue.

Now hey for home and vogue la galère. I'm going to work on Eliot about your Ingersollship as strongly as I can.[11]

· *To John Shaw Billings* ·

Cambridge
June 20th [1902]

Dear Dr. Billings,

I wrote some time ago to the Carnegie trustees in favor of Charles S. Peirce's Logic, as a good object for aid. Peirce writes me that he fears your vote may be cast against him, so I scribble this line to you to say once more that he seems to me a perfectly ideal case for help. Grant everything that can be urged against him in the way of character and practical eccentricity and irresponsibility—the plain fact remains that he is one of the first intellectual geniuses of our country, and that his writings invariably contain original contributions to thought of the highest value. This logic of his will certainly if published be one of the great human efforts in that line, in spite of whatever capriciousness and obscurity certain pages or parts of it may show.

I state this as my deliberate opinion. I know that my colleague Royce would say as much.

No answer! of course.

Yours sincerely,

Wm James[12]

· *To Charles William Eliot* ·

Silver Lake, N. H.
June 25th. 1902

Dear President,

Just home from Scotland, somewhat the worse for wear. I come up here, and almost my first act is to write an office-seeking letter!

I dislike to appear to pull wires for my brother in law—*another* brother in law this time—but not knowing just what changes Bôcher's death is likely to occasion, it occurs to me to suggest that Prof. Leigh R. Gregor of McGill College should not be left entirely unconsidered in case there should have to be a new Assistant Professor or Professor. I only fairly made his acquantance last winter, and his perfect gentlemanliness and liberality of character are such as would decorate our french department, or any of our departments. Concerning his scholarship I am not in a position to judge.

Pray take no notice of this in the way of replying!

You should have received my Gifford volume earlier. It was a mistake of my son's. The lectures were a great success as far as the audience's curiosity went, but the Scotch are unco cautious about committing themselves in the way of praise. I seem to myself to have made a very *objective* study of the subject. I judge this to be the case, because I can see what different reactions will inevitably be aroused by my pages in different readers' minds.

I am glad to hear of Mrs. Eliot's recovery—what an illness she must have had! With best regards to you both, I am ever truly yours,

Wm James[13]

Chocorua, N. H.
June 28. 1902

Dear Dr. Billings,

I never dreamed that you would answer my remarks about C. S. Peirce,—I hope it is not your habit in similar Carnegie matters, for too much correspondence has been the bane of lives less valuable than yours.

Since you *have* answered, however, I will make one more remark, which is that I fully appreciate your doubts as to Peirce delivering the goods "on time" if paid for in advance. Nevertheless I feel strong confidence in his finishing that book *some* time, for it is the nursling of his life; and I believe that if you should award payments chapter by chapter only, and only when the chapter is completed and sent in, you would supply a stimulus to punctuality which would in all probability be effective. A very considerable fragment of the book is already written out. A *severe* contract, from which you could peremptorily withdraw in case of non-fulfillment on his part, would in any case be necessary.

Your Institute will be collecting endless material for a future book on "the tragedy of genius"—especially that of semi-genius. Peirce is a tragic personality, but he is a *real* genius, of a discontinuous kind, and with all his arbitrariness, has a very lovable side to his character. I never knew a human being like him.

Sincerely and apologetically yours,

Wm James

Cambr.
July 14. 1902

I should long since have thanked you for your kind letter of end of June. I am glad you sympathize so much with my book, which I think must be a genuinely objective account of things, for it seems to confirm every one's prepossessions—making them loathe or love religion according to their bias. I got so deep into my own individualistic hobbies in composing it, that I found myself off your ground altogether and feel guilty at having given you only that contemptible little reference. But I left out much besides. I am now hoping to get well, having that long job behind me. I am here for two summer school lectures—family at Chocorua. Can't you come that way? I admire your vigor.

Wm James[14]

· *To Wincenty Lutoslawski* ·

Cambridge
July 18th. 1902

Dear Lutoslawski,

Your card of June 30th has just come to me. I suppose
that you will have received before now a letter which I
wrote to you (and my Gifford lecture book also) the day
before I left Edinburgh, addressing both if I remember
rightly, to Geneva (since that was given as your "regular" address in the little Mickiewicz pamphlet). I have
got home, and improved my neurological condition very
much by "living close to nature" on my little sylvan farm
in New Hampshire, for 3 weeks. I have had to come
down here to give a couple of lectures to the Harvard
Summer School of theology,—lectures *eigentlich* supplementary to my aforesaid book, and now that they are
over I feel free and as if that religious psychology phase
of my existence were wound up, and, the burden once
removed, I might get well with a good deal more *essor*
and stimulus, and address myself to more properly philosophic tasks. So much for the Ego. The family is well,
my two elder boys in especial, turning out very satisfactory indeed.

I rejoice in the news of your own better health. Also in
your being about to do some purely scientific work
again. I confide more in your scientific than in your
practical powers, but you're a great man anyhow and
must settle your true vocation with God.

Have you seen the review of your Plato by my colleague Santayana in the International Review of a few
months ago. I have but just discovered its existence, and

will send it to you, if you have it not. Good fortune attend you!

Yours affectionately

Wm James[15]

· *To Oliver Lodge* ·

Chocorua, N. H.
Aug. 8. [1902]

Your letter and paper about prayer came to me and were read a long time ago. Yours is what I call a philosophical mind *truly*—ready for any hypothesis whatever, provided it can be interpreted "pragmatically" and bro't to any experimental test. Keep it up! I've just been reading with great delight (though I'm afraid to throw away the whole molecular business) Ostwald's Vorl. üb. Naturphilosophie—also a big & free man. I'm delighted to hear from Piddington of a new automatic writing subject of great importance. Sorry for the delay in Myers's book.

Best regards to you all.

William James[16]

· To F. C. S. Schiller ·

(Chocorua)
August 29, 1902

Infinite gratitude for your contribution to the Nation.
For a eulogistic notice, I couldn't have imagined one that
better fills the bill, giving just the résumé required and
abounding in such adjectives as "incomparable." Thanks
again! The summer is waning and I still waxing, tho' I
remain finite ever. Am in the middle of the McTs Studies in Hegelian Cosmology which I greatly enjoy for its
pellucidity of manner. He's an Hegelian who is not a
prig. I envy you your mountain climbing powers.

Cordialest regards!

W. J.[17]

· To Jane Addams ·

Chocorua, N. H.
Sept. 17, 1902

Dear Miss Addams,

I have just been reading your Democracy and Social
Ethics, and with such deep satisfaction that I must send
you my tribute of thanks. It seems to me one of the great
books of our time. The religion of democracy needs
nothing so much as sympathetic interpretation to one

another of the different classes of which Society consists; and you have made your contribution in a masterly manner. I have learned a lot from your pages. But just whither the said religion of democracy will lead, who knows? Meanwhile there is no other, in human affairs, to follow.

Gratefully yours,

Wm James[18]

· *To Mary Corinna Putnam Jacobi* ·

95 Irving St.
Cambridge
Oct. 17. [1902]

Dear Mrs. Jacobi,

The "Roberts-Hawley Lymph-Compound" is the name of the animal extract. Dr. Joseph R. Hawley, 3421 South Park Avenue, Chicago is the medical promoter of it, and whether you use the stuff or not, you will find his book, analyzing the results of three years (or more) experience of it, and some of the Bulletins of the American Animal Therapy Association, very good reading. Hawley inspires me with confidence, and I advise you to write to him for the literature.

Dr. Baldwin of Rome, who first introduced me to the substance, told of the extraordinary rejuvenation of his father (78 years old) under its use. B. himself had Graves disease, badly, & is now practically well. I believe it to have softened to some extent my sclerosed arteries, and it *certainly* has had a *highly* beneficial effect on my acute neurasthenia.

The doctors here all seem shy of it, except J. J. Putnam, who has got differing results in different cases, some very favorable. I hope that, if you try it, you may be one of the appropriate subjects. With sympathy and warm good wishes, I am very truly yours

Wm James[19]

· *To Macmillan Co.* ·

I have read Mr. Strong's MS. of "Why the Soul has a Body," in its unrevised shape. I can unqualifiedly recommend it for publication, as a sterling work, admirable for clearness of statement, & thoroughness of discussion, luminous, and likely to be much used by students of philosophy.

Wm James

Harvard University
Oct. 22. 1902[20]

· *To Arthur Oncken Lovejoy* ·

Cambridge
Nov. 1, 1902

Prof. Arthur O. Lovejoy
Washington University
St. Louis, Mo.

I have just "got round" to reading your article on Rel. &
the T.–P. and cannot refrain from expressing my satisfaction with its conclusions, and my admiration of its
execution. You write as if you were 50 years old, and it
makes one proud of Harvard training to see such good
work done.

Wm James[21]

· *To Longmans, Green and Co.* ·

Cambridge, Mass.
Nov. 21, 1902

Messrs. Longmans, Green & Co.

Dear Sirs,

. . . As regards application for press copies, I suppose it
to be the cheapest way of advertising, and I am continually struck by the fact that the existence of books is
only revealed by accident to the persons who most need

them. Many have written to me to know where this book is published. In the case of a former little book of mine, published by Houghton, Mifflin & Co., I was literally bombarded one whole winter with letters from people (in *cities* too) asking *where* they might get it. The old fashioned bookseller seems either to have gone out of existence, or to have abandoned his function of keeping acquainted with the book market. In small towns he is replaced by the "periodical depot," with magazines, bananas, soda water, etc. Sad age!

Apropos to which, would it be worth while to advertize this book especially for Christmas? It might be a good sort of gift book.

Item, would a leaflet with contents & press notices do good? I could supply the latter out of all the clippings which you have sent me.

Sincerely yours,

Wm James[22]

· *To Henry Rutgers Marshall* ·

[late December, 1902]

My dear Marshall,

I am both touched and flabbergasted by your letter. There isn't a page more of possible psychological literature in this child's mental organism. Do you know Ladd's "primer" of psychology pub'd this fall, which I have not read, but which is called his best work by those who have read it? I have never got so many invitations to give lectures and write books as this winter. Our reputation first begins as our talent commences to decay. It is fortunate that there are such compensations! Thanks for thinking of me so kindly, and a merry Christmas to you, from yours always truly

Wm James[23]

IX

1903

Since the committee of the Carnegie Institution turned down Peirce's request for a grant, James renewed his efforts to have the decision revised, but to no avail. He did, however, secure Harvard's sponsorship of a series of lectures by Peirce in the spring. James argued that, since his students heard so much about Peirce in his new course, it would be helpful to them to hear Peirce himself.

In the early part of this year, James sent to some friends copies of the syllabus he used for his "Philosophy of Nature" course. He hoped to write a new book along the lines of this syllabus. The book would present his metaphysics, a "system of tychistic and pluralistic philosophy of pure experience" or "a pluralistic empiricism radically defended." One of the people to whom James sent his syllabus was G. F. Stout, who had asked James for a testimonial, since he was leaving Oxford with the hope of teaching at St. Andrews University in Scotland.

James did not teach the second half of the school year. He booked passage on a steamer for Genoa, Italy, on 28 February. However, he cancelled this trip and went to North Carolina in early April. While there he expressed his dislike for the architecture of the new Emerson Hall building that was to house the philosophy faculty and classes. Later in that month he was honored by being elected a member of the Royal Danish Academy of Sciences.

Now that James was mainly out of psychology, it is most interesting to see how he ranked the psychologists in the country at the request of Cattell, who along with Schiller, was an advocate of the "questionnaire" method of obtaining opinions.

In line with his own philosophic tendencies, James welcomed with enthusiasm the "school" of empiricism being developed at the University of Chicago under the leadership of John Dewey. James saw this movement fitting in closely with Schiller's philosophy as expressed in Schiller's collection of essays entitled *Humanism* (1903). At the end of August, James gave five lectures on his "radical empiricism" at Thomas Davidson's old summer school "Glenmore" in Hurricane, New York. This school was continued by Davidson's friend, C. M. Bakewell. James offered the lectures to "hear how the stuff would sound when packed into that bulk." While there he acknowledged the honor of election to the *Accademia Nazionale dei Lincei* of Rome, Italy, as well as putting his views on vivisection in a "nutshell" in reply to a request for his opinion. In the middle of October, while he was vacationing at Chocorua, James wrote an article containing his reminiscences of Davidson.

James felt very badly about the American government's treatment of the insurrectionists in the Philippine Islands. He belonged to the New England Anti-Imperialist League to protest such matters. He thought that "the great disease of our country now is the unwillingness of people to do anything that has no chance of succeeding."

In December James submitted his resignation from teaching, which was intended to become effective for the school year, 1904–05.

95 Irving St.
Jan. 1. '03

Dear Marshall,

Can you *immediately* write a word to the Carnegie Committee in favor of aid to Chas. Peirce whilst writing out the "Logic" which will be his magnum opus, & contain all his ideas?

He seems to me an *ideal* beneficiary, yet they have turned him down. A revision is yet possible, if his friends act *quickly* enough.

Send your line to Hon. H. D. Peirce, Department of State, Washington & mark it "personal." He is Chas.'s brother, & is collecting documents.

I hope you are well. I am vastly so, on the whole. A happy New Year!

Yours in haste

Wm James

Cambridge
Jan 5. 1903

Dear Russell,

Your letter is gratifying—I answer it before I have read
the New World article, (which must have come out in
my absence, for I never saw that number before) since I
am balled up just at present and can't read it for several
days.

We had a plan of asking you and Mrs. Russell to visit
us for the holidays, but we had to have a surgical operation and a "trained nurse" instead. No danger, only a
congenital hernia on our boy which this seemed the best
time to have cured, and all has gone well, though he
must keep his bed a fortnight more.

I rejoice in your own reported betterment. I too believe I ought to go on to a lighter diet, and what you say
inspires in that direction. I am vastly tougher nervously
than I was a year ago. I got pretty low again in September, and as soon as I returned I went back to the
Roberts-Hawley lymph & went up like a cork. I can't
possibly doubt the effect this time. It has carried me
through the winter so far.

Does your Dr. really know anything about it?

As for giving your Williams men a "talk," I am getting
shyer & shier of that sort of thing. *Writing* seems my
only channel of communication that is satisfactory, and I
am absorbed now in the metaphysical technicalities out
of which I hope someday to write a new book. They are
quite unfit to "talk" about to the young.

Later in the year we shall hope to have you with us. Best regards to Mrs. Russell & the young ladies.

Yours ever truly

Wm James

The looseness of *reasoning* in Royce's books staggers me, for the whole thing professes to be *reasoned*.[1]

· *To Henry Rutgers Marshall* ·

95 Irving St.
Jan. 7. 1903

Dear Marshall,

I am hoping to leave for N. Y. on Jan 21, and perhaps dine at the so-called National Institute of Arts & Letters. Are you not a member? It will give me great pleasure to go to your Philosophical Club the following night, and discuss if you like, monistic & pluralistic theories, though I think I won't *write* anything.

I shall be delighted, if it be still convenient to you, to be your guest on those two days.

You are very kind!

Yours, as always,

Wm James[2]

95 Irving Street
Cambridge
Feb 8 1903

Dear E. B. V. W.,

I return to you the Harbinger, rather reluctantly, since it would seem as if an "effort" of that kind all in my own handwriting ought to become the heirloom of my family rather than yours. Perhaps you'll leave it to my children in your will. They are filled with astonishment that their father's poetic genius should never have manifested itself after the age of 13.

I thank you for your kind letter. I haven't yet seen your boy—if you lived in Cambridge you would understand why—but I hope to do so before long.

It was a fine experience to see you again—but not exactly the physical type I should have expected of you. That would have been something more tall and lank and scholarly.

Affectionate regards!

Wm James[3]

95 Irving St.
Cambridge
Feb. 28, 1903

Dear President,

You may remember that some 5 years ago I asked the Corporation whether, in case I raised the money, they would appoint Chas. S. Peirce to give a short course of lectures on Logic.

The Corporation declined, and the lectures were given at Mrs. Bull's in Brattle Street, and were a great success, so far as arousing strong interest in advanced men went.

Peirce wants to devote the rest of his life to the writing of a logic which will undeniably (although in some points excentric) be a great book. Meanwhile he has apparently *no* means. I am willing to help financially again, & venture (since the Corporation has partly changed its composition) to renew my old question. My class in Phil. 3 has this year been dosed with some of Peirce's ideas at second hand, and is (I know) full of curiosity to hear his voice. I can't imagine the possibility of any personal clash with the authorities here, in case he lectured. He is one of our 3 or 4 first American philosophers, and it seems to me that his genius is deserving of some official recognition. Half a dozen lectures, at 100 dollars a piece, would seem to me about right.

Can't the Corporation change its earlier mind?

Respectfully *its*,

Wm James[4]

Harvard University
March 2, 1903

Dear Stout,

Your request of the 17th. puts me in a somewhat embar-
rassing position. I thoroughly disapprove of the Scotch
methods of candidacy, and the other day I finally struck
work on the pamphlets. I have been asked lately to contribute testimonials to all the chief candidates to all the
chief vacancies, and a couple of months ago, in answer to
David Irons I flatly refused, not because I disbelieved in
him, but because I think that we Americans at least may
make a beginning of protest against this absurd pamphlet
system. I forget whether his candidacy is for the same St.
Andrews place or not, and have written to him to know,
but get no reply. Perhaps he's "mad"! Under the circumstances, *cher et illustre maître,* I think I had better decline to testimonialize you also. You surely won't *need*
my word, and your case will be so splendid a precedent
to quote when I refuse all future comers.

Schiller says that they're in despair at the danger of
losing you, as well they may be. And apropos of that, is it
conceivable that, *le cas écheant,* you might accept an
invitation to Harvard? There are possibilities of a place
being vacant, and last year when we in the department
canvassed things, you ran strong.

I send you for your own private solace, what I wrote
the moment your letter arrived, and before I had written
to Irons, and decided to rally on my principles. I send
you also a copy of my syllabus, since you so kindly mention it. Much of it is unintelligible except to the class.

Yours with apologies & Glückwünsche

Wm James

I regard Mr. Stout as one of the foremost philosophers of our time. In psychology his work is admirable for clearness, subtlety & accuracy of analysis. His mind is preeminently independent and original, and I expect him to do constructive work in philosophy as important as that which he has already done in psychology.[5]

· *To George Herbert Palmer* ·

Victoria Inn
Asheville, N. C.
April 3, 1903

Dear Palmer,

An item in the Tribune announces a conditional 50,000 for Emerson Hall, which I suppose practically ensures the project, on which I congratulate you. I never cared for it as much as you seem to have cared.

What I confess I dread is becoming an accomplice in another architectural crime. Must the building go on Quincy St.? Isn't the Holmes field region, with "power" for the laboratory etc., accessible from outside, better? I think this question ought to be thoroughly threshed out, before any irrevocable step is taken. The only way of saving the Quincy St. site architecturally is by erecting an almost identical mate to Robinson Hall opposite it, where the two would form a frame for the absolutely heterogeneous Sever Hall. To introduce a third heterogeneity and discord there, would, I think, be an absolutely unpardonable outrage on the public eye.

Surely it isn't too late for both architect and site to be reconsidered. Longfellow is capable of any atrocity. I don't want to hurry back now to fight this, being completely "tuckered out," but I do hope that you won't through the mere inertia of the movement already begun lend yourself to architectural villainy,—just look at some of the recent work!—and beg you to show this note to Münsterberg and to the President.

I expect to be home by the end of next week.

Yours as ever
Wm James

You have a nice nephew here![6]

· *To Hieronymus Georg Zeuthen* ·

95 Irving Street
Cambridge (Massachusetts)
U. S. of A.
April 26. 1903

My dear Sir,

I have the honour to acknowledge the reception of your letter of April 4th. acquainting me with my election to membership in the Royal Danish Academy of Sciences.

I need not assure you that I accept with pleasure, and regard it as a very great honour to be connected with so illustrious a learned Society.

I am, with thanks, and high respect,

Yours very sincerely

Wm James

To Professor H. G. Zeuthen
Secretary of the Royal Danish Academy[7]

· *To F. C. S. Schiller* ·

Dear Schiller,

Of all the letter-writers I know, commend me for re-
pleteness with pith and moment, both subjective and
objective, to you! Promptitude also! I am myself more
stingy and costive, so I reply to your free and generous
effusion of the 22nd. ult. by just enough to meet the
practical needs. I am very glad in the first place that your
essays are so well advanced towards reprinting. What
under heaven has got into Miss Johnson—to cut out a
man like you! What next? She has just sent me proof of
my notice of Myers—so dead and dreary that I regretted
writing it. That book can't be *criticized* now—it will
have to breed its own criticisms as any good hypothesis
does, by being hung up and attracting around it the
facts, favorable or adverse, for the observing of which it
has sharpened our attention and faculties. *These* will
criticize it. Obviously it is now only a theory, which the
facts extant are insufficient either to establish or to condemn. It is a fine example of mental power as it stands
and thus I like to leave it.

What a pathetic, tragic and comic story you tell of poor
Mrs. Dyer. Dear old Louis Dyer doesn't seem to be
built on the right sort of lines for navigating these turbid
waters. I pity them both, but am very glad that she is

now well. An interesting result, from the psycho-physical point of view!

Now for your wonderful activity as "promoter" of my personal interests. Neither by "acclamation," proclamation, exclamation or declamation shall I ever be a don at Oxford. A younger and better man would have to be Stout's successor, even if you had the "living" in your personal gift. But the Gifford lectureship is another matter altogether and were I re-invited by any of the Scottish Universities, I should (I think) gladly accept. I am going to concentrate myself on that book anyhow. I believe popular statement to be the highest form of art and after next year, I expect to be free to choose my own times and places as I have not been before. So, if the spirit moves you to pull wires for me, I will not say nay. Everything would pull together to make such an appointment help the mountain to bring forth the mouse.

I am glad that Moore is your pupil. The Chicago School is doing well. Dewey is certainly growing to be a very "wise" man—the only trouble is that his style is over-abstract.

Affectionately yours,

Wm James[8]

· To James Mark Baldwin ·

Chocorua, N. H.
June 9, 1903

Dear Baldwin,

I am glad to see your handwriting again. Glad also that you can recommend two men from Harvard, even though they be Princeton nurslings. Perry has a berth with us for next year, & will probably not be tempted at all by Texas. He is now in Europe. Rogers made a good impression on me at his Ph.D. exam. I don't know him otherwise. Palmer, who manages that business, has I understand recommended to Mezes Dodson & Burnett, both Ph.D. of this year with us, & both older than Rogers, which probably was his reason for preferring them.

How you skip about! and how stagnant I remain. Mentally too! whilst *your* mind is an effervescing vat out of which truths are incessantly getting born. Your article in the May Psych. Rev. is germinative with directions of solution—but oh! that the Abschluss were reached! I feel so often, in reading you, as if I were in presence of a universe 1/2 born, and which I can't grasp with my categories, though quivering on the edge of doing so. Certainly you *stir up* more conceptions than any one else I know, and as deep ones.

With best regards to you both, I am very truly yours,

Wm James[9]

Chocorua, N. H.
June 10, 1903

Dear Cattell,

I have to eliminate 1st. a lot of philosophers whose contributions to "psychology" I am ignorant of, if they exist, taking psychology *sensu stricto*. 2nd. a lot of *dii minores* whom I know too little to compare or scale, although they *are* psychologists in the narrow sense. 3rd *your* name & *my* name, for obvious reasons.

There remain a small lot of names which, rating for probable *effectiveness* on their immediate generation, and *not* discriminating between origination and dissemination (for this is what I understand your circular to demand) I should be inclined to rank as follows: 1. Münsterberg; 2. Baldwin; 3. Hall; 3 1/2. Ladd; 4. Scripture; 5. Titchener; 6. Thorndike; 7. Calkins; 8. Sanford; 9. J. R. Angell; 10. Witmer; 11. Stratton; 12. Jastrow; 13. Stanley.

I am puzzled where to put the names of Dewey, Royce & Ladd. Ladd has been doubtless very effective in education. From that point of view he *might* come in between Hall & Titchener for ought I know. Royce and Dewey, so far as I know, haven't yet influenced psychological education at all (in the narrow sense), yet they have contributed ideas which psychology will be influenced by. All three are men of volume, and ought to go in the 1st batch, though I can't interpolate them and it seems absurd to put them after the first batch. I put them collaterally, in spite of Ladd being so deficient in originality. −On reflection, I think Ladd deserves, for his observations on visual imagery, a place in the more original series, so I make him number 3 1/2.

The next "batch" (batch 2) beginning with Allin and ending with Washburn, make on me the impression of being stronger men than any in Batch 3, but I doubtless have an erroneous impression as to certain individuals in both batches. I cannot scale them in either.

Starbuck I can't place—I think his book on Conversion to be an excellent contribution to the Science of human nature, but it is not homogeneous enough with other men's work to be comparable.

Permit me to say that in my private breast *you* stand lower now than you did before I got this problem from you! The variety of dimensions in which we estimate a man's eminence, the subjective bias, the accidents of acquaintance & ignorance, the subjective uncertainty are so tremendous, that when one gets away from ½ a dozen eminent names, I don't think that one can do more than make a few *groups*. I doubt whether the averages of individual rating will be of any value—the votes will be too few. Even with the 1st half dozen I doubt whether a lump rating of the men means much, they should be compared in single respects. My own uncertainty as to my own rating exists *in every* instance, almost.

I wish you joy of the task however. It will give you occupation enough.

Sincerely yours,

Wm James[10]

Chocorua, N. H.
July 29, 1903

My dear Sir,

I thank you for your "Introduction" which I have read with the liveliest interest and pleasure. It comes as a bolt "from a clear sky" for I had no previous knowledge of your existence, and here I find a thoroughly equipped new American philosopher, independent in thought and free in style. I admire particularly your informality & freedom from technicality. At first I thought you were going to be popular in the prolix sense, but the moment you get down to reasoning you are as concise as any one could wish, and as direct, and on the whole the impression the book leaves is predominantly that of rapidity and pithiness. It is a real comfort to see things *moving* again in our language.

All the pleasure which I have taken in the book is strangely enough coupled with a complete disbelief in most of its theses. I mean all your contacts with absolutism. I think your reasoning in the Chapters on Pluralism, Singularism and Causation are victims of the dangers (which you yourself warn against) of too *abstract* a treatment. I am sure that they are incoercive. But I am so accustomed to absolutism in others that I am resigned, and can enjoy the "points" in which one man excels another. You show so admirably empiricist a *temper,* and hold to so many of the essential features of my empiricism, that I still think you may *end* as a pluralistic empiricist.

How can you now, by the way, hold to atomism as an absolutely *imposed* belief, when so disparate an account of the same phenomena—equally mathematical too—as "energetics" competes? It seems to me that that is the worst kind of a priorism. But I don't mean to discuss, only to praise & thank.

Yours most sincerely

Wm James[11]

· *To Mary Whiton Calkins* ·

Chocorua, N. H.
July 30. 1903

Dear Miss Calkins,

I know not what imp mislaid your letter of inquiry, and has kept me from answering till now.

Dewey began to lecture on July 15th. Baldwin will lecture this week beginning—but lo, here is a Program which I enclose, the only one I have.

I should *admire* to have you in my audience, so pray come. The place is beautiful, and the company *rum*. I want one sane thinker while I am there. Mr. Weston writes me that the Glenmore accommodations are all *besetzt*. I advise you to write to the Willey House (if you go) for room. You can cross to Westport from Burlington, as well as get there by the West Shore. Stage goes from W. to Elizabethtown, & from Elizabethtown to Keene Centre, where for 1 dollar you can get hauled to Glenmore. Come, and demolish my system!

Ever truly yours,

Wm James

Chocorua, N. H.
Aug. 9th [1903]

I have just read with great satisfaction your "Structural & Functional" essay, and find it clear and illuminating. I wish I could say the same of Mead's, whose paper I *guess* to aim at something s'what similar, but cannot read out what. You have developed a full-coat of mature philosophic feathers around your psychological core, and live, as I perceive now, in the shape of a complete and well balanced philosopher. How few do! how few are not crude! Is Dewey much to be thanked for this? or only your maker? I fully agree to the truth of the position you maintain, and wish now that you or someone would write a psychology frankly on "functional lines." Well done, it would be a great relief.

Wm James[12]

· *To Pasquale Villari* ·

Cambridge (Massachusetts)
August 17. 1903

My dear Sir,

I have to acknowledge the honour of your letter of the 14th. of July, announcing my election as foreign associate for the philosophical Sciences, by the Class of moral, historical and philological Sciences of the Accademia dei Lincei.

I accept, I need not say with the greatest pleasure, the distinction so generously accorded to my small deserts by so ancient and eminent a body, and beg to remain, with high respect, your and the Academy's obedient servant,

William James

To Professor Pasquale Villari
President of the Accademia dei Lincei[13]

· *To Owen Wister* ·

Lee House
Port Henry, N. Y.
Aug 22 1903

Dear Wister,

I sent back your plays the other day, intending to accompany them with a line of thanks and comment, which, as usual, I neglected to compose. I now remember my default.

I think l'Evasion to be the most solidly constructed play I ever read, a perfect masterpiece of technical art, as well as a jolly good sarcasm on official medicine and professional officialdom at large. Reading a thing so well done makes it seem easy to do, but the number of ways in which one can fail is suggested by l'Avarié, which I imagine was no great stage success in spite of the tremendous wit & humor of certain scenes. It was a rather unpleasant picture to me of le maître's spiritual atmosphere, so to call it.

L'Engrenage was much the most banal play of the three, though equally solid technically. How late do you stay at Saunderstown? If through October, I shall feel tempted to run down for a night. Am now on my way to spend a fortnight (I hope) in Keene Valley N. Y. With warm regards,

Yours very truly

Wm James[14]

· *To Sarah N. Cleghorn* ·

Nodoneyo
Hurricane
Essex County, N. Y.
Aug. 29. 1903

My dear Sir,

Your inquiry of the 23rd. is just received. To call vivisection "altogether wrong" seems to me an impossibly sweeping and undiscriminating position. You probably would allow in the abstract that pain is a price that may be paid for certain goods, and you probably would not insist absolutely that one being must never be forced to serve other beings' ends.

The door being thus opened to the possibility that inflicted suffering may be right, it seems to me that the only question is the practical one, of *whose, how much, when, where*, etc. Absolutely irresponsible power to inflict pain on animals for human ends cannot well be entrusted to Tom, Dick, & Harry. I think that *in principle* vivisectors should be made responsible to some tribunal for what they do. They ought to welcome such responsibility. In practice it seems not easy to find a good tribunal to supervise the matter. The exasperated public opinion which you represent is in this state of affairs, I think, a healthy check upon the callousness of physiologists. There have undoubtedly been, and probably still are, especially on "the Continent," gross abuses of power, especially for lecture demonstrations. This is my opinion in a nutshell.

Sincerely yours,

Wm James

S. N. Cleghorn Esq.[15]

· *To F. C. S. Schiller* ·

Burlington, Vt.
September 4, 1903

I write thus at the P. O. on my way homeward after a 3 weeks trip. It suddenly comes over me that I haven't yet answered your last letter. Of course I accept the dedication, if you haven't meanwhile found a worthier recipient of so great and undeserved an honour. I have, inter alia, been spending a week at "Glenmore," Thomas Davidson's old summer school of Philosophy at Hurricane, N. Y. (above Keene Valley) and given 5 lectures on "Radical Empiricism," just to hear how the stuff would sound when packed in to that bulk. It sounded *queer* and I must make it sound less so to the common mind. Heartiest regards.

W. J.

· *To James Mark Baldwin* ·

Dear Baldwin,

On my return last night from "Glenmore," where you had been faithless as a lecturer, and I faithful, I find yours of August 30th awaiting me. I had been greatly disappointed on arriving at that glorious hillside to find that both you and Dewey were absent. I had hoped for some instructive interchange of views.

What you write me is quite startling. As a residence, I should think that Baltimore would be a poor exchange for Princeton, but in other respects the change probably amounts to a promotion. Students of the right sort will no doubt go to you, and if you don't have laboratory drudgery, you will found a "school." I am glad for the sake of our national philosophic activities, that you have accepted the charge of creating this new post. May it prosper and may you like it. Who can replace you, though, at Princeton? No one!

I had a fine time at Glenmore, though my lectures were, I fear, too technical for all but the few. It is a beautiful region—on the whole (the rest of Keene Valley included) the most beautiful one I know.

Good luck to you, and may Mrs. Baldwin's path (as a pioneer's wife) be made easy.

Yours always faithfully

Wm James[16]

· *To F. C. S. Schiller* ·

Chocorua, N. H.
September 9, 1903

Dear Schiller,

Reaching home, I get yours of the 26th. ult. and my son William at the same time. I thank you *herzlich* for treating him so kindly.

You enclose but one half a page of preface proof. I suppose the rest will follow. I am glad [the] thing is so far forward. I am sure that the times are now ripe for it to make a strong impression. I rejoice in the prospect of your visiting this country. I must try again for the third time to get the Ingersoll appointment. I don't know what bee has got into Eliot's bonnet that makes him so mistrustful.

As for the Psychological lectureship, I am glad if it means relief from your tutorial drudgery, but if not that, then curse it. You seem to me distinctively a metaphysician and "cosmologist" not to say "cosmogonist" à la Hesiod, but a non-experimental psychologist's chair can be wrested to any purpose and it won't hurt you to lecture on metaphysics under that umbrella. Have you read Strong's book *Why the Mind Has a Body?*—a very well knit thing, which somehow nevertheless fails to convince me, although it has bro't the panpsychic hypothesis fairly into the ranks of orthodox discussion. Morton Prince in his Human Automatism (Boston, 1884 or 5) set forth the same conclusions with almost identical arguments, so far as they go. Bergson is the cud which I keep chewing, though I can't yet get satisfying nourishment therefrom. Alas! that I can do so little straight forward work myself. The moment I get interested I get wakeful and used up and have to stop. So it is very slow a progress. Goodbye. Bless you!

W. J.[17]

· *To Pauline Goldmark* ·

Chocorua
Oct. 14. 1903

My dear Pauline,

About to leave these sylvan glories, what is more natural than to write a word to you, and express my sorrow that you had to return to town before they had developed? I have been fortunate enough to wait till yellow is beginning to be the prevailing colour, but the whole preceding month has been a spectacle of jewelry, as if the world were rubies and gold, and emerald & topaz. The thing has been at once violently sensational & exquisitely spiritual. I never saw so much of it, or such warm Americanism in the atmosphere, and I wish that you could have enjoyed it with me. It makes one patriotic!

I have been thinking of Keene Valley and East Hill the

past few days, for I have been writing, at Professor Knight's solicitation (a Saint Andrews professor—editor of Wordsworth) 37 pp. of reminiscences of T. Davidson, to go into a "life" of him which K. is about to publish. When once I got started, I enjoyed the writing greatly— with D. as a subject, it became so easy to be racy.

I see that a book by your friend Mrs. Kelley is about to be published—I shall read it, for your sake as well as the subject's, with great interest. Thank your sister Josephine for her nice letter. I devoutly hope that Susan's health is improving and will continue to improve indefinitely. *I* am in fine condition, almost like my own self again in spirit, as indeed I ought to be, for my outward duties etc. are now "fixed" so harmoniously. Good bye! Have a good winter, don't over work yourself, and keep a place in your affections for your ancient but faithful friend.

W. J.[18]

· *To James McKeen Cattell* ·

Cambridge
Nov. 29. 1903

Dear Cattell,

Yours of the 25th re Perkins's Automatism article, received.

I never thought of hinting at any special payment for him. Pay whatever usual price the magazine would pay for that much of a contribution. Send it to me, made out to his order. I mentioned his need of "realizing" to account for my having offered to get an author's fee for him if he would put his experience on paper. He seems a very respectable fellow indeed, but I doubt whether any other magazine than the Pop. Sci. would pay him anything at all for his "case."

Yours always,

Wm James[19]

· *To Mrs. Charles Russell Lowell* ·

95 Irving Street
Cambridge
Dec. 6. 1903

Dear Mrs. Lowell,

Many thanks for your delightful letter. I am glad you still have the gift of tears about our national soul. I cried, *hard,* when the hostilities broke out & General Otis refused Aguinaldo's demand for a conference,—the only time I've cried in many a long year, and I know one other person who did likewise, a man of 60.

As for these little leagues, of course they are ridiculous, and I only went to the meeting because I had heard the people ridiculed so much. It seems to me that the great disease of our country now is the unwillingness of people to do anything that has no chance of succeeding. The organization of great machines for "slick" success is the discovery of our age; and, with us, the individual, as soon as he realizes that the machine will be irresistible, *acquiesces* silently, instead of making an impotent row. One acquiescence leads to another, until acquiescence itself becomes organized. The impotent row-maker becomes, in the eye of public opinion, an ass and a nuisance. We get to live under the organization of corruption, and since all needful functions go on, we next treat reform as a purely literary ideal. We defend our rotten system. Acquiescence becomes active partnership. Against this the only remedy is that every little donkey like your correspondent should keep making a row. We want people who are willing to espouse failure as their vocation. I wish that *that* could be organized—it would soon "pass into its opposite." Believe me, with affectionate regards,

Yours faithfully,

Wm James[20]

· *To Charles William Eliot* ·

95 Irving Street
Dec. 12. 1903

To the President & Fellows
Harvard University

Dear Sirs;

I beg to place my resignation in your hands. Poor health of late has much impaired my working powers, and I believe that a "foot-free" condition will be better for me personally. I also believe that it will be better for our philosophical department to have a man who can bestow on it his undivided energies in my place.

I trust that you will accept this resignation as simply as I offer it. I have spent 30 (to me) pleasant and profitable years of teaching at Harvard. There is always sadness in severing such a connexion; but objectively I feel that in my case the hour has struck, and the time come for my successor to be appointed.

I am, dear Sirs, your obedient Servant,

Wm James

X

1904

IN THE NEW YEAR'S LETTER TO HIS COUSINS RODGERS, James mentioned his approval of the views of the dietician Horace Fletcher. James withdrew his resignation and agreed to teach a "half" course, "Metaphysics" (Philosophy 9), beginning in October and extending to February 1905. His "full" course, a 1903 Metaphysical Seminary, continued until June. Since he had had a severe and prolonged attack of influenza, he took a vacation in Florida, where he met T. M. Shackleford, the chief justice of the State's supreme court. While there James made an extremely revealing remark, in a letter to Schiller, about his own relation to "pragmatism," to which Schiller and Dewey were giving a scope that exceeded his more "timid philosophizing."

James did decline, however, to participate in the International Congress of Arts and Sciences to be held in St. Louis in September. He received visits from a number of foreigners who attended the Congress. In particular, he welcomed Harald Höffding of Copenhagen. James engineered the translation and publication in 1905 of Höffding's book, *The Problems of Philosophy.*

Financial conditions forced Harvard to let D. S. Miller go. James even promised to guarantee the money necessary to keep him another year. He also tried to encourage other institutions to accept Miller. James also tried to moderate a bit of misunderstanding between Miller and Münsterberg.

F. H. Bradley was Schiller's main adversary at Oxford University. He attacked Schiller's book *Humanism* in the Journal *Mind*. This called forth replies from both Schiller and James, who cautioned Schiller to avoid a polemic style of writing, which might damage the new empiricist movement in philosophy against the reigning "Absolutism" at both Oxford and Harvard. Unfortunately, Baldwin attacked Schiller's style as "vulgar" and this probably strained the James-Baldwin relationship. Their correspondence dipped to near zero after James "scolded" him gently.

In September James began to publish a series of articles, which centered on his philosophy of "pure experience," in the new *Journal of Philosophy, Psychology and Scientific Methods*. This journal was partly founded by J. M. Cattell after he broke away from the *Psychological Review*. In letters to Perry and Schiller, James interpreted some points made in the first article of the series.

A letter concerning the visit of Henry James reveals a rare occasion of the feeling of good health on the part of William.

A French exchange professorship with Harvard was inaugurated through the initiative and generosity of James H. Hyde. James declined to lecture at the Sorbonne University in Paris in 1905. Also, he recommended to president Eliot the German philosopher F. Paulsen to fill the new Berlin-Harvard exchangeship of professors. Finally, James finished this busy academic year by delivering his presidential address, "The Experience of Activity," to the American Psychological Association at its late December meetings in Philadelphia.

Cambridge, Mass.
Jan. 1, 1904

Dear Girls,

Here is New Year's day and nothing to show for many weeks in the way of correspondence between us! I suppose that you are back at the old apartment in Lausanne, and I earnestly hope that the winter is opening propitiously for both of you. It has gone on propitiously enough here, save that influenza is rampant, and this house has not been spared. I, in particular, am dictating this to you on the twenty-second day of my confinement to the house with it and with an attack of old-fashioned gout into the bargain. The latter is practically over, but the debilitating effects of the grippe seem interminable. I am going to send you as a Christmas present a little book by one Horace Fletcher on the art of regenerating one's life by chewing one's food superabundantly. I advise Henrietta in particular to lay it to heart. There is lots of important truth in it. It isn't simply not bolting your food; it is chewing and rechewing and overchewing until it is a perfect slush in your mouth before you swallow it. The physiologists here are very much excited about Fletcher's results. He is an extraordinary and admirable human being, and there is certainly, for some of us at least, salvation in his new gospel.

Billy is back and in the Medical School. His visits to you last winter were extremely pleasant episodes of his Swiss existence. Harry takes his bar examination to-morrow. Alice, save for an attack of the influenza, has had a good winter; but both she and I feel that our position in society is getting to be a little too considerable for us, and the old life at the Hotel Beaurivage and elsewhere, with no social complications except the Rodgerses, was a sort of Elysium in comparison. I shall practically give up all my college work next year and be free to come and go and spend fewer months in Cambridge and more in the country. I think that within two years I can foresee another trip to Europe, in which case perhaps the very first objective point would be the Rodgerses.

It will rejoice your hearts to know that Alice has found a very satisfactory dressmaker in Cambridge who takes care of her, though she has nobody to gossip with as she could gossip with you when we were on Lake Leman. Henry still writes of his hopes of coming to America. He is amazingly shy about it, dreading the expense as well as the social boredom. I imagine it will come off, and he and I will make a tour into the south and west country, enlarging our national consciousness. I have no idea what your social circle or sphere or level may be in the Avenue d'Eglantine, but I hope it is highly respectable. Henrietta is all right, but I never feel certain of Katie's being sufficiently conventional.

I am dictating this, with a lot of other New Year's letters. Don't count it as a genuine letter from heart to heart, but take it as an observance of the date on which it is written. When I get on my feet again, and hearty, I will write you something better. Meanwhile don't forget us or grow to dislike us, but consider me

Always your loving cousin,

Wm James

The Mesdemoiselles Rodgers[1]

· To James McKeen Cattell ·

Cambridge
Jan. 15, 1904

Dear Cattell,

I confidentially told you at your recent visit, of my having sent in my resignation.

The President and the "department" have *überredet* me to stay, and today I have decided to do so, giving, however, only one half course—on "Metaphysics." Nothing had better be said, therefore, about my having resigned.

I thank you for your letter about my election to the Presidency of the Amer. Psych. Assn., though the compliment sounds rather ironical to one who feels as if he had forgotten all the psychology he ever knew.

I have had to resign that office, and have just refused to be überredet, much as I dislike to disappoint such good-will.

Sincerely yours,

Wm James[2]

95 Irving St.
Jan. 22. 1904

Dear President,

Your letter of the 20th. is ultra-kind and considerate. I should call and speak to you about it, but I leave for Florida to night and am so pushed that I haven't time. Suffice it to say that I am confident (barring the accident of acute illness) of putting through the first half year of Phil 9, 3 hours a week and all the chores, without undue strain. I have read your letter to Royce, and he, (who gives the second 1/2 year) agrees that if there is to be any "relief" of me, *he* is the man to give it, just as I would be the natural man to give it to him in the second 1/2 year, if he broke down.

I thank you heartily and trust that your cold will not be of this obstinately virulent kind.

I expect to report at Chicago for the Harvard Club dinner on the 20th of February.

Always truly yours,

Wm James

President Eliot

Tallahassee, Florida
February 1, 1904

Dear Schiller,

By curious coincidence, your letter of January 15th. with the Times review, reaches me this A.M. at breakfast just nine hours after I mailed my own review of Humanism to the Nation. The Times review seems to me almightily cleverly done. Somethings about it suggest Rashdall but can he be quite as animated and epigramatic [sic] as that? Evidently it is the pouring out of a long smothered volcano of irritation at your general tone of belligerency and flippancy and of dislike of a philosophy which seems to the reviewer partial and shallow because he has never taken in the profounder vistas which it opens up. What do we mean by 'truth'? What is it known-as? Those are questions, which if once opened up for discussion, will make each side respect the other a little more. I am amused at the way *my* name has been dragged in as that of the Father of all this way of thinking. I recognize it as the continuation of partial thoughts which I have expressed; but "pragmatism" never meant for me more than a method of conducting discussions (a sovereign method, it is true), and the tremendous scope which you and Dewey have given to the conception has exceeded my more timid philosophizing. I welcome it, and admire it, but can't yet think out certain parts of it, although something inside of me feels sure that they can be successfully thought out and that it will then be a great day for Philosophic Man. "Humanism" (the term), which did not at first much "speak" to me, I now see to be just right. Vivat et floreat!

Apropos of your reviewer's animosity to your jokes, I confess that I was both startled and shocked to find lately how antipathetic they are to certain temperaments. One man recently said to me "I *hate* him"—another: "he is intolerable and odious." Poor Schiller—so good a man! It is well to know of these reactions which one can provoke and perhaps to use the knowledge for political effect. Now that you are the most responsible champion in England of what is certainly destined to be the next great philosophic movement, may it not be well (for the sake of the conversion—effect) to assume a solemn dignity commensurate with the importance of your function and so give the less excuse to the feeble minded for staying out of the fold? I confess that as I grow older I find myself believing more and more in the excellence of colorless *objectivity* of statement, keeping any personal oddity out and letting brevity and pellucidity do the work. The french ideal in short as against the germanic.

Now as regards my own poor little review, it is bound to disappoint you for three reasons: 1. its tardiness; 2. its brevity; 3. its neither analyzing nor quoting you. My excuses are: to 1) the "grippe," which for seven weeks has wholly knocked me out and only began to yield a week ago; to 2) the miserable short-winded requirement of the Nation—you can't get under way but you must stop; to 3) partly the fate of my pen which began in essay form and had to go on so, and partly my belief that it would really serve the interests of your book best to simply emphasize in general terms its importance and give an *apperception's masse* for its better comprehension. Heaven now knows how long Garrison will keep the thing in manuscript. I am sure, my dear Schiller, that this *is* the dawn of a really new era for the empiricist way of thinking.

I am returning the Times review to you *via* Miller, who will be interested in it. Royce has reacted beautifully on both you and Dewey, in a presidential address before the American Philosophical Association. He swallows you whole without a cough or hiccup, simply insisting that the Absolute surrounds you. Agreeable contrast to the smaller, shallower way of taking you. Royce, whenever he deals with details, works in good empiricist, pluralist fashion—his Absolute is only a surplus ornament which suits his humor.

The Ingersoll lecture is to be given this year by Osler, the Johns Hopkins clinician. I wonder what he has up his sleeve.

How can we live with this flood of new philosophic periodicals? Faith, we ought to start one of our own, to neutralize the others. Perhaps some day that will come.

I got your previous letter from the Engadin some 6 weeks or more ago. All this is its answer. Your vacation is robuster and more herculean than mine, who have come down to this humanistically decrepit debased and degenerate place to get warm, but find myself still shivering. The landscape is "rolling" and park-like and very beautiful—only man is vile, especially his speech which hath neither distinct vowels nor any consonants except *H* and *wk* and *w*. One brilliant exception however seems to be a Mr. Shackleford, chief justice of Florida, very deaf, but an âme d'élite, who called on me last night and proved that he had read all my works and Royce's, Personal Idealism, Myers's Human Personality, Podmore, etc. and had just ordered Humanism. With such a leaven the State of Florida is safe!

Goodbye! buckle down now to s'thing very solemn and systematic! Write your jokes by all means, but expunge them in proof and save them for a posthumous number of 'Mind!' I shall send my $5.00 for the Mind Association to your N. Y. bankers. I don't know how the publishers take cognizance but suppose it is all right.

Your review of Dewey was good. I suppose you saw my much less elaborate one. How I exult in this forward movement along the whole empiricist line, towards something which must be recognized in the end as more concrete and vital than any possible Absolutism! Woe is me that I can work so little. Four of my working days have gone to that miserable little Nation notice.

Ever thine,

W. J.[3]

· *To Arthur Oncken Lovejoy* ·

Richmond, Virginia
Feb. 7. 1904

Dear Lovejoy,

I get your letter here this morning, and must hasten to correct the error into which Münsterberg's printing of my name has led you. I told him unequivocally that I shouldn't go next September—probably the article which named me was written ere he had asked me, but I hope that his other American named are not similar creatures of hope.

As for the infinite, it is less simple than I once thought, or (as I now believe) than Renouvier tho't. But I can't see that all this Cantorian stuff that Royce wallows in so nowadays has the least bearing on the question of reality, nor does it seem to me to displace any of the old arguments, or to give any new turn to the old questions. Royce's Absolute self-reflecting himself an actualized infinite number of times seems to me the most trivial idol I ever conceived of. Couturat's book has left my own opinions unchanged.

I am sorry not to see you on your own heights at St. Louis, but am so finite a creature myself that I have to say no to everything.

Have you read Bergson? He is the puzzle for me just now. Such incessant gleams of truth on such an obscure background.

Are you never coming "East"? If so, don't forget me.

Yours ever

Wm James[4]

· *To Wincenty Lutoslawski* ·

Cambridge (Mass.)
March 2. 1904

Dear Lutoslawski

I have got into an inveterate *habit* of postponing reply to your letters, so that now I seem to be quite unable to answer promptly. The reason, I suppose, is that I want to send you a *good* letter; but good letters are with me *rarae aves,* so I wait for the happy moment to come, rather than write you immediately one of my dry words.

I am glad you are enjoying yourself so much at Port Said, and that you have a prospect of going to Palestine as well. How much of the world, first & last, you have seen! All for the sake of Poland! ! ! I have 3 cards from you unanswered, will look up Fabre d'Olivet.

I am recovered from my influenza, and at work again, though on my usual diminished scale. Am greatly interested in developing my system—but hardly attain to putting anything on paper—Leider!

The family is well, and there is no news whatever.

I am sending you your guinea back, with another one for your own charities or other uses, which I beg you to accept. It does not seem to me that you ought to be endowing America.

Mrs. Eddy personally is a rapacious humbug. She will never send you her book, I believe, and you had better forget it. There are so much saner expressions of the mind cure movement than hers. Good bye, & good fortune attend you. How you must have enjoyed the excellent Flournoy family.

Yours affectionately

Wm James

· *To Charles William Eliot* ·

95 Irving St.
March 21. 1904

Dear President,

I venture to write a word in re D. S. Miller, hoping that it may reach you before his dismissal has been announced.

Twice this winter quite spontaneously he has asked me whether I tho't it his duty in consequence of his repeated attacks of grippe (pure ill luck!) to send in his resignation, either direct, or conditional on a recurrence next year. I pooh-poohed the idea, thinking it due to morbid depression; but yesterday in a conversation I had with him he returned to the subject again, although quite unwitting that the worms were already banqueting on his remains as an instructor in this University.

By this last phrase I mean that the department at a meeting from which I was absent, has just revised the program of courses for next year, leaving his name out. As I learned from Münsterberg yesterday, one of his courses has been assigned to Dr. Woods, who, as M–g also informs me, is to serve gratuitously.

I write with no hope of Miller's ulterior retention, for I believe your mind to be already made up. But I am exceedingly anxious, and I think we owe it to the quality and fidelity of his work here, that there should be no unnecessary harshness in the circumstances of his separation from us, and that he should be left in the most favorable position for gaining a place elsewhere.

That Woods should have been asked to give one of Miller's courses gratuitously, without such an opportunity being even mentioned to Miller himself, seems to me a thoughtlessly brutal act of the department, one which it will doubtless be glad to revoke, assigning Woods elsewhere.

Could you not consider, (if it be not too late) some way of breaking the fall, & saving Miller's dignity in the eyes of other institutions? Since the quality of his work has earned nothing but praise from the students, might it be possible to offer him *next year as a final year here*, say on 500 dollars pay, the need of the reduction being explained, and the amount being raised by those interested?—I shall be only too happy to guarantee its being paid in.

If this be out of the question in your eyes, will you not *let me advise Miller to put in the directer resignation of which he spoke*, before you make any communication to him?

Once more, it seems to me that we owe him, for the

quality of his work and the excellence of his character, every indulgence that can facilitate his passage to another place.

Sincerely and respectfully yours,

Wm James[5]

· *To Charles Montague Bakewell* ·

Apr. 15 [1904]

Dear Bakewell,

I know nothing of Leuba as a *psycholog*. He is a dignified personality, but I have found him a little reticent & cautious in social ways. I haven't yet read his smashing of my Varieties in the I. J. of E.

How about Sanford?

Of the younger men I cannot judge, being too ignorant. Will speak to M—g. again to night. We have had to drop Miller from our forces as a consequence of retrenchment—$2500 knocked out from Phil. Eliot offered him $500 and a single course, but he declined. In case you do promote Rieber to Stratton's position M. wd. be rather a prize.

As for Dewey & pluralism, the case (for me) is not yet closed, for I can't think out certain aspects of Dewey's tho't.

In haste
Yrs.

W. J.

I have read your article on Strong, & think it a very strong article. Strong thinks he can easily reply to us both.[6]

· *To Charles William Eliot* ·

95 Irving St.
June 2nd. 1904

Dear President,

I feel like sending you in writing my impression of the Miller-Münsterberg affair while it is still hot. I wish it to go on record somewhere and also to have you hear it, though Heaven forbid that you should make reply.

On a first reading I tho't that for display of peculiar temperament the honours were even. It seemed to me simply extraordinary that Miller, instead of calling the department to hear the charges, should have embarked on those interminable letters to their author.

The temper displayed by Miller in the last pages seemed to me "morbid," but not unnaturally so, considering the situation. Miller felt like a toad under a harrow, he was bottled up, talk being forbidden, and the thing worked like madness in his brain, engendering extravagant suspicions & accusations.

A second more careful reading, after hearing both parties talk, has, however, made me think Miller's procedure much less excentric than I did at first.

His last and longest letter was evidently, though addressed to M−g., *written* for *nous autres*, and consequently no such anomalous *act*. The content of it also, (I mean the accusations of false dealing) were not unreasonable considering how few of the facts Miller knew. *We* knew of Münsterberg's active good will; Miller couldn't know of it except through M. himself, until now; and it was *a priori* so incredible that such a Dr. Jekyll should coexist with what for Miller was such a Mr. Hyde, that he disbelieved it altogether. Münsterberg's account of the Emerson-Hulls episode was on its face so incredible that he read everything more or less in the light of that incredibility.

I now believe that if the two earlier chances for an overt row had been passed by and a merely private correspondence had been entered on, *anybody* probably would have been swept on to conclusions like Miller's. Not every body would have expressed them so elaborately, but that comes of having a taste for a neat literary job!

All the while the antecedently improbable was literally true, and Münsterberg *was* the inimitable mixture of cruelty & good-will of which Miller couldn't credit the existence. I believe his *action* about Miller's affairs to have been unusually generous, and even in regard to the Emerson lecture, I think he told an essential truth, though in an extravagant way. He really wished Miller's glory to shine.

Miller's suspicions were then false; but granting a man with a strong sense of his rights and a strong sense of accuracy, they were neither unnatural nor 'morbid', as I at first supposed. I don't think that this episode ought in the least to affect our future recommendations of him. He is hardly likely again to meet a colleague so hard to understand. Moreover I imagine Münsterberg's charges of neglect of duty to be quite baseless—mere chrome work, in fact.

Of Münsterberg's rare friendliness to human beings I have the liveliest admiration. In this case, his consciousness of really seeking to help Miller has embalmed his whole procedure in his own eyes. This hapless incident ought, it seems to me, to be prevented from imperilling his connexion with the University. He is too valuable a man. It would be a calamity if this loosened the tie.

That his relations can be quite other, is shown in Holt's case. Holt told me that for him the profession of psychologist meant to be able to work with M–g. If he couldn't do that, he would become a business man, and give up psychology.

Through all our departments and their quarrels, I think you must be gaining a good deal of knowledge of human nature!

Ever truly yours

Wm James

· *To F. C. S. Schiller* ·

Cambridge
June 12, 1904

Dear Schiller,

Yours of the 3rd. reaches me this blessed morning as ever was, just as I am about leaving (tomorrow) to rejoin my family at Chocorua and begin my vacation from all the interruptions and frustrations of Cambridge life. Hurrah for Bradley's attack. I don't know what it is to be an attack upon, but if it be an attack upon the Schiller-Dewey school in favor of the older notion of "truth" as copying a standard, why then the Lord will have delivered him into our hands. Reflection has pretty well quenched my difficulties there and I shouldn't mind putting a finger into the pie. A. E. Taylor, whose book on Metaphysics I greatly admire for its extraordinary talent of exposition and for its many true things, has written the most sickeningly shallow criticism of my Will to Believe in the McGill Quarterly. I find it almost incredible. "Believe what you d . . n please and call it 'Truth'"—this is the "pragmatist" doctrine which he seems seriously to think that we defend. If I had a copy, I would send it to you. He never sent it to me, but another person did and I have returned it, annotated, to Taylor, from whom I get no reply. It seems to me that there must be in Taylor some discrepancy between the dialectic and the human endowments or he couldn't conceive of his opponents in so superficial a way. However, he has put Bradley's Absolute into a conciliatory, instead of a repellent, shape. It makes me think better of Bradley that he should sport such a disciple. I shall probably, unless Bradley is going for something irrelevant to my special interests, come up to the scratch in the October Mind. As regards tactics, I should think that the more of us there are to make reply the better—and independently. But everything will depend upon what Bradley's paper actually is. I have had a winter badly broken by acute maladies and an excessively tired month of May. But the shop is now closed and save a score of examination books my "duties" are *vorbei*. Thank heaven! I hate to think of you as a Civil Service examiner. Surely you ought not to consume yourself in such drudgery. Münsterberg's explanation of you, Small, and St. Louis is, that after Small's breakfast at Oxford, you said that you would be happy to come, which took him so aback that he replied that he should be delighted, etc. All the while the invitations of first choices and possible substitutes had been sat upon by Committee after Committee here and were so bolted, riveted and consecrated that none but Almighty power could change a jot or tittle. I said that, if Small had not proclaimed that fact at the breakfast, nothing could be more natural than your supposition that he wanted proposals. In any case you are well out of it. It seems to me little less than an insane exhibition of the schematizing impulse run mad. My wonder is that Münsterberg should have talked his co-committee men over so successfully to his ideas. I wouldn't touch it for 1000 dollars. Poor Miller leaves Harvard next year. We have had a big deficit for two years running and in almost every department men have been cut off. This is his natural place and he has done first rate work, so I hope he may get back. I have been so frustrated that 32 pages of MS is all I have to show for my winter's work. It is infamous!

Ever affectionately yours

Wm James

Royce's article: The Eternal and the Practical was in the March Philosophical Review. He told me he was sending you a copy. He adopts us, soul and body, merely surrounding us with his Absolute. His adhesion is practically important. His additions can be easily met.
PS I forgot to ask whether you had seen the account of Personal Idealism by that portentously solemn ass, G. E. Moore, in the Archiv für Systematische Philosophie, the number just out. A man who seems to think that one can solve questions of fact by making logical distinctions.

W. J.[7]

Chocorua, N. H.
July 7, 1904

Bradley's article has arrived and I have begun a general article on the subject of "Truth," leaving *him* to your tender mercies. It would be time wasted to polemize with him in detail, so remote is he from the subject, spending his great subtlety on inventing one straw-caricature after another of what you *may* mean and refuting that, instead of spending five minutes in sympathetically imagining what you *do* mean. It is piteous.

W. J.[8]

· *To F. C. S. Schiller* ·

Chocorua
[July 15, 1904]

Your second letter re Bradley is here and I hope you will send me a typed copy of your MS. I will make no comments, however, except on passages where I think you may throw yourself open to retort. (I don't expect to find any). I am just mailing my own article. It hardly mentions Bradley, who seems to me almost purely irrelevant. I have explained Humanism as *I* understand it—(I don't know whether you will fully agree), but I hope to have helped somewhat to a clearing of the atmosphere. You and Sturt and Dewey have at any rate forced on the philosophic public a revision of its current ideas of 'truth'.

W. J.[9]

· *To George Frederick Stout* ·

Chocorua, N. H.
Aug. 16, 1904

Dear Stout,

I send my proof back corrected to your brother—I would it were written in more architectonic form! I hope you sympathize with the 'new' view. I hope also that Schiller will mercilessly cut off *his* article's head and tail. Exert your editorial authority despotically to that effect!

I have read your paper in the Aristotelian Proceedings with great interest, instruction, & essential agreement. Only you ought to go farther, and I look forward palpitatingly to your 'conative' supplement, for it seems to promise something rather in my own line of thought. You are a real *investigator*, one of the few that be.

Hobhouse is *impayable!* To serve up an exact duplicate of my doctrine as an alternative and contradiction of the same, and to publish as an account of my thesis a travesty for which I defy him to find a single line of justification in my text! Apart from that, he has written a beautiful essay, and I have written him a letter to say how naughty he is.

I must have *100* reprints of this thing. I want to get it into my students' hands.

Believe me, ever sincerely yours—I would we might have a talk together—

Wm James[10]

· *To Ralph Barton Perry* ·

Chocorua
Sept. 9. [1904]

Dear Perry,

Thanks for your letter, and for your *adhesion!* We must start a 'school'. As for the marks of the two series to which the same experience can belong, I think it is the type of conjunctive relation that connects the terms of the series. In the physical series, terms do not interpenetrate and diffuse into each other, but are juxtaposed in space & successive in time, & have (or may have) causal connexions. In the mental series they tend to 'osmosis', so that each part is modified by its connexions, and they do not wear their qualities energetically or causally. It seems to me that these differences suffice. But a great problem is: how came they to arise.

I oppose transcendental Idealism to Berkeleyan idealism. It may however be that you mean s'thing different by empiricist & rationalist idealism.

Spiritualism is the classic name for the 'soul' philosophy, Spiritism for the medium religion.

Holt is a most delightful fellow, prejudices & all.

I congratulate you on being so near the end of your book which I hope will be a big success.

Yours as ever

W. J.[11]

Chocorua
September 14, 1904

Dearest Schiller,

Your letter from Engadin—still harping on my unfortunate attempt at diverting your lightnings from Bradley's
head—is just here. Would that I had never raised my
voice on the matter or given you all this *pech!*

What I write of now is California. If you are decidedly
not going, that will be the casting reason in my (at any rate
still possibly negative) decision. I don't want the *work*
there, which will be rather sharp while it lasts, but I
should like to have that period with you and Dewey. So
let me know the very moment your own decision is fixed,
one way or the other, and I can better make up my own
mind.

H. Höffding has just been here—a good but dull man
(socially). You should read his summing up of himself
(Philosophische Probleme, Reisland, 1903, 100 pp.)
which shows him to be a first rate pluralist and pragmatist. Sorley has also been here—a good fellow
enough, but professionally rather inadequate, I should
say.

Ever thine

Wm James[12]

· To Katherine and Henrietta Rodgers ·

Wentworth Hall
Jackson, N. H.
Sept. 20. 1904

Dear Girls,

I brought Henry up here last night (having left our
Chocorua home with him the night before) to see an old
Newport friend Miss Wormeley, who lives here, and at
the same time to give him a glimpse of the mountains.
The Hotel is as clean and good as any Swiss hotel, and
has moreover an Americanism all its own. Henry showed
us your recent letter from Caux, and the thought of you
which in any case would have resulted in a letter about
this time, combines with the propitious hour, the writing room of the Hotel being empty—the warm American September air flowing through the mosquito
screened windows from the dark piazza, the electric
lights overhead, the clean blotting paper beneath, Henry in his bathtub upstairs after a hot walk on a neighbor-
ing hill from which he came down at sunset 3/4 of an
hour ago, I having just finished an interesting medico-
psychological article, the feeling of good health in my
body, of enthusiasm for Japanese prowess, of the beauty
of the world, of Henry's satisfactoriness, and above all of
your dual incarnation of niceness,—all these things, I
say, seem to make a brief communication to you the
inevitable occupation for just this particular moment.
Can you understand that sentence? Sometimes thoughts
and feelings crowd on one so that grammatic expression
of them is difficult. I think that I have noticed that symptom in some of thy letters, O delightful Katherine. Now
to force myself down into statistical prose, let me say that

Henry's coming, so far, is a great success. He looks extraordinarily well, and attributes it mainly to his "Fletcherizing" *i.e.*, *over*chewing his food. Our Cousin Bay Emmet said that to avoid the shocks of New York he ought to be driven from the Steamer to 44th Street with blinders on. But so far from shocks, he seems to be delighted with everything he sees, especially with the prettiness of Chocorua, & in general with the feminine delicacy, charm, elegance, slenderness and sentimentality of *Nature* in America—especially here in the mountains. Certainly, although there is grandeur in Switzerland, there is little or no *Sentiment* in the landscape, or in fact anywhere in Europe north of the Alps. He will get impressions, and gradually write them down, having sold his pen (& his soul) in advance for that purpose. He will stay six months, go far and wide, and make a good impression on all who see much of him, for in sooth he is really an awfully nice creature—inheriting that from his Rodgers ancestry, I am sure. We have all been well, & had a cool summer, with a good deal of young company. Alice is *tired,* played the part of a sick nurse most of last winter, had a h–ll of a time with painters & plumbers & carpenters in Cambridge in May & June, ditto at Chocorua in August, etc. etc. I foresee that she and I will turn up before two more years are over, begging hospitality at 9 Avenue Eglantine, I the well one, this time, taking care of her. Henry has come down, & is standing about, waiting for me to get ready for summer [sic] [supper?]. So the sheet being filled, I will go.

Blessings on you both. *Keep yourselves!* for our sake.

Your loving

W. J.[13]

Cambridge
Oct 9. 1904

Dear Dewey,

Miss Jane Addams, who was here the other night, told
me that you had lost your boy. How sad a beginning of
your and Mrs. Dewey's new life. Pray receive the tenderest sympathy of both my wife and myself—there is
nothing more to be said in these pathetic situations. It
will doubtless spoil all the taste of Europe.

Faithfully yours,

Wm James[14]

· *To F. C. S. Schiller* ·

Cambridge
October 9, 1904

Dear Schiller,

I am just back on this weeping autumnal Sunday A. M.
from the P. O., reading your letter of the 1st. on the way
and sit down immediately for a word of reply.

First, I wrote to Wheeler immediately after last writing to you, to say that I would *not* go to California. So
don't let me be one of your inducements any longer.

Second, as to your strictures on my article on Consciousness. I am temporarily out of possession of any copy, so cannot verify your references in some instances. But one of your objections illustrates beautifully the difficulty of making one's self understood in these matters even to one's closest cronies. I refer to your difficulty about my paragraph on "breathing." You interpret it as if I were using just the method I try in the article at large to supersede. That is, when people say "I can feel consciousness directly," making it a kind of substance *sui generis*, I, making it a *function*, a way in which certain experiences work together in such a way as to have a collective character and deserve a name (in this case the name is "individual personal life"), point out that they mistake the part for the whole. Breathing is indeed a *part* of our personal life and free breathing or oppressed breathing makes our self-consciousness different. But breathing, like other experiences, enters also into the physical system of Nature. You (and most readers I suppose) only think of that when they read; so you chide me for making that equal to the whole of consciousness and for making "physiological" fact primary and not secondary, as if it were an immediate datum and thereby you of course convict me of swallowing my whole article. I am sure that on reflection you will find no inconsistency and that this particular objection will give you no more trouble.

I can't refer to Sec. VIII, but I doubt whether your reading is a right one. I never meant to imply that appreciation is a medium from which fact has to be extricated. I was far too short in that section and when I spoke of the evolution of the psychical from the physical I doubtless allowed all sorts of cursory misinterpretations.

No time for more. [St. Louis] Congress has come and gone. Ostwald and Harnack were for me the two most interesting personalities, especially Ostwald. But I saw only a limited number. Harnack is a duck of a man and we are hoping to have Lloyd Morgan spend a week with us.

Hastely yours

W. J.[15]

· *To Frederic Rowland Marvin* ·

95 Irving St.
Cambridge
Oct. 19, 1904

Dear Mr. Marvin,

I have to thank you for another very interesting communication. I have heard much about Blavatsky from my friend R. Hodgson, but wish I knew more about Andrews. My father, in my childhood, used to be interested in some of his ideas, and had I think some controversial passages with him in the Tribune. His name was then often sounded in our house in N. Y.— but you are the only person who has recalled it for many years. A sympathetic crank-biography, of people of gifts [who] are writ in water, would be valuable reading.
    I thank you again, and am sincerely yours,

Wm James[16]

· To James Mark Baldwin ·

Cambridge
Nov. 20, 1904

Dear Baldwin,

Since you use me as a foil for calling Schiller "vulgar" in a note to your article in the last Bulletin, I think I have a right to chip in. One may well be annoyed at Schiller's tending to jokes, even to puns, but that is the thinest iridescent film on a body of solid work, and to be blind to the admirable clearness of his writing, and his dialectical skill, and see nothing but that surface, seems to me sovereignly unjust. Moreover on behalf of our general literary manners, which, Bradley (and Schiller himself in his last Mind article) apart, are good, I think a protest is in order. Wholesale insulting epithets like that, merely pitched, without motive given, at an author whom we dislike, are not permissible, and least of all so when we are merely passing on a kick begun elsewhere.

Don't reply, but please be a better boy in the future! I am sure you feel sorry—and oblige

Yours every faithfully

Wm James[17]

Cambridge
Nov 21. 04

Dear Marshall,

I have but just attained to reading the whole of your recent Philosophical Review papers consecutively, and I must say that they make on me the impression of a fine system. The whole form of movement of your mind is so different from mine—I refer to your extraordinary fondness for putting everything into extreme abstract and schematic shape—while I can't bear to leave the concrete instance—that I have to overcome a certain primary repugnance for your statements. But this time your schematism carries you sweepingly over so much ground, that you seem to me to have achieved a big synthesis in a very radical way. I am not sure that the time paper carries us on to any much deeper level in the comprehension of that subject; but I do think that your way of putting the question of wider and narrower consciousness and of a possible cosmic consciousness is masterly—a real advance in that subject; and of course I welcome all that you have to say about will and belief.

If you could only introduce a clown to make jokes occasionally, against the classic architecture of your own logical construction, your success would be perfect.

Ever truly yours,

Wm James[18]

95 Irving St.
Dec. 5. 1904

Dear President,

I wrote to Hyde after you spoke to me, to get exact information, if possible, about the amount of work expected. I enclose his reply which shelves the matter for the present.

In case you think of me again, this is my decision:—

I won't go for next year (1904–5); I will *gladly* go for 1905–6 if the job be limited to the Sorbonne. If it necessarily involve 36 additional lectures in the Provinces, I feel very doubtful.

Thinking over the whole business has raised many doubts in my mind about the advisability of a permanent foundation of American lectures. The french standard of performance in that line is so *very* much higher than ours, that when 1/2 a dozen Harvard men had been told off, there would be no others to fall back on except such lecturers as would impress the French as strikingly inferior to themselves. Is it worth while for us to *challenge* the comparison?

The *Sorbonne* lectures, I am told, keep the tradition of fine literary form & structure. At the College de France & École des Hautes Études I believe they are less exacting.

Sincerely yours

Wm James[19]

95 Irving St.
Dec. 6. [1904]

Dear President,

Your note is received, with thanks.

Your mention of the Berlin affair is simultaneous with a conversation I have been having to day with Prof. Francke. Long ago we decided that Prof. Friedrich Paulsen was the man in Berlin of our acquaintance whom we should rather see come here. I still think so (of course I am ignorant of most of the other possible candidates) but Paulsen is a splendid *character, writer,* and *philosopher,* in the sense of making the subject alive and real rather than in that of introducing new conceptions. He is a very *finished* academic personality. I have heard him sneered at as "ober flächlich"—which only meant that he took too much pains with the manner of presenting the subject. The fact is that his work begins where that of his critics ends, and beneath his more humanized statements, all that erudition lies hidden which when served up raw, they call 'scientific' and 'profound'.

Sincerely yours,

Wm James[20]

XI

1905

THE RUMBLINGS FROM THE BALDWIN-SCHILLER AF-
fair continued for awhile. Also, James's articles on various aspects of his doctrine of "pure experience"
continued to appear this year in the journals. Included
was a reply to another British critic, H. W. B. Joseph,
again in defense of "Humanism." Some articles that appeared in a volume dedicated to Howison by his colleagues centered on the James-Schiller-Dewey movement.

On 11 March James sailed alone for a three months
vacation in Europe. The trip took him first to Italy,
where he visited Genoa, Naples, Pompeii, Capri, and
Sorrento. Then a steamer carried him to Athens. After
seeing the Acropolis, he noted in his diary, ". . . shows
that a human thing *can* be exactly *right*." Altogether he
spent about three weeks in Greece. He arrived in Rome
on 22 April. He was asked to give a speech at the Fifth
International Congress of Psychology. He wrote it in
French and delivered it on the 30th. He met a group of
Italian thinkers who were much interested in "pragmatism" and were starting a journal that featured such a
movement. He left Rome on 1 May; it took him six days
to arrive at Cannes via Orvieto, Siena, Pisa, and Genoa.
He spent a week there with C. A. Strong, whose conversation was always very profitable to James philosophical-

ly. Strong, along with Bergson, were two thinkers whose views greatly stimulated James to formulate his own views.

On 15 May James stopped at Marseilles to see Frank Abauzit who was translating his *Varieties of Religious Experience.* Then on to Geneva to see Flournoy, Claperède, and others; to Lausanne to see his cousins Rodgers; to Dijon to see his colleague Barrett Wendell; to Paris to see Dr. Rupert Norton and the "beautiful" Bergson; and to Oxford to see Schiller. He sailed for home on the "Cedric" on 2 June, cutting short his trip by a week.

Not long after reaching home on 11 June, James traveled to Chicago to deliver some lectures on "Characteristics of Individualistic Philosophy," from 30 June to 7 July. He spent the weekend of 1–2 July on Lake Geneva, Wisconsin, in the home of his friend, Mrs. Wilmarth.

Again, soon after returning to Cambridge, he and Mrs. James took off for Hurricane, Keene Valley, New York, in the Adirondack Mountains. He gave two lectures there at Thomas Davidson's old summer school "Glenmore." The rest of the stay was on vacation.

The American Philosophical Association met at Harvard on 27 and 28 December in the newly opened Emerson Hall for its fifth annual convention. Since James left for California on 28 December, he could attend only the meetings of 27 December. In the afternoon of that day, there was a joint meeting with the American Psychological Association. James was quite irritated at what seemed to him Münsterberg's excessive prominence at the dedication of Emerson Hall.

Cambridge
Jan. 1, 1905

Dear Baldwin,

I return the enclosures, and regret more than ever that you should have given occasion to Schiller's letter. My point is the *wholesale* application of such epithets—in print. Schiller's 'pages' are mixed, very superior ones, and others in bad taste. *Swamping* judgments do no good, and are untrue. Other critics had taken the serious pages seriously, and made protest against the others. But I don't think you have a right in print to indulge in such undiscriminating wholesale damn-words as one uses in familiar talk with a friend. Schiller has sinned in this way towards Bradley, and I have protested in private letters to him. Bradley sins against every one, but the best way to rebuke him is to treat him with better manners than his own. If you, an editor, set such examples, we shall soon be all at sea, vomiting our mere personal antipathies into the common pool. Delicate irony is far more effective as a weapon.

Yours as ever,

Wm James

Cambridge
Jan 1. 1905

Dear Shackleford,

Arriving home yesterday from 5 days spent in Philadelphia, at the Am. Psychol. Ass., of which I was president, I find your kind Christmas remembrance—the excellent and enormous cigars. Pray don't think that I regard this as a precedent to which I expect the Florida Supreme Court to live up in the future. I am grateful as an individualist and tychist, accepting whatever additions come to my universe, but storing up no claims.

The meeting was on the whole interesting and improving mentally. Too *much;* and little or no chance for serious talk with any one. I, however, by staying away from evening functions, managed to have two good evenings of talk with my friends H. R. Marshall & D. S. Miller respectively. Miller's two papers, Woodbridge's and Miss Washburn's were the best I heard. You will doubtless soon have them to read. A. E. Taylor was expected with an onslaught on Humanism; but it appears his pocket was picked of $75, his little all, at the Montreal Station, so he had to stay. Served him right say I! Perhaps it will make him believe in a world of chance. You will find Fullerton's System of Metaphysics very good reading. (The Macmillan Co). His range is limited, but he is amazingly clear. With a happy New Year to you all, in which my wife asks to join, I am with renewed thanks for the cigars, yours faithfully,

Wm James[1]

Cambr.
Jan. 22. [1905]

Dear Marshall,

I return to you S.'s letter which seems to me masterly for straight & concise statement. How foolish, when he can argue & write so well, for his detracters to go off the track about his "vulgarity." I say nothing about reality & realness, or of [reality] which we make. I don't fully understand Schiller's position, or yours,—or my own, *yet.*

Affectionately

W. J.

· *To F. C. S. Schiller* ·

Cambridge
January 23, 1905

Dear Schiller,

With my invincible epistolary (and other) laziness, I am damnably behind hand in writing to you. I always wonder at your alertness in all these regards. Your pressure per sq. inch is so much higher than mine, that steam escapes in constant puffs. I have your good letter from

Davos of Dec. 28. Also your article on Myers. Also a letter to Marshall sent by Marshall for my instruction and delectation. All read, pondered and admired, but not to be animadverted on in detail at this present writing, by reason of the laziness aforesaid. I *can't* write philosophy in letters—I need to get up too much steam. The Mind for Jan. arrived 2 hours ago. I haven't done more than glance at it. It is evident that our movement, like the liberal movement in Russia, will not down—it is spreading its influence and out of just such discussion in detail as this, a better understanding of the whole thing will come. I am sure that *I* don't half understand our own position yet, need to apply it to many cases and details first, etc. I enclose to you a letter from A. W. Moore, received by the same mail as Mind. Perhaps you had better return it.

Immediately on reading that insulting note of Baldwin's I wrote him a sharp protest, to which he replied impenitently. Such manners are an abominable intrusion into philosophic literature. Since then he has sent me the correspondence between you both. It is a deplorable incident. But I think good can accrue from it, if you take from it a certain practical hint. There can be no question that your jibes on the one hand and a certain old-fashioned or Germanic polemic *Schwulst* on the other (as in the beginning and end of your late reply to Bradley in Mind, the parts I wished expunged) have alienated many readers whose taste is hypersensitive; and that, if you will constrain yourself both to be perpetually solemn and never to come the big bow-wow in polemics again, you will exert a far wider influence for good. To me it is unspeakably sad that, when a man reasons and writes as you do, more clean and clear in style than any one, full of new insights and new handlings of the old on every page, people should consider themselves free to ignore your philosophy, because forsooth their taste doesn't quite relish your jokes and some of your other ways. One of them is mentioning *my* name too often—cut that out! Another is being obsessed too much by *F. H. B.* Cut him out also! His literary manners are bad enough, but I don't interpret them as you do, as the mark of a domineering spirit. I have had two letters from him this fall, of a very irreproachable tone. Bradley's intellect, to my mind, is perverse, but he is a sincere thinker and *works hard* for truth in all his writings. Quite *à l'encontre de* Münsterberg, who affirms everything that occurs to him, without let or hindrance, Bradley's mind seems to work under a perpetual sense of inhibition from possible objectors. He supposes and invents their objections when he has no text; isn't free to advance without refuting them; imagines all his readers hostile; and finally *à bout de force*, gets impatient and says "in such an atmosphere and in such company, etc."

It's all pretty harmless and on the whole pretty pathetic. If you would see each other face to face, you'd cease to be such mutual bogies, appear as men and not as demons and very likely love each other passionately for the rest of your lives.

Goodbye! enough for today. Hurrah for Japan! and how interesting are the convulsions in Russia. Republics are the only safe governments with their centre of gravity already at the lowest point.

Goodbye again, dear Schiller. Pray take my sermonizing in good part. I never should try to reform you, but for the strategic necessities of the hour. You should make all your force tell, not waste any powder or let any enemies get away, as they now are doing on these preposterous pretexts of taste.

Yours fondly

Wm James[2]

· 365 ·

Cambridge
February 7, 1905

Dear Schiller,

Being a graphophobe I have delayed comment on your interesting letter about Joseph's attack, which resembles the behavior of an ant crawling over a man and saying I can't find any "man," only some skin and nails and hairs. He takes too nearsighted a view! Meanwhile I have made a reply (*not*, please God, to his petty logic choppings but to the sources of his misapprehensions) and sent it to Stout and written also two other short articles for Woodbridge, one of them entitled the "Essence of Humanism," with which I devoutly hope that you will agree. I think that certain hasty expressions of yours and Dewey's have encouraged the notion that Humanism is "subjectivist" in the bad sense of waywardist, as if there were no anchorage at all. As I understand it, it only says that reality is still growing and in part by our thoughts. That the parts of it that have already grown are not [sic] fixed, *as such*, who doubts—and they enter *as such* into the whole which the grafting of the new upon them will bring. We need a more central and authoritative formulation or the discussion grows quite wild.

I got this morning the University of California publications with two articles mainly upon us by Rieber and Bakewell. I have only glanced them over but they seem also to be beating the air, from the lack of more definitely systematic statements on our part.

However, no more palaver now! *I may see you in May*, having taken passage for Naples on the 11th. of March, expecting to go to Greece for a month and return about

June 10th. from England. I must spend a month in France and possibly some time in Switzerland. Where shall you be in May? No more just now.

from yours til deth

W. J.

The Occult Review has arrived with your amusing skit.[3]

· *To Charles Montague Bakewell* ·

Cambridge
Feb. 22. 1905

Dear Bakewell,

I don't exactly know whom I have to thank for the California Denkschrift to Howison, but I write to you, to work the gratitude off. It is a stately volume, and I hope that Howison is pleased. So far, I have read only Rieber's article and yours. I leave Rieber to your tender mercies. You are so much farther advanced upon the road which leads to that humanistic fold where some day you will both lay down your weary heads in lamb-like rest. "Home at last!" At present, *you* are all but there, a touch and you are inside. And as you are now to Rieber, so will you soon be to your present self. What is this 'fixed' standard of yours that dominates purposively the process of experience and confines and pins it in, but the merest vestigial ghost of older rationalisms, interpretable now only as a very bad abstract way of naming the fact that

· 367 ·

experiences *do* concretely manage to work out combined results? Give it up squarely and come out into the air!

It will interest you to know that I have been named "Acting Professor of Philosophy" at Stanford U., for 1905–6, with leave of absence for the 1st 1/2 year. I look forward with great glee to being a working part of California after next January 1st. Of course I hope to see much of you and Howison. I hope to see you also next July, when I am expecting to revisit Keene Valley, for a fortnight at least. Meanwhile my cordialest regards to you both and to the Howisons, also to the Riebers, from yours,

faithfully,

Wm James[4]

· *To James McKeen Cattell* ·

Cambridge
Feb. 26 [1905]

How about Ostwald's proofs? I shall possibly take a trip to Europe in a fortnight—and had better get that job done ere I go.

Wm James[5]

Cambridge
March 2, 1905

Dear Schiller,

Yours of the 16th. ult. just in and is like a breeze from—
whence? Some good place anyhow. I thought I had acknowledged and praised your article on Myers, which I
read with both applause and profit. I don't know what
incomprehensible lapse of memory at the moment of
writing made me omit your article On Saving Appearances from the references in note 9, p. 35 of my
article on the Thing and its Relations. Such disagreeable
accidents will happen. I think that article *most* masterly.
I also squeal with delight at your deduction in 5 heads of
the indeterminateness of truth in this letter. I believe
every word of it; and, in general, the more I go on
thinking, writing and reading and hearing others on the
subject, that we have struck the fattest of possible leads,
leading practically to a new epoch. This philosophy is
susceptible of indefinite increase, usually you have only
the alternative of "take it or leave it" with a philosophy.

The hard place is Mind and Body and there I want to
conciliate Strong and Bergson.

It seems almost certain now that I shall sail on the
11th. Will write to you from somewhere on the Mediterranean. Haste!

W. J.[6]

Cambridge, Mass.
March 8, 1905

Dear Hibben,

I had already heard of your scheme, but find it hard to imagine its details, and on the details would depend the kind of men you want. If they are simply to nurse the students for your and Ormond's examinations etc. then they should be more young and transitory men, & of less ebullient, ambitious, hustling, Napoleonic and Caesarian natures. If, on the contrary, their instruction and inspiration is to be collateral and even competitive, you want another type. You start with very generous salaries for youngsters, and yet I don't see the *prospects* for oldsters. We have several good names of both sorts to recommend, but can't do so till you specify the requirements more.

Of course Dickinson Miller is the best disengaged man in the field, and he has been so unlucky of late that the pay might possibly tempt him. But he is *eigentlich* a man of professional calibre, and ought to be a professor. The same is true of Perry, of whom you ask.

I sail for Europe on Saturday for 3 months, so I can't continue the correspondence. I advise you to consult Royce. It is very interesting scheme, and I hope it will succeed.

Truly yours,

Wm James[7]

Cannes
May 12, 1905

Dear Schiller,

Thus far on the way (I am spending a week with poor Strong who is exiled here by his wife's illness) to England and the USA. I must sail on June 9th. at the very latest. Of course a conference with you is one of my justifications for leaving home, but the days are few, I am very fatigued and the Oxford Social System is immense and once in it, I might be drawn too far. Would it be consistent with your convenience to come to London to meet me or even better, perhaps, to meet me at Southampton, where at my hotel we might for 24 or 48 hours settle the universe's business forever? I go on Monday the 15th. to Lake Leman where I have business with poor Flournoy (who has just lost a grown up daughter) and with some ancient she-cousins, with whom I must spend three days. Thence, about the 23rd., to Dijon, where a colleague awaits me for 24 hours. Thence to Paris, where I can hardly arrive before the 25th. and where I ought to spend at least a week—which leaves but little time for England, with Liverpool staring me in the face on the 9th. Edward Carpenter has asked me to spend a night with him near Sheffield, an old friend another night at Liverpool and Douglas Fawcett invites me to visit him in Surrey. I shall have pretty surely to pass James Ward by at Cambridge, much as I long to see him. You see there is no time for "Oxford," as such. Write me therefore to the care of Mesdemoiselles Rodgers, 9 Avenue Eglantine, Lausanne, to say what place and time is most convenient to you.

Yours "for the truth"

W. J.[8]

· *To Patrick Geddes* ·

Paris
May 25, [1905]

I just got your letter of the 2nd. on arrival here. Am not well and am hurrying home, sailing in a week probably, to avoid social entanglements—*a fortiori* such diabolic things as you have the hardihood to suggest. Sociological Society, forsooth! As if I could instruct sociologists. No! let me off! When I come back in a more fighting disposition than the present finds me, I might try. I hope that you and yours are well, and that your various projects prosper.

Wm James

Professor Patrick Geddes, Dundee, Scotland[9]

28 Rue d'Offemont
Paris
May 26, 1905

Dear Lady Welby,

You are extremely friendly, and I should like above all things to make your acquaintance, although I am ashamed to say that long as I have known the outside, so to speak, of your writings, I have not even yet attained to reading them. I am a slow reader, and the pile of hopes deferred grows higher and higher.

I am hastening back to America, being far from well. I may have to sail on the 2nd, which will give me only two days in England, and make it impossible for me to get to Harrow. If I stay, as I hope to, till the 9th, I shall communicate with you in time to make an appointment for a call upon you at Harrow.

Sincerely yours, and with cordial regards,

Wm James[10]

Paris
May 27, 1905

I spent 2 amusing days at Dijon, where my colleague Wendell not only lectured, but we assisted at the public performance of a play "Raleigh in Guiana" written by him, and acted by the english department of the Lycée with an accent à faire pouffer de rire. The Hotel de la Cloche there is excellent, and Dijon is a charming town. Train not crowded at all thither; but the train thence at 5.35 P. M. all first class, was rather crowded, and there was no room at the H. des Sts. Pères, although I had written 2 days previous, so I put up for the night at a place quelconque. I am now at Rupert Norton's, very comfortable, but very seedy, though I sleep better. To England Wednesday night.

Affectionately,

W. J.[11]

· *To Katherine and Henrietta Rodgers* ·

Paris
May 29. 05

I am going by the Cedric, June 2nd.—and am very glad to head for home a week earlier, sleep being still bad, and me dreading a sort of vortex of sociability with which

I am threatened at Oxford, & wh. I shall now escape. I have had a delightful quiet time at Rupert Norton's pleasant apartment, and had a *very* satisfactory interview with my philosopher Bergson, as well as seen 4 more friends. Summer has come with a vengeance. I wonder if Henrietta has left.

Lovingly

W. J.[12]

· *To F. C. S. Schiller* ·

June 2, 1905

Euston Station, on train. Hey for America! I slept last night (very comfortably) in a bath room in a small hotel in London Street, all London being "full up." Have just read (rather languidly) Knox on Bradley—absolutely fatal, but really too thoro'—less elaboration wd. have sufficed. A Frenchman wouldn't have written so. The last 2 pp. are great. I'm glad to leave "Europe" on such a delightful impression as that of Oxford—and to find how extraordinarily complete your and my agreement is. God bless you.

W. J.[13]

S. S. "Cedric"
Mid-Atlantic
June 6, 1905

Dear Mr. Marvin,

I got your letter of March 7th just before starting for a
few weeks of holiday in Europe, and the holiday spirit
has held me so tight in its grasp ever since, that I have
been too lazy to answer it till now. I dare say that you
have long ago forgotten its contents. You said that my
definition of Humanism applied to all "transcendentalist" systems after Kant. I must confess that I didn't
emphasize enough the point (which however I intended
to make, and believe I made) that Humanistic experience is pluralistic, and its parts lean on each other *from
next to next,* whereas in all these post Kantian systems,
however conceived, it is *through the whole* that they get
connected with each other, that being the logical *prius.*
In "Humanism" as I understand it, no whole need be
realized at all, and the largest *ensemble* that is realized
may be a *sum* or *result.* I was culpable in not bringing
this out more plainly: it is such an essential part of *my*
humanism, that I take it for granted too much.

Your own definition of Humanism is that it "maintains
knowledge to be at any moment faultlessly true." It
seems to me that to judge of this, one needs to define the
word "true"—a thing which the critics of humanism sed-
ulously avoid doing. If it means simply "satisfactory"
then your definition will pass; but if it means "*stably*
satisfactory," I don't think it will. The word faultless
would seem to mean stable or inalterable, and your met-
aphor of the maps would lead one to say that anything in

an opinion that proves inalterable is part of permanent or faultless truth. Our knowledge surely becomes truer as it thickens up, provided the new relations modify our conception of what was first laid down.

I am extremely glad that you find yourself able to become a member of our philosophical department, though I don't yet know for which half of the year you are to come. I hope for *my* half, the first—for I go to Stanford University after the Christmas holidays. With you & Ostwald, we shall have a rich crew, even though Miller be gone, and Santayana be away.

Hoping to talk these things over with you erelong, I am very truly yours,

Wm James

· *To Robert Underwood Johnson* ·

Cambridge
June 26. '05

Dear Mr. Johnson,

I have duly pondered your most persuasively written letter of the 22nd. and admired the admirably serious way in which you interpret the Secretary's duties, but as Saint Paul (I believe) said, "None of these things move me." On the contrary, your picture of the Academy's duties and functions rather makes me feel glad that I wrote promptly enough not to be too late with my declension of the honour. I am an unassimilable barbarian, & there is an end of the matter.

Regretting to disappoint you personally, and thanking

you for your charmingly courteous letter, I am going to stand fast by both my resignations, and remain nevertheless yours most sincerely

Wm James

R. U. Johnson Esq.[14]

· *To Mary J. Wilmarth* ·

Cambridge
June 26, [1905]

Dear Mrs. Wilmarth,

Is it undignified to confess to you that only yesterday, asking my sister in law, Mary Salter, whether she had lately seen you, I proceeded to remark: "How I wish that she would invite me once more to Lake Geneva!"? I should most gladly come out on Saturday the 1st to stay over Sunday, but there is a movement on foot to "dine" me with a group of University colleagues, and I don't know what date they will have set. I will wire you as soon as I know, and define the date.

You are very good to have remembered me so long. I hope that your daughter may also be there.

Always sincerely yours

Wm James[15]

Cambridge
July 12. [1905]

Dear Bakewell,

Your good long letter of the 3rd. from Oliver's Mills, reaches me only this A. M. via Chicago. On reading it and the Glenmore circular, I go back on my recent announcement of arrival by the 24th. It will be more convenient to me to take the *last* 2 days of that week to lecture; so we probably shan't arrive before the 26th. I shall in this way miss your lectures which (I assume) can be given the 24th, –5th & –6th. But we can talk the universe over. Heaven knows what I can lecture about— I am thinking of working up some of Fechner's panpsychic speculations, but it means a good deal of work. Is Davidson's pupil Cohen to be thar?

I pine for the air and for the view, but especially to have a good gossip with you again.

Yours ever truly

Wm James[16]

· *To Charles William Eliot* ·

95 Irving St.
July 12. [1905]

Dear President,

Someone told my wife this afternoon that *you* had written to some newspaper to screen the Colleges from my indictment at Chicago that they were training schools of crime. I'm very sorry you should have been at any such trouble. What I said was a very brief and passing version of something I said much more emphatically at Commencement a couple of years ago—that intellectual training doesn't curb men's passions, it only gives them more instruments of service—the conclusion being that "education" is useful mainly as a critical spirit, enabling men to *know the better from the worse* in a sober hour, and thence fitting them to hold up the hands of the right leaders, when their private interests are not too much involved.

The practical purpose was to bid them support *my* philosophy rather than that of the rest of our department! I only saw one newspaper report, a single paragraph—but that was diabolical. It was sent me by an unknown correspondent who said he thanked God for raising "one man courageous enough to tell the truth about the Colleges," adding "I never had a College education, the blood of Jesus is enough for me."

Great hulking adult ploughmen & their feminine counter parts in the Chicago summer term. Splendidly earnest. I expected to lecture to 50 at the outside. There were 800 at my first lecture, and 500 at the last—on which occasion I felt them pulling on my line like one fish.

Best regards "from house to house,"

Yours ever truly

Wm James

· *To Thomas Mitchell Shackleford* ·

Cambridge
July 23. [1905]

Dear Judge Shackleford,

It is an age since I have written to you, tho' I have had it "on my mind" to do so since last March, when I carried an envelope addressed to you on to the Steamer that took me to Naples, meaning to fill it up when I got at sea. But neither that, nor any other good resolution, was fulfilled:—I fell rather into a trance of laziness towards all my customary activities. I spent a week at Naples, 3 weeks in Greece, and the other six between Italy, Switzerland, France, & England, and came home refreshed mentally but profoundly tired physically, as is always the case with me in the Spring of the year. But I escaped my writing table & the Ph.D. examinations, and now I am feeling comparatively well again. There was a psychological Congress at Rome, at which I was forced, rather unwillingly, to speak. What pleased me was to see what roots "pragmatism" is striking in Italy—in fact I was hailed there (to my surprise) as a kind of master, which was an agreeable experience. I had much talk with that monument of sincerity & veracity, Strong, at Cannes, a couple of very renumerative hours with Bergson, at Paris, and a day with Schiller at Oxford. The ferment is working—see the last Mind, the last Philosophical Review, and the last J. of Philosophy etc. I have written nothing for 4 months, but read some German books. We have let our Chocorua place, our children are scattered & the good wife & I are making our summer headquarters here, though with some absences in the shape of visits. In three days we go for a fortnight to Keene Valley in the Adirondacks. Schiller's article on Taylor in the July Mind (also Hoernlé's on Bradley) seem to me very masterly. I lectured, at the beginning of the month, at Chicago University, on "the Characteristics of an Individualistic Philosophy" and was delighted to find that it could be put into a shape that kept 500 auditors attentive—big truly sons & daughters of the prairie— mostly teachers.

I hope that you are cooling off in your Tennessee Mountains, and that you all are well. With warm regards, I remain truly yours,

Wm James[17]

· *To Henry Rutgers Marshall* ·

Cambridge
Aug 16. 1905

Dear Marshall,

I am glad your new book—which I fancy will be your greatest—is about to appear, clad in its native austerity of style. I must say that I think these recent articles of yours are very profound and luminous, though your whole system of thought is more *schematic* than I like. If you had injected a little of the lovely Fechner's concreteness into your last article, e.g., I should have rejoiced.

I have small experience of publishers, but the best has been with Longmans, Green, & Co. Their partner in this country, Mr. Mills, is an impeccable man to deal with, and I have found them liberal and obliging throughout. Rumour also ascribes to them a preeminent place for fair dealing. They have a regular printer arrangement for books published on commission, which is my way, though possibly you would prefer a royalty basis.

I hope you're well. I must settle down to work on that problem of psychic synthesis again.

Ever truly yours,

Wm James[18]

· *To Charles Montague Bakewell* ·

Cambridge
Aug 30. 1905

Dear B.–

Pray send me one word of news as to how Woodbridge's lectures went off, and what ground he took. Of course I don't expect an elaborate *compte rendu*, but just a page & a half.

I have been *absolutely* knocked out by the venemous

cold I bro't back from Ridgefield 2 1/2 weeks ago, though Alice is better. To day my catarrhal symptoms are on the wane; but the prostration of strength continues. We leave this noon for our friends the Merriman's at Intervale, where I doubt not the change of air will start me towards health again. It would have been absolutely impossible for me to go to either end of Keene Valley again, and I must give it up for this year.

I have just read Carveth Read's Metaphysic of Nature. Too *dumpf* in tone; but *honest*,—a real english book; full of felicitous epigrammatic sentences, but not destined to have an influence, in my opinion.

Yours—

Wm James[19]

· *To Charles Montague Bakewell* ·

Cambridge
Sept 22. 05

Dear Bakewell,

I got your long and interesting letter about Woodbridge, and it made me wish more than ever that I had been there. Thank you. I suppose that by this time you are at New Haven, getting settled before the struggle begins.

I write to day on account of a visit I have had from Dr. Angier of Berlin, who aspires towards the psychology place at Berkeley. He is one of our best Laboratory Ph D's—not, I fancy a 'philosopher', but a sterling good man. I am much influenced in my view of his value by

Holt's opinion. Holt is tremendously critical, doesn't usually let personal sympathy or friendship blind his intellectual judgments, and swears that Angier is the ablest man we've graduated in Psychology since we've been here. Angier says they are urging him to stay in the Berlin Laboratory. He goes back thither now with pay.

I believe that M–g has some dislike of A., tho' I know not on what grounds, nor do I suppose that it would make him withhold a fair judgment on his abilities.

Good luck to you, & regards to "the Missus"—if she will pardon the familiarity,

Yours,

Wm James[20]

· *To F. C. S. Schiller* ·

Cambridge
October 14, [1905]

I have just read in the Mind which came today, Hoernlé's second article, and I have rarely been more satisfied with anything than with his statement up to the last 4 or 5 pp. I think that something better may be done over that conclusion. But he is a master of statement as well as of thought and I wish you'd tell him, with my compliments, how much I have been "transported."

W. J.[21]

· *To George Frederick Stout* ·

Cambridge
Oct. 17. '05

Thanks for "Things & Sensations," which is clear and (as I understand it) I believe, true. Doesn't it tend to make *continuity* rather than substantial or "through & through" union, union by *co*, rather than by *in* or *of* an absolute "whole," the secret of the one and the many? I read your paper as if it meant s'thing like what I once tried to say in the Psychological Review, pp. 111–113, vol. 2. But very likely you will repudiate that. I am delighted with Hoernlé's paper in Oct. Mind.

Wm James[22]

· *To Charles William Eliot* ·

[Oct. 26, 1905]

Dear President,

Since you send me this letter, I make another remark or two on Sidis's case. He is (I fancy) 35 years old, is fully engaged in his own line of practice, and the certainty of his not becoming later a "general" practitioner is altogether different from that of (say) an ordinary candidate who should plead exemption from obstetrics on the ground of his intending to be an ophthalmologist.

It is in truth a very peculiar case. In the N. Y. Pathological Institute, he developed an interest in, and a great ability in treating, by what may be called suggestive methods (invented partly by himself) various nervous diseases and invalidic states. Working as he did, both there, and in the Woman's infirmary along with M. D. colleagues who could take the legal responsibility, he was all right. But naturally he must now take the M. D. degree. I regard it as *absolute pedantry* to make him spend three months (he being poor & the examination requirements anyhow interfering terribly with his serious work) of drudgery at labor cases, bandaging, and bronchitis cases. He is author of 3 solid & important books, two of them mainly clinical, and recognized (by all who know anything) as an authority in his own line of practice.

Sincerely yours,

Wm James[23]

· *To Henry Rutgers Marshall* ·

95 Irving St.
Cambridge
Dec 8. 05

Dear Marshall,

I trust you are coming to the meeting of the Societies. I offer you and Gardiner for your joint use, suite 56, Dunster Hall, belonging to two younger colleagues of mine, and one of the best sets of rooms in College. They said *I* might offer it to two of my friends, but won't give it to the swinish multitude of philosophers.

I leave for California on the 28th, so I can barely see you. I wish I could ask you to this house, but the gods have decided otherwise.

Truly yours,

Wm James[24]

· *To Charles William Eliot* ·

95 Irving Street
Dec. 28. 1905

Dear President,

Prof. Münsterberg has sent me a copy of a letter of resignation which he sent to you to day, in consequence of a letter which I wrote to him.

Since the matter has been bro't to your attention I enclose the copy I kept, of my own letter. I think that I had better have it back.

In my irritation at what seemed to me M–g's excessive prominence on that day (after the Emerson meeting he went on and introduced Dewey, the President of the Association meeting (!) in a speech, and Dewey, following the program, immediately called on *him* as the first speaker in the discussion—5 speeches in one hour, and all this with no opportunity afforded to the visitors of the Emerson meeting to escape!), I was ignorant of certain excuses which he had. In our committee we had discussed the ceremony of opening, and Palmer declined to take an active part. I, wishing to head off the chairman, proposed that no one of the department should speak; which was agreed upon; and we then decided to ask you & Edward E. I never dreamed of *your* requiring any words of introduction, and supposed that things were safe. To my astonishment, Münsterberg "bossed the show." I heard groans over it from influential people; and supposed at first that he had usurped the opportunity, in spite of the department's resolution. But Palmer told me he had given *his* consent or advice (which I think was wrong in him) and Münsterberg himself told me to day that the thing had been arranged with you. These are the excuses to which I refer. But I doubt whether either you or Palmer meant that his presiding should be so loquacious.

I much regret to have wounded Münsterberg's feelings, but it did seem to me well that he should get a reflection of what is being said of our department. His zeal and good intent are admirable, but in public utterances he does not strike the right quiet note. He has a splendid business head, and makes a first rate chairman (save for his unprovoked onslaught last year on Miller!). His willingness to do work and to assume cheerfully the heaviest burdens is extraordinary. His services with Emerson Hall have doubtless been great, and deserve our gratitude. If our sensibilities are grated on sometimes, the fault is in our own laziness in letting him do all the work. The remedy is in our hands, but we *are* a lazy crew, where business drudgery is concerned—all but him!

He must have felt my letter to be profoundly unjust and ungrateful; and of course his resignation must not be accepted now. I was surprised, after the Miller episode, to find Münsterberg still chairman this fall. If a new chairman should be appointed next year, I imagine that Perry had better be tried.

Very truly yours,

Wm James[25]

XII

1906

James served as "Acting Professor of Philoso-phy" at Stanford University in Palo Alto, California, for the first four months of 1906. He traveled there alone, since Mrs. James did not join him until 14 February. The main reason for this appointment was to help organize a philosophy department. The University had opened its doors to students for the first time in 1891. In recommending to President Jordan various candidates for a teaching position, James revealed a surprisingly extensive and personal knowledge of the philosophic scene in the United States. He especially recommended R. B. Perry. Also, James was quick to evaluate the strengths and weaknesses of Stanford and to identify the direction he thought it must take to become an ideal university.

During their stay in California, the Jameses enjoyed many new experiences: a new climate, new people, new activities, and new scenes, which included a trip to the southern part of the state during a short vacation. James wrote a syllabus to accompany his new course, a general introduction to philosophy, for a large audience of stu-dents and guests. He represented Harvard at the meet-ings of the Association of American Presidents, substitut-ing for President Eliot. All this idyllic living was shattered by the great earthquake that struck the whole

San Francisco peninsula on 18 April. Since all classes had to be cancelled due to the extensive damage to the university buildings, the Jameses left for home on 26 April.

After reaching home, James looked into the possibility of responding to an invitation to give a series of lectures at Columbia University, which had been offered some years before. The negotiations turned out to be an off-again, on-again affair, until the matter was settled finally in the affirmative.

James was shocked to learn in September that his cousin, Henrietta Rodgers, had died. He first heard of this through a graduate student, Horace Kallen, whom James had been urging to be sure to take the kind of vacation from studies and work as James had insisted upon for himself. When school did resume, James offered the same course, called "Philosophy 1 D," which he had developed at Stanford. However, he felt that he should resign from teaching. This time the resignation stuck, and James did retire the following year.

No doubt, the main reason that turned James in the direction of accepting the Columbia lectures was that in the meantime he had accepted an offer to give another Lowell series of eight lectures in Boston in November and December. These were then written out and repeated at Columbia in late January and early February 1907.

Sandwiched between these two series of lectures was James's presidential address, "The Energies of Men," which he delivered to the members of the American Philosophical Association at their late December annual meeting, also held at Columbia University.

Los Angeles
Jan 5. 1906

(Address, till next June, Stanford University, Cal)

Dear Cattell,

About a month ago I got a notification from the Secretary of the National Academy of Sciences, to the effect that you, I and a third person had been appointed a committee to report on some question which I now totally forget. You see what a good member I am! I pigeonholed the communication, expecting you to appear in Cambridge for the "Association" meetings, and waiting to confer with you then. But you were at New Orleans, and the thing escaped my mind till just now when, meeting with Mr. Hale the astronomer who is putting up the Carnegie Observatory here, we spoke of the Nat.l Academy, & that reminded me of that committee.

I am sorry to be so imbecile as to have forgotten the very problem proposed and still sorrier if my distance makes trouble for you. In general in these administrative matters, I have great confidence in your judgment, and if you send me a brief statement of what that is in this case, I make no doubt that I can easily subscribe.

Very truly yours

Wm James[1]

· *To F. C. S. Schiller* ·

Stanford University, California
January 16, 1906

Dear Schiller of my soul,

You see where I am—*seit 8 Tagen*—and I owe you for
two letters, one of which reached me only a few days
ago—that of December 24th. I exult in your continued
gaudium certaminis and beg you to send me the Quarterly and its article straight hither. I have ordered none
of my periodicals forwarded, so pray send me *item*, a
reprint of the Mind article, when you get one, hither. I
am writing to my wife to forward the Hibbert Journal
expressly. I saw Taylor just before leaving home, at the
American Philosophical Association, which met at Harvard University. He is companionable enough, apparently, but hasn't eaten of the fruit of the tree of life, a
logic chopper and ratiocinator, as I imagine, to the end,
with no *perceptions* of his own. "Where there is no vision, the people perish" as I hope will be the motto of
our new philosophic building, "Emerson Hall"—an architectural horror, by the way. I hope you won't spare
him. In spite of his marvelous power of straight clear
writing, he seems to me really very *crude. He won't do*
to be my successor at Harvard in a year or two. Do you
yet know any Briton predestinate to that glory? I take my
Journal of Philosophy here, so I shall see your article "Is
Absolute Idealism Solipsistic?" duly. I've bro't Poincaré's *Valeur* book with me to read, but haven't yet
looked into it. Have just read Mach's Erkenntniss und
Irrtum—excellent wise stuff and very pragmatic.

Poor Hodgson's death was the event, before I left.
Absolutely sudden, dropt dead while playing violent

handball. Had said to a friend, a week before, that he thought he could count reasonably on 25 more years of life. All his work unfinished. No one can ever learn those records as he knew them—he would have written certainly 2 or 3 solid books. Too bad, too bad! And the manliest, unworldliest, kindest of human beings. May he still be energizing somewhere—it's not a case of "requiescat."

Thank Heaven, I've said no to the Paris temptation for next year. I shall probably never go. I have been in very poor shape, *neurally*, ever since last Spring and have so little "margin," that I feel as if a feather could knock me out, sometimes; yet I'm booked to lecture here till mid-May to 300 enrolled students and (so far) more than 100 visitors. They are starting a serious philosophical department and I have to create an atmosphere. Hence the nice artistic problem of an interest-arousing introductory course. It is inspiring; but would be more so, if I didn't feel as if the breath were leaving my body. I trust I shall pull through. I will send you in a day or two a copy of a syllabus that accompanies the lectures, to show you the sort of way in wh. I begin. Of course it's a bare table of contents.

This University is absolutely Utopian. It realizes all those simplifications and freedoms from corruption, of which seers have dreamed. Classic landscape, climate perfect, no one rich, sexes equal, manual labor practiced to some degree by all, especially by students, noble harmonious architecture, fine laboratories and collections, admirable music, all these latter things belonging to the community as such, while individuals live in the simplest conceivable way. Yet so perverse is man, that, when I listen and hear the great silence of the historic vacuum that lies behind all, I almost wish I were in Oxford!

Have you read Chesterton's Heretics? There's truth for you, right in the pit of the stomach. Goodbye dear

Schiller. Remember me to all inquiring friends and believe me

Ever affectionately yours,

Wm James[2]

· *To Gilbert Keith Chesterton* ·

Stanford University
California
Jan 17, 1906

I have just read your Heretics and cannot withhold my word of applause. You certainly do know how to hit truth in the pit of the stomach, and bring it down. And what straight writing! Only beware of letting flat contradiction become a "mannerism" in your old age. You, of all men, can afford to speak classically and without exaggeration. Keep it up.

Wm James (permanently of Cambridge, Mass.)[3]

Stanford University
January 30, 1906

Dear Schiller,

Mind has come with Taylor's article, to which I am very glad you have a reply ready and *zwar* one characterized by unusual mansuetude of tone (for sooth to say I think you do habitually sin in the other direction and Taylor has probably some legitimate ground for complaint— your former article is out of my reach for verification as I write), because the ordinary reader will gather from this article of Taylor's, owing to his almost diabolic cleverness in putting things, that he has effectively knocked you out. Of course his way of taking your meaning is simply silly. Handling a big subject that requires some largeness of interpretation, with a mind narrowed to a spectrum slit. E.g., the 100th. decimal of Pi: as if *consistency* had no working value and as if the *kind* of inaccuracy that makes no difference in one case would not be fatal elsewhere, so that the *habit* of accuracy is a *habit* of truth. Compare great bank accounts, balanced to a penny, not for the sake of that penny, but for the value of the habit. Also I am sick of all his recent cram of mathematics and logic, which he takes so crudely. As if cardinal numbers had *refuted* ordinals! On the other hand, I think *your* statement of your general view of truth was originally unfortunately vague and sweeping. It ought to have discussed more types of case analytically and would then have given rise to less misunderstanding. Taylor's forte is his insistence on the fact that what we collectively call Truth does lean on fixed *perceptions*, inconvenient in many cases, yet which we submit to, because to deny or ignore them or be inaccurate with them would be more inconvenient still. They *are* perceptions and how can we live unless by perception; so here is a meeting ground for both Taylor and you. Perceptions *work;* and they work, because they are *true,* i.e., constant, coercive, etc. By perceptions, I of course mean 1) sense-perceptions, 2) perceptions of time- and space-order, and 3) perceptions of comparison, which latter give rise to logic, mathematics and classifications.

But in the wider sense of Truth, as including judgments building-out perception (theories, constructions, many metaphysical and other "principles," etc.) you seem to me to be wholly right and Taylor nowhere. He doesn't even seem to notice what you're talking about. In these things truth means what you say it does, satisfactoriness on the whole and in the long run, which satisfactoriness of course *includes* consistency with the various orders of perception, and so depends in part upon the narrower order of truth. Taylor seems to think it must be *unequivocally derivative* from the narrower order. The world of thought is wide enough for both opinions together. Taylor seems to make his opinion exclusive of yours and it isn't altogether surprising, if he and some of his friends have interpreted some of your earlier utterances as intended to be exclusive of theirs. But why not open yourself to the fruitful part of an adversary's meaning? I confess that I am staggered by the tight little contracted character of the rationalist mind. But Taylor's cleverness along his sharp little lines seems to me prodigious. No more today—the weather outside is refulgent, tho' perhaps no more so than at Davos.

Yours as ever,

Wm James[4]

Stanford University
California
Feb. 1st. 1906

Dear President,

I got your flattering telegram a couple of hours ago, and
my negative answer is on its way now. I am touched by
the confidence shown; but the truth is that I have too
little strength to put it on any but genuine work at present, and I can't believe that there can be much demand
that is solid at Berlin for my particular wares. It would
mean a great deal of wear and tear socially, and much
nervous trepidation, in an atmosphere not wholly congenial, and it would keep me away for another 6 months
at least from the writing of a text book which is my most
pressing duty. (This engagement *here* keeps me from
that, but they offered me 5000 dollars so I could hardly
say nay). I withdrew my candidacy for the Sorbonne for
next year from Hyde, on account of the text-book. If that
were offered for *1907–8*, I should very likely accept. I
could do much more real work at Paris than at Berlin.

This place is a wonder. The conditions seem to me
ideal for a man who wants to teach and study undis-
turbed for 9 months, and who is financially able to take 3
months away in the year. But the great surrounding
vacuum is curious. The historic silence fairly rings in
your ears.

I have 450 listeners, 300 of whom are regularly enrolled. Assistants take charge of the chores. No red tape.
No rank lists. Instructors keep absences or not, mark
as they like, etc. In short we are refreshingly individualistic, and the tone of study seems decidedly more

earnest than at Cambridge. I ask myself whether it be not partly cause and effect, & whether our red tape doesn't partly defeat its own ends.

Believe me, again with thanks & regrets,

Faithfully yours,

Wm James[5]

· *To F. C. S. Schiller* ·

Stanford University
February 17, 1906

Quarterly Review just rec'd. Also wife arrived, simultaneously, with your post card to her about Hibbert Journal. I believe that I acknowledged that, sent on by her previously, by my direction and expressed due satisfaction to you. The Plato article is *grossartig*, one of the boldest, straightest and of course most impressive as being 'scholarly' things that you have written. So simple! I find it *most* instructive. I'm down with bad *gout*—if it isn't one thing, it's another!

W. J.

· To F. C. S. Schiller ·

Stanford University
February 24, 1906

Dear Schiller,

Your letter of the 4th. about Hodgson, etc. came yesterday and along with it Woodbridge's Journal of Philosophy with your article on Solipsism, which adds to the
enlightenment, doubtless, of the young. Of course
Royce has always agreed that the Absolute himself is a
solipsist, but insisted that finite minds can't be so until
they merge in the Absolute by absorbing the totality of
content. As long as there is any *content of which you are
ignorant*, you mustn't try to imitate the Absolutist's
solipsism.

I am pressed with examination reading—250 students
and me convalescing but slowly from a bad attack of
gout. I send you, to *égayer* you, some specimen replies
and also in another cover my syllabus so far. The students have to read Paulsen, read the syllabus, and hear
my lectures—then "combine their information."

Your article on Plato chimes still through my intellect.
Keep on diversifying yourself in this way and you will
lead everything!

Affectionately thine

W. J.[6]

Stanford University
California
Feb. 26. 1906

Dear Perry,

Dr. Jordan tells me that you have at last been invited formally hither by action of the trustees, and asks me to make you come. I can't quite undertake that commission, but I will set things down in black and white as fairly as I can, for your & Mrs. Perry's choice.

The *pros* that one sees immediately are the exquisite landscape hard by, the splendid climate, both for comfort and for work, the simplification of all things which is so favorable to work, the excellent wholesome, earnest, though relatively to Harvard somewhat immature, tone of the students, and the existence of what seems to me a very good looking superior faculty, relatively young.

Further more, in your case, headship of the department, freedom to make your work in your own way, and possibility of making an important mark for all future time if you should stay here long, with things in this plastic condition.

I assume that they are offering you 4000 dollars.

The *cons* are that rents & supplies seem little cheaper here than in Cambridge. There are fewer temptations to spend money, however, in small ways, altho that great trade-centre San Francisco is only 70 minutes away by rail. The great economy here is fuel, on which one spends much less than at Cambridge. Hired help being so hard to get, the wives suffer from too much housework. The human vacuum and fewness of elements (exquisite tho many of them are) ends by making a change necessary occasionally, *especially* for wives, who haven't the stimulus that the instructors get from their teaching function. Travel requires money; and salaries, so far, have been so small that a bad grumbling habit has set in, which is demoralizing to the tone of the teaching body.

Apparently neither trustees nor president have so far had the right kind of imagination. The exquisite "plant" and conditions point to a University of *quality,* unique all through, though not necessarily large. Whether that will ever be the policy, I know not. It means big salaries. You can't count on it. All talk from above seems tainted with vagueness. Don't trust any *generalities,* only engagements in black and white. Things may turn out for the best, they may not. The thing hinges mainly on money; and the U. *may* be pinched—I can't get anything definite in the way of facts. They ought to have two big men in the philosophy department. Jordan talks vaguely of adding to the force; but don't you *count* on anything! He means well, but is vague, talks impulsively, and can't live up to his intentions.

This is the seamy side, and the faculty is demoralized in consequence. A *somewhat* better era is *certain;* the future *may* be a *fine* one—it depends on what counsels get uppermost.

My *total* advice to you is *come* by all means. It will enlarge your knowledge of your own country, educate you grandly in that respect, even if your stay should be transient. You are just as much in the running (or almost as much) for a higher eastern place (e.g. at Harvard) here as you would be there. And if you stay here and identify yourself with Pacific civilization, it means more of a career than you could hope for on the Atlantic coast. You can be a really vital influence.

There are really utopian *beginnings* here, it all depends on the turn things take. The students, both female

& male, make on me a better impression than do the Harvard undergraduates—for earnestness and simplicity.

In haste to catch the mail & with love,

Yours ever,

W. J.

I will send you some syllabus stuff I give my class.[7]

· *To Ralph Barton Perry* ·

Stanford University
California
Feb. 27. 1906

Dear Perry,

I wrote in a great hurry last night, to catch the mail, omitting certain things.

I wrote also *wholly from the point of view of your own interests. Our* interest is to keep you; and I dare say that pressure will be bro't on you to stay, so that your decision will not be an easy one. Were I at your age and the temptation to come here came to me, I think I should yield to it, in spite of some uncertainties.

One drawback here is the small library. If you accept, you must make a *positive condition* of your coming that you be allowed to spend 250 or 300 dollars a year on books for the library (exclusive of the periodicals now taken) to be designated by yourself. I was surprised on arrival to find so good a lot of philosophical books in the library for students' use. Most of the needful things, and no dead wood. It is a *live* library, though a small one.

We, by great good luck, have just stept into a little furnished flat on the campus, just big enough for a married couple ($250 for 6 months). A Swedish woman comes in once a week and sweeps etc for 50 cents—*sonst* we take care of things ourselves; and step across the way to a somewhat unappetizing college boarding house, where, however, the company is agreeable, and where one pays 16 dollars a month for 2 meals or 21 for 3 meals daily.

Most of the faculty live in the village of Palo Alto, a mile away. The clay mud is fierce during the rains (as now) and in summer it is dust unto dust and under dust to lie. But the fine weather is exquisite, the hills divine and never to be invaded by much civilization. The climate is queer. It has made me intensely wakeful, yet I *stand* the wakefulness as I never should at home. All this, however, without any feeling of excitement such as our N W weather brings. I *feel* absolutely *let alone* by the climate, it is simply *comfortable*.

As usual, my d—d health spoils everything. A *bad* attack of gout, unable to walk today, after 3 weeks of it, and an itching urticaria all over my skin with fever, s'thing I never had before in my life! 400 listeners, very appreciative and earnest, 275 of 'em enrolled, and examination books perhaps as good as those at Harvard. They give one meanly paid 'assistants' for the drudgery of the course, exams (account keeping etc). Very little red tape, tho' of course it will grow. At present instructors keep absences or not, give what tests & exams they please etc. There is no rank list but they drop delinquents easily, and the tone of study, ambition etc is distinctly superior to that at Harvard. Co-education seems to work here quite ideally, the relations being friendly and whole-some in a high degree. I guess this is about all.

Yours as ever,

W. J.

· *To George Herbert Howison* ·

Stanford University
California
March 7th. 1906

Dear Howison,

I know of no "out" whatever to Hocking. My only re-serves would be that he is as yet untried in big tasks and "one never can know;" likewise a certain "preciousness" of style in his first article in Woodbridge's Journal. Al-together, I regret (sic) [regard] him personally as per-haps the most *distingué* young fellow we've had in recent years. All his personal traits, so far as known to me, are of a superior order. Handsome, good manners, ready to joke—in short a "gentleman." The only fault I can find is that like so many Americans, he is afraid of letting out his voice. As for whether he would "consider" $1000, I haven't the least idea, one way or the other.

I have been so poorly that in common prudence I had to back out from my promise to address the Union on the 23rd. I expect to be at S. F. next week, and shall cer-tainly go out to Berkeley & see you.

Affectionately yours,

Wm James[8]

St. Dunstan's
Van Ness and Sutter St.
San Francisco, California
March 13. 1906

Dear Perry,

Dr. Jordan has just informed me of your refusal of both his propositions—so I can now sink back into satisfaction that Harvard has you for good. I am a little surprised, though, that you couldn't come for the single year— probably they wouldn't let you off.

My letter to you was written solely from the point of view of your own interests, you having asked me to advise you from that point of view. I have to confess that if *I had been consulted* about candidates in the interests of the University here, immediate as well as future, I should have advised their going in for Dewey. What they need now is a leader established in the public eye. They have been too shy, hitherto, and relied on younger men, to grow up, but the time for that is over.

You must have had a trying time deciding, you & Mrs. P. especially, for the wives have the second best time here. I hope they gave you securities at Harvard. In haste,

always truly yours,

Wm James

Stanford University
California
March 18th. [1906]

Dear President,

I have to report that the Association of American Universities had a harmonious meeting, rather strenuous so far as hospitalities went, and closed yesterday. The paper you sent me arrived in the very nick of time, and on the whole the paper on the same subject by President Wheeler agreed with it. He made much of interchange as a way in which the guild of teachers were made mutually acquainted, leading to rapider exchanges of place and promotion, which he regarded as normal.

Jordan's paper made very good literature and was full of sense. The Cornell contribution was an "elaboration of the obvious." The only really important paper was Dean West's of Princeton, yesterday. Masterly in both form and matter, it ought to have a wide circulation. Practically it recommended our Harvard constitution (not naming us, however) as the sole path of salvation.

There were no resolutions, no differences of opinion developed, nothing to lock horns over, for every one seemed of essentially the same mind on all the subjects. It was not worth crossing the Continent for, except for the sociability. The attendance was small, the only eastern men being President Remsen, President van Hise, Carpenter of Columbia, Burton of Chicago, Woolsey of Yale, & West of Princeton.

The Spring advances here, but it's rain, rain, rain! I'm glad you didn't come—I went off at 1/2 cock in writing to urge you. Things here won't admit of reform *yet*, and a volcanic explosion of some sort will probably have to occur first. But the potentialities of the place are exquisite.

Always sincerely yours,

Wm James[9]

· *To Ralph Barton Perry* ·

Stanford University
California
April 11. 1906

Dear Perry,

Your excellent letter explaining your refusal, etc. is at hand, and very welcome. I confess that we had both of us been a little curious to know what had been going on behind the scenes, especially what made you decline the invitation to come for one year. At present all is made perfectly clear, and the decision was certainly the safest, and possibly, even as regards the remoter future, which is the big gambling stake in California, the wisest you could have made. I am mighty glad that Harvard still possesses you, though I am unaccustomed to imagine you in Palmer's chair. You must have been pleased at his adoption of you as his successor.

I am down for a general Introduction next year, which will certainly be my last as lecturer. I wish that I could see my way to using your book, but I can work Paulsen easier. I have read yours again while here, and admire it

more than ever as a synopsis, and retrospective summing up of philosophic wisdom, wonderfully pregnant
paragraphs & sentences, but don't see how (in my hands
at any rate) it can be made a means of working the subject in to the inanimate minds of beginnings. What they
need is a few problems very concretely treated. You
cover too much ground (in my opinion) and often too
abstractly. This is not to "rub in" my ancient criticism,
but only to excuse myself for not using a book which for
your sake I should have liked to use above all others.

Only 4 more weeks of lecturing now for me. Less than
for you 'uns! but I am *orfle* tired.

Yours in haste

W. J.

Shaler's death is a *great* shock—the best loved man in
our university.[10]

· *To Josiah Royce* ·

Stanford University
California
April 22. 1906

Dear Royce,

Not knowing whether McVare still presides over the
destinies of the tabular view, and requiring at any rate (I
suppose) the approbation of our department for my
proposition I write to you to say that I am willing, and
should *like*, to give my Introduction to Philosophy at 8

o'clock. It would cut down the men, but leave me with the more earnest ones, and it would be of edifying example. Seeing them begin here at 8 this winter has made me more ashamed than ever (and that is saying a good deal) of our slugabed practice.

Henceforward I am prepared to *pose* at afternoon teas and other social gatherings as an authority on earthquakes. The critter herself was very *vivid*, and the San Francisco story is *historical*. I spent 6 hours there on the morning. No harm done to *us*.

In haste, yours, as ever

W. J.[11]

· *To Frank Angell* ·

Cambridge
May 13. 06

Dear Angell,

We have been home 10 days, and I think the time has come to notify our safe arrival to you. The "East" looks very solid, dark, and complex compared with the civilization of Palo Alto, & Harvard seems tremendously tremenjusly so after sweet little Stanford. Everything in this world—even you and I—has its *p'ints;* but has to go without the p'ints of something else: which arrangement increases the richness of alternatives in the Universe. I find the Ph D. examination season on here now, the thing I most detest in my academic life, partly because it comes at the fatigued end of the year, and partly because of the amount of humbug on *our* part connected with it. There is not much humbug on the part of the poor candidates, for although their theses usually make one grovel with admiration of their industry and learning, the oral examinations send the daylight into all their crannies. *I* invariably ask them questions which I can't my self answer, and feel mean that they should have no opportunity to show me up.

We have talked little except earthquake since our return, and are thoroly accustomed to the "pose" of heroes. With you all in California the state of excitement must have worn itself out, and in poor San Francisco the stage of unutterable fatigue with the number of decisions and the comfortless conditions must have set in. The next six months will make many nervous victims surely. It will be a new sifting out of those who are natively adapted to triumph in such a strenuous situation, from those who are not adapted. I should suppose that many citizens who could have been happy and prosperous at S. F. in quiet times will now simply bow their heads, and fall back on humbler conditions of living, in the country or in smaller towns, and there find perhaps a more genuine contentment than they ever had in the city. Blessed conditions of California, that make such rearrangements easy!

My regret is that we never got to Ben Lomond, never drove to La Honda, never saw the Santa Cruz mountains or paid a visit to Car-*mell*. Perhaps hereafter! I think the climate did have something adverse to me—I began to sleep immediately on my return and am now sleeping quite normally.

I enclose you a check on the Palo Alto Bank (solvent ?) for $100.00. Please make any balance not needed for Palo Alto relief over to the San Francisco relief fund. When I receive my pay for April from Stanford, I shall be generous abundantly, but I must wait for that. I left $100 at Berkeley. We are hoping to go to Milton in a couple of days to give Mrs. Angell news of you and see your children. Believe me dear Angell with my wife's warm regards,

Yours ever truly,

Wm James[12]

· *To James McKeen Cattell* ·

95 Irving St.
Cambridge, Mass.
June 3, 1906

Dear Cattell,

Thanks for the Sciences of which a dozen (enough!) have arrived. As for the lectures, after writing my last letter, I had relaxed into a state of holy peace as regards my future thinking of that chalice as averted from my lips, but now your letter comes; I will say immediately "yes" to your proposition of six lectures. I hate them, and they're thoroughly *bad* for me. But I love your Columbia "Department," and will contribute to its grandeur, so count me in. I wish I could tell you how many thousands of dollars worth of jobs I've declined in the past 6 years. But no matter! The *time* will have to be last 1/2 of Jan. or 1st 1/2 of Feb. I note that I may have 3 consecutive days on 2 consecutive weeks, but it *might* prove better to space them, every other day for two weeks. When can that be definitely decided?

Truly yours,

Wm James[13]

· *To F. C. S. Schiller* ·

Cambridge
August 3, 1906

Dear old Schiller,

How you keep it up! I have read your reviews of Sturt and Joachim in the Nation and your article on Taylor in the July Mind. I could almost wish the latter had been less elaborate. When one has construction in hand, polemic writing may well take a second place. Taylor will be effectively superseded if we once get out a perfectly clear expression of what we believe, without all this labor of refuting him. I'm not sure that he will himself succumb to what you say of the Pi case. To my mind his talk about it was absolutely childish. Does he not see that a *habit* of neglecting fractions may be so pernicious that the "truth" of even useless decimals is worth contending for? That granted, all your remarks about the 100th. decimal follow.

Sturt has sent me his book, but I have hardly had time to look at it. I wish it were less polemic and more constructive. But out of all this polemic writing advance in clearness must result. I find Dewey's article in the same Mind *most* illuminating and masterly. Mackenzie excellent too, but he fails to take the last step, after leading right up to it, being unwilling to admit that what experiences "mean" and "know" may just be other experiences in the *plural*. He leaves us with a monistic Absolute, only not idealistic. But things are drifting tremendously in our direction. It reminds me of the Protestant reformation![14]

[rest missing]

Cambridge
August 24, 1906

You blessed old Schiller, here comes in your letter of
August 9 from Sils Maria, redolent of vigor and good
spirits and fight. What a godlike life you lead, between
Oxford and the Engadin peaks. And what a contrast with
my penurious tide of health and energy. No matter,
while there's life, there's hope. I'm off for a fortnight in
the Adirondacks tomorrow, where I can't climb, but
where I can at least lie on the *ground* instead of sitting
on a "piazza," and where I shall read Sturt, among other
things. I've just read Joachim, a beautiful piece of composition and clear writing. But *hasn't* the Lord delivered
him into pragmatism's hands, just? I think it ought to
clear up the situation amazingly. I'm overjoyed at the
table of contents that you are sending me. I didn't realize
that things were as far forward as that. And I'm particularly rejoiced that Plato is to occupy so central position. I
hope that the whole Quarterly Review criticism gets in
bodily. The most effective way of turning the tables on
our particular adversarys is to fling Plato's Theaetetus
right into their teeth. They treat us now as little street
boys and ignoramuses, of which I indeed am one, but
they can treat you as such no longer if you emphasize
and develope that particular criticism, which their lop-
sided training will lead them especially to respect.

Young Barlow shall be welcome! Hurrah for Goldstein! I didn't know a German *could* be anything but a
dogmatist.

The ghost of dear old Hodgson is reappearing through
Mrs. Piper and I am to co-ordinate his utterances and
make report. *Not* convincing, to me: but baffling exceed-

ingly. I send you a pretty memorial of him, read at the Tavern Club by de Wolfe Howe.

Ever thine

W. J.

Possibly I may get to Europe for a few weeks next Spring. In haste and with hearty admiration for the Aristotelian Society fragment also.[15]

· *To Horace Meyer Kallen* ·

St. Hubert's
Sept 4. [1906]

Dear Kallen,

I meant to write to you yesterday but forgot about it. And here I am, about to leave tomorrow at 7 A.M. I hope that you may be getting better adapted to the climate of Glenmore. If not, there is a *Broe* boarding house about a mile before you reach here in Keene Valley where the beauties of this nature would be open to you. I can't find anything about its prices etc. You have, as intermediate stations, Elizabethtown (Maplewood house) or Lake George, where there must be s'thing cheap alongside of the fashionable parts, but I am ignorant of conditions there. Possibly you are getting information at Glenmore. The main thing to me seems to be that you should get the whole month of Sept. in the country somewhere and that means making your cash go as far as possible. And not doing any study after 4 P.M.!!!

I enclose a card to Adler, in case you should come along to this part of the Valley. I spoke to him of you, and I think he would be glad to see you. He is very jealous of his time, and the best time to call is about 4.30 or 5 P.M.

Good luck! and to a happy meeting in October!

Yours truly

Wm James[16]

· *To Horace Meyer Kallen* ·

95 Irving St.
Sept. 9. '06

Dear Kallen,

Reaching home last night I find your letter of Thursday. I re-enclose Mr. Boardman's to you.

I cannot believe that Henrietta Rodgers is dead. I should *certainly* have heard of it direct. I advise Mr. Boardman not to write to Katherine about it till it is confirmed. It might shock Henrietta to learn of such a rumor.

I am *very* sorry that your vacation is being cut short by such a call. I do think that your recuperation is more important than these civic troubles which are always with us, and your particular share in which can certainly be postponed till you have got a "position" of some sort which will make your influence greater.

Your first duty is to keep yourself in decent condition so as to gain the position. I don't mean that you should get nervous about your health, but that you *should* get what is a prime element of mental as well as bodily hygiene in the long run, *one rural month* at least in the year.

You mistake my praise of Joachim. What he has done is to save us from a big lot of critical labor, and to open our door wide.

> Great haste,
> Yours truly
>
> W. J.

· *To Ralph Barton Perry* ·

> 95 Irving St.
> Sept. 10. 06

Dear Perry,

Just touching Cambridge between Keene Valley and Chocorua. I have informed the office that *you* will answer questions concerning my new introductory course D. in Paulsen, on *Tu. Th. & Sat.*, at 9. Will you do so? Probably none will be asked. I don't wish, for good reasons, to get home here till Thursday night. I will meet my students on Saturday at the 9 o'clock hour.

You, I believe, are Dean now, and I hope that you will relish the fierce light that beats on that throne. I got your points about "K.," and will reserve them till I get energizing again on the subject. Kind regards to Mrs. P. Pray let me know if aught transpires, addressing "Chocorua."

> Yours as ever
>
> W. J.

Chocorua, N. H.
Sept. 23. 06

Dear President,

I find myself in a very awkward situation. For a year past my infirm "heart" has been giving me trouble again, and within the past fortnight something like the bad symptoms of seven or eight years ago have broken loose. The obvious indication is to spare it. Much of the trouble is doubtless "nervous," and sure to ameliorate when I get home and treat myself as I know how. I *can*, no doubt, carry through my half year's course as advertized.

I *can;* but the question is how far I *ought* to subject an organ which is going back and losing its tone, to a deleterious strain? Next to carrying trunks up stairs the most *angreifend* thing I know is lecturing, especially to large classes. The cumulative effect of it is very great on me.

Under these circumstances it is natural that I should find myself wishing that I had forced my resignation through, last year. Is it too late for it to take immediate effect now? The course, Phil. 1 D, I advertize is a supernumerary novelty. If dropped, it would leave our traditional program in no essential particular altered. I might resign then, and let the course drop altogether.

That is one alternative. The other would be to start the course as advertized, on the express understanding that I shall be free at my conscientious discretion to stop lecturing whenever I think it is having damaging effect. Fortunately we have this year Apthorp Fuller Ph.D., already licensed as lecturer, a man very sympathetic with my general attitude in philosophy, who would undoubtedly be glad enough to step into the breach in case

I called on him. *I* should have absolutely to determine the amount of help required; and to notify the students on meeting them next Saturday that they cannot count on my uninterrupted ministrations.

I should also expect Fuller to be paid out of my salary.

I rashly accepted an appointment last winter to give a short course of lectures at Columbia. This of course I shall resign from. But a Lowell course to which I have also been appointed, I shall only resign from under stress of necessity, for the fee ought to more than cover the expense of Fuller, and I need my income.

I ask you either to accept my resignation outright, or to authorize the arrangement with Fuller, experiment being left to decide the amount of help I shall require of him. I haven't yet written to sound him! Use your own preference, and I shall be satisfied; though my own abstract preference is decidedly for the first & most decisive solution.

It might be that the department would like to have Fuller give the course wholly, in his own name. This would be a 3rd solution.

I shall return home Wednesday night, and report to you promptly.

Sincerely yours,

Wm James

If there is anything I hate it is this perpetual crying "baby," and I probably seem so vivacious when in action, that others can't well believe in the lack of solidity with which I am beset. If the earthquake hadn't closed Stanford a month too early last year I don't know how I should have got through the lecturing, it fatigued me so.[17]

Chocorua, N. H.
Sept. 25, 1906

Dearest Katie,

From Henry comes a letter last night enclosing one from you to him and giving the terrible news. He, it appears, had known it from the first, but had not notified it to us, thinking we would get it in a directer way—we write pretty infrequently to each other.

Three weeks ago a student of mine told me that a friend of his had asked him to ask me if Miss Dorrington Rodgers was dead. I replied of course not—I should have heard. It gave us a twinge of anxiety, and I felt like writing, but refrained because I tho't that such a rumor, if false, and it was pretty certainly false, would give pain to Henrietta. So now, dear little Katie, the day whose possibility must have often haunted your imagination, has really come, and life for you must be a great readaptation. It isn't the death, it is the *suffering* the poor child must have gone through and borne, as you say, so heroically & patiently, that is the shocking feature of the news your letter brings us. It doesn't seem exactly compatible with our notions of divine wisdom that a person as frail and innocent as poor Nettie should be reserved for so heavy a punishment at the end. But she is safe now, and as a mortal, gathered into the world of our tender memories, of *your* very tenderest. For myself, Katie, I am glad that *you* are the one preserved, and who knows, whether the new life now forced upon you may not awaken some resources of energy and health not drawn on hitherto? You say nothing of your plans; and I suppose they are not yet fully settled. Whatever you incline to do, I hope you will let us know. Do it through Henry, since that will save double writing and you must be rather overwhelmed at present with epistolary calls. To think of beautiful Lake Leman and Lausanne having now this intimately pathetic association! How I recall every *minute* of the days spent with you 18 months or less ago! If you come home, dearest Katie, you must make a good long stay with us and get wonted to our family ways. Our own plans after next spring are some-what doubtful. I am "down" for a Paris lectureship, but it is not at all certain that I shall toe the mark. In that case, whether next summer gets passed here, or abroad, or if abroad, *where?*, is all a mass of uncertainty. But you must keep close to us, dearest Katie, in spirit if not in body, and believe us both, with warmest sympathy and love,

Yours ever

Wm James[18]

· *To James McKeen Cattell* ·

Cambridge, Mass.
Oct. 29, [1906]

Dear Cattell,

If I succeed in giving the lectures at all (as I hope I shall) it will have to be during our mid year recess, which usually runs from about Jan 20th to Feb. 8th.

I put in the *if* because I've had a very disagreeable recrudescence of heart symptoms this fall, and next to carrying trunks up stairs, lecturing is as bad a duty as I am called on to perform. Along with this is a ragged state of nerves, and in view of both conditions I am carrying on my Harvard instruction only from week to week, another man being engaged to take my place in case it seems best for me to stop.

Meanwhile I'm trying to get ready some Lowell lectures for next month—lectures which for financial reasons I don't like to back out from. So you see how I am squeezed, & why I say "if."

But I *hope* to come up to the scratch. So you had better advertize the course, and let me disappoint expectation, if need be, when the time comes.

I positively can't do duty as President of the Amer. Society of Naturalists, but this is a small matter.

As President of the Amer. Philosophical Association, I can in any case send a written "address" but I hope to be there in the flesh as well.

Sincerely yours,

Wm James

P.S. I think you said I might lecture on 3 successive days of two weeks (successive). On the whole this might suit me best. The title of the course had better be: "The Pragmatic Movement in Contemporary Philosophy."[19]

Cambridge, Mass.
Nov. 10, 1906

Dear Cattell,

I have deferred answering your letter of the 3rd till I could interview Santayana, and the time has sped. He says that he is to give six lectures on "the appreciation of Art" at the Brooklyn Institute in January & February, and will be ready at very short notice to give them, if required. Of course I don't propose to start *my* lectures without a reasonable certainty of putting them thru. Therefore, if you approve of Santayana's subject, and don't require more than the six that I bargained for, I will let you know in time for the announcement of change to be made 10 days in advance.

As for the *time*, my time would naturally be the last week in Jan. & the first in Feb. The days are indifferent. In view of an eventually possible change on Santayana's part, need the days & hours be advertized *now?* Morning is best for me, but I suppose it has to be afternoon.

The address I shall write for the philosophers will be of general human interest enough to do for the general Society of Naturalists. But it will last 50 minutes, I fear. I had hoped to do something on "composition" in "consciousness," which would have been highly technical. It won't pan out in time, so I fall back on a popular talk with concrete illustrations of the reserves of energy in people that they habitually don't draw upon. I have notified you all i.e. Castle & thru him the other members of the executive committee that they need expect nothing from me as president. Angell also. As I told you, I think it likely that I may have to send my address to the philosophers to be read. Very sorry to put you out and I won't, unless compelled by *force majeure*.

Truly yours,

Wm James[20]

· *To F. C. S. Schiller* ·

Cambridge
November 25, 1906

Yours of the 11th. rec'd. How glad I am that your 500 pp. are to appear so shortly. I'm sure that *that* vol. will give a great shove to the cause and to your reputation. I have decided to *write out* my Lowell lectures and have done 1 1/2 already. Splendid audience—but they'll be much better as written. *Very* sorry for your examinership, tho' you seem exultant. Poor Strong's wife is dead and he's back in America. Affectionatest greetings.

W. J.

P.S. What do you say to the following dedication of my vol. of lectures?—"To Schiller, Dewey, and Papini." Don't you think Papini deserves it? With his *Uomo-Dio* he certainly has given a new kind of shove to the doctrine. I hope you have enjoyed Chesterton's Dickens and Wells' Days of the Comet.

W. J.

· To Herbert George Wells ·

Cambridge, Mass.
Dec. 4, 1906

Dear Mr. Wells,

I've delayed acknowledging the double present you have made me till I should have read both books *thru*. Which I've now done with unallayed delight. The "America" will start up a lot of thinking in brains capable of it, which will eventually take effect, and on the whole, with its tact & brilliancy to boot, is as good a service as a foreigner has ever performed. It breaks conventional crusts.

The "Comet" is very great—written out of *perceptions; & such* words to hit them off by! But you're an artist & philosopher & not a statesman, thank Heaven, and the present of fact and future of vision in both books are rather *unmediated*. The *real* future won't be discontinuous, or quite as much of a breach with the past as the Comet made. Meanwhile you deal in *possibles;* bring them home *alive &* hot, and wake us from our dogmatic slumber.

With you & Chesterton & Bernard Shaw no one can now accuse this age of lack of genius.

Keep it up!
Yours fondly

Wm James

You're a *pragmatist!* I'm writing a small book with that message.[21]

1907

AFTER RETURNING FROM THE PHILOSOPHICAL ASSO-
ciation meeting, James wrote that New York City, where
he was born in 1842, seemed to him to have changed
very much over the years, becoming in fact a "permanent earthquake." Before returning to New York, James
held his last class at Harvard on 22 January. A week later
he was lecturing at Columbia University until 8 February. The lectures were published in book form in May as
Pragmatism: A New Name for Old Ways of Thinking.

No sooner was James back home than Cattell suggested that James give another series of lectures at Columbia. After some leanings in that direction, James decided in August against such a venture because he found
it difficult to try to put his metaphysical speculations into
popular form.

James did find the time and interest to serve as an
agent in America to find a suitable candidate to be part of
a committee to establish an international language. Such
prominent men as Alexander Graham Bell and Thomas
Raynesford Lounsbury were asked. But the real enthusiasm was for Bergson's new book; *L'Evolution Créatrice*.
This book was to have a deep influence on James's
thought. He also welcomed Schiller's second collection
of essays *Studies in Humanism* and Stout's review of it.

In the correspondence from now on, the name of the

young Harvard Ph.D. candidate in philosophy, Horace Kallen, appears frequently. Kallen took some time off from Harvard to study under Schiller at Oxford. There he became a good friend of Bertrand Russell, who lived near Oxford. Kallen became something like an intermediary between James and Russell during his seven months stay at Oxford, beginning in October.

Two honors came to James in July. He was elected to the British Academy as a Corresponding Fellow and the Carnegie Foundation voted to pay him a retiring allowance.

G. Papini, whom James had met in Italy during his 1905 visit, had written an article on *pragmatism,* which James had Mrs. Royce translate, and which he urged Cattell to accept for republication. As to the book *Pragmatism,* the sixth chapter was devoted to the pragmatist conception of truth—what James called the "wider sense" of the word *pragmatism.* James's view, along with those of Dewey and Schiller, was criticized in journals. James was surprised and, at times, became annoyed at what he took to be a lack of understanding of the doctrine, despite his efforts to be clear in his replies to some of his critics.

Though he had turned down the Columbia offer, James did accept on 29 November the invitation to give the Hibbert lecture series at Manchester College, Oxford University, in 1908. Finally, the debate over 'truth' was carried on at the annual meeting of the Philosophical Association in late December at Cornell University. James was a member of a symposium on the topic of truth.

Cambridge, Mass.
Jan. 1, 1907

Dear Cattell,

I'm fairly ashamed to be such a tergiversator whenever you are concerned, but I *will take the lectures* in spite of what I said to you and Thorndike last Saturday night. Miller got hold of me on Sunday morning and made me wish I had held on till I were away from N.Y. at least, and now, my wife also consenting, and my recollection of that delightful Columbia philosophical circle pulling, I say yes instead of no. I will go into cold storage *after* instead of *before* the Columbia lectures! My organism can stand *that* extra strain, surely, before taking its eternal repose from the lecturing function.

What really tempts me is the prospect of converting all you Columbians into enthusiastic advocates of pragmatism as I conceive it. And since I have eight lectures all accurately mapped out, it will be easier to give the full eight as they stand, than to do any work of condensation into six upon them. Eight lectures then, $400 dollar fee, O Basilisk Cattell (who always has his way) on "Pragmatism, a new name for an old way of thinking," to be given on 4 successive days in each of 2 successive weeks, as soon as possible after January 23rd.

Believe me, very much yours, & with a happy New Year,

Wm James[1]

Cambridge
Jan 1. 1907

Dearest Katie,

A happy New Year to you, or as happy a one as circumstances permit! Your last letter gave an impression of the circumstances being rather disconsolate, and the need of inner self-support great, but also of the healthy mind and will being there to meet the emergency, and, on the whole, of the strong soul being on deck. I am 36 hours back from New York, where I went to attend a meeting of our "philosophical Association," and where I spent a pleasant hour with your sisters Kit & Lizzie. They looked rather startlingly older than when I last saw them (no one knows how many years ago), and poor Lizzie complained of arterio-sclerosis (wh. is my trouble too) but said that her recent iodide-medication was already producing its effect. They agreed fully in the wisdom of your staying abroad, and in sooth they seemed themselves rather *dépaysées* in N. Y., with so many of the old circle passed over to the majority, and the city grown by leaps and bounds beyond all recognition. It isn't a *place*, or a *city*, but an infinite railroad station or factory of monstrous buildings, tearing down and going up wherever you look. I never wish to set foot in the place again—it looks so awful to the mere visitor, who doesn't see all the god fearing old fashioned domestic happiness that lots of those house-fronts conceal. And you, if you came back, would never cease to be the mere visitor. You'd never get used to it; and you will really have *far more* intimate sociability with your friends and compatriots in Lausanne or elsewhere in Europe than you could ever have here. Compare your relations with *us*, for example, with your sisters'! And that is only one specimen of what happens. I am going back to N. Y. in 4 weeks to give eight lectures at Columbia University, and after that I shall try not to go there any more. This will be my last lecturing exploit in this vale of tears. I finish my Harvard duties forever on the 23rd of this month— then Columbia, and then emancipation! I almost tremble at the freedom. You will have heard that the Paris scheme is absolutely abandoned. Fortunately! I don't see how I could have entertained it for a moment. My thoracic organs have been going back on me lately, so an uneventful life, an egoistic life, not trying to influence others by spoken word, or acted deed, is my cue. After 35 years of teaching, one has earned a day to one's self! But I hope to *write*.

Our family news is good. Peggy is home for the holidays from Bryn Mawr, much consolidated and improved in soul for the 3 months experience. She has a just way of looking at things; and belies Godkin's epigram (when he said the trouble with women is that they haven't got the instincts of a gentleman). She has, after a fashion. Alice has had unusually little headache this fall, tho she has one this very day. She is too sociable, & hospitable, wants to fill the house with strangers while I want to empty it of every one but her and myself—whence fearful scenes of recrimination and accusation! But we love one another in spite of it all, and I must say that her moral excellence and "accommodating"–ness under the continuous regime of W. J. will entitle her to a high rank in the scale of saints hereafter. Aleck is a schoolboy, Harry more and more a busy lawyer—both healthy. Of Billy you know as much as we, probably. It is a lovely clearing from the South to day, after a real European December, in point of darkness. Hardly a ray of sun the whole month. Well, Katie dear, keep up health and heart, and believe in the constant affection of both Alice & your loving

W. J.[2]

· *To James McKeen Cattell* ·

Cambridge, Mass.
Jan. 25, 1907

Dear Cattell,

I seem to be only too well taken care of socially by the Columbia friends. As I also have other friends in N. Y. I shall have all the conviviality I can stand under. Pray leave Columbia non-philosophers out, but let me see the younger men in the department. Better set that for the week beginning Feb. 3rd, as most of my evenings till then are already pre-empted.

This is evidently going to be my final flare-up, the bangout of the fireworks! I enjoy the prospect very much.

Yours faithfully

W. J.

95 Irving St.
Cambridge, Mass.
Jan 25, 1907

Heartiest thanks for your tears and for your ultra cordial
letter. My resignation doesn't mean moribundance but
more abundance, rather, in more useful forms of energy
than teaching, which after 35 years begins to pall. Send
me a sample of your Nautilus work.

Truly yours,

Wm James[3]

· *To Jane Addams* ·

Cambridge, Mass.
Feb. 12, 1907

Dear Miss Addams,

I am just back from a fortnight in New York, where, in
the intervals of "energizing" in the rhythm of that active
city (or trying to), I soothed myself by the perusal of your
book. I find it hard to express the good it has done me in
opening new points of view and annihilating old ones.
New perspectives of hope! I don't care about this detail
or that—it is the *new setting of questions.* Yours is a
deeply original mind, and all so quiet and harmless! Yet

revolutionary in the extreme, and I should suspect that this very work would act as a ferment thru long years to come. I read precious little sociological literature, and my *opinions* in that field are worth nothing—but I am willing to *bet* on you.

Of course you have sent it to Wells, and to Carpenter. Possibly to Chesterton, but I doubt whether it has occurred to you to order it sent to Bernard Shaw. I *bet* (again) that it will stimulate his genius in the most extraordinary way. The publishers have sent me a second copy (wasteful things!). May I send it, with a note (and your permission) to Bernard Shaw?

Gratefully and sincerely yours

Wm James

Bernard Shaw is a fanatic moralist of the new type, and will some day be cared for as such.[4]

· *To James McKeen Cattell* ·

Cambridge, Mass.
Feb. 13, 1907

Dear Pertinax,

I admire the way in which you seize the Psychological Moment, before I've cooled off! Yet I think it far too early to say yes even conditionally—I might and mightn't—the great difficulty now being to see what next to lecture about. "Pragmatism" made a very well subdivided little chunk. Leave it till your last moment for announcement purposes, and ask me again!

Thanks for your compliments—but the single word "I believe" would be worth them all! Hard hearts, hard hearts, in the Columbia philosophical department!

Fondly yours,

Wm James

· *To F. C. S. Schiller* ·

Cambridge
February 20, 1907

Hurrah for the book, just come! It looks *stattlich* with its 500 pp. I'm sorry you say what you do of the "correspondence-with-reality" view of Truth, on p. IX. It perpetuates misunderstanding. Better to *explain* "correspondence," as *taking account* in any profitable way, and "reality" as (1) sensations, (2) relations among ideas and (3) previous truths. I got your letter and the typescript of my article, which I didn't need back. Also the Journal of Philosophy with the Mad Absolute. Terribly busy and fatigued, which accounts for brevity. Better be reviewed by an enemy than by me.

W. J.[5]

To Alexander Graham Bell

95 Irving St.
Cambridge, Mass.
Feb. 21. 1907

Dear Mr. Bell;

It never rains but it pours, so here I am, writing to you again.

Are you interested in the project of an International language,—not necessarily Esperanto, but any other candidate, if more successful?

I have a letter from the eminent french logician and mathematician Couturat, asking me to say who in my estimation would be the best American to ask to serve on an international committee of nine, to organize definitely the propaganda.

Naturally *your* name suggests itself. We need a person—not necessarily a philologist—rather the contrary!—whose example would win respect for the cause, and whose reputation is national. Exempt too from the suggestion of crankiness! President Eliot, and several others whom I have consulted, suggested your name independently.

I myself believe that this is one of the great "causes" of the future. The ease with which Esperanto is learned appears quite marvellous.

There is to be one member of this Committee of nine from each country. The point is to organize the movement towards the adoption of the international language as a public school study in the different countries. The Committee is to have its first meeting in Europe, in May or June probably, at the best convenience of its members.

· 436 ·

Can I ask M. Couturat to propose your name to the delegation which elects this Committee?

Sincerely yours

Wm James

Ostwald is on for Germany. Villareal of Lima for the South American Spanish countries. If you can't serve, who do you next think of?

· *To James McKeen Cattell* ·

95 Irving St.
March 10, 1907

Dear Cattell,

I was surprised yesterday at receiving about a hundred reprints of my lecture in the March Pop. Sci. I don't think I asked for them, so I owe them entirely to your liberality, but I don't mean to circulate these lectures in advance of the book, so I shall need only 6 or 8 copies of the Pop. Sci. itself when my 2nd lecture comes out.

I *did* ask for 50 copies of Science with my energy article in it—but they have not yet come.

Yours as ever,

Wm James[6]

95 Irving St.
Cambridge, Mass.
20. 3. 07

Dear Mr. Bell;

I thank you for your two kind replies to my two letters. I am glad you are well enough again to write. I am very sorry you can't see your way to being on the International language committee. I will write to Prof. Lounsbury of Yale to sound *him*.

Exceedingly obliged for the promise of $50 yearly (D.v., of course!) for C. S. P. I am now sure of my 500 dollars; and with as much on the relatives' side, his future safety is made sure. As we are proposing to start payments early in April, a check from you would be welcome now.

Sincerely yours,

Wm James[7]

95 Irving St.
Cambridge, Mass.
March 20, 07

Dear Professor Lounsbury,

An international committee (to consist of one member from each of twelve countries) is being formed at Paris, to organize definitely the movement in favor of an International language—not necessarily Esperanto! I have been asked to advise concerning its American member. The committee is to meet some where in Europe in May or June next, it is hoped. M. Couturat, the distinguished mathematician, is the Secretary at present.

Were I a frenchman, I would now enumerate the gifts of nature and the resources of art, the academic authority, public fame and political influence that infallibly point *you* out as the worthiest possible American member of such a committee. But I refrain! I hope that you care for the *cause*, which I believe to be tremendously important. If you do, should you be willing to serve on such a committee? I should like to be able to urge you upon my correspondent Couturat, if he hasn't already written to you independently. In all seriousness, I believe that your name would add much prestige throughout our country to the project.

Very sincerely yours,

Wm James[8]

Cambridge
March 22, 1907

My pragmatism book (MS now with printer) should appear in both countries by June 1st. I have read only 25 pp. of your book as yet (being balled up with labor and having lent it to one Kallen, an enthusiastic Pragmatist who is writing a Ph.D. thesis on that subject). I shall get at it soon now. No chance of Europe for me for the next twelve months.

W. J.

· *To Thomas Raynesford Lounsbury* ·

95 Irving St.
Cambridge, Mass.
March 25, 1907

Dear Professor Lounsbury,

I am exceedingly sorry to hear of your poor "shape," cerebrally, and regret that I should have troubled you about the International Language scheme at all.

A. Graham Bell also declines, so, you and he being my only candidates, I will write to Couturat that my cards are played.

I hope you'll get well speedily. Beware however of resting your brain *absolutely*, for too long. After 3 or 4 months, I believe that a certain amount of one's "life-work" is indispensable for recovery.

Very sincerely yours,

Wm James

· *To Mary Whiton Calkins* ·

Cambridge
May 20. 07

I don't think there has been any literature of the kind you write of, unless possibly Bergson's new book (wh. is probably "epochmaking") l'Evolution Créatrice, Alcan, contains it. I have done nothing. I see you take pluralism [sic] as necessarily monadistic, wh. I don't see as a necessity. The last 2 essays in Schiller's Studies in Humanism are a beginning of pluralistic evolutionism. If you start with tychism, you can have relations between terms vary, as well as terms, so you needn't remain monadistic. Yours, in haste, W. J. who hasn't yet had time even to look at your Persistent Problems.[9]

· *To F. C. S. Schiller* ·

Chocorua
June 13, 1907

Yours of the 27th. ult. rec'd and highly appreciated. I'm glad you relish my book so well. You go on playing the Boreas and I shedding the sunbeams, and between us we'll get the cloak off the philosophic traveler! But *have* you read Bergson's new book? It seems to me that nothing is important in comparison with that divine apparition. All *our* positions, real time, a growing world, asserted magisterially and the beast intellectualism killed absolutely *dead!* The whole flowed round by a style incomparable, as it seems to me. Read it and digest it, if you can. Much of it I can't yet assimilate.

[unsigned]

· *To Horace Meyer Kallen* ·

Bay View, Maine
July 12, 1907

I advise you to write fully to Schiller for advice. I will simultaneously write to him to introduce & commend you. So Royce is using my Pragmatism-book already— bully for him. I shall be here till the 22nd at least, and then for a couple of days in Cambridge. I wish you joy of the Aesthetics, & hope you'll get a fair audience.

W. J.

Bay View House
Bay View, Maine
July 15, 1907

Dear Schiller,

A student of ours named Kallen, candidate for Ph.D., is about writing to you for advice about whether to go to Oxford next year—he has one of our fellowships. He is a Russian Jew by birth, very intense in character, very able and with high potentialities of all round cultivation, an enthusiastic and aggressive 'pragmatist', an active political worker, a *decidedly* original mind, neurotic disposition, but sails indefinitely long close to the wind without losing headway, a man with a positive future and possibly a great one and in good directions: *Revers de la médaille: sticky*, conceited, censorious of all institutions. Nevertheless faithful, candid, goodlooking and in favor of all good things. I shouldn't wonder if these eastern jews formed the chief ferment of ideality in our future America—they seem quite different from the more materialistic German hebrews.

If you want that kind of a man for a *famulus*—encourage him; if not, discourage. He gains lots from experience and will gain lots from Oxford. I value Kallen very much, but have been disappointed in the portions of his thesis he has got ready this year. Too much general program and denunciation—too little hard work at discriminations.

The July Mind is just in and I have read most of it, including you on Bradley cursorily again, in spite of my aversion for minute polemics. Taylor is a regular little *monkey*, monkeying first with Bradley's absolute and now with the new mathematical logic, wh. he understands as an ontology. Heaven help him! He has no more *weight* than a thistle down, in spite of his admirable power of expressing himself. See how they are beginning to sing small and take their hats off, in consequence of our recent writings, to wh. Dewey's article in this number will add its strong effect, tho' I could wish him to be a bit less obscure or less one sided rather, in his writing, wh. is solely from the point of view of his own problem of how *problems* are solved, whereas there is truth and knowledge apart from solving problems. However, the day is dawning and in a year or two even, I seem to foresee that states of mind like Joachim's and Taylor's will seem absolutely senile. But Bergson will be the *great* intellectualism-smasher!

Yours as ever,

W. J.[10]

· *To Charles William Eliot* ·

Bay View, Maine
July 20, 1907

Dear President,

I have your note enclosing one from President Pritchett, and the one relative to Mr. Hoernlé which I re-enclose.

The vote of the Carnegie Committee is exceedingly gratifying to me—not only because the sum implied (which you name as $3000) is 400 more per annum than what you had announced to me as my due from Harvard, but because of the exceedingly gracious terms in which the appropriation was couched. Graciousness *tells!* And as for the compliments, etc., they make me think of the french saying "La renommée vient à ceux qui ont la patience d'attendre, et s'accroît à raison de leur imbecilité." When you're just about defunct, people awaken to your powers!

As for Hoernlé, I don't know that *his* powers concern us particularly, just now, for if we are to take up a younger man for purposes of eventual promotion, I don't know what we can do better than stick to Fuller, with whom we are making a beginning. But Hoernlé is a splendidly promising fellow, with whom I have had a little correspondence about some extraordinarily clearly written articles of his in Mind. He is now a candidate for a Capetown professorship, but he oughtn't to be buried in Africa.

We have got some very competent younger philosophers in America now, and a few of them write clearly. But their competence is critical wholly, and no one shows any strong originality. I fancy that from that point of view Perry and Holt will pan out as well as any one.

With best regards to both you yourself and Mrs. Eliot, I am

always faithfully yours,

Wm James[11]

95 Irving St.
Cambridge
July 31. '07

Dear Miss Calkins,

I have just "got round" to the reading of your Persistent
Problems, and must testify to my admiration. It is excellently planned & splendidly executed, something to feel
that you have "left behind" when you are called to higher spheres. And what a relief it must be to you to have
got it all "off"—I hope you're having a splendid holiday.
What strikes me as most admirable in the composition of
the thing is the "persistent" way in which you have limited your subject to the evolution, step by step, of modern idealism, and then the completeness with which you
have handled it within the limits. You have marked
every step on that line of progress so distinctly, and
secured it so candidly, that the reader is kept perpetually aware of his position in the journey, and the
result is a great clearness aided by the cleanness and
perspicuity of the style everywhere. Really a splendid
piece of composition—and what careful reading of your
authors also! Upon my word you're a wonder! Of course
you dislike praise—all philosophers do! but I can't help
praising. By reason of the cleanness and dryness and
straightforwardness of its statement, it seems to me that
your exhibition of the transcendentalist argument must
supersede all others. Bradley and Royce have created it,
but you have made it plain and accessible, both to assent
and criticism. You must have felt proud of your paraphrase of Hegel. The Descartes chapter seems to me
splendid, and the one on Kant very good; but haven't

you rather *forced* your interpretation of his transcendental ego?—I never read quite as much into it. I regret to have to say, after all this, that you haven't converted *me* to belief in the absolute self, sincere and candid as your argumentation is. It still remains to me only an interesting and sublime *hypothesis,* and the reason why it isn't more is the non-conducting character (to my mind) of the argument from "relation" (middle paragraph of p. 419). I don't see how you can hold that seriously—but I will do naught but praise, so I say no more, prudently.

With hearty congratulations and kind regards,

Yours always truly,

Wm James

P.S. What a triumph also for your downtrodden *sex!*

· *To James McKeen Cattell* ·

Cambridge, Mass.
Aug. 21, 1907

Dear Cattell,

I send herewith a translation of a clever & instructive article on Pragmatism by G. Papini of Florence. The original is in "Leonardo" for last February, and Josiah Royce being in California, I seized the opportunity to alienate the loyalty of his wife from his famous Absolute, and to prevail on her to perpetrate the translation, which has been revised by me. It seems to me to be rather in the right line for the Pop. Sci., so I offer it to you, and hope you may think it fit for publication therein. It accentuates more than I have done the pragmatic notion that Reality is there not so much to sit for its unaltered portrait at our hands, as to be *changed* by us into something richer & better. With faithful portraiture intellectualism says that our relations to reality are consummated.

Since I am writing to you, let me speak of another matter, my Columbia lectures next winter, namely. It is more and more evident that I *cannot give them*. No subject heaves in sight as even remotely possible for popular treatment and I am sure that after this no subject will. My mind is occupied now solely with *Spitzfindigkeiten* that can interest the fewest. I accepted the appointment on the chance that something might turn up, and felt that you were safe in any event, because Royce is to deliver 8 Lowell Lectures anyhow and, I failing, you could turn him on with them. They are sure to be entertaining and popular. Unless you have somebody better in mind, you had better engage him to repeat his Lowell course as I did mine last year. In any case release *me* without further delay, and make other provision.

I hope that you and yours are all well. I dare say that you may be haunting (as I am not) the Zoological Congress. I am actually at Lincoln, Mass., but return to Cambridge on Friday, en route for Bar Harbor.

Truly yours,

Wm James[12]

· To James McKeen Cattell ·

Cambridge
Aug 31. 07

Thanks for yours of Aug 24.—Please have the proof of Papini sent direct to Mrs. Royce. I am leaving for Keene Valley, for (I hope) 3 weeks—I will think of your idea of highly "dialectical" course—repulsive to the swinish multitude; maybe I can work it.

W. J.[13]

· To F. C. S. Schiller ·

Cambridge
August 31, 1907

I have just read your controversy with [J. E.] Russell in the Journal of Philosophy. I think your part is admirable for breadth and clearness. Poor Russell is honest and sincere but absolutely stone-blind to *everything, after* he had seen that the thought must be "as" the object. No use! but some readers will take it in. Keep it up!

W. J.[14]

· *To Horace Meyer Kallen* ·

Chocorua, N. H.
Sept. 29, 1907

Dear Kallen,

I thank you for your decidedly elaborate review of my "Pragmatism" in the Transcript—full of misprints as it is. It will probably do good to the "cause." I fully accept the correction administered in the last 1/2 column. The distinction you make is sound and important, and when the "truth" definition is spread out at due length will have to have all justice done it. The whole "will to believe" business has also to be revised in the light of it. The *total* goodness of a belief for the believer depends on its relation to his other beliefs and *their* goodness, and you can only call a single good belief true with the reservation "ceteris paribus." Those who defend the Kantian "as if," teleology, etc. mean that a view of the world's purposiveness that *combines with everything else we know* can pass for "true." It is surely neither "false" nor "irrelevant."

Let me know when you leave for "abroad." I will keep my financial promise by remittance after you're there. I hope you are rested a bit. I shall stay here at the hotel till about the 14th. Thank you again and truly yours

W. J.[15]

Cambridge
October 16, 1907

Dear Schiller,

Yours of Sept. 25th. is very welcome. Likewise Mind with your flamboyant account of my book, for which thanks. Strong also enjoyed very much meeting you. He is a clear thinker, devoted to truth, and *may* do great things—how great I can't now tell.

[J. E.] Russell must be about 70, a dear good honest man, dry in teaching and utterly stupid as to what you and I mean. Hopeless!

As to Bergson, I admit all you can say as to his unsatisfactoriness and non-finality, but he has *opened new horizons,* surely, and he has as surely *given intellectualism its coup de grâce.* Who else has done either in our time?

Your friend Goldstein has written me an enthusiastically cordial letter about *Pragmatism* and Prof. Jerusalem of Wien is translating it into German, hopes it to appear next month. If that nation ever does take hold, it will do so with its usual ponderosity and disgust us with our own work.

I rejoice very much in Stout's review of you in Mind. At last we have something really clarifying and helpful from an outside source. It will tend to sober the others, I doubt not. Is "Philosophy or Bluff?" in the Saturday Review by G. E. Moore? There is a certain suggestion of his way of thinking, ass that he is. Do you know whether the contemptuous review of Pragmatism in the N. Y. Nation came from Oxford? I ween it did, but have been too polite to ask. Who cares? I think, Schiller, that such reviews, of which *you* can't complain on the score of manners, show the advantage of more conciliatory tactics. They are absolutely uninstructive and add to the confusion lamentably, but would justify themselves, if asked to, by alleging the need of castigating your swagger and "side." The whole recriminative polemic simply wastes *time.* I wonder who is going to review me, to neutralize your review, next January. I wish it might be Stout; and I am very curious to see how his next article will handle the subject. I hope he may find some stronger objection than the one at the end of the present article, which he certainly ought to have known better than to urge. After saying that we are "interested" in the ejective life of our fellows, he proceeds to treat the satisfactory "working value" of our belief concerning our fellow beings as if it might pragmatically be allowed to violate this interest! Perhaps the most important need of our mind is to have it satisfied. In my California address, partly reprinted in *Pragmatism,* lecture II, I said that "matter" and "God" were synonymous, so far as they both were conceived as making the same world. I have always had a bad conscience about that, but added nothing, partly because the illustration cleared up what I meant, partly to avoid complication of statement. But from the first the "automatic sweetheart" difficulty was strong. Would she, if devoid of consciousness, "work" as "satisfactorily" as one *with* consciousness, even tho her outward acts were exactly the same. No! and why? Because our social interest in her soul is a positive factor. We wish to be sure of *her interest in us,* and that her responsive caresses are *meant* and *felt.* That conception of her prompts other conduct from *us*—less "cold, dull & heartless" as Stout would say, thus conforming to Peirce's criterion. That is part of the game; and part of Stout's case. How absurd to imagine you as leaving such an interest out. The purely theoretic interest of thinking consistently, even tho inconsistency might not impede us "practically" in the narrow sense, is like unto this interest in each other's souls. Stout is as bad as the common herd here. Truth, *we* say, is the property of *conceptions that are satisfactory*. He keeps the "satisfactory" and drops the "conceptions," as if the satisfaction per se constitutes the truth, according to us. But the satisfaction cleaves tight to the special conception. It simply *doesn't work* satisfactorily to conceive our fellows as soulless, it does work so to conceive them with souls. Wherefore we believe it *true that they have souls*, and carry that belief into life as our theoretic act. Surely that is Stout's only way of believing this; and why he should cut you off from the privilege is to me absolutely unintelligible in the man who could write the rest of that article. Or am I myself the dunderhead? I should like you to send this to Stout, the rest of whose article I greatly admire.

Poor Kallen. I hope you will find some position of equilibrium for him, and get along well together. I wrote him a letter in return for his review of "Pragmatism" which I fear arrived too late, and was not forwarded to the Steamer. I will wait now till I hear from him. Please give him my regards.

Affectionately,

W. J.

I can't guess what you mean by saying that you find my paper "A Word More about Truth" obscure. I tho't it cleared things a good deal.[16]

· *To F. C. S. Schiller* ·

Cambridge
Oct. 17. [07]

Your 2 cards just in. I have sent Murray's query about 1st use of pragmatism to C. S. P. I sent my copy of P's original article to Papini (I think) who has never returned it. *Where* is your handling of McKenzie? Article on Freedom and R. in Oxf. and Camb. Rev. also just in. Looks tempting.

W. J.[17]

· *To Horace Meyer Kallen* ·

Cambridge, Mass.
Oct. 26, 1907

Dear Kallen,

Yours of the 12th is just in, and I am glad to hear of your safe arrival and prosperous settlement. Glad also that Schiller pleases so. I had hoped to send you a hundred dollars today, but since you say you are in no immediate need of more cash, I refrain, and will rely on you to notify me *in time* as soon as you are likely to need it. Don't fail in this. With best wishes,

Yours as ever,

W. J.

· To Charles Montague Bakewell ·

Cambridge
Nov. 6, '07

I have read your review of me with great pleasure and interest. Sweetly written! and I thank you for the praise. As for the censure, if you have found nothing harsher to say, it seems to me a good omen for "pragmatism." On the whole I count you as in the fold and am glad of it.

W. J.[18]

· To James McKeen Cattell ·

95 Irving St.
Nov. 7. 1907

Dear Cattell,

I thank you for your invitation to the Century Club, but I'm not going to the meeting after all. A virulent catarrh and an attack of gout are on me, and I feel so seedy that New York will be too strenuous a bath. Colchicum seems to be getting a "holt" on to the gout, which may prove a light attack. A bad one is no joke. One at Stanford kept me on crutches for 6 weeks.

I hope you will enjoy the Academicians.

As ever, yours,

Wm James

95 Irving St.
Cambridge
Dec. 31. 07

Dear L.–

Just back from Ithaca, where I heard nothing of any paper by you. Either it didn't arrive or it was crowded out. Gardiner told me that he had hoped for your presence—that was all! The meeting was good, all epistemological. The *discussion* of pragmatism didn't come off for the symposium consisted of 5 independent essays with no talk. A warning for the future.

What glorious surroundings you are in! Go in & conquer! A big mail awaits me on my return, so I must be brief, so with a happy New Year to you, I subscribe myself.

Yours as ever,

W. J.[19]

XIV

1908

BESIDES WRITING THE HIBBERT LECTURES, JAMES CON-
tinued writing on 'truth.' He had a very short and exact
statement of his view privately printed in February and
circulated among his friends. It was entitled "The Meaning of the Word Truth." He also published an article,
"Truth versus Truthfulness," in March. A copy of the
latter was sent to Schiller, Kallen, and, through Kallen,
to Bertrand Russell, who had published an article
"Transatlantic Truth" in January. James continued to be
disturbed by some of the reviews of *Pragmatism.*

Before James sailed for England on 21 April, he had
committed the manuscript of seven lectures to the University Press. He had still to compose the eighth lecture.
He thought of giving the series the title "a critique of
intellectualism" or "the present situation in philosophy."
He delivered the lectures to large audiences from 4 May
to 28 May. He received from Oxford University the honorary degree of Doctor of Science on 12 May. While at
Oxford James of course saw much of Schiller and his
friends. He and Mrs. James also visited the Bertrand
Russells at their home near Oxford. Their social life was
full and overwhelming with lunches, teas, and dinners.

After the lectures were completed, the Jameses stayed
two days with Mrs. Fiske Warren, who had recently won
a "first" in "Greats" at Oxford. She was from Boston.

Then they spent four days at Miss Sands' home, "New-ington House," at Wallingford, Oxford. There they met, among many others, Lady Ottoline Morrell and her husband. She was often referred to as the "high priestess of Bloomsbury."

On 10 June the Jameses left this whirl of activity for some relaxation and rest in the country. They spent nine days at Bibury, two at York, three and a half at Durham, where on 23 June James received another honorary degree, Doctor of Letters, from the University. They spent two weeks in the Lake District of England, particularly Patterdale. On 9 July they arrived in London for a week's visit with friends. With his daughter "Peggy," James took off for Rye on 17 July. Mrs. James went to Harrow to see some friends. While at Rye, James visited H. G. Wells and G. K. Chesterton, who lived next door to Lamb House. James was much pleased with a volume of essays written in his honor by some of his friends. On 21 August he left for Ostend to join his wife and daughter, who had been visiting Switzerland, for a two week tour, mainly of Holland. This trip, if for no other reason, prevented James from attending the Third International Congress of Philosophy at Heidelberg, Germany, 1–5 September.

With Rye as a home base, James made several trips to London—once to show the city to his son "Aleck" who had come abroad to study for a year; another time to attend the Moral Education Congress at the University of London on the 25th. Then there was a last visit to see Schiller again before they sailed for home on 6 October.

The Jameses reached home in mid-October. In November James repeated his Hibbert lectures at Harvard. He was almost enticed by Cattell to give a talk on Darwin at the December meeting of the American Association for the Advancement of Science. A few other letters also deal with James's membership in scientific societies.

· To F. C. S. Schiller ·

Dear Schiller,

I got your letter re my Hibbert lectureship a week or more ago. I have been too busy, variously, to reply; also too ½ hearted, meaning by that that my damned arterial degeneration (which gives me pectoral anguish when I make efforts or get badly fatigued) may in the end wreck the enterprise. For that reason I am saying nothing about it over here, having told Strong and Miller only. I accepted because I was ashamed to refuse a professional challenge of that importance, but I would it hadn't come to me. I actually *hate* lecturing and this job condemns me to publish another book written in picturesque and popular style when I was settling down to something whose manner would be more streng "wissenschaftlich," i.e., concise, dry and impersonal. My free and easy style in *Pragmatism* has made me so many enemies in academic and pedantic circles that I hate to go on increasing their number and want to become tighter instead of looser. These new lectures will have to be even looser; for lectures *must* be prepared for audiences; and once prepared, I have neither the strength to re-write them nor the self-abnegation to suppress them. What I dread, however, more than the actual lectures, is the hospitality and sociability of Oxford. I find too many hours a day spent in talking, very fatiguing and in the month of May my tide of nervous energy is invariably at its lowest—a regular annual cycle. I must rely on *you* then, my dear Schiller, not to add one jot or tittle to my social burden by inviting *anyone* to meet me. Let me see first how I stand the more ordinary and official sociability. If well, then you may take your turn. But I positively *veto* any engagements from your quarter made in advance. Now take me seriously as to this or there is danger that I may not go at all. I am a thoro invalid and have to live accordingly, in spite of my appearance of animation to people who see me briefly. So much for that damned disagreeable topic!

I got back a week ago from the meeting at Cornell U. of the Philosophical Association. *Very* nice: almost all the papers read were epistemological, but the 'symposium' on 'truth' was abortive, not being a discussion at all, but a delivery of five unconnected general essays on the subject, of which I gave the first. I enclose for your perusal a paraphrase of what I said, which I have just sent to be published in the report of the meeting. (My remarks at the meeting were unwritten). Your name was in many mouths, no one persuadable that you could possibly admit an 'objective' reality. I, being radically realistic, claimed you to be the same, but no one believed me as to either of us. Wouldn't you subscribe to the paper I enclose? Isn't the *hulé* which you speak of as the primal bearer of all our humanized predicates conceived by you, epistemologically, as an independent *that* which the *whats* qualify and which (in the ultimate) may be decided to be of any nature whatsoever? I hope so, for that position seems to me invulnerable and in the end must win against all the muddlers and misunderstanders. Don't answer me too minutely; if tempted to do so, refrain; I only want to be able to quote you as agreeing. If you *don't* agree, the bare fact suffices, the reasons can come later.

Taylor was in great force and very jolly, on his feet, rapid, incisive and interesting, apropos of almost anything. His own paper shows him to have left his *Elements of Metaphysics* far behind him. He called Avenarius the greatest philosopher (so, by the way, did

Norman Smith in his paper), advocated a sort of monadistic pluralism and realism, defended external relations, and professed belief in (as I understood it) indeterministic "freedom!" If he goes on monkeying, he will get a vision of his own in ten years and then have the personal weight and authority he now lacks so greatly. His intellectual liveliness and jollity gave me an impression that, if he and I lived near each other, we should get along very well together socially, if not philosophically. Meanwhile I am told that he lets himself out freely on the vulgar tone of my *Pragmatism*.

Kallen writes great things of you, somewhat at the expense of the rest of Oxford. He needs to have his sentiments of *respect* developed! Pray show him the enclosed sheets, as well as the proof I mailed you 10 days ago. Give him my love and a Happy New Year also. Ditto to your inestimable self. If I heave in sight about May 1st., 'twill be with my wife and possibly our daughter. College rooms not to be tho't of therefore. We shall be best suited by "lodgings." I suppose there are plenty.

Addio! "Yours for the truth"

W. J.[1]

Cambridge, Mass.
Jan. 5. 07 [1908]

Dear Kallen,

Your jolly good letter arrives yesterday, and gives a good account. I'm glad you find so much in Oxford, particularly as to Schiller and Russell. I had mailed a letter to Schiller an hour ere yours came in asking him to communicate its content to you, so I won't reduplicate any of it, being very busy and tired. Ask him for the whole letter. I send you a revision of the paper on truth which I sent Schiller. I ticked it off this A.M. I don't see how any one can misunderstand it in so simplified a shape. Possibly you might show it to Russell, since he has been writing on the subject. Odd, to be called a scoundrel for saying such reasonable things.

Keep the paper, and the moment need of that 100 is in sight let me know.

Yours always truly

Wm James[2]

· To Arthur Oncken Lovejoy ·

Cambridge, Mass.
Jan. 11, 1908

Dear Lovejoy,

Thanks for your letter and enclosure returned. The great thing to aim at now among all us discussers of "pragmatism" is *ein Verständigung*. Calling each other scoundrels ought to stop—(this is not meant as a damper on the project of publishing your letter as a last atmosphere-clearing thunder clap!). So I send you the shortest statement I have made yet; please return it. It is practically just what I said at the Cornell 'symposium', and the longer statement which you return I am sending to Woodbridge as an independent article.

I can see no difference between what I call 'truthfulness' and verifiability; nor can I augur havoc from an infinite regress of certifications. I only call your attention to this: that if the statement now enclosed is admitted to pass muster in its present shape, then everything else about truth that Schiller and I have contended for must also be admitted. I confess I am sick of such *blind* criticism as McTaggart's in the current number of Mind. No one can write for readers who are resolved not to understand. They will always find their opening in the dot omitted from some *i.*

Yours truly,

Wm James[3]

95 Irving St.
Cambridge
Jan 14. 08

Dear Wister,

I now "twig" as to the connexion between pragmatism &
incredibility—truth happening etc.

There *do* seem to be a germ of sterility in Boston.
Only I don't think it lies mainly in Cabot & Putnam but
in the whole medical crew which regards them as dangerous cranks and sentimentalists.

Poor Gay Waters! The most humble-minded of
cranks. Were I able, I would pension him. As things are,
I have to avoid even "whistling" to him. I've no doubt he
did shed real salt tears over your letter.

Faithfully yours,

Wm James[4]

· *To F. C. S. Schiller* ·

Cambridge
[January 17. 1908]

Laid up with a *bad* attack of grippe (6th. day). I find myself at last growing impatient with the critics of *Pragmatism* and beginning to share your temper towards the reigning Oxford influences. McTaggart, e.g., in this month's Mind, means to be perfectly annihilating, but some of his interpretations wd. be discreditable to my terrier dog. Ditto Lovejoy in the Journal of Philosophy. I'm getting tired of being treated as 1/2 idiot, 1/2 scoundrel and beginning to assume an *écrasey l'infâme* state of mind. *Écrasons l'infâme!*

W. J.[5]

· *To F. C. S. Schiller* ·

Cambridge
January 26, 1908

Dear Schiller,

Your splendid letter from Rome of the 10th. arrives this morning. I am grateful for your praise of my "Misunderstandings" article—also for your strictures. I agree with both! You see that you and I are following different tactics and I believe that your strategy will gain rather than lose by my simultaneous operations, tho' they are dictated not wholly by strategic considerations but partly by personal ones. What I define as the "pragmatic conception of truth" is my old one publisht in Mind in 1885. It assumes the notion of "reality" uncritically. This seems to me a necessary preliminary step towards your far more inclusive doctrine of Humanism (treated separately therefore in my lectures), which in part is an account of reality as well as of truth. I naturally fight with zest for my own peculiar doctrine. It is the easiest first step to make. Once made, the way to Humanism lies open. But I think that one great trouble so far has been that everyone was fighting all over the lot at once. If "Pragmatism" gets settled, "Humanism" follows in due course. Certain opponents, like Strong, are thoroly friendly in spirit, but they are *incapable* of using the *word* "truth" in a concrete way. It will always mean for them that resident thing *in* a belief that *makes it potentially susceptible* of verification, a quality *ante rem*, not *in rebus*. Meanwhile they don't deny any of the pragmatic *facts*. It seems to me that when things have come to this pass, of pure loyalty to a word used in one way rather than another, the only thing to do is to keep on writing in one's own way and wait for the next generation.

This last article of mine will probably do some good to the younger crew. Even Royce has already changed his purely ironical tone and went so far as to say to me the other day, that after reading it he had thought it well to give some account of it to the young men at his seminary whom he had not long previously treated to another account of what I was driving at. McTaggart in Mind is simply infamous, so (to a great extent) is Lovejoy in the Journal of Philosophy. I agree with you now in full that our enemies of the absolutist school deserve neither respect nor mercy. Their stupidity is only equalled by their dishonesty. Kallen writes me that the egregious G. E. Moore has been annihilating me at the Aristotelian

Society. Kallen has been much imprest by B. Russell. It seems to me that, if the pragmatic notion of truth has any merit, it is to have rid the world of such diseased *Wucherungen* as the Moore-Russell-Meinong epistemology. It cuts under them so completely. Don't think, dear Schiller, that I don't see as in a blaze of light, the all embracing scope of your Humanism and how it sucks my pragmatism up into itself. I doubt if I shall trouble myself to write anything more about Pragmatism. If anything more about truth, it will be on the wider humanistic lines. This is my 15th. day of the grippe and the biggest intellectual effort I have made in that time. I don't feel much as if I were going to lecture at Oxford just now! The job I have set myself is a hard one and, unless I can pull it off handsomely, I won't try at all. It depends on how long this grippe will prove to have thrown me off the working track. My "margin" in these days is very narrow indeed.

My regards to the Thaws. How I wish I were at Rome with you!

Yours fondly

Wm James[6]

Cambridge, Mass.
Feb. 1, 1908

Dear Thilly,

I sent you one page of type-writing for the report of our
Association meeting. I had a duplicate which the person
I lent it to has lost. It is so compact a statement of my
account of truth that I wish to have a copy on hand, since
your report won't appear till April. Will you kindly send
me what I sent you? I will then copy & return.
I duly got the longer statement back.

Sincerely yours,

Wm James[7]

· *To Mary Whiton Calkins* ·

95 Irving St.
Cambridge
Feb. 1. '08

Dear Miss Calkins,

I have been a-reading of you in the J. of P. Jan 30th., as
well as in the Psych. Bull., Jan. 15. The vividness with
which your mind focusses on everything is extraordinary. Also your good faith, I mean candor etc.

You bring me nearer to the "Self" in the J. of P. than I have ever been before. But as between you and Pillsbury, isn't it a palmary case for treatment by the pragmatic method? *What difference* in the particulars of anyone's experience is implied by our saying "Self" or saying "dynamic entirety of experience," etc.? Can't you work your contention along those lines? I still fail to see any great difference, and "Self" and "Stream" seem to me but two names for the same facts.

But I didn't write to say this—only to urge you most vehemently to become intimate with Bergson's writings. His last book will at least entrance you as literature. It may be that his way of representing the life of the individual (discarding intellectualist categories altogether and) representing the actual past as telescoping into the actual present, is the promising way out of what seems to me at present a somewhat loggerhead position in psychology.

I fully admit that the term "Self" should have the right of way.

Pardon my garrulity![8]

[unsigned]

· To Arthur Oncken Lovejoy ·

Cambridge, Mass.
Feb. 12, 1908

Dear Lovejoy,

I have read your "Pragmatism & Theology" with great interest, and high admiration for your literary style. You are one of our very few first rate philosophic *writers.* I also find some of your distinctions to advance the subject. Naturally I like your anti-monistic adhesion.

I agree to your conclusion about pragmatism No. 1, at the bottom of your page 129—at any rate the *main* pragmatic use of that principle is to distinguish concepts whose differences are futile from those whose differences are weighty. Even *verbal* differences have emotional consequences, so you can't say that any concepts don't differ at all in meaning, so long as they are *spelt* differently! So, vigorously, I agree to your p. 131. As for "matter" and "God," I am glad I forestalled you in my "misunderstanding" paper in the note about "automatic sweethearts," tho your pp. 132 & 133 are vastly more telling.

But we are both on pragmatic ground here, both applying the pragmatic method to find the meaning of the concepts under discussion. I have therefore much fault to find with your pp. 122–124, in which you take "ejects" (W. J.'s consciousness) as a case of concepts not explicable, as to their meaning, into particulars. I wish you would define *my* consciousness, so as to distinguish it from John Smith's, without employing its empirical consequences. "My" consciousness is only *known as* that which animates a certain body, expresses certain sentiments, does certain acts. These are not "future" necessarily, but *your* relations with each and all of them may be future, so futurity, on which you insist so, must be allowed for. Abstracting from these, *my* "that which" means the same as John Smith's—both shrivel into a contentless locus to be recognized by you as *existent*. And what does "existent" mean except another "that which," that which we must acknowledge and take account of. An object of knowledge that had *no* relations, not even relations of kind, to anything in the world except your "true" knowledge of it would be an absolutely indeterminate object. What would be meant by knowing that object *truly,* or knowing *it* rather than any other object, I can't imagine. So I continue thinking that the pragmatic method No. 1 holds good radically. And why you (and almost everybody else) keep churning the irrelevant question of *futurity* into the discussion, I can't well imagine.

Enough! I am sending you tomorrow a revision of my remarks at Cornell. I thought well to print them.

Yours, as ever,

Wm James[9]

[marginal addition on the letter] Have Leicester, Elizabeth, & marriage no pragmatic contents of meaning, and even if that marriage be not verifiable directly, does it not belong to things of a verifiable class, and may it not pass for true if its falsity is unverified?

Cambridge, Mass.
Feb. 12. 1908

Dear Kallen,

I have to thank you for 2 letters, of which the 2nd came this morning along with Russell's article. I have already ordered a copy of the Albany from England, so I return your sheets with some marginal scribbling on them, which Russell may read if you think fit to show them to him. I thank you for sending them. Russell's article is splendidly written, but R. errs from failure to have grasped my central position. The only way to understand anything is to jump into its centre and work outwards. Poor childish Moore! Thank you again for sending me his Aristotelian paper, which I keep—he might have had the grace to send it himself! He is too weak & silly for any comment at all, so I won't waste a minute on him. A monument to the folly of pretending to have no *vision* of things, but to admit anything as possible and then select by "logic" which is most probable! He crawls over the outside of my lecture like a myopic ant over a building, seeing only the spot he touches, tumbling into every microscopic crack, and not suspecting even that there *is* a centre or a whole at all. Bah! Non ragionam di lui, ma guarda & passa!

As for Russell, I find fault with his insisting on the word "useful" in the narrower sense (for so the reader will take it) to show how absurd I am in saying that the truth is what is "expedient" or "what pays." Much truth *is* useful in the narrower sense, so is much falsehood; but much truth "pays" without being "useful" in *that* sense. A developed pragmatism will have to discriminate the various types of truth-making satisfactoriness. Our critics try to head us off from doing this by insisting *in limine* that we *shall* recognize no other kind than the economically or emotionally satisfactory. Then Russell, because I say that truth means "satisfactory leading towards an object," first equates "the true" with "the satisfactory" at large, then "the satisfactory" with the "useful," and performs his reductio ad absurdum by the mathematical process of substitution, leaving all reference to the "object" out!! The real way to refute me would be to offer a tenable and intelligible alternative, but this no critic tries to do.

However, we shall certainly win thru, and I personally have no fault to find with the tone in which they handle me. Russell's article tickles me by the splendid style of it, so clear and english. Lovejoy also is writing very well, tho' fearfully off the track in parts.

I am in funds again, owing to "Pragmatism," and take great pleasure in sending you the $100 I promised. Spend it for luxuries! My grippe is over and 4 days ago I began to work again. The lectures at Oxford look more possible, but a clear 4 weeks have been lost.

Yours ever truly

W. J.

You don't mention my "Misunderstanding" paper, which I sent you. I hope you think it conducive to clearing up. I will send you tomorrow a copy of my remarks at Ithaca, which I have tho't it well to have printed, so much misrepresentation is in the air.

· *To F. C. S. Schiller* ·

Cambridge
February 22, 1908

Thanks for your delightful letter and paper on exams.—
Still giddy from the grippe. Can hardly think or work, so
I only say this, that in my opinion we have perfectly
definite "theoretic" interests distinct from the "practical" ones, but that they themselves *have a utilitarian
and humanistic history.*

W. J.[10]

· *To F. C. S. Schiller* ·

Cambridge
March 20, 1908

Dear Schiller,

Another letter to thank you for, and the Albany Review
with your article, and the splendid Protagoras pamphlet
in addition. The latter ought to clinch the nails in the
absolutist coffin. Have you, by the way, read Münsterberg's onslaught on 'relativismus' in his new book, Philosophie der Werte? So childish! as if you altered your
relation to a reality by saying of your statements they are
absolutely true rather than by saying they are *true!* The
reply to [B.] Russell is very clear and simplified. You
work the distinction between truth as claimed and truth

as validated more than I do and to great effect. You write that you shrink a little from my use of independent realities, etc. No need of shrinking! They are an indestructible common sense assumption and the discussion is kept on terms more intelligible to the common man, if you also assume them. Moreover, in relation to the *individual man* the object *is* an independent reality with which his thought can "agree" only by its pragmatic workings. Allowing it prejudges in no whit a final humanistic treatment of the whole of the reality thus assumed. Your note on p. 17 covers the ground.

Ever thine

W. J.[11]

· *To Herbert George Wells* ·

Cambridge, Mass.
April 15, 1908

My dear Wells,

You enrich the lean earth on which you have consented for awhile to incarnate yourself! I have just read New Worlds for Old and am unable to restrain my loud and prolonged applause. The bigness of its temper! the persuasiveness of its method! the artfulness of its construction! the sincerity of its spirit, and the excellence of its style, will probably render it an "epoch-making" and tremendously influential document. I say no more.

I doubt whether you have made quite enuf allowance in the last chapter for the necessary austerity of life. I myself believe that a compulsory blood tax paid in mines, or freight-trains, winter cod fisherman, garbage collecting and dish washing at the Club and hotels will have eventually to take the place of the military blood tax, and will make the race more manly but no one can foresee the exact way in which the socialism of the future will realize itself.

Yours admiringly,

Wm James

I sail on the 21st. to give some Hibbert lectures at Manchester College, Oxford, during May.[12]

· *To F. C. S. Schiller* ·

68 Banbury Road
May 20. [1908]

Dear Schiller,

Have you by any chance kept some "Syllabuses" that I sent you from Stanford University? I am trying to patch up a last lecture and should like to help myself out with the last few pp., on the Will to Believe, if you have them. I forgot the number of the sheets and forgot equally to bring a copy with me. If you have that last sheet (4 or 6 pp.) I should be greatly obliged for the loan of it.
Wicksteed is a brick and writes a first rate letter.

Yours ever,

W. J.[13]

Sunbury Lodge
68 Banbury Rd., Oxford
Sunday P.M.
[May 24. 1908]

Dear Russell,

In a nutshell my opinion is this: that instead of there being one universal relation sui generis called "truth" between any reality and an idea, there are a host of particular relations varying according to special circumstances and constituted by the manner of "working" or "leading" of the idea through the surrounding experiences of which both the reality and the idea are part.

It is the particularity of these experiences that I have always had in mind when I have called the workings "practical," for only with particulars and concretes do we have practical relations. One ought thus *to be able to define empirically* what the truth-relation *consists in* in every instance, and one will probably find it different in most instances.

The ordinary conception makes it the same abstract thing in every possible instance. Direct verification by sensible presence is one kind of leading. Where no kind of verification is possible to us it seems to me that the question of our idea being true is irrelevant, except as meaning accord with some enveloping authority who *has* the verification which we are cut off from, and our accord with that observer has itself to be defined pragmatically. I imagine that these views are Schiller's.

Truly yours

Wm James[14]

· To Lady Ottoline Morrell ·

The Swan Inn
Bibury (Glos.)
June 13, 1908

Dear Lady Ottoline,

It is needless to say that your friendliest of notes has gone to the right spot. "C'était cette voix du coeur qui seule au coeur arrive"—and if the U.S.A. had been the scene, and *you* the visitors, it is the sort of letter you would have received first from us. We should not so modestly have waited! How good the personal sympathies are that overleap the national boundries and local differences. Those days at Newington House have been the climax of our visit, and the family relation, so to speak, with so many good people, you and your husband *imprimis*, have meant a real enlargement of our moral horizon.

Alice has sent for one of Prentice Mulford's volumes as a specimen, and perhaps will have the pleasure of laying it in your hands later. I have ordered Jane Addam's two volumes to be sent to Miss Sands, and she will doubtless make them over to you duly.

We were well advised in coming to this Cotswold region. The villages and towns, the streams and views, are endlessly perfect in their way and interesting. A country in equilibrium with itself, and to Yankee eyes, fabulously antique & finished.

We shall certainly let you know, and call at Bedford Square when in London—unfortunately I can't set dates yet—and either on this continent or ours keep you in sight. As "advanced sociologists" Mr. Morrell and yourself must make the obligatory American tour some day,

· 478 ·

and then see the inside of our humble abode, where no one will ever have been more welcome.

Believe me, dear Lady Ottoline, with warmest regards "to both from both," yours and Mr. Morrell's most sincerely,

Wm James[15]

· *To F. C. S. Schiller* ·

Bibury (Glos.)
June 15, 1908

Dear Schiller,

Your letter, inclosing Knox's (wh. I return) is very welcome. It is funny that the intense and rapid fire logician Knox should be standing up for "psychology" against me the slow witted logical waddler. I think I see his main point, but I think it is too fine for this rough world and I wish he could be drafted off to silence Joseph who, at Mrs. Warren's last dinner, seemed to need a kind of correction which my addled brain was in no condition to apply on that occasion. As things now appear to stand between you and Knox on the one hand and myself on the other, I think that the whole ground is strategically covered as it would not be, if either your statements or mine were the only ones used by our party. We and our critics are all alike born into a mental world which has long since evolved the notion that statements are *about* something and that to be 'true' of that something, they must in some sense "agree" with it. You start with the psychological subject claiming a statement of his to be 'true' and verifying it by working towards conclusions which lead him to say 'these *are* the something or the proximate marks of agreement with the something, wh. my statement meant'. I start with the something (calling it 'reality') and ask what makes the statement 'true' of it, replying by instancing your verifying workings, as constituting the agreement in concreto. We both deal with an identical universe, given us by common sense and traverse it in opposite directions. We are both abstractionists in starting with one pole only and filling in the rest. Our critics don't demur to the filling in as such, they only call it a psychological concomitant of the truth relation and deny that in *your* statement it leads to any possible reality or belief on your part in a reality. They fail to see that what 'satisfies' in the workings is just *that belief* and that, apart from what our beliefs postulate, reality there is none for either pragmatist or absolutist. But because I *start by postulating* the reality which you only *end by verifying*, they are willing to say that I talk sense (at least some of them are!) but that you mean something different. From my point it is easier to make them see that the notion of agreement may after all mean nothing but the concrete workings, especially if you gladly admit (as I do, but you seem less willing to make the admission explicit) that the workings may be purely 'theoretical', in the sense of having other truths as their termini, or as terminating in the direct inspection of such 'eternal' realities as triangles and numbers and the relations of likeness and difference among them. Thus, it seems to me, is the whole arena of 'truth' successfully and exhaustively occupied and in the way that minimizes opposition. But I'm in such a 'dopy' and confused state cerebrally, being only in my 4th. day of relaxation after the steady tension of the last few months, that I can't tell whether I write anything intelligible.

Our last 4 days at Oxford were spent at Miss Sand's, at Newington House, Wallingford, a beautiful place and humanly very delightful from the unworldly atmosphere and the presence of some very interesting people, high bred and well bred M P's who were radicals, etc.

This country is exquisitely lovely, tho' cold and sunless from the American point of view. We stay till Friday morn. and then go to Durham via York. On the 24th. to London for a few days. Address Coutts & Co., 440 Strand

Ever thine,

W. J.[16]

· *To Horace Meyer Kallen* ·

Bibury (Glos.)
June 16th. 08

You have sent a plenteous shower of notes, to wh. I make this scant return. Glad Santayana likes your thesis—I shan't read it till at Rye, possibly a month hence. The Oxford tutors woke up during the last week of my stay, and I heard a good deal of philosophy discussed, but my own brain was too confused and addled to play any effective part. It is a uniquely precious bit of furniture in the world's showroom, but the world is not all showroom, and I doubt whether other places ought to emulate Oxford, except in this detail or that. Any how, they could never catch up if they did! The social whirl is over—both its instruction & its fatigue, and the summer opens restfully in the country. But little sunshine! Bad for an American skin. Love to all "inquiring friends."

Yours,

W. J.

· To F. C. S. Schiller ·

Bibury
June 17, 1908

Your letter is satisfactory tremenjusly. *Your* tactics are doubtless much the best ones for Oxford, where to smash the malevolent adversary is the thing required, mine the best for America, where to convert the perplexed truth-seekers is the problem. Let us each stick to his line! What I mean by calling your starting point an "abstraction" is that the "claim" of "truth" belongs to a universe of which the notion of a *reality to be true about* is also an integral member. You abstract *vorläufig* from *it*, altho' the content claimed and verified is only our statement of what it is.

W. J.

· *To F. C. S. Schiller* ·

Ullswater Hotel
Patterdale
July 6th, [08]

Just one line to report biography since we parted: 9 good days at Bibury (Glos); 2 at York, 3 1/2 at Durham (which was tremendously impressive) and where I found Jevons very *simpatico*, likewise the splendid old liberal minded octogenerian of a "Dean." Since then here in the lake district, where my nervous condition makes little progress owing to a virulent and pestilential "cold." Shall be at Garlant's Hotel, Suffolk St., from Thursday to Monday, when I go to Piddington for a few days. Thence to Rye. I dare say that you're already on the Continent. I don't think of "Truth" any more!

W. J.[17]

· *To Herbert George Wells* ·

Lamb House
Rye
July 18th, [1908]

Cher et illustre maître,

Your hospitality is evidently genuine—not that I ever suspected it wasn't. Arriving here last night I find your note, bulging with Chesterton, whom my brother hasn't yet seen, though he lives next door. I shall myself admire to see him (as we say in New England) if the chance be allotted, but I shall probably see you first. My wife unfortunately cannot, being for the next ten days with some friends at Harrow; which makes me ask whether I might not bring our daughter (aet. 20) instead, and ask also whether from next Wednesday p. m. to the friday morning would be a propitious and convenient time to yourselves. Pray address me here, and believe me most sincerely yours,

Wm James[18]

· *To Herbert George Wells* ·

Lamb House
Rye
July 25, 1908

My dear Wells,

This is to report our safe arrival home from our most delightful visit, with which we have regaled our respective wife and mother, who got back yesterday afternoon from her week at Harrow, making her wish she had been "along." To reward you for your hospitality I have caused a copy to be made of a letter which the postmaster of Rye gave my brother yesterday, as a specimen of the sort of information which he is expected to supply to the population of the Kingdom. It seems to me a precious document in illustration of the phase you dwell on so much in our present civilization—the survival of the habits and gestures of something that once was strong, in microscopic form. This lady goes through the form of requiring things on account of her innate gentility, and of shedding bene-factions, tho she has nothing either to pay or to give. Dreadful person!

I am sorry to have to ask you to return the letter.

Peggy also sends her joyous regards, and I am, with the same to you all, including the ferocious redskins,

Very truly yours,

Wm James

P. S. It has occurred to me that if you should come and spend a couple of years in America, say in California, you'd get all sorts of nutritious lights on the way the future is being made. Think of it! Even one year might do.

· *To F. C. S. Schiller* ·

Lamb House
Rye
August 4, 1908

Dear Schiller,

I've been here for a week and feel much more like my natural self again. I shall stay for 10 days longer, wife and daughter being at present at Geneva. I suppose that you are also in Switzerland by this time and hope that you're *secouer*-ing the dust of pupils and examination books. Would I had your vigor. I write now merely to say that I have just read the vol. of Essays in my "honor" in Henry

James's copy and that the excellence of its content makes the volume trebly honorific. Dewey's article seems to me uncommonly massive and weighty and I write mainly for the purpose of telling you not to fail to read it. The day will come when people will wonder how there could have been any different notion of truth held by anyone. So let's hammer away.

Yours as ever

W. J.[19]

· *To James McKeen Cattell* ·

Lamb House
Rye, Sussex
Aug. 5, 1908

Dear Cattell,

"The proudest moment of my life" was that in wh. you handed me the volume dedicated to my memory, but I am prouder still since reading it. Your copy was too handsome to travel, so I have only mastered the contents of it now, in my brother's copy, which Miller sent him. It's a masterly book, full of vigorously original thought, beautifully exprest. I've no doubt that it marks an epoch, or just the *eve* of an epoch, in American philosophy. I say the eve for one connecting touch is needed to make all that epistemology shoot together. Who will make the spark shoot?

I find your own contribution extremely suggestive. Along with my pages on inhibitions, etc in the 2nd vol. of my Principles, with Münsterberg's "Actions Theorie," with W. McDougall's chapter on mental retention, with Bergson's general account of the brain's function, etc. it seems to me to force on us a general revision of the whole subject of "consciousness" in relation to brain activity. Difficult enough! You have certainly thrown in a lot of points of view to be taken account of.

I thank you, each and all, most heartily for the splendid volume.

Yours ever truly

Wm James[20]

· *To Arthur Oncken Lovejoy* ·

Lamb House
Aug. 6, 1908

Dear Lovejoy,

I write to express my tremendous gratification over the Essays "in my honor," and to thank you for your share in their production. Owing to certain circumstances, I have only just got round to reading the volume, which seems to me masterly throughout, and almost to eventuate in a definitive epistemology. At any rate the essays on that subject bring one up to the very *verge* of a pragmatistic realism. Almost without exception too, they are excellently well-written. You and Adler on Kant are very strong. I didn't know how much of him had been anticipated in this country—Cudworth I knew about but not Collier. I doubt whether Kant knew either, he seems to have read so little philosophy. A delightful old *crackle* about his mind; but the only thing that ever seemed to me to have any permanent value in his system was his argument for Idealism based on the antinomies, and now you show that that was anticipated by an englishman:—hurrah! Of course Kant developed the idea more thoroly—with his pun on gegeben & aufgegeben.

Did Lamont send you a card of inquiry of mine as to who wrote the review of Duncan's Spencer? It was you, and a *most* masterly thing indeed! Are you a fixture at Columbia, or are you going to Wisconsin?

Very truly yours

Wm James[21]

· *To F. C. S. Schiller* ·

Charing Cross Hotel
London
September 15, 1908

Dear Schiller,

I got your letter from Dresden duly a few days ago and I suppose that this will find you already arrived at Oxford. I had heard nothing of the Heidelberg meeting and was very glad to learn from you that Pragmatism was so much to the fore. I had never supposed that the German mind would even look at it. But that mind is shoreless and measureless, so who knows? Are you sure that other topics were, as you say, "nowhere" in comparison? Of course where *you* were, Pragmatism was the foreground, for you were the foreground. So I wait for impartial or inimical corroboration! I'm sorry that Bergson didn't go. Strong is back in N. Y. Our own departure has been postponed for a fortnight, till October sixth, on the daughter's account, and we shall be at Oxford again for a few days, at the end of next week probably, when I can hear more of the Congress, and of the Truth generally from you. I will therefore write no more now, but will notify our day of coming and place of abode to you in advance.

I am going to spend a night with James Ward tomorrow—thence again to Rye. We had a very pleasant 2 and 1/2 weeks on the Continent, mainly Holland.

Yours as ever

W. J.[22]

· *To F. C. S. Schiller* ·

Charing Cross Hotel
London
[October 5, 1908]

I had an exquisite evening and morning, so far as weather and landscape went, at [William] McDougall's and a very satisfactory talk—but I forget that I told you that at the Station! Superb weather and landscape at Torquay, too. No hope for Bergson at Oxford. He can't go there this week, but wishes that you could notify him when next you pass thru Paris. He will meet you anywhere. He is a marvel intellectually and a very easy talker, I found him, but very shy and timid I think, with bad nerves and habitual fear of their playing him tricks. Like *me*, du reste!

Yours

W. J.[23]

· *To Ralph Barton Perry* ·

95 Irving St.
Oct 27 '08

Dear Perry,

I am off again to Chocorua, sorry not to have seen you yet. I shall be back on Wednesday Nov 4th. at latest. I send to you the program of my lectures at Oxford, rather than send it to the office direct, for you may know some reason why one day or hour is better than another. They ought, I suppose, to be "open to the public," tho they are rather abstruse. Scheffer seems to block the way to Mondays & Fridays. I don't know when Kallen means to chip in. Any hour except 2.30 will suit me, and any day you may appoint, after Nov 4th.

I devoutly hope that you are *much* better, but hang all summer schools, say I! With greetings to the Missus,

Yours ever

W. J.[24]

Chocorua, N. H.
Oct. 30, 1908

Dear Lady Ottoline,

Your extremely pleasant & friendly letter to my wife was duly received in the last days of September, and I volunteered to write you a word of reply and farewell. In the press of getting off it got postponed, & that bred farther postponement—until now! The envelop that covers this was as far as I got, on our homeward pitching steamer. You express the divine discontent of the reforming mind with many of your nation's things and ways. Were you to come to this country you would realize, as we have done since arriving, that the general environment spread out before a people's eyes has more to do with the value of their lot in life than the sociologists, with their exclusive attention to income & expense, old age provision and other immediately personal conditions, are apt to realize. And the tidiness, beauty, stimulating power, & general interestingness of this environment are to a great extent the work of very rich or powerful men with ambitious plans of their own, executed by the toil of others. In this country of small peasant proprietors, the only adjective that the face of nature brings to one's lips is 'scurvy'. The most unnatural mixture of rawness and decay, perfectly shocking after the stoutness, roundness, tidiness, and endless feast for the eyes of all the English landscape I was in this summer. England has *done* things well, *some* of which *some* of us are at most hoping that we *may* some day do! Ah me! One oughtn't to be torn both eastward and westward in this heartbreaking way. Please give my warm regards to your husband. Those three days at Miss Sands' were an oasis in the desert of life, and the best thing in them was making your acquaintance. My wife is in Cambridge. I have been here since Oct 17 when we landed.

Believe me, dear Lady Ottoline, with sincere affection, yours,

Wm James

· *To James McKeen Cattell* ·

Silver Lake, N. H.
Oct 30. [1908]

Dear Cattell,

After a day devoted to heavy scientific papers on evolution, the three evening speeches ought to be short, the shorter the better. You may put me down for a maximum of 10 minutes. God help us all!

I was much struck by Simon Patten's recent remarks apropos of pensioning professors, etc. It seems to me that the concept of improving environment is one of great utility. "Scurvy, scurvy, scurvy!" is the one adjective that has risen to my lips at the sight of our American environment after my five months spent mainly in rural england, where the poorest farm laborer has spread-out permanently before his eyes the environment of tidiness and beauty and "interestingness" which the American millionaire has to spend thousands of dollars to go & see.

Woodworth writes me that you are taking your sabbatical year. Prithee *where?* & *how?* This invitation to me doesn't look much like it.

I hope that you are all well at Garrison. With best regards, I am always,

truly yours,

Wm James[25]

· *To John Shaw Billings* ·

Cambridge
Nov. 7. 08

Dear Dr. Billings,

I am just back from 6 months in Europe with a mountain of arrears to attend to, and consequently can't go to the National Academy meeting at Baltimore. Count me absent, therefore, from the Anthropological committee's deliberations.

Truly yours,

Wm James

95 Irving St.
Cambridge
Nov 25. 08

Dear Cattell,

I accepted your invitation to make an after dinner speech
on Darwin the other day as the bird accepts that of the
"fascinating" serpent to fall into his jaws. I was just back
from Europe, and disposing of my accumulated mail
with lightning speed; I knew your diabolical per-
severance and ultimate success (also I felt grateful for
your part in the memorial volume), so I just said yes as
the coon came down. But I've been repenting of it ever
since, for I haven't found a single word to say about
Darwin, and the thought of the whole thing has become
an obsession. Last night I went to another dinner where
I had to make a speech about some one else, and the
whole kind of thing disagrees with me so profoundly,
morally and intellectually as well as physically, that I am
writing to Howard that I am not to be at the meeting,
and that he must look to inviting someone else.

More and more I perceive that big crowds are not my
proper element. There are lots of men who like it, so
why should I feel any duty. Therefore, dear old Cattell,
say to me *"absolvo te"* and look among the names in your
American Men of Science for some one more worthy
than yours always truly

Wm James[26]

95 Irving St.
Cambridge, Mass.
Dec. 19. 08

Dear Dr. Billings,

Replying to yours of the 12th (after a delay of which I am ashamed) I concur with the criticism of Dr. Minot's suggestion. *Biology* & medicine are the best partners.

I also think that "anthropology" covers too much ground (unless as a legal pretext for certain otherwise excentric nominations) and that the proposed 3 subdivisions are a logical improvement.

As for the names, Dewey is one of the 2 first philosophers whom we have, the other being Royce. Bowditch is too much of an amateur gentleman. Fewkes has work't hard, but I don't know whether his general power of mind is up to standard. I doubt it, but haven't followed his career at all of late.

Sincerely yours,

Wm James

Unofficial P. S.! I think seriously of resigning from the Academy. I appreciate the distinction of being a member, but my use for it ends there, and my only relations with it till I die will probably be in the line of helping to peddle out the distinction to other people. But isn't that rather childish, and can man live by distinctions alone? Moreover, if I resign now I shall do one human being a concrete service—Royce namely who if I remain will in all human probability have the onerous task of writing my *éloge funebre*. I really don't see (with so many other organs of publication provided) what function except that of drawing a social line between the "ins" and the "outs" the National Academy subserves. I don't suppose that any member has resigned yet, but I suppose that one *can* resign, if so perversely impelled.

Very sincerely yours,

Wm James[27]

XV

1909

IN THE BEGINNING OF 1909, JAMES DECLINED TO EN-
gage in further public debate about "Pragmatism,"
though he continued to applaud Schiller's vigorous
efforts. He also suggested to Cattell that he publish in
the *Popular Science Monthly* an article by Shackleford,
which Cattell accepted in exchange for James's article,
finished on 12 February, entitled "On a Very Prevalent
Abuse of Abstraction." On 1 March James corrected the
proofs of his "Report on Mrs. Piper's Hodgson-Control,"
which appeared later in July. He began to write his
"Introduction to Philosophy" textbook, but did not get
very far due to distractions and poor health.

"To lighten life's baggage," he resigned his membership in the National Academy of Sciences. He also
dropped his subscription to the journal *Science* because
he could not any longer read all the literature that came
his way. Another sign of James's slower pace was his
decision in June not to accept an invitation to attend a
Jubilee of the University of Geneva in Switzerland and
to receive a rumored doctor of divinity degree. He did,
however, receive instead the degree of Doctor of the
Natural Sciences *in absentia* on 9 July.

James's Oxford lectures were published in April as *A
Pluralistic Universe: Hibbert Lectures at Manchester
College on the Present Situation in Philosophy.* He

thanked Kallen for his review of the book in a Boston newspaper. Also, in April Bertrand Russell's second article on "Pragmatism" appeared, which, James noted in June, had a marked difference in tone from Russell's first article in 1908.

While on vacation at Chocorua, James continued to receive, read, and praise both articles and books sent to him by his friends, especially the books by Perry and Douglas Fawcett. In September his own book appeared, *The Meaning of Truth: A Sequel to Pragmatism.* This was a collection of essays evoked in response to many criticisms of his conception of 'truth'.

In the early part of September, James journeyed to Clark University in Worchester, Massachusetts, to attend a congress of scientists to celebrate the twenty years of the University's existence and achievements. There he met Sigmund Freud and Carl Jung. The president of the university, G. Stanley Hall, had conducted some psychic experiments and wrote to both James and Sir Oliver Lodge of the British Society for Psychical Research about them.

Another event more significant for either the scientific success or failure of the psychical research movement was the visit to this country of the Italian psychic medium, Eusapia Palladino, under the direction of Hereward Carrington. The first séance was held in New York City on 13 November. Münsterberg was present at the 13 and 18 December séances in New York. James was most interested in the way the scientists would react.

His own views of mediumistic phenomena were published in the article "The Confidences of a 'Psychical Researcher'" for the October issue of the *American Magazine.* A writing of another kind resulted from the invitation of Nicholas Murray Butler to contribute to the *International Conciliation* series. James took this opportunity to formulate in print his thoughts on war and peace which he had considered for years. The "Moral Equivalent of War" was the product of his efforts.

· *To Paul Carus* ·

95 Irving St.
Jan. 3, 1909

Dear Dr. Carus,

If to attract public attention is a mark of greatness, I must be becoming a 'great' man. This last number of the Monist suffuses me with blushes.

You may wonder at my having made no reply to your first article on my pragmatism. The fact is, and renews itself now apropos of this second article of yours, that I am deadly weary of polemic writing on the subject, either private or for publication. If I haven't already made my meaning clear by all that I have printed, I shall certainly never succeed in doing so. Outsiders generally end by judging between disputants rightly, and I leave the issue to them. Meanwhile, dear Dr. Carus, the world is wide enough for both you and me to live on our differing philosophies therein, so I hold my tongue still! You will pardon me, or rather applaud me, I know, for simply subscribing myself

Very sincerely yours

Wm James[1]

Cambridge, Mass.
Jan. 12, 1909

Dear Cattell,

Will you kindly cast your eye over this and see whether
it is fit for the Pop. Sci.? The author (Hon. Justice
Shackleford, Tallahassee, Florida) has been for 6 years
past Chief Justice of the Florida Supreme Court—a
splendid old fellow who, all alone in his state keeps up
with philosophic reading in the most extraordinary way,
and wants to publish a volume of essays. Judicial duties
retarding him, he has sent me this one and another for
my personal gratification; but it seems to me, in view of
the incredibly stupid attacks that have been made on my
ideas, that this defense, altho superficial, has a certain
timeliness and merits publication. I say this in spite of
the compliments lavisht on my unworthy self.

Truly yours,

Wm James

P. S. He agrees that I should send it to you. If you can't
accept it, pray return it to him at Tallahassee.[2]

Cambridge
January 17, 1909

Dear Schiller,

I have a letter and p. c. from you, both unanswered;
also, if I remember aright, a previous letter. The spectacle of your *unverwüstlichkeit* fills me with admiration of
the creative energy. But the only thing I am writing for
now is to applaud your contribution to this month's
Mind. The tone of it is *perfect* and you never did a
cleaner, clearer or more complete piece of work. That no
one else should chime in heartily as yet on either side of
the Atlantic, is to me one of the paradoxes of my experience. Possibly the words "as yet" cover the key to the
riddle!

Yours heartily (and hastily)

W. J.[3]

· *To F. C. S. Schiller* ·

Cambridge
March 10, 1909

Dear Schiller,

I have just read your "Rationalistic Conception of Truth"
for which I thank you. It is ergötzlich and I don't think
your pen was ever both so sharp and so light before, or
your logic so inclusive of all the possibilities. It won't
make converts, but it will make adherents shamefaced
and in the Oxford atmosphere of fencing logically, wrangling and scoring points, it will increase your influence
on the young and the prestige of your power. *I*, as you
know, despise logic, where the material is inductive, and
I think that if one wants to see what sorry tricks it will
play with a man of genius one need only read over again,
as I have recently done, the epistemological contributions of Bertrand Russell. Really pathological stuff, in my
opinion. Your recent letter shows you working like a
marine engine and snorting destruction to God's enemies like a cyclone. I am getting on fairly well, but
doing almost no work, as the condition thereof.

I enclose an advertisement of my Oxford lectures,
which I hope to send you in three weeks or so. We both
thank you for your friendliness to our boy.

Yours ever,

W. J.[4]

95 Irving St.
Cambridge, Mass.
21. III .09

Dear Mr. Hague,

I wish to offer my resignation as member of the National Academy of Sciences.

I was acutely sensible of the honour, when elected; and hoped, when I accepted, to play some active part. But as time goes on, it looks more and more as if my only active relations to the Academy would probably be the voting (or neglecting to vote) for the addition of new members, or the writing of some one's necrological notice, or inflicting upon someone the burden of writing mine. I feel more and more, as I grow older, like lightening life's baggage, and this occurs to me as one of the places where I may harmlessly take in sail. I therefore respectfully beg the Academy to accept my resignation from its membership, and remain its and your

Obedient Servant,

Wm James

Mr. Arnold Hague
Home Secretary of the National Academy of Sciences
Washington, D. C.[5]

95 Irving St.
April 3, 1909

Dear Cattell,

I substituted this year the Pop. Sci for Science, as member of the A.A.A.S. I ought to take both, but I find it physically impossible to read so much, and it muddles me to *see* so much that I can't read.

I observe that the Pop. Sci. is *bound with wires* instead of being sewed like any self-respecting periodical with a circulation of less than 250,000. Don't you think this is too low toned, blackguardly and infamous a thing for you as editor to be held responsible for? The saving of expense must be very small. The big 10 cent monthlies excuse themselves by saying that their enormous editions make sewing too *zeitraubend* to be possible—it would take half the month to sew them. *You* unfortunately have no such apology to offer; and the wires must be an annoyance to every reader, to say nothing of the eventual binder, who hates them like poison. I am a busy body, I know, but you ought to thank me for being one in this instance.

Yours as ever,

W. J.

Don't answer this unless by acting on it!

· To James Gibbons Huneker ·

95 Irving St.
Cambridge
26. IV. 09

Dear Mr. Huneker,

What blindlings we are! 'The idea' of your being bro't up under the influence of my father's writings seems to me most strange. I am ordering to be sent to you my last literary adventure, publisht last week, and too technical in matter for me to expect any but co-professors to read it.

I have to beg your pardon about Huysmans, of whom you have direct personal knowledge. I only know 3 things of his, a novel about a man's troubles in finding a decent mistress after his wife left him, the book 'à Rebours', and a pamphlet of art-criticism. All 3 made my gorge rise, and I suppose that his later catholicism was only a sort of insincere pose & mystification. I defer to your judgment—the categories of human beings are beyond classing. My brother in law W. M. Salter carried off your volume almost immediately after I received it, and I have only had that one look at it as yet. I've just read an extraordinarily brilliant article of yours on Violinests in Everybody's Magazine.

Believe me,
Very sincerely yours,

Wm James[6]

Cambridge
April 27, 1909

Dear Schiller,

What a ripping good letter writer you are—even from
Rome. I congratulate you on your pluck in reading your
lecture in Italian to *orecchii romani!* Also in your advances in formal logic and pragmatism as a denial of the
same. What you tell me of Taylor doesn't either surprise
or elate me. He seems to be the nimble flea of contemporary philosophy, which doesn't however detract either
from his cleverness or his candor. I shall never expect
him to be an *ally*, for his mind seems to be merely
ratiocinative and Humanism needs the feeling for reality. The good [J. E.] Russell is a genuine convert. I
never heard of *What is Reality?* Can't you give me the
author's name? Meanwhile I can inquire at Houghton-
Mifflin's. I have just sent you a little squib on 'Relativismus" which I hope you'll approve. I am poorly as to
my precordial symptom and want to get to Nauheim, but
doubt whether I can compass it.

Affectionate regards,

Wm James[7]

95 Irving St.
Cambridge
30. IV .09

Dear Mr. Huneker

What a reader you are, and what a rememberer!—to say nothing of what a letter writer! I haven't seen Gaultier's Pragmatisme, of which you write. To tell the truth I'm tired of reading even what I say myself, let alone what others say, in elucidation of that unhappy word. I don't think I mention it once in my last book. Papini, I hear by rumor, recently died insane. Too bad! for he was indeed a genius. The *freest* I have known, even if he did delight a bit too much in *épater*-ing the *bourgeois.* Salter disappeared to N. H. yesterday, carrying your book with him, to my dismay, as his wife tells me, so I can't read your Stirner or Nietzsche till I get it back from him. I read a life of Stirner a few years ago, by some conscientious German. Strange epigram! This man, so exalting of the self, seems to have been the most effaced and *null* of God's creatures, in his actual personal incarnation. So null, that almost nothing can be collected to tell about him. I am impatient to get at your articles on him and on N–.

Very sincerely yours,

Wm James[8]

· To F. C. S. Schiller ·

Cambridge
May 15, 1909

To your card, just in, I say "Yes, Knox is *magnificent.*"
[Bertrand] Russell has evidently taken great pains, but is
absolutely ineffectual. I think he'll give in, he's on the
brink of the precipice. I wrote to him yesterday. I've
been seeing J. E. Russell—glorious old boy for innate
liberalism of mind. My reference to Theaetetus in
Relativismus paper was a quotation from current opinion. I am sorry you took it for my own view. Of Witmer
don't for Heaven's sake write! He's a dwarf and should
be totgeschwiegen.

W. J.[9]

· To Horace Meyer Kallen ·

Silver Lake, N. H.
June 19, 1909

Dear Kallen,

I hardly ever look at the Transcript, but yesterday I
stumbled accidently on last Wednesday's issue with your
long review of my Oxford lectures, for which please accept my thanks. I am not sure that you haven't elabo-
rated the Hebraic-Hellenic contrast at too great length,
or at any rate used those words too absolutely. Your

remarks on "evolution" vs. Darwinism are worth making, and under whatever names the *devenir réel* and the *statically true* have to be contrasted. When you get down to my text, you are successful, &, I imagine, *interesting*. It must have been difficult, but for *me* of course the two paragraphs before the last are the important ones. In the knife-simile you have supplied an essential link in the Bergsonian argument for which he ought to be grateful. And the penultimate paragraph is profound, to me, and must be kept account of in future.

Yours as ever,

Wm James[10]

· *To F. C. S. Schiller* ·

Silver Lake, N. H.
June 22, [1909]

Dear Schiller,

Your card of the 5th. has duly come and makes me sorely wish that I had been at the Aristotelian Society to hear the debate. I hope you didn't get off there your diabolical moremonistic pun! I have been up here with my brother-in-law, Salter, breathing the sylvan fragrance for 3 weeks past, the family still at Cambridge. The simplified life and the natural beauty do me good and I find that by walking slowly enough, I can get about much as I please. A note rec'd last night from Woodbridge reveals the thickness of the night which our rays have got to dispel. "I wish Truth could be let alone," he writes; "I am still convinced that there is something profoundly absurd in an inquiry as to the true conception of truth and something intellectually comic (and tragic) about a controversy between rival conceptions of it." Such an utterance is well calculated to make us realize how genuinely original and really "epoch making" our doctrine is.

I had an extraordinarily courteous and reasonable letter from Bradley the other day. He makes concession after concession, so far as our works go and were he younger and in better health, I shouldn't be surprised to see him make a volte-face as regards the citadel and embark on a new career. Knox's article continues to look great and [B.] Russell's to grow smaller and smaller as my mind looks back.

I am correcting the proofs of my collected writings on "Truth" to form a volume about as big as *Pragmatism* and to be published in September. Seen together, they have a decidedly solid look to me and I hope may close a certain period of Woodbridgian darkness in the history of opinion on the subject, when they once get digested by the reader. Certainly the change of tone is already marked—vide a clipping from yesterday's Boston Herald which I enclose. Think of the change of tone from B. Russell's Transatlantic Truth to his article in the Edinburgh Review.

I hope that you will have a fine Swiss vacation. I finally declined only two days ago the invitation to the Geneva Jubilee in July. Country life here agrees with me better, tho' I confess I should have liked to exchange chaff with Royce about the D. D. degree which Flournoy whispers has been in store for me.

Yours, dear Schiller, as ever,

W. J.[11]

Silver Lake, N. H.
June 24. 09

Beloved Katie,

Think what you have lost (or gained?)! I have refrained from writing to you for many weeks past because I have been weighing the arguments for and against my accepting an invitation to the Jubilee of the University of Geneva next month, at which, as Flournoy whispered to me in a confidential note I should probably have gained a doctor of divinity degree (!!). A week ago, at the last possible moment, I definitely decided *not* to go, so thou and I are not to meet this side of next summer, when I hope we shall. Apart from the expense of making such a trip which (with the children costing what they do in these days) is prohibitive, I am better, under home conditions, in the country, than trying to keep up with the procession at Jubilees in towns, even tho you and Lausanne are near to retreat to. But next summer I intend fully to make it up, for I fairly thirst for the Swiss scenery and civilization, and think that we shall all come over for a couple of years. At the age of 67 one begins to earn the right to enjoy the greater finish of european conditions. Fighting the fierce American summer fight should be reserved for youth. Exhausted with the Cambridge winter, and with the sociability that redoubles there in Spring (people trying to make up what they had deferred in that line), I have been up here with the Salters (Alice's sister is Mrs. S.) who live very primitively on a superb hill top, for three weeks. I have enjoyed greatly the simplified life, and the beauty (not so much the insects!) and go down tomorrow to bring up

Alice & Peggy on July 2nd., to open our Chocorua house & abide there for the summer. Our *healthes* are all good (mine is so if I go *slow*) but our prospects are a little uncertain, owing to Aleck who came over here hot to go off with Billy for a year in a Paris studio, but who has been fired by the sight of so many of his schoolmates in College to re-enter the lists for Harvard. I don't know how it will turn out. As for myself, I have another book coming out in September, & have begun to write another one still. I am beginning to be *acknowledged*, in more than one country, and must live up to my reputation and not get down from my pedestal. I find it a pleasant enuf perch. I haven't been to N. Y. all this winter, so can tell you nothing of your family there. You will of course write, and communicate what you are going to do this summer. But for the tourists, what a paradise Switzerland would be! Believe me, dear Katie,

ever lovingly yours,

W. J.[12]

· *To Thomas Mitchell Shackleford* ·

Chocorua, N. H.
July 11. 09

Dear Shackleford,

I have your long letters of the 5th & 6th. & hasten to reply.

As regards the Wallace, I think there was an Edwin

Wallace who did something but I forget what it was—
may be Butler meant him.

My 8 lectures on Exceptional Mental States were
given at the Lowell Institute in the late '90s, covering
hypnotism, degeneration, genius, double personality,
witchcraft, etc, and no part of them has been printed. I
have grown into a distaste for the morbid side of life, to
wh. I once paid much attention.

Keep the article from the Republican!

My new book will be called "the Nature of Truth, a
Sequel to Pragmatism."

Keep those english reviews as long as you wish to!

As regards the "finite God," I have just finisht reading
the proof sheets of a book by Douglas Fawcett (author of
the "Riddle of the Universe") which runs on lines most
astonishingly congruent with Bergson's, Fechner's and
mine. He goes at great length into the question of a finite
Deity, and it seems to me that no one has defended that
view so well. He is an amateur in philosophy, his serious
occupation being automobiling up the Alps(!) in wh. he
has broken all records, but his book, which is soon to
appear, is an extraordinarily rich case of "vision." You
must read it without fail.

You are an extraordinarily *scholarly* mind, which I am
not—a fact that makes me tremendously glad to be no
longer a "professor" where I was always made to feel my
deficiencies by the demands of students for bibliographic
references for their theses etc. It tickles me to have my
own writings treated as a "source"—as you treat them!
But I fear that your summer program is going to lead you
to overwork yourself badly, and I wish that you would
take the scholarship of the subject more lightly—so
much of the literature is worthless that it is best killed by
silence. Moore's article in the Aristotelian Society, e.g.,
is the painful crawling of an ant over the outside of a
subject whose centre he gets no glimpse of. It shouldn't

be *mentioned.* Nevertheless I will send it to you on my return to Cambridge, if you insist on reading it.

It sometimes seems to me that the history of filosophy consists essentially of two parts, first the wanton creation of difficulties and artificialties by intellectualism, and the struggle back to the dramatic concreteness of common sense after remanding intellectualism to its proper subordinate place. But that place, which we are just beginning properly to apprehend, is not fully *comprehended* yet.

Yours ever truly

Wm James

· *To F. C. S. Schiller* ·

Chocorua, N. H.
July 17, 1909

Dear Schiller,

All hail to yours of the 5th., summoning me to a public constatation of Bradley's weakening estate. Not I! I've done with polemicizing on the subject of truth and leave the job to other hands. Moreover, Bradley's symptoms of giving out are chiefly in private letters to me and the poor fellow, who is evidently in very bad case with his kidney, complains that he is intellectually defunct, etc., so that I see no need for further rubbing it in to him, by anyone. In general I think one can easily overdo *explicitness* in controversies like the present one. Truth makes its way silently, well enough, and if after 10 years a certain kind of attack stops, that army may be considered beaten.

I shan't see the July Mind or the Hibbert for 3 weeks or so, when I revert for awhile to Cambridge. The Greats paper on Logic, which you enclose, is an example to me of the terror of examinations. I'm glad to be quit both of passing and of giving them. There is hardly a question on this paper that I could even begin to answer and I should surely flunk it. Where is Knox on Pratt to appear? Had I gone to Switzerland, I could have seen not only him, but you and Strong and last [but] not least Douglas Fawcett who has sent me the proof sheets of his forthcoming book *The Individual and Reality*—an amateurish thing but all the better for the impression of sincerity which that gives and most astonishingly congruent all over with your positions and mine. He spends most of his time ascending [the] Alps in a motor car! and his last headquarters were at the "splendid" Hotel, Les Praz, près Chamonix. You two ought to meet. I don't repent not going, for I can stand but little fatigue in these days and the life here suits me best.

Affectionately yours

Wm James

Chocorua, N. H.
July 17. 09

Dear Perry,

I got your letter, which touches me very much, invoicing your "Economy" book weeks ago, up here. The book remained in Cambridge, and I have only now got round to reading it, in part aloud with Alice & Bill. I need hardly say that I "agree" with about everything in it, but I should like to say what a splendid trumpet blast of liberalism in Ethics it seems to me to be, and how the style in which certain pages are written fills me with admiration, as if the elevation of the argument had given wings to the pen. It goes deep, and is indeed the Gospel instead of the law. It will immediately give you a Master's place—yet all the while you kept us ignorant (me, at any rate) of this most important stream of constructive effort that was going on inside of you!!

The leading idea, of the field of ethics being that of the human interests allied against the material environment, and the consequent appeal to reasonableness all round seems to me unconquerable truth and common sense, and the way in which you handle egoism is the *endgültig* way, and quite in the line of your epistemological realism. For the man who simply *obeys* his egoistic interests there is no theoretic refutation. But when he *reflects* on them, comparing them with others, the conceptual commutability of all egos instantly appears, and argument can have only one result, and that the reasonable one. Just so "solipsism" vanishes, the moment one *thinks* of other thinkers at all, for then they are as real as the objects which one supposes themselves to know, and which for oneself are real. Morally as well as epistemologically solipsism as a system is a preposterous abstract from the concrete psychology of men—the only *real* solipsisms are practical, selfishness namely, & dogmatism. Your table of virtues is tremendously fresh, unconventional, and stimulating. I care least for the fine-art chapter. What I care most for is the reasoned faith in radical democracy, and the smiting and sweeping sentences in which every now and then it comes to the fore, scouting the pedantic, conventional, and scholastic alternatives, whatever they may be.

It is really a *splendid* book!

I suppose that Mrs. Perry is stationary at Norwell, but can't you and Holt, (or you alone, if Holt can't do it) manage to come up here for a week end, or for any 2 or 3 days before August—*better* the *last* week?

Ever truly yours,

Wm James[13]

· *To James McKeen Cattell* ·

Chocorua, N. H.
July 31. 09

Dear Cattell,

Apart from the general difficulty of rating men serially (after the two or three *sommités* have been told off) I have neglected my psychological reading so utterly in the past ten years that I feel myself to be a back number and quite out of touch with the progress of that branch of learning. I actually could make no reply. Get a younger and more wideawake man in my stead! I re-enclose the printed slip, and hope that you're enjoying your vacation.

Yours always truly,

Wm James

· *To F. C. S. Schiller* ·

Chocorua
Aug. 4, 09

Dear Schiller,

This country is being eaten up by innumerable host of caterpillars (unknown here before) they swarm and defoliate all our trees. I am reminded of them by an exquisite specimen of professional philosophy by H. Rickert in *Kantstudien*, XIV, Heft 2, Zwei Wege der Erkenntnisstheorie. Ignoring all phenomenal intermediaries between mind knowing and thing known he swarms over the subject with innumerable scholastic distinctions, etc., etc. in the most diseased way. I wish you would review him. He has a couple of most insulting pp. about pragmatism wh., if it have no other advantage, has at least that of decaterpillarizing epistemology from such work as Rickert's.

Yours ever,

W. J.

I wish you might meet Douglas Fawcett. I have just had a very interesting letter from him.[14]

· *To F. C. S. Schiller* ·

Chocorua, N. H.
August 22, 1909

Dear Schiller,

I re-enclose poor Schinz's letter which is pathetic in its benighted sincerity. I am sorry I spoke hard-heartedly of your review. I have reread it, but still think that more urbanity and ingenuity were never wasted on an unworthier object. He was not worth mentioning at all and is *not* a fair protagonist of our adversaries.

I have read Bradley's article in Mind for July and agree with it fully, finding it excellent pragmatic doctrine, expressed in parts just as you or I might have exprest it, but compatible also with his own previous system, it seems to me. I don't remember Stout's or [B.] Russell's sensationalist absolutism which he seems to be criticizing. I don't think they can possibly have meant anything as absurd. Of course to work with the system is the mark of truth, but the system itself has central pins, points of anchorage, to which the rest is coordinated and *on the whole* the sensational order is the least moveable of these, but for pragmatism sensations must work with concepts and with other sensations to be accounted real and many of them fail thus to accredit themselves. I don't myself see much use in crowing over Bradley about this article. When we prevail, it will be by our own views doing more work than others and so leaving them high

· 519 ·

and dry without explicit notice. I confess that I should like most to be able to show the pragmatic method at work and then let follow consequences as they will on public opinion. Any number of concepts remain to be interpreted by that method, the Self, consciousness, etc., even more than the religious concepts.

I am having a rather poor time with my health this summer, but it may mend. Last summer "abroad" made me turn a corner in my life. I no longer want pioneer conditions, but all the establisht comforts of civilization to take care of me. This summer our trees defoliated by a new invasive caterpillar named heterocampa, our lawn completely desiccated by the long drought, 3 chimneys having to be rebuilt and today our spring of water (which has supplied the house for 20 years) gone dry, so that we must either return to Cambridge or haul water from the lake (which we are now doing) and get drinking water from another spring. Precarious "help" and in general always living under "emergency" conditions! How different was the little Inn at Bibury, Gloucestershire where Alice and I spent a fortnight last year! How different the hotel at York! But I'm in a bad mood owing to loss of sleep, so I will rail no more, but sign myself,

Yours as ever,

W. J.[15]

95 Irving St.
Cambridge
Sept. 11. 09

Dear Hall,

I had to take my train yesterday before I got a chance to say good bye to you. I suppose that what you wished to speak to me about was the Lodge affair. Write to me at Chocorua, and I won't write to him till I shall have heard what you say.

I congratulate you on the evidently *great* success of your 2nd international Congress—vastly better than the bigger affairs. The program for next weeks seems to me in particular important, and I hope that the newspaper reports will be full.

Yours, as ever,

Wm James[16]

95 Irving St.
Cambridge
Oct 17. 09

Dear Mr. Whitehead,

I have read your article in the N. C. R. with much interest. The quotations on p. 344 & 345 interested me particularly as connecting S's experiences with others more common. My bad health prevents my taking up any active work in psychics; but I hope that you will yourself all alone make the exhaustive study of Swedenborg, which you suggest.

Of course I agree as to Swedenborg being a bearer of light. I am staggered however by his hugging so close the scriptural text.

Sincerely yours,

Wm James[17]

95 Irving St.
Oct 29. '09

Dear Marshall,

Your "Consciousness" looks as enticing as it is formidable. I thank you "von herzen" for the inscription. I am ordering you my latest in return—you may not get it promptly; the first edition is out of print.

Lucklessly I can't look at your book or at any other serious thing, for I don't know how long, being at present in the trough of the sea, with nervous prostration & anginoid sensibilities—*alg-* but not *hed-*onic!

Good luck to your book!

Yours affectionately

Wm James[18]

· *To F. C. S. Schiller* ·

Cambridge
October 30, 1909

Dear Schiller,

Yrs. of the 20th. along with a ripping good letter from Knox, came yesterday. I have been silent of late because, under the most splendid hygienic conditions in

New Hampshire, I have been getting worse and worse as to my pectoral pain and dyspnoea and have at last gone into regular nervous prostration such as I had 10 years ago after Nauheim. I have written only 26 pp. of MS in the past month and nothing before that for six months, but my brain has now "struck" entirely and I am to lie by and "isolate" myself for many weeks. I haven't yet read Bradley's October article. I wrote to Stout (in reply to your question) proposing *him* for my reviewer, if he would accept. Nothing could *please* me more than a review from you, but I think it would profit the situation more to *draw out* the objectors and *make* them define themselves or give up. Pringle-Pattison would be my second choice. *Your* assent can be discounted and you ought to be kept for better things than praising me.

As for psychology and logic cf. The Meaning of Truth, pp. 152–3. I should like to have your opinion as to my reply to [B.] Russell and [R.] Hawtrey ("2 Engl. Critics.") I don't mind Ladd, anyway.

Your phrase that our critics think it "impossible that for us *experiencing* a real thing should be experiencing a *real* thing" is splendid. Goodbye! write when you can, irrespective of my replying and shed no tear, for I expect to come out of this hole.

Yours ever affectionately

Wm James[19]

Cambridge
November 6, 1909

Dear Schiller,

Your card of the 26th. ult. telling that you review me, etc., just arrives. Of course I entirely assent to the treatment you propose. Your form of attacking the problem is doubtless logically more shipshape than mine, but I think that mine *works* perhaps more easily on the philosophic rabble.

On p. 265 "regulative" would have been infinitely better than "constitutive," tho' you can hardly treat it as a "misprint." Evidently my mind groped for regulative, but blindly took up the other term of the Kantian pair.

No matter for the proof of you on Bradley. I'll await the Jan. number. I write in bed with an inflamed knee—so must stop.

Yours ever

W. J.

95 Irving St.
Cambridge
Nov. 10. [1909]

Dear Kallen,

Your article is a *splendid* one, puts a number of points in a clear and new light, and I am very glad indeed that you've written it.

I enclose Bergson's letter with the passages I spoke of marked. You can return it without comment.

Yours,

W. J.[20]

· *To Nicholas Murray Butler* ·

Cambridge
Dec. 2. 09

I will send you in a week the peace article you ask for, tho I fear it may possibly not be 2000 words short, and otherwise not be exactly what is needed. No matter! it will serve then for elsewhere.

Wm James[21]

· *To Mary Cadwalader Jones* ·

95 Irving St.
Cambridge
Dec. 5. 09

Dear Mrs. Jones,

What a pleasure to hear from a lady who knows how to write a letter!! I have already mailed the 'Talks', with my name on the title page, and have just read the account of the accident, in the Isis, which I return to you. Being myself of the kind who, when they are on the roof of a piazza, lie down on their stomachs and call for their mother to take them away, you may imagine how *my* imagination is fired with admiration of the Arnold Lunn type. I am glad you met him, and he you, and I hope he will be spared for more cliffs & more philosophy still.

 With best regards to you both, and gratification that I should still exist for you, believe me, dear Mrs. Jones,

Very sincerely yours

Wm James[22]

95 Irving St.
Cambridge
Dec. 13. 09

Dear Miss Addams,

I have just read your Spirit of Youth, and think it "simply great." Hard not to cry at certain pages! The fact is, Madam, that you are not like the rest of us, who *seek* the truth and *try* to express it. You *inhabit* reality; and when you open your mouth truth can't help being uttered. I think that this book will have a great and vital influence. I am proud that you should have thought of sending it to me.

   Believe me, dear Miss Addams, your faithful colleague and pupil in sociology,

Wm James[23]

· *To Ralph Barton Perry* ·

95 Irving St.
Dec. 27. 09

Dear Perry,

Miss Emmet needs but 2 (or 3) more sittings to finish my picture. If left to her unaided lights, she will come on January 10th to do so. But if the picture is *needed* earlier she will come earlier. She ought in the latter case to be informed promptly—perhaps you will phone me.

You spoke of a presentation banquet, and I may have chilled you by expressing horror. What I *should* like would be a dinner (*here, I the host*) of the department, visiting committee, and whoever else you wish to ask (*you* the *inviters*). We can seat 12 comfortably in our dining room, and four or 5 more, if required, in the library. The great thing is to define the date, so let us know.

Yours ever,

W. J.[24]

· *To Oliver Lodge* ·

95 Irving St.
Cambridge
Dec 29. 09

My dear Lodge,

I thank you for the copy of Stanley Hall's letter, in the terms of which I find nothing objectionable. I hope they will write their book, and I'm glad that you invited him vainly to contribute to the Proceedings. They become *responsible* now, whereas hitherto Hall & Münsterberg have enjoyed the otium cum dignitate of irresponsible little sneers & digs from a safe distance. Münsterberg has also made himself responsible at last, by having two sittings with Eusapia in N. Y. I am told (not by himself) that he thinks he has caught her—which I doubt! I have

just been talking with Robert Wood (the physicist at the
J. H. U.) & found him in a most satisfactory state of
mind, convinced subliminably, I think, but waiting for
proofs. He has seen her but twice, and proposes now
(this "not for publication"!) to x-ray her and have an
observer read *all* her movements on a fluorescent screen
behind the wall. If the arrangements will work this will
be crucial; and if Wood gets anything crucial, scientific
respectability won't be the thing to close his mouth.

A happy New Year to the whole Lodge family from
yours faithfully,

Wm James[25]

XVI

1910

On 12 January James called on Carrington and Eusapia Palladino at a Mr. Adam's house. He experienced a "queer twisting of my chair." Münsterberg's article in the *Metropolitan Magazine*, received on 21 January, evaluated his own visits. James characterized this writing as "a buffoon article."

In his Oxford lectures, James had devoted a chapter on the influence of Henri Bergson on his thought. One of his letters reveals how deeply this influence touched his own personal life. Later in the month an article appeared by James on "Bradley or Bergson?"

James was honored by a dinner on 18 January with friends to celebrate the presentation of his portrait painted by his cousin "Bay" Emmet. He replied to the speeches by Palmer, Royce, Eliot, and Lowell. Another honor was his election to the *Institut de France* (Academy of Moral and Political Sciences). The announcement was made by Bergson by cable on 22 January. In one sense it was also an honor to receive from a friend a complete set of Shakespeare's works, which James intended to read in their chronological order.

Some of the letters deal with James's efforts to help Schiller win the Waynflete Professorship of Philosophy at Oxford, which unfortunately he lost. James was involved, to the extent that his poor health permitted, in the attempt of others to have the thirteenth International Congress of Psychology meet in the United States in 1913. Academic politics caused the failure of this venture.

Mr. and Mrs. James sailed for England on 29 March to visit his brother Henry who was ill and depressed. While there, he worked a bit on his "Introduction to Philosophy" manuscript. He also wrote an article on his friend Benjamin Paul Blood, which turned out to be James's last article.

From 5 to 16 May James was in Paris on his way to Nauheim. There he met Strong, Bergson, and J. M. Baldwin. Professor Boutroux, who had lectured at Harvard in March and stayed with the Jameses, took James to a meeting of the French Academy. The main reason James was in Paris was for a medical experiment that did not work out. He was alone on this stage of the trip, because Mrs. James stayed with Henry. Both of them did not join William at Nauheim until 8 June.

While at Nauheim James continued to write to his friends, always showing great interest in their activities. One new interest of his own was meeting a young German philosopher, Julius Goldstein.

They all left Nauheim on 23 June. It took them a month to reach Rye via Constance, Luzern, and Geneva in Switzerland, then Paris and London. At Rye James was too weak to see Schiller. It is very sad to read that he had not received any word, even from Blood, about his article on Blood, which he must have thought was well done. Ironically, the last word in that article was "Farewell."

The Jameses, with Henry, left for home on 12 August. The ship docked at Quebec. From there they traveled to their summer home "Chocorua," where on 26 August William James died.

Cambridge, Mass
Jan. 4, 1910

My dear Savage,

It gives me great joy to hear from you again. I have been ignorant of what had become of you, knowing only that since I saw you in California (Redlands, was it?) you had gone into a still worse nervous and mental breakdown. You had used yourself harder than anyone I ever heard of during the previous years, and I suppose you have paid the price. I hope the thing now is liquidated, and that you are well on the way to a stable equilibrium again. It is a pity, it seems to me, to get into the more poisonous *labyrinths* of philosophy, the first thing, but perhaps you have to. I have acquired emancipation from the labyrinths by following the example of Bergson, who has, I think, successfully shown that antinomies & puzzles all come from a misapplication of concepts to the immediate flow of sensible experience. The latter (which is the only *concrete reality* given us), is a continuously changing much-at-once, of which however each of us realizes very little at a time. We enlarge the perspective of it by building it out conceptually, and thus not only learn vastly more *about* it, but control it practically in a wonderfully successful way. But the concepts, being abstracts, are *inadequate;* yet philosophers make the mistake of supposing that they are truer and deeper, that they should be *substituted,* and that as *they* are related to *each other,* so to the profounder philosophic eye the parts of the sensible flux must also be related. This gives rise to the puzzle of dialectic. The concepts are discontinuous and static. The flux is continuous and full of activities. Concepts can only be *compared,* nothing *hap-*

pens among them. The flux is one long happening etc. In brief the remedy is to take up the flux, bodily and *tel quel into the content of philosophy*, and to allow that its peculiarities, novelties, activities, continuities, etc. are a legitimate part of reality. This has, as I said, been a great emancipation to *me;* and if you haven't got my book called A Pluralistic Universe, I should like to send it to you for the sake of the Lecture in it on Bergson. Let me know! It seems to me that this short-circuits Kant, and successfully disposes of Spencer's book on the unknowable. I think one is entitled after this to pass them by entirely, unless one be a historian of philosophy by profession. It is a great joy to me to revert to the concrete flow of my experience, to believe in activities, and think that reality is really being worked out there and growing. All this liberty is denied me by the 'eternal' type of filosofy.

Of *course* truth is relative to the trower, and yet the thing most relative to him at times may be that he should frame to himself a duplicate copy of the reality. At other times not a copy, but some idea which proves a satisfactory *substitute* for the reality would be what best expresses his cognitive relation to the latter.

All that *my* pluralism contends for is that there is nowhere extant a *complete* gathering up of the universe in *one* focus, either of knowledge, power or purpose. *Something* escapes, even from God. This is a purely formal statement. The material specification of the situation is for all science, philosofy & theology to work out together.

Write again, dear Savage, and tell us more about yourself. Such a life as yours used to be ought not to go into eclipse!

Believe me, with all good wishes for 1910,

Yours faithfully,

Wm James[1]

· *To Paul Carus* ·

Dear Dr. Carus,

I send herewith as a candidate for publication in the Monist a paper by Mrs. Fiske Warren on the relation of "science" to absolute reality, which seems to me personally well worth publication. She shows that the universality by which scientific concepts give us so much "control" of nature is paid for by an inadequacy due to their abstractness. Mrs. Warren lately distinguished herself at Oxford by going through the "double first" examinations with flying colours. Being a woman, she got no degree.

Her address is: Mrs. Fiske Warren, 8 Mount Vernon Place, Boston and you will of course deal with her directly as regards the article's fate. I thank you for your recent friendly note.

Truly yours,

Wm James[2]

· To Ralph Barton Perry ·

95 Irving St.
Jan 5. '10

Dear Perry,

It has occurred to me that if Lowell is to be invited to the great portrait banquet Eliot ought not to be left out. Lowell was my pupil but Eliot was my 1st teacher (in the chemical dept. of the L. S. S. in 1861). He appointed & promoted me, and has always shown confidence in me and been an excellent friend. Shouldn't he be asked? I saw Dorr last night who said he had a dinner engagement on the 18th. & hoped our date might be the 17th.

Yours, as ever,

W. J.[3]

· To F. C. S. Schiller ·

Cambridge
January 5, 1910

Dear Schiller,

I have had your long letter of the 19th. ult. a couple of days. We are no wise *at variance*, since we differ only as to a point of exposition and I have freely admitted that your method potentially includes mine. But I won't give mine up for all that, for I realize in every actual discussion what an advantage it is to me to take the opponent midway in the cammin di nostra vita, where he already believes in things that survive his own existence (or his exit from the room) and to call "truth" a relation of someone's belief to such things. Let us each keep on his own way—yours is the more consistently logical and radical!

I have just read Royce's Heidelberg paper, which I find a charming piece of literary composition (all but the mystifying end, about "will"). As an *approach to* stating our view (I think he has tried to) it is feeble; as a *correction* of our view, it is pitiful and inexcusable after all that we have printed. I think the active mainspring of Royce's philosophizing is to be always able to get in some *Wortschwall* of a semi-religious-mystificatory character before he closes. He always does it.

I have just read 75 pp. of Sturt's new book and am hot for the rest. It seems to me a great ethical document so far—just the sort of word that 1000's are waiting for, to be instantly emancipated thereby. It is the expression of such a whole and honest human individuality and what an admirable straight & simple style!

I have been quite ill again, but no matter. I keep cheerful. A happy New Year to you, Knox and the allies.

Yours ever,

W. J.[4]

· To F. C. S. Schiller ·

Cambridge
January 16, 1910

Dear Schiller,

'Tis a great letter that comes from you this morning. Your tho't is far finer grained than mine and I wish it were not too late to incorporate some of your marginalia on the proof into my article on Bradley or Bergson. But I understand it to appear this week, so it must go in without them. As regards Bergson, it is barely possible that I am overdoing his rôle as a pragmatist. I confess that there is much that I fail to understand in his way of thinking, in particular, I don't understand how much his 'intuition' as the philosofic attitude, differs from the usual 'mystical' enlargement of immediate perception. But I don't understand him (as you seem to) to treat that same intuition as in any sense *copying* reality—it is, I think, an immediate experience of reality, only in a wider form than the naif man uses.

If you could see a chapter I have just been writing on 'percept and concept', I think you would be satisfied with my vindication of the conceptual function. I make it 'consubstantial' with perception. I have just re-opened a page to copy a phrase or two of your letter (you didn't say it was copyrighted) and to refer to your article on Thought and Immediacy which I have just re-read. I found it all marked up by my pencil, but quite forgotten! I am better in health than I've been for a year or more. All the result of being forced by a fiendish cold to stay in doors and stop all work for a month! This gave my heart a thoro rest and caused abatement of all its symptoms. Evidently all I need is to be *sedentary* enough and I shall be comfortable. A few years ago and I should have felt like suicide at such a state of affairs—now I welcome it! But how different from *your* life of mountaineering and skiing.

Ever thine,

W. J.[5]

· *To Oliver Lodge* ·

95 Irving St.
Cambridge
Jan 22. '10

Dear Sir Oliver,

I am mailing you, along with this, a "Metropolitan Magazine" which will show you the depth to which the "scientific" mind can descend, in the person of my impudent colleague Münsterberg. It is a buffoon article, as if written by a bagman. The worst of it is that I can imagine no process by which he could possibly be made ashamed of it, so essentially dogmatic is his mind that he will remain convinced to the end that he has "opposed" Eusapia and be proud of the literary performance. Absolutely the *only* "observation" was the catching of the foot by the man on the floor. M–g insinuates that this was done in consequence of his advice, but in point of fact he knew nothing of it till he was told after the sitting. I hope the article will amuse you more than make you angry.

Yours as ever

W. J.[6]

95 Irving St.
Cambridge
Jan 27. '10

Dear Doctor Furness,

It will be hard for you to imagine the degree of pleasure which your letter to my wife has given to us both. That you and Owen W. should both have a stomach for the rather nasty and squabbly dialectics of a good deal of that book of mine is a surprise, but also a reassurance as regards the rest of the world. I am less surprised at Wister's digestion than at yours, however, for after that examination-paper in Philosophy 4, I have known him to be *capable de tout.* I am glad his health is improving, and I hope that yours will never deteriorate. The sight of your smooth and youthful countenance at poor Chas. Norton's funeral was good. It was extra good of you to yield to the impulse to write. We remember the impulse that made you give a mug to our new born girl so many years ago.

I suppose you have read Frank Harris on Shake-speare—be it true or false, I care not, it is at least a *possible* interpretation, and there is more vitality in that kind of handling of the divine William than I have met with before. It has set me on to reading S. in chronological order, which I have never done, and wh. I find intensely interesting. He *was* assuredly an erotic genius and ladies' man of the first order. I don't care what they say. I fear that you will despise the book, and all readers who take it serious. But no matter, if you don't despise *my* works—I am sending you 'Pragmatism' as still worthier of being read aloud than the Pl. U. But you must render no account!

With the love of both of us, especially *hers*, I am very sincerely yours,

Wm James[7]

· *To T. Herbert Warren* ·

Harvard University
January 31st, 1910

My Lords and Gentlemen,

I take the liberty herewith of recommending Mr. F. C. S. Schiller for the vacancy to which he writes me that he is a candidate.

His theories and mine agree on so many points that I may well be supposed to have a partisan prejudice in his favour. I may have one; but I can also see objective features in the situation, and it is only of these that I shall presume to write. Our day has become metaphysical again; publication abounds in all departments of philosophy; the interest both of scientific and of religious circles is awakened and the more thoughtful part of the rising generation everywhere follows developments intently. I know not what rival candidates may be in the field; but I know of no living English philosopher whose works are quoted in Italy, France and Germany with the frequency with which Mr. Schiller's are quoted; and in my country Messrs. Bradley and James Ward are the only authors who compare with him in this respect. His learning, clearness, acuteness, and originality, are recognized and honoured wherever English philosophy is read.

A University like Oxford is looked upon so critically that it must henceforward appoint *leaders* in philosophy, as well as in science, or suffer in the esteem of the competent; and Mr. Schiller is a *leader*, by the voice of enemies as well as of friends. He and Mr. Bradley are by common consent the philosophic leaders at Oxford to-day.

Mr. Schiller's writings, influential and copious as they are, have largely been polemical and occasional-probably because his College duties have forbidden work of a more sustained kind. It is poor academic economy to keep a productive mind busy with tutorial drudgery, if a post be available with leisure for original systematic work. In my humble opinion Mr. Schiller has well earned a right to the amount of leisure which a professorship brings. This seems to me the dominant objective feature of the situation; and my opinion so little depends on my own sympathy with Mr. Schiller's doctrines, that if Mr. Bradley were a candidate, I would urge it just as emphatically on his behalf.

It is hardly possible that the Electors should not be fully alive to this aspect of the situation. But a disinterested voice from abroad often reinforces an opinion; and it is because of the chance that my words may emphasize a little the rank in which Mr. Schiller is held abroad, and the importance of his literary productivity to Oxford's reputation, that I take the great liberty of laying them before you.

Believe me, gentlemen, with great respect, your obedient servant,

Wm James[8]

95 Irving St.
Cambridge
Feb. 16 '10

Dear Mr. Furness,

You return bread for a stone, a fish for a serpent!
Cleopatra and Charmian are more fun than "Truth" and
"Pluralism." The world of Plutarch and Shakespeare is
the absolutely real world, and it is the whole purpose of
my preposterous abstractions to make the common herd
of philosophers believe it.—Only they *won't!* d—n 'em!
I'm sure *you* believe it "on instinct."—Ah! me! if Shakespeare could only have been less *fluent* on certain nights
or mornings, and no less fluent on others, his opera
omnia would be worth more today. With hearty good
wishes and repeated thanks for the monumental edition,
I am ever faithfully yours,

Wm James

95 Irving St.
Cambridge
Feb. 18. 1910

Dear Cousin Bertha,

I was greatly pleased to get your letter three or four days ago. I have heard no news of any member of your family for so many years. I think we are seeing in our family how rapid the process is by which collateral descendants of one person may soon cease to know whether they are related or not. I fear that your children and mine know nothing of one another's existence. Where and how are your sisters?—I hesitate, thinking one of them may be no longer living!

I am growing old, and receiving flattery—but I don't think it hurts me. What does hurt me is a poor condition of my circulatory apparatus, which stops all active exercise—and has reached such a pass this winter that I don't dare to go to New York, for fear of the consequences.

My bro. Henry, who lives at Rye in England, has been quite ill and my eldest son Harry, who is a lawyer aged 30, sails tomorrow to spend a fortnight with him.

Let us keep each other informed hereafter at intervals of not more than a year! I thank you heartily for writing, and congratulate you on the married daughter (what name?) and the well son. I venture, in my wife's absence, to join her regards with my love.

Affectionately yours,

Wm James[9]

· To James McKeen Cattell ·

95 Irving St.
Mch. 9. '10

Dear Cattell,

Yours with enclosure rec'd. I am sorry you don't feel satisfied. I yielded to the combined suggestions of Baldwin and Pillsbury, thinking that the initiative of one man (who in this case seemed to be "officially" designated) is usually the best way out of a quandary. I think the machinery of the Association would have proved too cumbrous for any clear results. I doubt whether either Hall or Ladd wd. have got a majority. I can see reasons for either being president; but I confess that Hall would go against my grain, on account of his essential deviousness of nature and behavior. Münsterberg would probably *organize* the Congress better than any body; but he has also too many foes; and I think that Titchener, whose books have made him as favorably known in Europe, as his Cornell record has here, will be an altogether unexceptionable man. His real rival in my eyes was you, not only because you were one of the vice-presidents, but because of your organizing power, and credit all over this land. After you I should myself have *preferred* Judd, though if both you & Titchener had refused, I should perhaps have thought it my duty to propose Hall.

My own refusal was imperatively conditioned by the state of my circulatory organs. I had to introduce Boutroux to his audience 2 days ago, and could hardly speak for dyspnoea.

Yours ever,

W. J.[10]

· 545 ·

· *To Edward Bradford Titchener* ·

Cambridge
Mch 19. 1910

Dear Titchener,

Amen! I am forwarding your last, rec'd yesterday, to
Cattell, with my approbation, and saying that I am too
busy getting off to Europe to write any more on this
matter, except to notify Pillsbury and Watson of how
things stand, and to leave the matter in their holy
keeping.

My refusal to *act* is not a free-will performance. My
health opposes an absolute veto to all public
appearances.

Yours, with every hope,

Wm James[11]

· *To James McKeen Cattell* ·

95 Irving St.
Cambridge
Mch. 27. '10

Dear Cattell,

I send you the enclosed the moment it arrives, not
knowing whether it may not contribute to make your
journey hither unnecessary.

I confess I shuddered at the idea of both T. & you resigning and Hall or Ladd being the only alternatives, for no one but myself seems to think of Münsterberg as available!

I am exceeding glad that Titchener says yes.

Faithfully yours,

W. J.

· *To F. C. S. Schiller* ·

Lamb House
Rye Susses
April 8, 1910

Divine Schiller,

You will be surprised to hear from me at this address. My brother Henry has been quite ill and my wife and I landed on Thursday at Liverpool, first to spend two or three weeks with him and then to get on to Paris and thereafter to Nauheim for treatment of my bad circulatory apparatus, which has been progressing backwards rather nastily during the past year. Have the electors spoken? And to what effect? I think the decision must have been made. It seemed to me that your only serious rival should have been Taylor; but after reading your testimonials and knowing that neither he nor any other could muster anything half as imposing, I fell to believing that with every allowance made for ill will on acct. of punning, polemic virulence, anti-absolutism and your whole criminal record, they simply would not dare to

choose an inferior man. Heaven grant they may have
been cowards! Let me know quick! I shan't get to Oxford
this time, tho' I dare say that you are ready to give a
series of banquets in my favor. I am so badly broken up
thoracically that I prefer to wait till the therapeuts have
patched me up and to see my friends (or such of them as
I expect to see at all) on my way back in August, re-
surgent like a phoenix from his Nauheim bath. Of course
you are the one I shall chiefly enjoy seeing. Hoping to
hear good news from you speedily, I am

ever truly yours,

Wm James

· *To F. C. S. Schiller* ·

Lamb House
Rye, Sussex
April 22, 1910

Dearest Schiller,

I shake Oxford and its ways from the soles of my shoes—
whatever one may say of America, such an election
would have been out of the question in any of its institutions of learning. A real scandal! But the electors were
courageous! By the way, *at what college is J. A. Smith
tutor?* I am announcing the momentous event to Woodbridge, for an item in the Journal.

As regards the MS, which you send me, the matter of
it is *splendid*—on pp. 9, 10 and 11 you strike into the
very bowels of the subject and I hope that your "logic"

will start exactly on those lines. "Confusion of the judgment when *in use* with the *potential meaning of its words*"—that is göttlich indeed! I borrowed the April Mind from Sydney Waterlow, who lives here, in order to read your review of me, which I duly and submissively did. Incidentally, I tried to read Bradley's article, but whether the fault were his or mine, I couldn't follow its subtleties with any comprehension and postponed it to a later day, returning the number to S. W. I can't recall now what Bradley said of designation, but you appear to have him on the hip most fatally and the *exceedingly* simple terms to which, between Bradley's frankness and your *scharfsinn*, the issue is now reduced, ought to be a great clearer of dust out of the atmosphere. For my own part I find this paper immensely instructive, original and eye-opening.

As for the *manner* of it, I am much less pleased. [D. S.] Miller wrote years ago of Bradley that "he pinches and cuffs his reader like a nasty-tempered child." Don't you keep-a-doing something of the same sort to Bradley? And isn't that apparent "hatefulness" of temper in you (in addition to the punning vice!) perhaps the real ground for J. A. Smith's election instead of F. C. S. S.'s? Bradley never was a rationalist *pur sang*. In his *Logic* the recognition of reality in feeling and in his *Appearance [and Reality]* the passing beyond intellectual relations have made him one of the worst foes of the classic rationalism. Moreover, he is *candid* and becometh ever more so; and methinks the proper tone in which to accept this recentest candor is not that of standing off and triumphing, but of greeting and holding out the hand. If Bradley is a *pistist* with his vision (as of course he now avowedly is and is worth most for being so) speak not of *him* at all, if possible, but solely of the objective value of the vision. You have the best of him in point of truth; he is, I fear, a dying man; why then not let your tone be brotherly and kindly? Such a tone in this article might also heap coals of fire on the electors, if any of them were influenced by the reasons I have suggested. I have accordingly made some pencil scribblings in the margin suggestive of this spirit of conciliation. They are not meant for definite proposals, but only to show the line I would recommend and you will of course disregard them according to your *bon plaisir.*

Since you are at work on a logic, I have yielded to the temptation to send you some pages on "percepts and concepts" from the MS of my introduction to Metaphysics. Heaven forbid that you should assume the labor of *commenting* on the stuff. It simply occurred to me that you might possibly find some of the statements helpfully simple. Return at your leisure, but don't let the stuff get used for lighting your fire!

We are happy enough here, but a yankee misses the absolute privation of *warmth* in the climate. Not positively cold, but *warmthless.*

Ever thine,

W. J.

My MS consists of about 200 pp. so far. I hope about 1/2 of the book. I hear from Paris that my *Pluralistic Universe (Philosophie de l'Expérience)* just out is selling very fast. Who'd 'a thunk it? I don't know whether I wrote you that I am now (along with Teddy R) an associé étranger of the Académie des Sciences Morales etc.—in short a full *membre de l'Institut*—its only foreign *philosopher!*[12]

21, Rue de Surène, Paris
May 9, 1910

Dear Schiller,

I rec'd your interesting letter a couple of days ago and read it to Strong who is himself working on very similar ground—the bleakest of human *characters*, but of monstrous integrity and candor, inhabiting a world of logical "thou shalt *nots*," to talk with whom causes me continual pectoral agony, but equally continual intellectual profit, so I keep it up! He has read me his late correspondence with you about the Will to Believe and I have just copied the major part of your admirable first letter to him for future use of my own. I will make no comment on your letter to me, not being im Stande just now.

You ask about Dr. [Alexandre] Moutier. He is exactly the reverse of a quack, but he performs genuine *Wunderkuren* on a certain type of arterial case to which, alas, he says, I don't belong. Of my case he says cela serait bien plus grave que ce serait bien moins ennuyeux. He advises me to repair to Nauheim again; but at my request, not by his advice, he is giving me some of his electric treatments, just to see what will occur. It is a discouraging experience for me, because Moutier has worked genuine wonders where the arterial tension is very high.

No more today—but assurance of my ever growing sense of the importance of the philosophic work of your pen!

Yours,

W. J.

Villa Isolde
Bad-Nauheim
May 20, 1910

Just this line to let you know that I am settled, taking baths, etc. for the next 6 or 8 weeks and *safe* after a fierce 10 days at Paris, which quite used me up. The wife is still at Rye, but I hope to lure the brother here (and her with him) before the end of the month. Great and calm is Germany. I love to see it. No more today.

Yours ever

W. J.

· *To Horace Meyer Kallen* ·

Bad-Nauheim
May 22, 1910

Thanks for your good letter, sorry for no better news about your prospects, but the sun will rise—"time & the hour" etc. I am here for 6 weeks more of bathing, Germany great & calm about me. I'm glad you take up the cudgels for me against Pitkin. Bergson does the same. I have to confess but partial understanding of Bergson's view of matter, however. Warm regards!

W. J.[13]

· *To Ralph Barton Perry* ·

Nauheim
May 28. 1910

Dear Perry,

Jacobson's article has caused this letter to him to trickle out of my pen—will you kindly address it, as I have no knowledge (which you probably have) of where he may be. He evidently has a gift for clear writing, tho I find a good deal of muddle in his statements here.

Lectures must be on the point of ending, and I hope that you are not reduced to pulp. How glad I am that you're out of the summer school scrape!

I am here alone, taking baths, & considerably depleted by the same. I have a definite objective diagnosis now, of aortic enlargement, which perfectly explains my symptoms, banishes the spectre of "nervousness" which has always confronted me, and will enable me hereafter to live in a much more comfortable way—*convenienter naturae*, in fact. The baths won't cure, but will help to adapt the heart. There's life in the old dog yet!

My love to the Missus and the youthful prodigy, as well as to yourself—may you have a productive summer!

Yours ever,

W. J.[14]

· *To F. C. S. Schiller* ·

Nauheim
May 29, 1910

I have just had a most refreshing 4 hours with Goldstein who is truly an âme d'élite and whom I found one of the easiest men to talk with whom I have ever met. I have had 7 baths and feel rather weakened as always, by them. The chief trouble is in my *aorta* and it is a comfort to have something so definite to serve as an excuse for saying "no" to disagreeable invitations. I am alone here, the wife still being with the brother. Dr. Moutier at Paris immediately said that I didn't fall within his competency. I enjoy the sweetness of this place but can do almost no walking. Goldstein seems to me a great discovery—he makes me feel as if I were myself a great philosopher!

[unsigned]

· *To Ralph Barton Perry* ·

Nauheim
June 12, 1910

I am forwarding to you in another cover a couple of articles by Prof. J. Goldstein of the technische Hochschule in Darmstadt, a man of 35, who seems to me to have an astonishing intelligence, and probably a big future. I think these articles will probably strike you as extraordinarily suggestive of the concrete way in which secular change comes over the ethical world. I hope you'll get a decent vacation, & wife & baby too. Look out for some splendid stuff by Blood in the July Hibbert.[15]

[unsigned]

· *To F. C. S. Schiller* ·

Nauheim
June 12, 1910

I have told Mr. K. Ashida, a Japanese who has been studying in our divinity school, that I would give him a note of introduction to you. Let this be the note—you will recognize the name on his card when he sends or brings it. He is a mature man, speaks admirable English and is genuinely interested in *our* point of view. It would be well if Japan could lay hold of it to *start with* in philosophy—its critical backlook would save them a lot of useless reading!

Wm James

Nauheim
June 22, 1910

Just read carefully Nunn's and your Aristotelian contribution. Nunn, in spite of much good, is simply silly in his ultimate conceptions, and the way you put him underground, playful as a jovial young burying-beetle, does my heart good. All the more pity to waste such powers on desultory polemic work, that counts so little on the formation of *opinion*, when you might be working on a systematic and dogmatic treatise.

My baths are ended and we go to Constance tomorrow, soon to Luzern and thence to Lake Leman, in England last week in July. Address me c/o Coutts & Co. We *ought* to meet! I will notify you direct of any relatively permanent address.

W. J.[16]

· *To F. C. S. Schiller* ·

Lamb House
Rye, Sussex
July 25, 1910

Dear Mr. Schiller,

William is here, very ill and weak. He can neither write or converse. His nights are dreadful and the hours one long fortitude. The Nauheim experiment has been all disaster and every move seems to diminish his slight strength. Dr. [James] Mackenzie, in London, has been a very angel of helpfulness and wisdom. He regards William's condition as one of acute neurasthenia complicated and intensified by his poor heart. We are to sail on August 12th. from Liverpool on the Empress of Britain. Henry goes with us.

William bids me give you his blessing and tell you that you will have the brunt of the good fight henceforth.

I "keep a good hope to the future" for him, for he never was more *vital* in spirit, or wiser in thought than now. Help me, our dear friend, to believe that his work here is not yet done.

Always sincerely yours

Alice H. James

· To F. C. S. Schiller ·

Lamb House
August 8, 1910

Dearest Schiller,

Your offer to come to London to see us is lovely, but my condition had better go without a meeting. Five minutes would mean little and anything more serious would add too much to the fatigue of my journey, rather hasardous [sic] at any rate, to Liverpool. This is the 2nd. note I've written in a month—the 1st being a card to Piddington yesterday. Heart proper not so bad, but atrocious reflex dyspnoea, weakness and anorexia. I leave the "cause" in your hands, yours and Goldstein's in Germany. I don't feel sure about Kallen yet, tho' he's a "noble" fellow. Goodbye and God bless you! You shall hear of our safe arrival. Keep your health, your splendid health! It's better than all the "truths" under the firmament.

Ever thy

W. J.

If you want to write another line, we shall be at Garlants Hotel, Suffolk St., Pall Mall, Thursday night or on steamer Empress of Britain, by Canadian Pacific Line, Liverpool Friday or (I suppose) Queenstown, Saturday. What do you think of Blood in my article in the July Hibbert?

· *To Horace Meyer Kallen* ·

Lamb House
Rye, Sussex
Aug. 8, 1910

Dear Kallen,

Your letter was a great delight and I return immediately the Bergson enclosure. All four of us except Pitkin may well feel satisfied.

I have been very ill for a month, abominable weakness and dyspnoea, unable to write or even to talk beyond necessaries, but I expect to land alive at Quebec about the 19th and proceed to Chocorua. I have been unable to see Schiller, but in writing he takes his Waynflete defeat lightly. What you write of Shackleford warms me up. If angeldom owns a supreme court he certainly is in it—extraordinary scholarly gifts also with all his modesty.

I sent you proof two months ago of my article on Blood in the July Hibbert Journal. Neither you, Blood, nor anyone else makes mention of it to me, barring Goldstein in Germany. It seems to me big literature and I hoped that it would please Blood to see it. Jacks was delighted, but my letter may have missed Blood.

No more, dear Kallen, but affectionate regards to you from us both, and congratulations on your having scored so well in the Bergson-Pitkin matter.

Yours always truly

Wm James[17]

· *To Thomas Mitchell Shackleford* ·

Chocorua
Aug. 21, 1910

Dear Shackleford,

Got safely home but too desperately ill to converse with anyone, least of all with a man so close to me philosophically as you. It grieves me much to forego your visit here, but it is out of the question.

Make the best of Cambridge from where we hear naught but praises of you and your wife, and preserve a tender thought of yours affectionately,

Wm James[18]

Notes

CHAPTER 1

1. G. Stanley Hall (1844–1924) was born in Ashfield, Massachusetts. At the age of thirty-four, he was the first to receive the Ph.D. degree in psychology at Harvard. He taught psychology at the Johns Hopkins University (1881–1888) and at Clark University (1888–1920), of which he was the first president. George Herbert Palmer (1842–1933) was James's colleague in the philosophy department. The letters to Hall are at Clark University.

2. Helen Bigelow Merriman (1844–1933), author and painter, wrote "The English pre-Raphaelite and poetical school of painters," *Andover Review* 1 (June 1884):594–612. The two letters to her are at the Massachusetts Historical Society.

3. Charles Marseilles (1846–1920) was a journalist and a member of the American Society for Psychical Research (afterwards, A. S. P. R.). The letters to him are at the New Hampshire Historical Society.

4. William Benjamin Carpenter (1813–1885) was an English scientist. He published *Principles of Mental Physiology* in 1874. James had reviewed this work in the *Atlantic Monthly* 34 (1874):495.

5. Alexander Graham Bell (1847–1922) was the famous inventor of the telephone and was also outstanding in the education of the deaf. The letters to him are at the Library of Congress.

6. Katharine Barber James Prince (1834–1890) was a cousin, the daughter of the Reverend William James (1797–1868). About 1861 she married Dr. William Henry Prince, as his second wife. He died 15 May 1883 after years of practice as a psychiatrist. After his death "Kitty" moved to Amherst, Massachusetts. The Jameses went to see Shakespeare's play *Julius Caesar* produced by Harvard students in their Sanders Theatre on 19 May. The letters to Mrs. Prince are at Colby College.

7. The baby, Hermann, died on 9 July. About 18 June the James family had moved to 18 Garden Street, the home of Alice's widowed mother, Eliza Putnam Gibbens, and Alice's two sisters, Mary and Margaret.

8. Hall, "Motor Sensations on the Skin," *Mind*, o.s. 10 (October 1885):557–72. Dr. James Jackson Putnam (1846–1918) taught neurology at Harvard. He married Marian Cabot on 15 February 1886.

9. Another cousin, Katharine Temple (1843–1895), married Richard Stockton Emmet in 1868. They lived in Pelham, New York. Mr. and Mrs. Edmund Tweedy were close friends of Mr. and Mrs. Henry James, Sr. Mrs. Prince's sister, Elizabeth Tillman James (1833–1881), married Julius

H. Seelye (1824–1895), who was president of Amherst College (1877–1890). They had four children.

10. Simon Newcomb (1835–1909) delivered his presidential address to the A. S. P. R. on 12 January 1886. In it he made reference to Edmund Gurney's investigations of some "blind drawings" published in the *Proceedings* of the English S. P. R. This reference was the basis of an editorial note in the 29 January issue of *Science*. This editorial evoked from James a reply of "unjust" in the 5 February issue, p. 123. James's letter to the editor in turn was commented upon by Newcomb in the 12 February issue, p. 145–46. The letters to Newcomb are at the Library of Congress. Wilhelm Thierry Preyer (1841–1897) was a German painter, child psychologist, and graphologist.

11. Hiram Miner Stanley (1857–1903) was an instructor in philosophy and art at Lake Forest College (1887–1892). Charles Augustus Strong (1862–1940) was an instructor in philosophy at Cornell University (1887–1889), associate professor of psychology at the University of Chicago (1895–1903), and professor of psychology at Columbia University (1903–1910). Ira Remsen (1846–1927) was professor of chemistry (1876–1913) and president of the Johns Hopkins University (1901–1912). He became editor of the *Journal of the American Chemical Society* in 1904. Charles Loring Jackson (1847–1935) was professor of chemistry at Harvard (1881–1894). Henry Barker Hill (1849–1903) also taught chemistry at Harvard (1874–1903).

12. Edmund Gurney (1847–1888) was one of the founders of the British Society for Psychical Research.

13. John Forrester Andrew (1850–1895) graduated from Harvard Law School in 1875. He made an unsuccessful bid for the position of Governor of Massachusetts in 1886. He was a member of the United States House of Representatives (1889–1893). Richard Hodgson (1855–1905) was born in Australia. He graduated from Cambridge University, England, and lectured there on Herbert Spencer. He was a member of the English S. P. R. (1882–1887). He became secretary and treasurer of the American S. P. R. in 1887. Elena Petrovna Blavatsky (1831–1891) was a Russian theosophist. This letter is at the Massachusetts Historical Society.

14. Lake Chocorua was in New Hampshire. The Jameses occupied their new summer home in September. They called the place "Chocorua." "Howard jr." was probably another cousin, Howard James (1866–1920) who was a graduate of the Georgetown School of Medicine in 1893.

15. The Jameses named their daughter Margaret Mary ("Peggy") after Mrs. James's two sisters. The "image of Mar." refers to her sister Margaret. The letter was addressed to Aiken, South Carolina. This letter is at the University of California, Berkeley.

16. Tamworth Iron Works was the nearest post office to "Chocorua." Dorothy Ross, *G. Stanley Hall: The Psychologist as Prophet* (1972), p. 170, misdated this letter as 1886. Also, on the same page Ross says that Hall's *American Journal of Psychology* first appeared in October, instead of November, 1887. Eduard Pflüger (1829–1910) founded the *Archiv für die gesamte Physiologie* in 1868.

17. Jacob Gould Schurman (1854–1942) taught philosophy at Cornell University (1878–1892) and was its president (1892–1920). James reviewed his book *The Ethical Import of Darwinism* (1887) in *Nation* 45 (1887):376.

Schurman criticised the views of J. F. McLennan and other authors. James's own paper "The Perception of Space" appeared in *Mind*, o.s. 12 (1887):1–30; 183–211; 321–53; 516–48. This letter is at Cornell University.

18. Victor Kandinsky (1849–1899), a Russian psychiatrist, wrote *Kritische und Klinische Betrachtungen im Gebiete der Sinnestauschungen* (1885). Wendell Phillips Garrison (1840–1907) was the literary editor of *Nation*. Joseph Jastrow (1863–1944) obtained his Ph.D. in psychology at the Johns Hopkins University in 1886. He taught psychology at the University of Wisconsin (1888–1927). A note on Mrs. Ladd-Franklin will follow. George Trumbull Ladd (1842–1921) taught psychology at Yale University. His *Elements of Physiological Psychology* appeared in 1887. Jules Ochorowicz (1850–1918) was at one time professor of philosophy and psychology at the University of Lwów (Lemberg) in Poland and from 1907 co-director of the *Institut Général Psychologique de Paris*. He wrote *De la Suggestion Mentale* (1887). Eleanor Mildred Sidgwick (1845–1936) and her husband Henry Sidgwick (1838–1900) were active investigators in the English S. P. R.

19. James McCosh wrote *Psychology: The Cognitive Powers* (1886). John Dewey wrote *Psychology* (1887). Borden P. Bowne wrote *Introduction to Psychological Theory* (1887). Charles S. Peirce wrote the article "Logical Machines." George Croom Robertson (1842–1892) was editor of *Mind* (1876–1891).

20. Felix Adler (1851–1933) founded the New York Society for Ethical Culture in 1876. He was professor of political and social ethics at Columbia University (1902–1933). Wendell Phillips (1811–1884) was a lawyer and reformer in Cambridge. Francis Greenwood Peabody (1847–1936) taught both in the Divinity School and in the philosophy department at Harvard. Adler's lecture "Ethics and Culture" was delivered on 9 January 1888 in Sanders Theatre under the sponsorship of the Harvard Philosophical Club. This letter was sent to me by Mrs. Ruth Adler Friess and is now at Columbia.

21. David Jayne Hill (1850–1932) wrote *The Elements of Psychology: A Text Book* (1888). He was president of Bucknell College (1879–1888) and of the University of Rochester (1888–1896), where this letter is kept.

22. Christine Ladd-Franklin (1847–1930) wrote "A Method For the Experimental Determination of the Horopter," *American Journal of Psychology* 1 (November 1887):99–111. She lectured both in logic and psychology at the Johns Hopkins University (1904–1909) and at Columbia University (1914–1927). The letters to her are at Columbia. Jean Martin Charcot (1825–1893) was a French neurologist.

23. James refers to "Oil on Troubled Waters," *Science* (July–December 1887):61, 145, 191.

24. James, "The Consciousness of Lost Limbs," *Proceedings of the A. S. P. R.* 1 (December 1887):249–58. James studied under Hermann Ludwig von Helmholtz (1821–1894) in Germany in the 1860s.

25. Martha Carey Thomas (1857–1935) was dean and professor of English (1885–1894) and president (1894–1922) of Bryn Mawr College, where James's letters to her are kept. The reference is probably to Edwin Doak Mead (1849–1937), author of the *Philosophy of Carlyle* and the *Influence of Emerson*. He was editor of the *New England Magazine* (1889–1901). In his previous 5 March letter to Thomas, James refers to Mead, whom he was

recommending for the teaching position at Bryn Mawr, as one "who is a most accomplished philosophical scholar and writer, and an experienced teacher." George Santayana (1863–1952) received his Ph.D. from Harvard in 1889 and taught philosophy there until 1912. Alys W. Pearsall Smith, "A Women's College in the United States," *Nineteenth Century* 23 (1888):918–26. This article is about Bryn Mawr. Miss Smith married Bertrand Russell in 1894.

26. George W. Ross was the Minister of Education of Ontario, Canada. George Herbert Howison (1834–1916) taught philosophy at the Massachusetts Institute of Technology (1871–1879), Michigan (1883–1884), and the University of California (1884–1909). James Gibson Hume was appointed to the chair of the History of Philosophy and Ethics (1890–1926). The address at the head of this letter is that of Henry James. William was visiting him and their sister Alice. This letter is in the Archives of Ontario, Toronto, Canada.

27. George Paxton Young (d. 1889) taught philosophy at the University of Toronto. The letters to Howison are at the University of California, Berkeley.

28. James Mark Baldwin (1861–1934) received his A.B. (1884) and Ph.D. (1889) from Princeton University to which he returned after a three year stay at Toronto. James refers to Baldwin's *Handbook of Psychology,* vol. 1 (1889). Francis Landey Patton (1843–1932) was president of Princeton (1888–1902) and James McCosh (1811–1894) taught philosophy there. Francis Bowen (1811–1890) held the Alford Professorship of Philosophy at Harvard (1853–1889). Josiah Royce (1855–1916) was James's colleague, dear friend, and neighbor. Sidney Edward Mezes (1863–1931) received his B.S. degree from the University of California (1884), his A.B. (1890) and Ph.D. (1893) from Harvard. From 1894–1914 he successively taught philosophy, was dean and president at the University of Texas. In 1914 he became president of the College of the City of New York. Leon J. Richardson (1868–1966) taught Latin at the University of California.

CHAPTER 2

1. On 15 May 1890, while Hall was away in Ashfield, his wife Cornelia and daughter Julia were accidently asphyxiated.

2. Katharine Peabody Loring was about to visit Alice James in England. For this close relationship, cf. Jean Strouse, *Alice James* (Boston, 1980). This letter is at Stanford University.

3. Kenneth Mackenzie (1853–1943) was rector of the Memorial Church of the Holy Trinity, Westport, Connecticut (1891–1926). This letter is at Yale University.

4. *Rapporteur Esthétique* (1888) and *Cercle chromatique* (1889) by Monsieur Charles Henry (1859–1926) were reviewed in *Nation* 51 (9 October 1890):290–92. The dating of this letter assumes a week's interval.

5. Auguste Comte (1798–1857) was a French philosopher.

6. James Mark Baldwin gave a summary of his experiments with his child on the origin of righthandedness in *Science* 16 (31 October 1890):247. James

discussed the matter in the 14 November issue, p. 275. Baldwin's letter followed in the 28 November issue, p. 302. James's 7 December letter is long and complicated. The letters to Baldwin are at the Bodleian Library, Oxford University.

7. Samuel Pierpont Langley (1834–1906), astronomer and physicist, was secretary of the Smithsonian Institution (1887–1906). He was a member of the A. S. P. R. Dr. Christian A. Herter, "Hypnotism what it is and what it is not," *Popular Science Monthly* 33 (October 1888):755–71. The "Mr. Forbes" mentioned might be John M. Forbes, the wealthy merchant and builder of railroads. This letter is at the Smithsonian Institution.

8. Thomas Sergeant Perry (1845–1928) was James's life long friend from boyhood. He was the author of *Greek Literature* (1890). This letter is at the American Academy and Institute of Arts and Letters.

9. Henry Rutgers Marshall (1852–1927) was an architect and psychologist. He wrote "The Physical Basis of Pleasure and Pain," *Mind* 16 (July 1891), 327–354; (October 1891):470–97. The letters to Marshall are at Smith College. Carlo Matteucci (1811–1868) was an Italian chemist, physiologist, and physicist. He wrote *Traité des phénomènes electro-physiologiques des animaux, etc.* (Paris, 1844).

10. Henry Sidgwick, "The Feeling-Tone of Desire and Aversion," *Mind,* n. s., 1 (January 1892):94–101. Marshall's "rejoinder" appeared in *Mind* 1 (July 1892):400–403, under the title "The Definition of Desire." Joseph R. L. Delboeuf (1831–96) was a Belgian philosopher and psychologist.

11. Mrs. Ladd-Franklin studied under the psychologists G. E. Müller in Gottingen and Hermann von Helmholtz in Berlin. Ewald Hering (1834–1918) taught physiology at Leipzig University.

12. Hugo Münsterberg (1863–1916) taught psychology at Harvard 1892–95 and 1897–1916. Herbert Nichols (1852–1936) was an instructor in psychology at Harvard (1890–95) and at the Johns Hopkins (1896). He then retired to Brighton, Massachusetts. James Rowland Angell (1869–1949) taught psychology at the University of Chicago (1894–1921) and was president of Yale University (1921–37). This letter is at the Boston Public Library and should be read as of 9 August 1892. Charles William Eliot (1834–1926) was president of Harvard (1869–1909). The Second International Congress of Experimental Psychology was held in London, August 1–4.

13. Frederic William Henry Myers (1843–1901) was one of the founders of the English S. P. R. James met him in England in 1882. This letter's date should read 9 August 1892.

14. Schurman was editor of the *Philosophical Review* until 1902. William James, "Thought before Language: A Deaf-Mute's Recollections," *Philosophical Review* 1 (November 1892):613–24. Theophilus Hope d'Estrella was an instructor of drawing and the first student to enter The California Institution for the Education of the Deaf and Dumb, and the Blind. This post card is at Cornell University. William James, "Review of Alfred Fouillée's La Psychologie des Idées-forces," *Philosophical Review* 2 (November 1893):716–20.

15. Carlo Francesco Ferraris (1850–1924) was professor of law and rector of the University of Padua (1891–96). James received on this occasion two honorary degrees from the University, a Ph.D. and a Litt.D. He wrote "The Galileo Festival at Padua," for *Nation* 56 (5 January 1893):8–9.

16. George Frederick Stout (1860–1944) was editor of *Mind* (1892–1920). He was Lecturer in the Moral Sciences, Cambridge (1894); Lecturer in Comparative Psychology, Aberdeen (1896–98); Wilde Reader in Mental Philosophy, Oxford (1898–1903); professor of Philosophy, St. Andrews (1903–36). E. Ford, "The Original Datum of Space-Consciousness," *Mind* 2 (April 1893):217–18. James's reply with the same title appeared in the July issue, pp. 363–65. Francis Herbert Bradley (1846–1924) was a philosopher at Merton College, Oxford. In the April issue of *Mind*, he published an article, "Consciousness and Experience" on a view of the English psychologist James Ward (1843–1925). The "proof" James refers to is the proof of his article against Ford in *Mind* for 1893. For an account of the Bradley controversy, see my article, "William James's *Essays in Philosophy*," *San Jose Studies* 6 (May 1980):90–105. Alan K. Stout possesses James's letters to his father.

17. Katherine and Henrietta Rodgers were James's cousins who lived in Switzerland. His letters to them are at Harvard. Henry James stayed in the Hotel National in Lucerne about five miles away from his brother. This was Henry's second visit with the William James family.

18. G. F. Stout, "The Herbartian Psychology," *Mind* 13 (1888); "Herbart Compared with the English Psychologists and with Beneke," ibid., 14 (1889); "The Psychological Work of Herbart's Disciples," ibid. (1889). Alexander Faulkner Shand (1858–1936) read a paper, "The Nature of the Subject," to the Aristotelian Society on 20 February 1893, but it was not published.

19. G. F. Stout, "Apperception and the Movement of Attention," *Mind* 16 (1891); "Thought and Language," ibid., (1891); "The Genesis of the Cognition of Physical Reality," ibid., (1890); "Belief," ibid., (1891). Robert Adamson (1852–1902) was appointed to the Chair of Logic and Psychology in the University of Aberdeen.

20. Samuel Alexander (1859–1938) succeeded Adamson to the Chair of Logic and Philosophy in Owens College.

21. Viscount James Bryce (1838–1922) was the famous jurist, historian, and politician who became ambassador to the United States (1907–13). James was elected to the American Academy of Arts and Sciences (Boston) in 1875, but resigned in 1882. Bryce was elected a member in 1893. Josiah Parsons Cooke (1827–94) was the Erving Professor of Chemistry and Mineralogy at Harvard. This letter is at the Bodleian Library.

22. Dickinson Sergeant Miller (1868–1963) received his M.A. degree from Harvard (1892) and his Ph.D. from the University of Halle in 1893. He taught philosophy at Bryn Mawr College (1893–98), was an instructor in philosophy at Harvard (1899–1904), and taught at Columbia University until his retirement. His article, "The Meaning of Truth and Error," appeared in the *Philosophical Review* 2 (July 1893):408–25.

23. Parke Godwin (1816–1904) was an author and editor of the *New York Evening Post* (1836–86). Francois Pillon (1830–1914) and Charles Bernard Renouvier (1815–1903) were French philosophers and editors of *L'Année Philosophique* (1867–72; 1890–) and *Critique Philosophique* (1872–1889). Arthur Schopenhauer (1788–1860) was a German philosopher. James McKeen Cattell (1860–1945) was a professor of psychology at Columbia University (1891–1917). He became editor of *Science* in 1894; of *Popular*

Science Monthly in 1900; of *American Men of Science* in 1906; of *American Naturalist* in 1907 as well as co-owner and coeditor with Baldwin of the *Psychological Review* (1894–1903). This letter is at the New York Public Library.

24. In the beginning of this letter, James is referring to the second annual meeting of the American Psychological Association held at Columbia on December 27 and 28. Edward W. Scripture (1864–1945) taught psychology at Yale at this time. He wrote, "Psychological Measurements," *Philosophical Review* 2 (1893):677–89. The letters to Cattell are at the Library of Congress.

25. G. T. Ladd gave the President's Address, which was printed in the *Psychological Review* 1 (January 1894):1–21.

CHAPTER 3

1. Ferdinand Canning Scott Schiller (1864–1937) at this time was an English philosopher teaching at Cornell University. He had been introduced to James through a letter from James Bryce. The dating of this letter is based on a remark ("A sharp attack of tonsillitis keeps me from writing myself") on 31 December 1893. Cf. *The Letters of William James to Théodore Flournoy*, edited by Robert C. Le Clair (1966), p. 30. The letters to Schiller are at Stanford University.

2. Pierre Janet, *État Mental des Hystériques* and *L'Amnésie Continue* were reviewed in the *Psychological Review* 1 (March 1894):195–99, along with reviews of J. Breuer and S. Freud, *Ueber den Psychischen Mechanismus Hysterischer Phänomene*, ibid., p. 199, and L. E. Whipple, *Philosophy of Mental Healing*, ibid., p. 199–200. G. T. Ladd's *Psychology: Descriptive and Explanatory* was reviewed by James in the May issue, pp. 286–93.

3. F. H. Bradley, *Appearance and Reality* (1893). The "correction" was of erroneous statements about the relation of the *American Journal of Psychology* and the *Psychological Review* and about the unduly restricted scope of the latter. Cf. *Philosophical Review* 3 (March 1894):256.

4. H. R. Marshall, *Pain, Pleasure and Aesthetics* was reviewed by James in *Nation* 59 (19 July 1894):49–51. George Stuart Fullerton (1859–1925) taught philosophy at the University of Pennsylvania. James saw "proof" of Fullerton's article which appeared as "The Psychological Standpoint" in *Psychological Review* 1 (March 1894):113–33.

5. The home address on this letter suggests that it is misdated, since James was in Europe in February 1893. John White Chadwick (1840–1904) was pastor of the Second Unitarian Church, Brooklyn, New York. He graduated from the Harvard Divinity School in 1864. Charles Christie Salter (1839–70) and Joseph May (1836–1918) graduated a year later. Chadwick had referred to James's *Principles of Psychology* in his sermon, "The Price of Moral Freedom," which, along with other sermons, was published in book form in 1893. This letter is at Brown University.

6. Bradley's *Appearance and Reality* was reviewed by Alfred Le Roy Hodder in the May issue of the *Psychological Review*. Hodder (1866–1907)

entered Harvard's Graduate School in 1890. James Edwin Creighton (1861–1924) taught philosophy at Cornell and became editor of the *Philosophical Review* in 1902.

7. Alfred Binet (1857–1911), French psychologist. Frédéric Paulhan (1856–1931), French psychologist, published *Les caractères* in 1894. Baldwin was responsible for a revised edition of *Johnson's Universal Cyclopedia*.

8. James contributed two articles to the *Cyclopedia*—"Person and Personality" 6 (1895):538–40 and "Telepathy" 8 (1895):45–47.

9. The reference is to Baldwin's *Handbook of Psychology* (1889–91) in two volumes.

10. George Malcolm Stratton (1865–1957) taught psychology at the University of California (1896–1935), apart from four years at Johns Hopkins (1904–08).

11. S. W. H. are the initials for South West Harbour, Maine. Ladd's "retort" to James's review of his book was his article, "Is Psychology a Science?," *Psychological Review* 1 (July 1894):392–95.

12. Alpheus Hyatt (1838–1902) was professor of zoology and paleontology at the Massachusetts Institute of Technology. W. Bateson, *Materials for the Study of Variation* was reviewed by James, *Psychological Review* 1 (November 1894):627–30.

13. Dr. Worcester's article, "Observations on Some Points in James's Psychology. II Emotion," appeared in the *Monist* 3 (January 1893):285–98. The other "medical man" was Dr. Henry J. Berkley. The letters to Stratton are at the University of California, Berkeley.

14. Louis Comfort Tiffany (1848–1933) was an artist famous for his work in glass.

15. Alfred Georg Ludwig Lehmann (1858–1921) wrote *Die Hauptgesetze menschlichen Gefühlslebens* (1892).

16. James's article was "The Physical Basis of Emotion," *Psychological Review* 1 (September 1894):516–29.

17. The reference to Münsterberg's *Beiträge zur experimentellen Psychologie* was added to the "note."

18. It does not seem that James wrote an article on the English scientist Francis Galton (1822–1911), who wrote "Discontinuity in Evolution," *Mind* 3 (July 1894):362–72.

19. Carl Stumpf (1848–1936) was a German psychologist and a good friend of James. Grace Norton lived across the street from the Jameses.

20. Edward Bradford Titchener (1867–1927) came to the United States from England in 1892 to accept a teaching position in psychology at Cornell. He reviewed both Wilhelm Wundt's *Grundzüge der physiologischen Psychologie* and Oswald Külpe's *Grundriss der Psychologie* in the journal *Brain* 17 (1894):90–102.

21. William James, "Review of Report on the Census of Hallucinations (H. Sidgwick, etc.)," *Psychological Review* 2 (January 1895):69–75.

22. Baldwin was professor of psychology at Princeton University (1893–1903). The third annual meeting of the Psychological Association was held at Princeton. James delivered his President's Address, "The Knowing of Things Together," on 27 December. He reviewed W. Hirsch's *Genie und Entartung* in the May 1895 issue of the *Psychological Review*.

23. Hodder taught English Literature at Bryn Mawr College (1895–99). D. S. Miller taught there until 1898.

24. Edmund Clark Sanford (1859–1924) taught psychology at Clark University (1889–1920). James's own summary of his presidential address "The Knowing of Things Together" was published in the *Philosophical Review* 4 (May 1895):336–37. This letter is at Harvard.

25. Charles Montague Bakewell (1867–1957) taught philosophy at the University of California (1897–1905) and at Yale (1905–33). Arthur Henry Pierce (1867–1914) taught psychology at Smith College (1900–1914).

26. Hodder received his Ph.D. degree from Harvard in 1897. In James's article "The Ph.D. Octopus" in the *Harvard Monthly*, 1903, he refers to Hodder and Bryn Mawr without naming either.

27. Paul Carus (1852–1919) was the editor of the *Monist*. The letters to Carus are at Southern Illinois University. Albert Gehring (1870–1926) received his M.A. degree in philosophy from Harvard in 1895.

28. James reviewed John L. Nevius, *Demon Possession and Allied Themes*, in the *Psychological Review* 2 (September 1895):529–31. His review of G. Sergi, *Dolore e Piacere*, appeared in the November issue, 601–4. Baldwin's *Mental Development in Child and Race* was published in 1895. Cf. my article "William James's 1895 Visit to Colorado," *San Jose Studies* 5 (May 1979):33–40, for an account of his visit.

29. Külpe's *Grundriss der Psychologie* appeared as *Outlines of Psychology* in July 1896. The letters to Titchener are at Cornell University.

30. H. R. Marshall, *Aesthetic Principles* (1895). James's "notice" appeared in *Nation* 61 (12 September 1895):192–93. James stayed in the home of Mrs. Elizabeth Cass Goddard during his visit. Marshall was the architect of the First Congregational Church in Colorado Springs, 1887–88.

31. Since Münsterberg left Harvard in the summer, James resumed direction of the psychology laboratory. James Edwin Lough (1871–1952) received his M.A. in 1895 and his Ph.D. in 1898 in psychology from Harvard. Edgar Arthur Singer, Jr. (1873–1954), received his Ph.D. from the University of Pennsylvania in 1894. He was an assistant in the Harvard psychology laboratory (1894–96). He taught philosophy at Pennsylvania (1896–1946).

32. This incomplete letter is at Yale. It is dated from a copy of Marhsall's 22 October 1895 letter to James. The symbols are: 'a' represents the psychic side of a physical activity 'A'; 'S' represents the stimulus; 'S plus n' represents pain; 'S minus n' represents pleasure. Marshall was the architect of the home of Rudyard Kipling (1865–1936), when the English novelist lived in America. In writing to a friend on 16 June 1895, James remarked: "The Kipling visit went off splendidly."

33. Daniel Coit Gilman (1831–1908) was president of the Johns Hopkins University (1875–1901). This letter is at Johns Hopkins. Nichols did receive the appointment.

34. E. W. Scripture published *Thinking, Feeling, Doing* in 1895. Titchener accused him of plagiarizing part of his translation of Wundt's *Human and Animal Psychology*. The fourth annual meeting of the Psychological Association was held in Philadelphia in late December. James was overheard to remark: "The best way to settle the matter was by a psychological duel. Let them both react at a given signal; and the one whose reaction

time is longer shall be declared psychologically dead." Cf. Howard C. Warren, *History of Psychology in Autobiography*, ed. Carl Marchison, vol. 1, p. 457. James also refers to President Grover Cleveland and his secretary of state, Richard Olney, in their dealings with England concerning the boundary dispute between Venezuela and British Guiana.

CHAPTER 4

1. *Riddles of the Sphinx: A Study in the Philosophy of Evolution* (London: 1891; second edition, 1894).

2. At the Philadelphia meeting, there was a discussion "On Consciousness and Evolution." Cf. *Psychological Review* 3 (1896):129, for a note on James's participation in the discussion.

3. Edmund Burke Delabarre (1863–1945) received his Ph.D. in psychology from the University of Freiburg in 1891. He taught at Brown University (1891–1932) and was the director of the Harvard psychology laboratory for the academic year 1896–97 on each alternate day of the week.

4. Arthur Allin (1869–1903) taught psychology at Ohio University (1895–96) and at the University of Colorado (1897–1903).

5. David Peck Todd (1855–1939) taught astronomy at Amherst College. He was the editor of the Columbian Knowledge Series. Notice of the third and last volume of the Series appeared in the 7 March 1896 issue of the *Publishers' Weekly*. Hence, the basis of the dating of this letter, which is at Yale.

6. Schiller, "Lotze's Monism," *Philosophical Review* 5 (May 1896):225–29; 232–37; 240–45. Rudolph Hermann Lotze (1817–81) was a German philosopher.

7. Baldwin attended the Third International Congress of Psychology in Munich, 3–7 August. He also was gathering contributors for his planned Dictionary of Philosophy and Psychology. James gave his course of lectures on psychology to the Chicago teachers from 31 August to 6 September. 'M–g' is the abbreviation for Münsterberg. James further refers to Charles Judson Herrick, Henry Herbert Donaldson, and George Howard Parker.

8. Wincenty Lutoslawski (1863–1954), a Polish author and patriot, had visited James in October 1893. He wrote "In Search of True Being," *Monist* 6 (1895–96):351–55. The second "article" (7:156) was just a review of his paper on the chronology of Plato's dialogues. His paper *Un peuple individualiste* (1896) appeared under the pseudonym Henri Erami. James's copy, with his notes in it, is at the Harvard Library. The letters to Lutoslawski are at Yale University.

9. Schiller had become a candidate for a teaching position at Firth College, Oxford, but the position was cancelled. James is referring to the political campaigns of William McKinley and William Jennings Bryan.

10. Nichols, "Professor Baldwin's 'New Factor in Evolution'," *American Naturalist* 30 (1896):697–710. Benjamin Ives Gilman (1852–1933) taught for awhile and then became secretary of the Boston Museum of Fine Arts (1893–1925). James is possibly referring to the neurologist, Dr. Henry Head, who had written several articles on pain in the journal *Brain*.

11. Schiller read his paper "The Relation of Pessimism to Ultimate Philosophy" at the fifth annual meeting of the Psychological Association, and also spent the Christmas holidays with the James family.

12. This letter deals with James's view on the possibility of Münsterberg's return to Harvard. Lightner Witmer (1867–1956) taught psychology at the University of Pennsylvania (1892–1937); he was founder and editor of *The Psychological Clinic* in 1907.

13. Solomon J. Silberstein, *The Disclosures of the Universal Mysteries* (1896), was reviewed by James Seth of Cornell in *Philosophical Review* 6 (1897):325–26. "The story of the book" involved James's financial aid to get it published.

14. Richard Watson Gilder (1844–1909) was editor of *Century Magazine*. This letter is at the New York Public Library. Degeneration and Genius were topics treated in James's October–November 1896 Lowell Institute lectures on "Abnormal Mental States." The lectures were never published by James.

15. Henry Churchill King (1858–1934) was professor of philosophy (1891–97), professor of theology (1897–1925), and president of Oberlin College (1902–27).

16. Marshall, "The Religious Instinct," *Mind* 6 (January 1897):40–58; "Function of Religious Expression," ibid. (April):182–203. George Santayana, *The Sense of Beauty* (1896), was reviewed by James in *Nation* 65 (22 July 1897):75.

17. Schiller was appointed as a tutor in philosophy at Corpus Christi College, Oxford.

18. Henry Charlton Bastian (1837–1915) was an English neurologist. It does not seem that James reviewed a paper of his. Baldwin attended the British Association for the Advancement of Science in Toronto.

19. Münsterberg returned to Harvard for the fall semester and stayed on until his death in 1916. The effective date of James's change of title was 31 October 1897. John Joseph Hayes (d. 1902) was an instructor in elocution at Harvard from 1886 until his death.

20. James B. Peterson, "Empirical Theory of Causation," *Philosophical Review* 7 (January 1898):43–61. This letter is at Harvard.

21. The sixth annual meeting of the Psychological Association was scheduled to meet at Cornell University, Ithaca, New York, in late December. James is referring to the possible successor to Baldwin as president of the Association. James H. Hyslop (1854–1920) taught psychology and logic at Columbia (1889–1902), originated the American Institute for Scientific Research in New York, and was editor of both the *Journal* and the *Proceedings of the American Society for Psychical Research* (1907).

22. Frank Thilly (1865–1934) taught philosophy at the University of Missouri (1893–1904), psychology at Princeton (1904–1905), and philosophy at Cornell (1906–), where he became associate editor of the *Philosophical Review*. Leo Wiener (1862–1939) taught at the University of Missouri (1892–95) and at Harvard (1896–1930) in Slavic languages. Friedrich Paulsen (1846–1908) wrote *System der Ethik* (1889). Thilly's translation, *A System of Ethics*, appeared in 1899.

23. James delivered the Ingersoll lecture on 10 November 1897, not in

1898 as both R. B. Perry (*Thought and Character of William James* 2:132) and G. W. Allen (*William James*, 393 of paperback edition), say. Charles Carroll Everett (1829–1900) taught theology and was dean of the Harvard Divinity School.

CHAPTER 5

1. Santayana was made assistant professor of philosophy in 1898 after nine years as instructor. His lecture, "Platonism in the Italian Poets," was delivered to the Contemporary Club on 5 February 1896.

2. James was elected to the Institut de France (Academy of Moral and Political Sciences) as a "corresponding" member. This letter is at the Institut.

3. William Pepperell Montague (1873–1953) was an instructor of philosophy at the University of California before establishing a career at Columbia (1903–41). Arthur O. Lovejoy (1873–1962) received his M.A. in philosophy from Harvard in 1897. He taught philosophy at Stanford (1899–1901), at Washington University (1901–08), at Missouri (1908–10), and at Johns Hopkins (1910–38).

4. Cf. my article "William James's 1898 Visit to California," *San Jose Studies* 3 (1977):7–22.

5. James received on 12 December 1897 a copy of Lutoslawski's book, *The Origin and Growth of Plato's Logic* (1897). Paul Shorey (1857–1934) was professor of Greek at the University of Chicago. He reviewed Lutoslawski's book in the *Monist* 8 (July 1898):621–25. Lutoslawski replied in the October issue, pp. 140–41. Shorey also wrote a review for *Nation* 67 (1 September 1898):168. The "genius," whom James mentions, might be Charles S. Peirce, who was interested in Lutoslawski's book.

6. H. B. Merriman, *Religio Pictoris* (Boston, 1899). William Torrey Harris (1835–1909) was founder and editor of the *Journal of Speculative Philosophy*. Helen married the Reverend Daniel Merriman (1838–1912) in 1874. They lived in Boston.

7. Elizabeth Glendower Evans wrote "William James and His Wife," *Atlantic Monthly* 144 (1929):374–87. James refers to James B. Peterson, who wrote "The Forms of the Syllogism," *Philosophical Review* 8 (July 1899):371–85. This letter is at Radcliffe College.

8. James was interested in the Boston medium, Mrs. Leonore Piper (1859–1950), and wrote about her. This letter is misdated. The quote "straight scientific path" is from E. B. Titchener's article, "The Feeling of Being Stared At," *Science* 8 (23 December 1898):896–97. This article provoked a reply from James by way of a letter to the editor, *Science* 8 (30 December 1898):956. Then a letter from Titchener followed, *Science* 9 (6 January 1899):36. This debate centered on the relation of involuntary whispering and telepathy as discussed by Henry Sidgwick and Alfred Lehmann.

9. Abraham Jacobi (1830–1919) was a New York City physician and author. The reference is to Paul Flechsig (1847–1929) and his book *Die Lokalisation der geistigen Vorgänge* (1896). This letter is at Radcliffe College.

10. Adolf Meyer (1866–1950) was a psychiatrist and neurologist. This letter is at the A.M.C. Archives of the Johns Hopkins University School of Medicine.

11. Alfred Francis Buck (1868–1924) received his M.A. degree in philosophy in 1894 and his Ph.D. degree in 1906 from Harvard. He taught psychology at the University of Chicago, Union College, and the University of Vermont (1908–?). William James, "Letter on the Philippine Tangle," *Boston Evening Transcript* 1 March 1899 (written on 26 February).

12. James's book, *Talks to Teachers on Psychology and to Students on Some of Life's Ideals*, was published on 22 April 1899.

13. D. S. Miller, "'Will to Believe' and the Duty to Doubt," *International Journal of Ethics* 9 (January 1899):169–95. H. R. Marshall, "Belief and Will," ibid. (April):359–73. William Caldwell, "The Will to Believe and the Duty to Doubt," ibid., pp. 373–78.

14. William James, "Lehmann and Hansen on Telepathy," *Science* 9 (5 May 1899):654–55.

15. Münsterberg, "Psychology and Mysticism," *Atlantic Monthly* 83 (January 1899):67–85. Schiller, "Psychology and Psychical Research," *Proceedings of the English S. P. R.* 14 (1899):348–65. Pauline Goldmark (1874–1962) was secretary of the National Consumer's League and was on the Industrial Board of the New York State Labor Department. She graduated from Bryn Mawr in 1896. James's letters to her are published in Josephine Goldmark, "An Adirondack Friendship," *Atlantic Monthly* 154 (September 1934):265–72; (October):440–47. Roger B. Merriman was the son of a close friend of the James family. Louis Dyer (1851–1908) taught Greek at Harvard (1881–87) and at Balliol College, Oxford.

16. Titchener, *Science* 9 (12 May 1899):686–87. James, ibid. (May 26):752–53.

17. Titchener wrote a personal letter to James on 28 May 1899. His letter to the editor of *Science*, 2 June, ended the "controversy." To the amazement of the examining committee at Cornell, Schiller failed his oral examination for his doctoral degree on 26 May 1897. He did not take a recommended substitute written examination because he had received his offer to teach at Corpus Christi College, Oxford, and the degree would now have only "a sentimental value." Arthur Chase Nutt (1874–1938) was a graduate student in philosophy at Harvard for the academic year 1898–99. His career was spent in teaching English and working with neglected children. George Alfred Cogswell (1869–?) received his Ph.D. in philosophy from Cornell in 1898.

18. Ralph Barton Perry (1876–1957) received his Ph.D. in philosophy from Harvard in 1899 and later returned there to teach (1902–46). He published *The Thought and Character of William James* in 1935. While climbing in the Adirondack mountains, James suffered further damage to his heart, as he had done the previous summer. The letters to Perry are at Harvard.

19. James wrote a preface for the English translation of Lutoslawski's book *Seelenmacht* (1899), which did not appear until 1924 as *The World of Souls*. F. Max Müller published a translation of Kant's *Kritik der reinen Vernunft* in 1881 (reprinted in 1896). Lutoslawski visited the Jameses about the middle of September.

20. The Jameses arrived in Geneva on 29 or 30 September.

21. Münsterberg, *Psychology and Life*. This book was reviewed by Schiller in *Mind* 8 (October 1899):540–43. This review was to raise a storm of protest. James Ward, *Naturalism and Agnosticism* (1899).

22. Henry Havelock Ellis (1859–1939) was editor for the "Contemporary Series." Edwin Diller Starbuck (1866–1947) wrote *Psychology of Religion* (1899) for this series, and James wrote the preface. Starbuck taught philosophy at Stanford (1897–1904), Iowa (1906–30), and Southern California. This letter is at Yale.

23. Schiller, "Philosophy at Oxford," *Educational Review* 18 (October 1899):209–22. Edward Caird (1835–1908) was master of Balliol College, Oxford (1893–1907). J. Royce, *The Spirit of Modern Philosophy* (1892).

24. James had declined to give the Gifford lectures for 1898–99, and had recommended Royce instead. This letter is at the New York Public Library.

25. Howison was in Europe on a sabbatical. Baldwin was spending six months there to work on his dictionary.

26. The "Nauheim baths" were taken in London. Stout, *Analytic Psychology* (1896). "The Common-Sense Conception of a Material Thing" was Stout's presidential address to the Aristotelian Society on 5 November. It was published in the Society's *Proceedings* 1 (1900–1901):1–17. Stout, *A Manual of Psychology* (1899). James Sully (1842–1923) was an English psychologist.

27. James left out "professor of psychology" after Münsterberg's name.

28. The word "undignified" was used by Münsterberg in his "Psychology and Mysticism" article. J. H. Hyslop, "Prof. Münsterberg on Mysticism," *Psychological Review* 6 (May 1899):292–98.

29. John Edward Russell (1848–1917) taught philosophy at Williams College.

CHAPTER 6

1. James quoted from Andrjes Towianski's book (without title, Turin, 1897) in one of his Gifford lectures on "Saintliness." The "little volume" was a copy of Starbuck's book.

2. J. Royce, *The World and the Individual*, vol. 1 (1899). This covered the first series of Royce's Gifford lectures. James saw Royce on about 5 January. Allen (p. 412) mistakenly puts the visit in France in February.

3. The Jameses were at West Malvern, northwest of London, from about 3 to 15 December. Théodore Flournoy (1854–1920) taught psychology at the University of Geneva and was coeditor of the *Archives de Psychologie* (1902–).

4. Allen (p. 408) has written in complete error, "The Jameses made the trip to Hyères, in Provence, by way of Rome, where they made a stopover lasting from early January 1900 until about the middle of the month."

5. Royce was then giving the second series of his Gifford lectures at the University of Aberdeen. Professor Charles Richet (1850–1935) was a French physiologist, who lent to the Jameses his Château de Carqueiranne

near Hyères, where they stayed from 22 January to 2 April. Frederic W. H. Myers has already been noted. The letters to Royce are at Harvard.

6. Arthur Auwers (1838–1915) was director of the Observatory of Potsdam. This letter is in the Archives of the Academy in East Berlin.

7. Schiller, "Note on Prof. Münsterberg's Psychology and Mysticism," *Proceedings of the English S. P. R.* 15 (1900):96–97.

8. Actually, the Jameses stayed in the Hotel Costebelle until 23 April and arrived in Geneva on 24 April.

9. Schiller had read in the magazine *Light* that J. H. Hyslop was to be turned out at Columbia on account of his investigations of the medium, Mrs. Piper.

10. William Ritchie Sorley (1855–1935) taught philosophy at various British universities.

11. Josiah Willard Gibbs (1839–1903) was a mathematician and physicist. Henry Augustus Rowland (1848–1901) taught physics at the Johns Hopkins. Richard Heinze (1867–1929) was a German philosopher.

12. Charles Edward Garman (1850–1907) taught philosophy at Amherst College. Perry taught at Smith College (not Amherst), 1900–1902. L. Clark Seelye (1837–1924), a Congregationalist minister, was professor of rhetoric and English history at Amherst (1865–1873), and then became the first president of Smith College. The Jameses stayed in Nauheim for the month of May. Harry Norman Gardiner (1855–1927) taught philosophy at Smith (1884–1924).

13. William G. Smith taught ethics and psychology at Smith (1895–1900). He then moved to England. Arthur Henry Pierce (1867–1914) taught at Smith before and after receiving his Ph.D. in psychology from Harvard in 1899. This was the third series of "Nauheim baths" (including London), but only the second visit to Nauheim. The Jameses spent June and most of July in Switzerland.

14. Bernard Bosanquet (1848–1923) taught philosophy at the University of St. Andrews. He had previously taught at University College, Oxford. Shadworth Holloway Hodgson (1832–1912) was an English philosopher. Henry Sidgwick died of cancer on 28 August 1900. Dr. Steven William Driver lived at 5 Farwell Place.

15. Benjamin Ide Wheeler (1854–1927) became president of the University of California, 18 July 1899. Evander Bradley McGilvary (1864–1953) was an instructor in philosophy there (1898–99), and then taught at Cornell (1899–1905) and Wisconsin (1905–34). William Jennings Bryan (1860–1925) was the Democratic candidate for the presidency in 1900.

16. Ostend (Oostende) is in N. W. Belgium, where Schiller met the Jameses.

17. The Jameses were at Nauheim from about 24 August to 7 October. Schiller's essay, "Axioms as Postulates," was published in 1902. Münsterberg dedicated his book, *Gründzuge der Psychologie,* to James.

18. William Mackintire Salter (1853–1931) married Mrs. James's sister Mary on 2 December 1885. He lectured for the Society for Ethical Culture of Chicago, 1883–92; 1897–1907. Horatio Willis Dresser (1866–1954) was an author whose writings James used in his Gifford lectures. Mary Baker

Eddy (1821–1910) founded the Christian Science Church. This letter is at Yale.

19. Lutoslawski's "text" was the English translation of *Seelenmacht*. Schiller sent to James a large number of texts from John William Mackail's *Select Epigrams from the Greek Anthology* (1890). James used some of them in his Gifford lecture, "The Sick Soul." Baron Carl Romanovich von der Osten-Sacken (1828–1906) was the Russian consul-general in New York City (1861–70). He then lived in Heidelberg, Germany (1887–98).

20. Thorstein Bunde Veblen (1857–1929), American sociologist and economist, published *The Theory of the Leisure Class* (1899). Maurice Maeterlinck (1862–1949) was a Belgian poet, dramatist, and essayist. Possibly his *Wisdom and Destiny* (in translation), 1898, is being referred to. This letter is at Stanford.

21. Schiller, "On the Conception of *Energeia akinesias*," *Mind* 9 (October 1900):457–68. The Jameses did not leave Rome until 6 March 1901. Mrs. Frazer was the wife of James G. Frazer, author of *The Golden Bough*.

CHAPTER 7

1. Hendrik Christian Andersen (1872–1940) was a sculptor and author. He was a close friend of Henry James. This letter is at the University of Virginia.

2. Sarah Helen Whitman was a Boston friend. Owen Wister (1860–1938) wrote *Ulysses S. Grant, A Biography* (1900). Joseph Thacher Clarke (d. 1920) was an American architect who wrote on archaeological topics. He moved to Harrow, England, where "Peggy" James lived in 1900 and 1901 while her parents lived elsewhere. Thomas Davidson (1840–1900), philosopher and wandering scholar, conducted a summer school for adults in "Glenmore," East Hill, Hurricane, New York. This letter is at the Library of Congress.

3. Perry, "The Abstract Freedom of Kant," *Philosophical Review* 9 (November 1900):630–47.

4. James, "Frederic Myers's Services to Psychology," *Proceedings of the English S. P. R.* 17 (1901):13–23. On their way to Lamb House, the Jameses stopped off at Perugia, Assisi, and Florence in Italy; Luzern, Montreux, and Geneva in Switzerland.

5. Schiller and others wrote *Mind!, A Unique Review of Ancient and Modern Philosophy*, edited by A. Troglodyte, with the cooperation of the Absolute and Others (London, 1901).

6. The "raw Greek" was the word *hule*, a Greek term that Schiller made use of in his philosophy. The reference is to Hugh D. Leigh, one of the contributors to *Mind!*.

7. John George Piddington (1869–1952) was an officer in the English S. P. R. He changed his name from Smith. Mrs. R. Thompson was Myers's medium.

8. Schiller's "dialogue" was published as "Useless Knowledge: A Discourse Concerning Pragmatism," *Mind* 11 (April 1902):196–215. Charles Sanders Peirce (1839–1914) was the founder of Pragmatism.

9. James gave the first series of the Gifford lectures at the University of Edinburgh, Scotland, 15 May to 18 June.

10. The fourth Nauheim visit lasted from about 3 July to 13 August.

11. C. M. Bakewell's article on Davidson, "A Democratic Philosopher and His Work," appeared in the *International Journal of Ethics* 11 (July 1901):440–54. Howison, *The Limits of Evolution and Other Essays Illustrating The Metaphysical Theory of Personal Idealism* (1901). The letters to Bakewell are at Harvard and copies at Yale.

12. Frank Abauzit (1870–1938) translated James's *Varieties of Religious Experience*. Alexander Herzen (1812–70) was an author and publisher. His son Charles, also called Alexander (1839–1906), was a professor of physiology at the University of Lausanne. Rudolf Eucken (1846–1926), German philosopher, wrote *Der Wahrheitsgehalt der Religion* (1901). Kurd Lasswitz (1848–1910), German philosopher, wrote *Wirklichkeiten, Beiträge zum Weltverstandnis* (1900). The Jameses could not find a hotel in the higher places of the Vosges, so they went on to Rye.

13. Mary Everest Boole, "Suggestions for Increasing Ethical Stability," *Monist* 12 (January 1902):236–72. Major General G. R. Forlong lived in Edinburgh.

14. Mary Whiton Calkins (1863–1930) passed all her Ph.D. requirements at Harvard, but in those days, Harvard did not award degrees to women. In his 29 June 1895 letter to a certain "Madam," James wrote, "Miss Calkins certainly did pass, all things considered, much the most brilliant examination for Ph.D. that we have had at Harvard." This letter is at Smith College. Dr. Calkins taught Greek, psychology, and philosophy at Wellesley College (1889–1929). The "masterly book" was *An Introduction to Psychology* (1901). The letters to Calkins are at Wellesley College.

15. Ernest Howard Crosby (1856–1906) wrote *Plain Talk in Psalm and Parable* (1899). This letter is at the Boston Public Library.

16. Edith Franklin Wyatt (1873–1958) wrote *Everyone His Own Way: Short Stories of Chicago* (1901). This letter is at the Newberry Library.

17. Edward Carpenter (1844–1929), author of *Towards Democracy,* third edition, enlarged (London, 1892). Crosby wrote *Edward Carpenter: Poet and Prophet* (Philadelphia, 1901). This letter is in the Michigan State University library. Professor Perry E. Gianakos, of the Michigan State University faculty, kindly called my attention to this letter. He has worked on the Crosby papers, which were deposited in the library by Crosby's granddaughter, Helen Crosby Glendening.

18. Boris Sidis (1867–1923), a Russian-born psychologist, received his Ph.D. from Harvard in 1897 and his M.D. in 1908. In his 15 May 1903 letter to Dr. Mary Putnam Jacobi, James had the following to say about Sidis: "As for B. Sidis, I have known him intimately, admire greatly his high and disinterested character, and think his work *decidedly interesting and important.* He is intractable in harness with others, on account of the intensity with which he sees his own aim and the tenacity with which he defends it. But, so far as I have known him, it has always been a good aim, and if you give him his head a bit, he ends by proving reasonable—at least so far as I have known him. It is a terrible handicap upon him now not to be an M.D. in N. Y. He would undoubtedly if free to carry out his present ideas, have a useful career of psychopathological work." This letter is at

Radcliffe College. The letters to Meyer, as has been noted, are at the Johns Hopkins School of Medicine.

19. J. Royce, *The World and the Individual*, vol. 2 (1901).

CHAPTER 8

1. This letter, which is at the University of Virginia, is to the printer of James's Gifford lectures. James did add an appendix called "Postscript."

2. Perry accepted the offer to teach philosophy at Harvard and remained there until 1946.

3. Oliver Joseph Lodge (1851–1940), physicist, was active in the English S. P. R. The letters to him are at the Society for Psychical Research, London.

4. James wrote "Ingersoll" instead of "Gifford."

5. Edward Lawrence Godkin (1831–1902) was editor of *Nation* and of the *New York Evening Post*. James did not receive an honorary degree from the University of Durham in 1902 because he sailed for home on 10 June. Cecil John Rhodes (1853–1902) was a British administrator and financier. He founded the Rhodes Scholarship Fund at Oxford University.

6. Schiller's "Essay" was "Axioms as Postulates." It was soon published, along with essays by seven other Oxford professors, in *Personal Idealism*, edited by Henry Cecil Sturt (London, 1902). Albert Venn Dicey (1835–1922) was the Vinerian professor of English law at Oxford. Louis Dyer (1851–1908), an 1874 graduate from Harvard, taught Greek at Harvard, Cornell, and Balliol College, Oxford.

7. This letter seems misdated by a day or two. James reviewed *Personal Idealism* in *Mind* 12 (January 1903):93–97.

8. James H. Leuba (1868–1946), born in Switzerland, taught at Bryn Mawr College (1898–1933).

9. Schiller's manuscript probably dealt with the question of eugenics on which he often wrote. Sir Francis Galton also wrote on eugenics. Alexander Campbell Fraser (1819–1914) taught philosophy at Edinburgh (1856–91), and was the editor of Bishop George Berkeley's (1685–1753) *Works*.

10. This letter is probably addressed to Sir George Archdall O'Brien Reid (1860–1929) from Scotland. It is found among the H. G. Wells papers at the University of Illinois. Two entries in James's diary in 1905 refer to this Reid. Herbert George Wells (1866–1946) was the English novelist. James is probably referring to Wells's *Anticipations of the Reaction of Mechanical and Scientific Progress upon Human Life and Thought* (1901). James's lectures were published in the middle of June as *Varieties of Religious Experience: A Study in Human Nature*.

11. In his 13 August 1902 letter to Eliot, James wrote about Schiller and the Ingersoll lectureship: "Your strictures on his circular of information seemed to me . . . based on misapprehension. He is a big man, and he has a lot of fresh 'human documents', and I know of nobody who is prepared to treat the subject in so unconventional a manner, or who would be likely so to arouse public attention."

12. John Shaw Billings (1839–1913) was a surgeon, librarian of the New York City Public Library, and chairman of the Board of the Carnegie Institution. On this topic, cf. my article "William James's Aid of Peirce," *Transactions of the C. S. Peirce Society, A Quarterly Journal in American Philosophy* 12 (1976):71–76. This letter is at the New York Public Library.

13. Leigh R. Gregor married Mrs. James's sister, Margaret M. Gibbens, 1 June 1899. Ferdinand Bôcher (1832–1902) was a professor in the modern language department at Harvard (1871–1902).

14. In the "Conclusions" to his book, James referred to chapters 8 to 12 of Marshall's book, *Instinct and Reason*.

15. James lectured on 14 and 15 July. Santayana, "The Search for the True Plato," *The International Monthly* 5 (January–June, 1902):185–99.

16. Wilhelm Ostwald (1853–1932), chemist and philosopher, wrote *Vorlesungen über Naturphilosophie* in 1901. James was to review Myers's book *Human Personality and Its Survival of Bodily Death*.

17. Schiller reviewed *Varieties of Religious Experience* in *Nation* 75 (21 August 1902):155. John McTaggart Ellis McTaggart (1866–1925) taught philosophy at Cambridge University. His book was published in 1901.

18. Jane Addams (1860–1935) was the founder of the Hull House settlement in Chicago; she was a social reformer and peace worker. She met James when he visited Chicago. The letters to her are at Swarthmore College.

19. Mary Putnam Jacobi (1842–1906) was a medical doctor in New York City, as was her husband, Abraham Jacobi. This letter is at Radcliffe College. The date assigned seems to fit James's state of health at this time. Dr. Joseph Roy Hawley (1871–1922) wrote *The New Animal Cellular Therapy* (Chicago, 1901). Dr. William Wilberforce Baldwin met James in Florence, Italy, in 1892.

20. C. A. Strong's book was published in 1903. This letter is at the New York Public Library.

21. A. O. Lovejoy, "Religion and the Time-Process," *American Journal of Theology* 6 (1902):439–72. This letter is at the Johns Hopkins University.

22. This firm published James's *Varieties of Religious Experience*. His "former little book" was *Human Immortality* (1898). This letter is in the possession of Longman, Inc.

23. G. T. Ladd, *Outlines of Descriptive Psychology* (1902).

CHAPTER 9

1. This letter is incorrectly dated as 1908 in *The Works of William James: Essays in Radical Empiricism* (Harvard, 1976) This letter is at Williams College.

2. James was an original member of the National Institute of Arts and Letters which was founded in 1898 as an offspring of the American Social Science Association.

3. Edgar B. Van Winkle (1842–1920) was an engineer and longtime friend. This letter is at the University of Rochester.

4. Peirce lectured on "Pragmatism as a Principle and Method of Right Thinking," 26 March to 14 May 1903.

5. Stout was attempting to change from Oxford to St. Andrews University. David Irons (1870–1907), born in Scotland, received his Ph.D. from Cornell in 1894. He was professor of philosophy at Bryn Mawr College (1900–1907).

6. Emerson Hall houses the Harvard philosophy department. This letter is at the Boston Public Library.

7. Hieronymus Georg Zeuthen (1839–1920) was a professor of mathematics and secretary of the Academy. This letter is at the Academy in Copenhagen.

8. Schiller soon published a collection of his essays entitled *Humanism*. Miss Alice Johnson was secretary of the English S. P. R. and editor of the Society's *Proceedings*. She refused to publish one of Schiller's reviews. James, "Review of F. W. H. Myers's *Human Personality and Its Survival of Bodily Death*," *Proceedings of the S. P. R.* 18 (1903):22–33. Mrs. Dyer attempted suicide. Addison Webster Moore (1866–1930) taught philosophy at the University of Chicago (1895–1929). He studied under Schiller while at Cornell. John Dewey (1859–1952) at this time also taught at Chicago.

9. S. E. Mezes has been noted before. David Camp Rogers (1878–1959) stayed on at Harvard until 1909, when he went to the University of Kansas (1909–14) and then to Smith College (1914–42). George Rowland Dodson (1865–1939) taught at Washington University until 1934. Charles Theodore Burnett (1873–1946) taught psychology at Bowdoin College (1904–44).

10. Edward Lee Thorndike (1874–1949) taught psychology at Teachers College, Columbia University (1899–1941). Margaret Floy Washburn (1871–1939) taught at Vassar College.

11. Walter Taylor Marvin (1872–1944) taught philosophy at Adelbert College, (Case) Western Reserve University (1899–1905), at Princeton (1905–10), and at Rutgers University, where this letter is found. He wrote *Introduction to Systematic Philosophy* (1903).

12. J. R. Angell, "The Relations of Structural and Functional Psychology to Philosophy," *The Decennial Publications of the University of Chicago*, first series, vol. 3 (1903):55–72. George Herbert Mead (1863–1931), "The Definition of the Psychical," ibid., pp. 77–112. Mead also taught at Chicago. This letter is at Yale.

13. This letter is at the Academy in Rome.

14. James is referring to the plays of the French writer Eugène Brieux (1858–1932): *L'Evasion* (1896); *Les Avariés*; *L'Engrenage* (1894). This letter is at the Library of Congress.

15. Sarah N. Cleghorn was a leader in the antivivisection movement. James assumed that the writer was male, since only initials of the name were used. This letter is at the New York State Library, Albany.

16. Baldwin left Princeton for the Johns Hopkins in Baltimore.

17. Schiller had sent the preface proof of his book *Humanism*, which was published in November. Morton Prince (1854–1929), physician and psychiatrist, wrote *The Nature of Mind and Human Automatism* (1885). Prince was professor of neurology at Tufts College, and became editor of the *Journal of Abnormal Psychology* in 1906. Henri Louis Bergson (1859–

1941). At this time James was reading his *Essai sur les donnés immédiates de la conscience* (1889), *Matière et mémoire* (1896), and "Introduction à la Metaphysique," *Revue de la Metaphysique et Morale*, January 1903. On 6 February 1903 James wrote to Bergson expressing a desire to meet him in Paris, but later cancelled such a plan.

18. James, "Reminiscences of Thomas Davidson," published in *Memorials of Thomas Davidson*, edited by William Knight, 1907. This letter is at Columbia University.

19. James, "A Case of Automatic Drawing," *Popular Science Monthly* 64 (January, 1904):195–201. This letter identifies the "case" as Mr. C. H. Perkins.

20. Josephine Shaw Lowell also belonged to the New England Anti-Imperialist League, which protested the American government's treatment of the insurrectionists in the Philippine Islands under the leadership of Emilio Aguinaldo. This letter is at Harvard. The "General" was Major General Elwell Stephen Otis (1838–1909).

CHAPTER 10

1. Horace Fletcher (1849–1919) published a number of books on diet and nutrition.

2. James also retracted his refusal to be president of the Psychological Association for 1904.

3. James (unsigned), "Schiller's *Humanism*," *Nation* 78 (3 March 1904):175–76. Royce, "The Eternal and the Practical," *Philosophical Review* 13 (March 1904):113–42. William Osler (1849–1919) at this time was at the Johns Hopkins University Medical School. Hastings Rashdall (1858–1924) taught at New College, Oxford (1895–1917). Thomas Mitchell Shackleford (1859–1927) was Chief Justice of the Supreme Court of the State of Florida at this time and widely read in philosophy.

4. Münsterberg, "The International Congress of Arts and Science," *The Journal of Philosophy, Psychology, and Scientific Methods* 1 n. 1 (7 January 1904):1–8. James's name appeared on page six. Cattell was the joint owner of this new journal after he broke away from coownership of the *Psychological Review*. This point has been developed in my article "William James's *Essays in Philosophy*," *San Jose Studies* 6 (May 1980):98–101. Georg Cantor (1845–1918) was a German mathematician and logician. James probably was referring to Cantor's *L'Infini mathématique* (1896).

5. James Houghton Woods (1864–1935) was appointed an instructor in philosophy at Harvard in 1903 without a salary. He later became chairman of the department. Miller went to Columbia University.

6. J. H. Leuba, "Professor William James's Interpretation of Religious Experience," *International Journal of Ethics* 14 (April 1904):322–39. Charles Henry Rieber (1866–1948) taught logic (1903–21) and philosophy (1921–36) at the University of California, Berkeley. Bakewell reviewed Strong's book *Why the Mind Has a Body* in the *Philosophical Review* 13 (March 1904):220–29.

7. Alfred Edward Taylor (1869–1945) wrote *Elements of Metaphysics* in

1903 and "Side Lights on Pragmatism," *McGill University Magazine* 3 (1903–4):44–66. Albion Woodbury Small (1854–1926) was professor of sociology and dean of the Graduate School of Arts and Literature at the University of Chicago. He was partly in charge of the St. Louis Congress. Schiller thought that he had been invited to attend. George Edward Moore (1873–1958) taught philosophy at Cambridge University. He wrote, "Jahresbericht über Philosophy in the United Kingdom for 1902," *Archiv* 4 (1904):258–64.

8. F. H. Bradley, "On Truth and Practice," *Mind* 13 (July 1904):309–35.

9. James, "Humanism and Truth," *Mind* 13 (October 1904):457–75. Schiller, "In Defense of Humanism," ibid., pp. 525–42.

10. Stout, "Primary and Secondary Qualities," *Proceedings of the Aristotelian Society* 4 (1903–4):141–60. Leonard Trelawney Hobhouse (1864–1929), British sociologist and philosopher, wrote "Faith and the Will to Believe" ibid., pp. 87–110.

11. Perry gave his "adhesion" to James's article "Does Consciousness Exist ?", *Journal of Philosophy, etc.* 1 (1 September 1904):477–91. Edwin Bissell Holt (1873–1946) stayed on at Harvard until 1918 to teach psychology, and then moved to Princeton University as a visiting professor (1926–36).

12. President B. I. Wheeler of the University of California had invited James, Dewey, and Schiller to teach in the 1905 summer school. Harald Höffding (1843–1931), Danish philosopher, visited James before and after the St. Louis Congress. James had Höffding's book translated and published as *The Problems of Philosophy* (1905).

13. Henry James visited America from 30 August 1904 to 5 July 1905. Katherine Prescott Wormeley was the American biographer and translator of the novels of Honoré de Balzac.

14. The Deweys lost their eight year old son, Gordon, while they were vacationing in Europe prior to Dewey's joining the faculty of Columbia University. This letter is at Southern Illinois University.

15. K. G. Adolf von Harnack (1851–1930) was a German theologian. C. Lloyd Morgan (1852–1936) was an English psychologist, biologist, and philosopher.

16. Reverend Frederic Rowland Marvin (1847–1919) was an author. Stephen Pearl Andrews (1812–86), reformer and linguist, debated with Henry James, Sr., in the pages of the *New York Tribune* in 1850–52. This letter is at the Huntington Library.

17. J. M. Baldwin, "A Word of Rejoinder to Professor A. W. Moore," *Psychological Bulletin* 1 (15 November 1904):424–29. The reference to Schiller is on page 426, footnote.

18. H. R. Marshall's eight articles (running from 9 June to 10 November 1904) appeared in the *Journal of Philosophy, etc.*, not in the *Philosophical Review*.

19. James Hazen Hyde (1876–1959), philanthropist, inaugurated a French exchange professorship with Harvard. James declined to lecture at the Sorbonne University in 1905.

20. Kuno Francke (1855–1930) taught German at Harvard, 1884–1917.

CHAPTER 11

1. This is a typed copy of the lost original letter. It is at Harvard. Frederick James Eugene Woodbridge (1867–1940) taught philosophy at Columbia (1902–37). He was a co-owner and editor of the *Journal of Philosophy, Psychology, and Scientific Methods*. G. S. Fullerton, *A System of Metaphysics* (1904).

2. Cf. J. C. Kenna, "Ten Unpublished Letters from William James to Francis Herbert Bradley," *Mind* 75 (July 1966):309–31. This complements Bradley's letters to James as found in R. B. Perry.

3. Horace William Brindley Joseph (1867–1943), English philosopher, wrote "Prof. James on 'Humanism and Truth'," *Mind* 14 (January 1905):28–41. In reply James wrote "Humanism and Truth Once More," ibid., (April 1905):190–98. James also wrote "The Thing and Its Relations," *Journal of Philosophy, Psychology, and Scientific Methods* (later, just *Journal of Philosophy*, as is now common) 2 (19 January 1905):29–41; "The Essence of Humanism," ibid. (2 March 1905):113–18. C. H. Rieber, "Pragmatism and the a priori," vol. 1 (1904):72–91; C. M. Bakewell, "Latter-day Flowing Philosophy," ibid., pp. 92–114.

4. For the background leading up to this appointment, cf. my article "William James and Stanford University: 1898–1905," *San Jose Studies* 1 (February 1975):9–23.

5. An unsigned article "Professor Wilhelm Ostwald" appeared in the *Popular Science Monthly* 67 (October 1905):571–73. This letter suggests that James wrote it. Ostwald was a visiting lecturer at Harvard, both in chemistry and philosophy, 1905–6 academic year.

6. Schiller, "On Preserving Appearances," *Mind* 12 (July 1903):341–54.

7. John Grier Hibben (1861–1933) taught logic at his alma mater, Princeton University (1891–1912), when he became the fourteen president of the University. Hibben was instituting a tutorial system at Princeton and needed five tutors for the fall semester. Alexander Thomas Ormond (1847–1915) was professor of mental science and logic at Princeton until he became president of Grove City College in 1913. This letter is at Princeton.

8. James was returning home after visits to Greece and Italy. His cousins were Katherine and Henrietta Rodgers. His colleague was Barrett Wendell (1855–1921), who was a professor of English at Harvard (1880–1917), and was lecturing in Dijon. Edward Carpenter (1844–1929) was an English writer on social subjects. Edward Douglas Fawcett (1866–1960) was an English author.

9. Sir Patrick Geddes (1854–1932) was a biologist, sociologist, and educator. This letter is at the National Library of Scotland.

10. Victoria Lady Welby was a friend of both Schiller and Peirce. In 1903 James received a copy of her book *What Is Meaning?* James did not have a chance to visit her. This letter is at York University.

11. Wendell's play was published in 1902. Dr. Rupert Norton (1867–1914) at this time was the medical director of a large American life insurance company in Paris. In 1906 he returned to the Johns Hopkins Hospital

in Baltimore to become its assistant superintendent. He was the son of James's Cambridge friend Charles Eliot Norton.

12. For the first time in his life, James met Bergson on 28 May in the apartment of Dr. Norton.

13. James spent the night of Wednesday, 31 May, and the day of Thursday, 1 June, with Schiller at Oxford. Mistakenly quoting James's diary for 31 May, Allen (p. 446) dramatically wrote that James slept in a "bathtub." All that this letter and James's diary for 1 June say is that he slept in "a bath room"—perhaps on a cot, but this is only guessing. Howard Vincente Knox (1868–1960), a military friend of Schiller, wrote "Mr. Bradley's 'Absolute Criterion'," *Mind* 14 (April 1905):210–20. A sure topic of conversation with Schiller was "Pragmatism." Schiller had written "The Definition of 'Pragmatism' and 'Humanism'," *Mind* 14 (April 1905):235–240, and C. S. Peirce had written "What Pragmatism Is," *Monist* 15 (April 1905):161–81. He sent a copy to Schiller. Cf. my article "Peirce and Schiller and Their Correspondence," *Journal of the History of Philosophy* 11 (July 1973):363–86.

14. In 1904 the American Academy of Arts and Letters was founded as an inner body of the National Institute of Arts and Letters. Robert Underwood Johnson (1853–1937) was secretary of both. He was an editor of *Century Magazine* (1873–1913). This letter is at the Institute. It is the follow-up to James's 17 June 1905 letter now printed in Geoffrey T. Hellman's article "Profiles" in the *New Yorker* 52 (23 February 1976):43–81.

15. After James returned from Europe, he went to Chicago to give a series of five lectures at the University from 30 June to 7 July. He spent the weekend of 1 and 2 July at Glen Arden, the name of the estate of Mrs. Wilmarth on Lake Geneva, Wisconsin. Her daughter Anna married Harold Ickes, secretary of the interior in the cabinets of Roosevelt and Truman. James had visited Mrs. Wilmarth previously in August 1896. This letter is at Stanford. Mary Salter and her husband William lived in Chicago at this time.

16. On 27 July James lectured on "Witchcraft," and on the following day on "Indvidualism," according to his diary. This letter also mentions only two lectures. However, the editors of James's book, *Pragmatism* (Harvard, 1975):296–98, included in an appendix James's notes for the latter lecture, but all the evidence contradicts their raising the possibility that James even intended to repeat the entire five Chicago lectures at "Glenmore" ("Plenty of opportunity existed for the rest of the series to be given," p. 279), the first of the alleged possible series being on "Individualism." Gustav Theodor Fechner (1801–87) was a German philosopher, physicist, and psychologist. James had been recently reading his *Tagesansicht* and *Seelenfrage*. Morris Raphael Cohen (1880–1947) was born in Russia, received his Ph.D. from Harvard (1906), and taught philosophy at the City College of New York (1912–38).

17. R. F. Alfred Hoernlé (1880–1943) was born in Germany, educated at Oxford, taught philosophy at Harvard (1913–20) and in South Africa, where he died. He wrote "Pragmatism versus Absolutism: Part I," *Mind* 14 (July 1905):297–334.

18. It does not seem that Marshall published another book until 1909.

19. Carveth Read (1848–1931) taught philosophy at the University of London. He wrote *The Metaphysics of Nature* (1905).

20. Bakewell was beginning his tenure at Yale University (1905–33). Roswell Parker Angier (1874–1946) received his Ph.D. from Harvard in 1903. In 1906 he joined the Yale faculty in psychology and remained there until 1941.

21. Hoernlé, "Pragmatism versus Absolutism: Part II," *Mind* 14 (October 1905):441–78.

22. Stout, "Things and Sensations," *Proceedings of the British Academy* (1905). James, "The Knowing of Things Together," *Psychological Review* 2 (1895):105–24.

23. In 1898 James wrote an introduction to Boris Sidis's *The Psychology of Suggestion*. This letter is dated from a note from Jerome D. Greene, Eliot's secretary, to James, 25 October 1905.

24. The American Philosophical and Psychological Associations met at Harvard 27 and 28 December in Emerson Hall, which had just been opened. Allen (p. 450) incorrectly wrote: "On New Year's Day James started alone for California."

25. Dewey was president of the Philosophical Association for that year. Edward Emerson was present for the occasion of the dedication of the building to his father's memory. Perry did become chairman of the department in 1906.

CHAPTER 12

1. James was elected to the National Academy of Sciences in 1903. George Ellery Hale (1868–1938), astronomer, was the director of the Mt. Wilson Observatory in Pasadena, California.

2. Schiller, "Plato and His Predecessors," *Quarterly Review* 204 (January 1906):62–88. Schiller, "Faith, Reason and Religion," *Hibbert Journal* 4 (January 1906):329–45. Henri Poincaré (1854–1912), French scientist, published *La Valeur de la Science* in 1905. Ernst Mach (1838–1916) was an Austrian physicist and philosopher. His book also appeared in 1905. Richard Hodgson died on 20 December 1905 in Boston. James declined to give a course of lectures at the Sorbonne University in Paris in 1906–7. Gilbert Keith Chesterton (1874–1936), English author, published *Heretics* in 1905.

3. This letter was supplied by Miss Dorothy Collins, Chesterton's literary executor.

4. A. E. Taylor, "Truth and Consequences," *Mind* 15 (January 1906):81–93.

5. James declined the Berlin University exchange professorship for 1906–7.

6. Schiller, "Is Absolute Idealism Solipsistic?" *Journal of Philosophy* 3 (February 1906):85–89. James used Friedrich Paulsen's *Introduction to Philosophy* as a text. Copies of the syllabus for this new course are preserved both at Harvard and at Stanford.

7. David Starr Jordan (1851–1931), scientist, was the first president of Stanford University. For the details of James's stay at Stanford, cf. my article, "William James and Stanford University: 1906," *San Jose Studies* 1 (May 1975):28–43.

8. William Ernest Hocking (1873–1966) taught philosophy at the University of California (1906–8) before moving to Yale and then to Harvard. He wrote "The Transcendence of Knowledge," *Journal of Philosophy* 3 n. 1 (4 January 1906):5–12.

9. James represented Eliot at the meeting of the Association of American Universities in San Francsco and Berkeley, 14–17 March. Andrew Fleming West (1853–1943) was dean of the Princeton Graduate School. Charles Richard van Hise (1857–1918) was president of Wisconsin University. William Henry Carpenter (1853–1936) was professor of Germanic philology at Columbia University. Ernest De Witt Burton (1856–1925) was professor of New Testament literature at the University of Chicago. Theodore S. Woolsey (1852–1929) was professor of international law at Yale.

10. Perry wrote *The Apporach to Philosophy* (1905). Nathaniel Southgate Shaler (1841–1906), a geologist, was dean of the Lawrence Scientific School at Harvard.

11. James is referring to the great earthquake that struck the city of San Francisco and the entire peninsula on 18 April. Since classes were cancelled, the Jameses left for home on 26 April.

12. Frank Angell (1857–1939) taught psychology at Stanford (1892–1923). This letter is at Harvard.

13. Cattell was the editor of *Science*, in the May issue of which appeared James's article "Stanford's Ideal Destiny."

14. Schiller reviewed Henry Sturt, *Idola Theatri*, in *Nation* 83 (26 July 1906):85–86 and H. H. Joachim, *The Nature of Truth, ibid.* (July 12):42. Schiller's article on A. E. Taylor was entitled "Pragmatism and PseudoPragmatism," *Mind* 15 (July 1906):375–90. John Dewey, "The Experimental Theory of Knowledge," *ibid.*, 293–307; J. S. Mackenzie, "The New Realism and the Old Idealism," *ibid.*, 308–28.

15. Schiller was preparing to edit another volume of essays. Julius Goldstein (1873–1929) taught philosophy in the Technische Hochschule in Darmstadt, Germany. Mark Anthony de Wolfe Howe (1864–1960) was an author and editor.

16. Horace M. Kallen (1882–1974) at this time was a graduate student at Harvard. Later he taught philosophy at the University of Wisconsin (1911–18) and then at the New School for Social Research in New York City. The letters to Kallen are at the American Jewish Archives.

17. Benjamin Apthorp Gould Fuller (1879–1956) received a Ph.D. in philosophy from Harvard in 1906. He taught intermittently at Harvard (1906–20), at the University of Cincinnati (1924–30), and at the University of Southern California (1931–47). He wrote *A History of Philosophy*.

18. James did not accept the "Paris lectureship" for 1906–7 at the Sorbonne University. Henrietta Dorrington Rodgers died on 25 August at the age of 62.

19. The Lowell lectures were delivered in Boston from 14 November to 8 December. James resigned the presidency of the American Society of Naturalists prior to its annual meeting in late December. C. B. Davenport (1866–1944), a biologist, is listed in the Society's records as president for 1906.

20. On 27–29 December at Columbia University, four groups met to-

gether: the Philosophical and Psychological Associations, the American Society of Naturalists and the American Association for the Advancement of Science. James read his presidential address "The Energies of Men" to a joint meeting of the philosophers and psychologists. His paper was published in the *Philosophical Review* 16 (January 1907):1–20. William Ernest Castle (1867–1962), who taught zoology at Harvard, was on the executive committee of the American Society of Naturalists.

21. H. G. Wells, *The Future in America: A search after Realities* (1906) and *In the Days of the Comet* (1906).

CHAPTER 13

1. James gave his lectures at Columbia University from 29 January to 8 February 1907. D. S. Miller was then teaching at Columbia.

2. James retired from teaching at Harvard on 22 January 1907.

3. Henry Guy Walters (1856–1921), a writer, came to Boston from London in 1876. He seems to be the person (under the pseudonym "Albert Le Baron") James wrote about in his article "A Case of Psychic Automatism," *Proceedings of the English S. P. R.* 12 (1896):277–79. This letter is at Rutgers University.

4. Jane Addams, *Newer Ideals of Peace* (1907). The reference is to Edward Carpenter.

5. Schiller's *Studies in Humanism* appeared in February. Schiller, "The Madness of the Absolute," *Journal of Philosophy* 4 (3 January 1907):18–21.

6. James, "A Defence of Pragmatism: I. Its Mediating Office," *Popular Science Monthly* 70 (March 1907):193–206; "A Defence of Pragmatism: II. What Pragmatism Means," ibid. (April):351–64. James's presidential address "The Energies of Men" also appeared in *Science* 25 (1907):321–32.

7. "C. S. P." are the initials of Charles Sanders Peirce.

8. Thomas Raynesford Lounsbury (1838–1915) was a famous Shakespeare scholar at Yale University, where James's letters to him are preserved.

9. M. W. Calkins, *The Persistent Problems of Philosophy* (1907).

10. This letter was shown to Mr. Kallen, and he saw no reason why it should not be published. Schiller, "Mr. Bradley's Theory of Truth," *Mind* 16 (July 1907):401–9. J. Dewey, "Reality and the Criterion for the Truth of Ideas," ibid., pp. 317–42.

11. Henry Smith Pritchett (1857–1939) was president of the Carnegie Foundation for the Advancement of Teaching (1906–30).

12. G. Papini, "Introduzione al Pragmatismo," *Leonardo* (February 1907) was translated by Katharine Royce as "What Pragmatism Is Like," *Popular Science Monthly* 71 (October 1907):351–58. The Seventh International Zoological Congress met in Boston, 19–24 August 1907.

13. James did not give another course of lectures at Columbia University.

14. Schiller, "Pragmatism versus Skepticism," *Journal of Philosophy* 4 n. 18 (29 August 1907):482–87; John E. Russell, "A Last Word to Dr. Schiller," ibid., pp. 487–90; Schiller, "Ultima Ratio," ibid., pp. 490–94.

15. Kallen reviewed James's *Pragmatism* in the *Boston Evening Transcript*, 21 September 1907. James refers to the distinction between the propositions "all good ideas are true" and "some good ideas are true."

16. Schiller reviewed James's *Pragmatism* in *Mind* 16 (October 1907):598–604. Wilhelm Jerusalem (1854–1923) taught philosophy at the University of Vienna. Stout reviewed Schiller's *Studies in Humanism* in the same issue of *Mind*, pp. 578–88. G. E. Moore did not review *Studies* in the *Saturday Review*. The second half of this letter is in the possession of Alan K. Stout. James, "A Word More about Truth," *Journal of Philosophy* 4, n. 15 (18 July 1907):396–406.

17. C. S. Peirce's "original article" was "How to Make Our Ideas Clear" in the *Popular Science Monthly* (January 1878). Schiller reviewed J. S. Mackenzie's *Lectures on Humanism* in *Mind* 16 (October 1907). Schiller, "Freedom and Responsibility," *Oxford and Cambridge Review* n. 2 (1907):41–73. David Leslie Murray, *Pragmatism* (London, 1912). Schiller wrote the preface.

18. C. M. Bakewell reviewed *Pragmatism* in the *Philosophical Review* 16 (November 1907):624–34.

19. In late December James went to Cornell University to attend the annual meeting of the Philosophical Association. He was a member of a symposium on the topic of truth.

CHAPTER 14

1. The title of the "discussion" was "The Meaning and Criterion of Truth." The other four participants were: J. E. Creighton, C. M. Bakewell, J. G. Hibben, and C. A. Strong. Abstracts of this discussion were published in the *Philosophical Review* 17 (April 1908):180–86. The "paper" James enclosed was an early version of "Truth versus Truthfulness," which later appeared in the *Journal of Philosophy* 5 n. 7 (26 March 1908):179–81. Norman Kemp Smith (1872–1958) taught logic and metaphysics at the University of Edinburgh (1919–45). Richard Avenarius (1843–96) taught philosophy at the University of Zurich. James had sent to Schiller the proof of his article, "The Pragmatist Account of Truth and Its Misunderstanders," which was published in the *Philosophical Review* 17 (January 1908):1–17.

2. "The paper on truth" was "Truth versus Truthfulness." Kallen showed this version to Bertrand Russell, whose comments on it are also found among Kallen's Papers in the American Jewish Archives. The year 1907 is an obvious slip of the pen, because Kallen did not go to Oxford until early October 1907. Bertrand Russell wrote "Transatlantic Truth," *Albany Review* 2 n. 10 (January 1908).

3. The "longer statement" is again "Truth versus Truthfulness." J. McT. E. McTaggart reviewed *Pragmatism* in *Mind* 17 (January 1908):104–9.

4. Wister had sent James a letter from Walters, to which Wister added the note: "It's inexpedient to whistle to a lost dog unless you are prepared to house him." Walters wrote under the pseudonyms "Gay Waters" and "Salvarona." He was listed as a member of the American S. P. R. from Langhorne, Pennsylvania, in 1907.

5. This post card is dated from the date on the postal cancellation stamp. A. O. Lovejoy, "Thirteen Pragmatisms, Part I," *Journal of Philosophy* 5 n. 1 (2 January 1908):5–12. Part 2, *Journal of Philosophy*, 5 n. 3 (16 January 1908):29–39.

6. James, "On the Function of Cognition," *Mind* o.s. 10 n. 37 (1885):27–44. G. E. Moore, "Prof. James's Pragmatism," *Proceedings of the Aristotelian Society* 8 (1907–8):33–77. Alexander Blair Thaw (1860–1937) was a Harvard M.D. in 1886, a member of the S. P. R., a poet and, with his wife, Florence, lived many years abroad. Alexius Meinong (1853–1920) taught at the University of Graz, Austria (1882–1920).

7. Thilly was an associate editor of the *Philosophical Review*.

8. M. W. Calkins, "Psychology as Science of Self: Part I, Is the Self Body or Has it Body ?", *Journal of Philosophy* 5 n. 1 (2 January 1908):12–20; Part II, "The Nature of the Self," ibid., (30 January 1908):64–68. In the *Psychological Bulletin* 5 n. 1. (15 January 1908):27–30, appeared Calkin's discussion of W. B. Pillsbury's (1872–1960) address, "The Ego and Empirical Psychology," as president of the Western Philosophical Association. This letter is incomplete.

9. Lovejoy, "Pragmatism and Theology," *American Journal of Theology* 12 (1908):116–43. The revision of James's "remarks at Cornell" appeared as "The Meaning of the Word 'Truth'," when privately printed.

10. Schiller, "Examination versus Research," *Nature* 77 (February 1908):322–24.

11. Schiller, "The Tribulations of Truth," *Albany Review* 2 (March 1908):624–34. This was in reply to Russell's article "Transatlantic Truth." Schiller, *Plato or Protagoras?* (Oxford, 1908).

12. H. G. Wells, *New Worlds for Old* (1908).

13. James delivered his lectures at Manchester College, Oxford, from 4 May to 28 May. On 12 May James received an honorary degree of Doctor of Science from Oxford University. The pages of the Stanford syllabus, which James requested, are printed as an appendix in James's *Some Problems of Philosophy* (1911). This is possibly Joseph Hartley Wicksteed (1842–1919), who was associated with Leeds University.

14. The evidence for the dating of this letter is the entry in James's Diary for this date: "Russell's Bagley Wood 1.30." Also, Russell's appointments diary has the entry: "Sunday 24th James's lunch." The original of this letter is at McMaster University. The editors of the new critical edition of James's *The Meaning of Truth* (Harvard: 1975):appendix 4, p. 299, published only the typed transcript which contains two crucial mistakes. That is why the letter merits reprinting here in addition to the dating of it.

15. Cf. Sandra Jobson Darroch, *Ottoline: The Life of Lady Ottoline Morrell* (1975). Newington House, Wallingford, Oxford, belonged to Miss Ethel Sands and not to Lady Ottoline, as Allen (p. 463) mistakenly states. The Jameses stayed with Miss Sands, 6–10 June. Prentice Mulford (1834–91) was a journalist. The letters to Lady Morrell are at the Humanities Research Center, The University of Texas at Austin.

16. The Jameses had dinner with Mrs. Fiske Warren on 5 June. She was an American from Boston, who studied philosophy at Oxford at this time.

17. Frank Byron Jevons (1858–1936) was professor of philosophy and the

principal of Bishop Hatfield's Hall. Allen (p. 462) incorrectly identified him as "William Stanley Jevons." George W. Kitchin (1827–1912) was dean of the Cathedral and Lord of Durham University. James received here the honorary degree of Doctor of Letters on 23 June. J. G. Piddington has already been noted.

18. For the humorous description of the meeting of James and Chesterton, cf. Wells, *Experiment in Autobiography* (1934), pp. 453–54. Margaret Mary ("Peggy") James had joined her parents on 27 June, after school was over at Bryn Mawr.

19. *Essays Philosophical and Psychological in Honor of William James* by his colleagues at Columbia University (N. Y., 1908). Dewey's paper was entitled "Does Reality Possess Practical Character?"

20. William McDougall (1871–1938), psychologist, taught both in England and in America.

21. Lovejoy, "Kant and the English Platonists." Felix Adler, "A Critique of Kant's Ethics." Ralph Cudworth (1617–88), philosopher of the Cambridge Platonist School. Arthur Collier (1680–1732), English philosopher. Hammond Lamont (1864–1909) was an editor of *Nation* (1906–09), where Lovejoy reviewed David Duncan's *The Life and Letters of Herbert Spencer* (1908).

22. The Third International Congress of Philosophy was held in Heidelberg, Germany, 1–5 September.

23. On Sunday, 27 September, James and his daughter had dinner with Schiller and others. On the next day, he lunched with Schiller, Knox, and Leonard Nelson, a young German philosopher.

24. James repeated his Oxford lectures at Harvard, 6–30 November. Henry Maurice Sheffer (1883–1964), Harvard Ph.D. in 1908, taught logic there until 1952.

25. Cattell asked James to read a paper on Darwin at the sixtieth meeting of the American Association for the Advancement of Science in Baltimore on 1 January 1909. James had become a member of this Association in 1902. He was a member of Section 1 (Social and Economic Science). Simon Nelson Patten (1852–1922) was a professor of political economy at the University of Pennsylvania (1888–1917). Robert Sessions Woodworth (1869–1962) was a psychologist at Columbia University.

26. Leland Ossian Howard (1857–1950), entomologist, was permanent secretary of the A.A.A.S. (1898–1920).

27. Dr. John Shaw Billings was responsible for nominations to membership in the National Academy of Sciences. Charles Sedgwick Minot (1852–1914) taught anatomy at Harvard. The reference is probably to Charles Pickering Bowditch (1842–1921), who was a student of and author on archeology. Jesse Walter Fewkes (1850–1930) was an ethnologist and archeologist.

CHAPTER 15

1. Carus, "Pragmatism," *Monist* 18 (July 1908):321–62; "A Postscript on Pragmatism: In Comment on Prof. James's Review of M. Hébert's Book,"

ibid. 19 (January 1909):85–94. James had reviewed Marcel Hébert, *Le Pragmatisme et ses Diverses Formes Anglo-Americaines*, in the *Journal of Philosophy* 5 n. 25 (3 December 1908):689–94.

2. T. M. Shackleford, "What Pragmatism Is, As I Understand It," *Popular Science Monthly* 75 (December 1909):571–85.

3. Schiller, "Humanism and Intuitionism," *Mind* 18 (January 1909): 125–28.

4. Schiller, "The Rationalistic Conception of Truth," *Proceedings of the Aristotelian Society* 9 (1908–9):85–99. James's Oxford lectures were published in April as *A Pluralistic Universe*. Alexander R. James ("Aleck") had joined his parents at Oxford and stayed on for a year of study.

5. Arnold Hague (1840–1917) was a geologist. This letter is at the National Academy of Sciences.

6. James Gibbons Huneker (1860–1921), American musician and critic, wrote *Egoists, A Book of Supermen* (1909). Joris Karl Huysmans (1848–1907) was a French novelist. The letters to Huneker are at the Historical Society of Pennsylvania.

7. Reverend Francis Howe Johnson (1835–1920) wrote *What Is Reality?* (1891). James, "On a Very Prevalent Abuse of Abstraction," *Popular Science Monthly* 74 (May 1909):485–93. When this article was reprinted in *The Meaning of Truth* (1909), the title was changed to "Abstractionism and 'Relativismus.'"

8. Jules de Gaultier de Laguionie (1858–1942) wrote "Pragmatisme," *Mercure de France* 77 (1 February 1909):408–28. "Max Stirner" was the pseudonym of Johann Kaspar Schmidt (1806–56). Friedrich Wilhelm Nietzsche (1844–1900) was a German philosopher.

9. Bertrand Russell, "Pragmatism," *Edinburgh Review* 209 (April 1909):363–88. James's letters to Russell are at McMaster University. James visited J. E. Russell at Williams College, 8–10 May. Witmer's criticism of James appeared in "Reviews and Criticisms," *Psychological Clinic* 2 (1909):285–97.

10. Kallen reviewed James's *A Pluralistic Universe* in the *Boston Evening Transcript*, 16 June 1909.

11. H. V. Knox, "Pragmatism: The Evolution of Truth," *Quarterly Review* 210 (April 1909):379–407. James's "collected writings on Truth" appeared in September as *The Meaning of Truth: A Sequel to Pragmatism*.

12. James began to write his planned *Introduction to Philosophy* on 28 March. He was elected, as has been noted, to Academies in Denmark, France, Germany, Italy, and England.

13. R. B. Perry, *The Moral Economy* (1909).

14. Heinrich Rickert (1863–1936) was a German philosopher.

15. Albert Schinz (1870–1943), born in Switzerland, was a professor of French literature at Bryn Mawr College (1899–1913). Afterwards he taught at Smith College and the University of Pennsylvania. He wrote *Anti-Pragmatisme* (Paris, 1909).

16. James attended an International Congress of scientists at Clark University, which was celebrating in this way its twenty-years' existence and achievements. In his 6 July 1909 letter to Hall, James wrote: "George B. Dorr has told me of your interest in Mrs. Piper. My report on the Hodgson

Communications that I have seen will doubtless interest you." Sir Oliver Lodge had also written a report on Mrs. Piper in the S. P. R. *Proceedings* (1909). Possibly the "Lodge affair" had to do with this report on Mrs. Piper.

17. John Whitehead (1850–1930), theologian, wrote "A Study of Swedenborg's Psychical States and Experiences," *New Church Review* 16 (July 1909). This letter is at the University of Virginia.

18. H. R. Marshall, *Consciousness* (1909). In his preface Marshall used the term "algedonic" to mean "any phase of pain [*algos* in Greek]-pleasure [*hédone* in Greek] experience." Beginning 9 November James paid nineteen visits to Mr. L. C. Strang for Christian Science treatments.

19. For James's letters to Knox, cf. Marjorie R. Kaufman, "William James's Letters to a Young Pragmatist," *Journal of the History of Ideas* 24 (1963):413–21. Andrew Seth Pringle-Pattison (1856–1931) taught philosophy at St. Andrews University (1887–91) and at Edinburgh University (1891–1919). James's "reply" to Bertrand Russell and Ralph George Hawtrey (1879–1975) is chapter 14 of James's *The Meaning of Truth*. G. T. Ladd, "The Confusion of Pragmatism," *Hibbert Journal* 7 (1909):784–801.

20. H. M. Kallen, "The Affiliations of Pragmatism," *Journal of Philosophy* 6 (25 November 1909):655–61.

21. Nicholas Murray Butler (1862–1947) was president of Columbia University (1901–45) and on the Executive Committee of *International Conciliation*, which was published monthly by the American Association for International Conciliation. James's "The Moral Equivalent of War," appeared as No. 27 (February 1910):3–20. This letter is at Columbia.

22. Mary Cadwalader married and divorced Frederic Rhinelander Jones. They lived in New York City. Arnold Lunn (1888–1974), author and leading English authority on skiing. While a philosophy student at Oxford University he edited *Isis*. In the 16 October 1909 issue, pp. 4–6, he narrated his fall and severe leg injury which occurred while climbing on Cader Idris in North Wales on 26 August. This letter is at Yale University.

23. Jane Addams, *Spirit of Youth and the City Streets* (1909).

24. Ellen Gertrude ("Bay") Emmet was born in 1875 to Ellen James Temple and Christopher Temple Emmet. She was a well-known painter and married William Blanchard Rand in 1911. The dinner for the presentation of James's portrait took place on 18 January 1910.

25. Hall wrote an Introduction, which mentions Mrs. Piper, to Amy E. Tanner's *Studies in Spiritism* (1910). Münsterberg attended two séances with Eusapia Palladino on 13 and 18 December. Robert Williams Wood (1868–1955) taught physics at the Johns Hopkins University. He attended the séances of 12 and 22 November. Cf. Hereward Carrington, *The American Séances With Eusapia Palladino* (New York, 1954).

CHAPTER 16

1. Maxwell J. Savage (1876–1948) was an Unitarian minister in Redlands, California, where James met him on a visit from Stanford University in 1906. This letter is at Princeton University.

2. Mrs. Fiske (Gretchen Osgood) Warren, "A Philosophical Aspect of Science," *Monist* 20 (April 1910):217–30.

3. A. Lawrence Lowell (1856–1943) succeeded Eliot as president of Harvard in October 1909. James graduated from the Lawrence Scientific School of Harvard. George Bucknam Dorr (1853–1944) was very active in the field of psychical research.

4. Royce, "The Problem of Truth in the Light of Recent Discussion," *Proceedings of the Heidelberg Congress*, pp. 62–90. H. C. Sturt wrote *The Idea of a Free Church* (1909).

5. James, "Bradley or Bergson," *Journal of Philosophy* 7 n. 2 (20 January 1910):29–33. James is referring to a chapter in his planned *Introduction to Philosophy* textbook, which was published posthumously in 1911 as *Some Problems of Philosophy: A Beginning of an Introduction to Philosophy*. Schiller, "Thought and Immediacy," *Journal of Philosophy* 3 n. 9 (26 April 1906):234–37.

6. Münsterberg, "My Friends, the Spiritualists," *Metropolitan Magazine* (February 1910). James himself had visited Eusapia along with Carrington on 12 January. Allen, p. 471, incorrectly says it was on 11 January.

7. Horace Howard Furness (1833–1912) was a Shakespeare scholar and editor of his works. Owen Wister wrote *Philosophy 4* in 1903. Charles Eliot Norton (1827–1908) was professor of the history of art at Harvard. Frank Harris (1855–1931) wrote *The Man Shakespeare and His Tragic Life-Story* (1909). The two letters to Furness are at the University of Pennsylvania.

8. Schiller was a candidate for the Waynflete Professorship of Moral and Metaphysical Philosophy at Oxford. T. Herbert Warren (1853–1930) was vice chancellor of the university. He once visited James at Harvard. This letter is at the Bodleian Library.

9. Bertha King Post (1854–1920) descended from Ellen James (1800–1823). She married Franklin Bartlett in 1872. James refers to his recent election to the *Institut de France*. This letter is at Trinity College.

10. The background for this letter and the following two letters has been supplied by Rand B. Evans and myself in our article "The 1913 International Congress of Psychology: The American Congress That Wasn't," *American Psychologist* 33 (August 1978):711–23. C. H. Judd (1873–1946) taught psychology at Yale (1902–9) and at Chicago (1909–38). Émile Boutroux (1845–1921), a French philosopher, lectured at Harvard in March. Allen, p. 472, says it was February.

11. John B. Watson (1878–1958), psychologist, was secretary of the committee to plan the congress. James and Alice left for England on 29 March to visit his brother Henry, who was ill, and to visit Nauheim again.

12. John Alexander Smith (1863–1939), an Aristotelian scholar, held the Waynflete Professorship until 1936. The announcement of his appointment appeared in the *Journal of Philosophy* 7 (12 May 1910):280. Sydney Philip Waterlow (1878–1944) was a diplomat and friend of Henry James. Schiller reviewed *The Meaning of Truth* in *Mind* 19 (April 1910):258–63. "Teddy R." is the former president, Theodore Roosevelt, who with James was elected to the *Institute de France* (Academy of Moral and Political Sciences) on 22 January 1910.

13. Walter Boughton Pitkin (1878–1953) lectured in psychology in Co-

lumbia University until 1909. He then became a journalist. He wrote "James and Bergson," *Journal of Philosophy* 7 n. 9 (28 April 1910). Kallen, "James, Bergson and Mr. Pitkin," ibid., n. 13 (23 June 1910):353–57. Bergson, "A propos d'un Article de M. Pitkin," ibid., n. 14 (7 July 1910):385–88.

14. Edmund Jacobson, "The Relational Account of Truth," *Journal of Philosophy* 7 (12 May 1910):253–61.

15. James, "A Pluralistic Mystic," *Hibbert Journal* 8 (July 1910):739–59. This was the last article James ever wrote. It was devoted to his friend Benjamin Paul Blood (1832–1919).

16. Sir T. Percy Nunn (1870–1944), a professor of education, and Schiller discussed the topic "Are Secondary Qualities Independent of Perception?," in the *Proceedings of the Aristotelian Society* 10 (1909–10):218–31.

17. Lawrence Piersall Jacks (1860–1955) was editor of the *Hibbert Journal*.

18. This dictated letter is probably the last letter James composed. He died at Chocorua on 26 August 1910.

Name Index

Lovejoy, Arthur Oncken, 171, 465, 466, 473, 572 n. 3, 579 n. 21, 589 nn. 5, 9, 590 n. 21; letters 296, 336–37, 463, 470–71, 487–88

Lowell, A. Lawrence, 536, 593 n. 3

Lowell, Josephine Shaw (Mrs. Charles Russell), 581 n. 20; letter, 324–25

Lunn, Arnold, 527, 592 n. 22

Lutoslawski, Wincenty, 238, 570 n. 8, 572 n. 5, 573 n. 19, 576 n. 19; letters, 147, 173–74, 195–96, 212–13, 261–62, 291–92, 337–38, 456

Mackail, John William, 576 n. 19

Mackenzie, James, 557

Mackenzie, J. S., 414, 454, 586 n. 14

Mackenzie, Kenneth, 564 n. 3; letter, 68

Macmillan and Co., 98, 133; letters, 201–2, 295

McCosh, James, 50, 60, 563 n. 19, 564 n. 28

McDougall, William, 487, 489, 590 n. 20

McGilvary, Evander Bradley, 234, 575 n. 15

McKinley, William, 149, 570 n. 9

McLennan, John Ferguson, 46, 562–63 n. 17

McTaggart, John McTaggart Ellis, 293, 463, 465, 466, 579 n. 17, 588 n. 3

Mach, Ernst, 394, 585 n. 2

Maeterlinck, Maurice, 241–42, 576 n. 20

Marseilles, Charles, 561 n. 3; letters, 29, 30, 31, 55

Marshall, Henry Rutgers, 106, 362, 364, 565 nn. 9, 10, 567 n. 4, 569 nn. 30, 32, 571 n. 16, 573 n. 13, 579 n. 14, 582 n. 18, 584 n. 18, 592 n. 18, letters, 79–80, 81, 116–17, 131–32, 133–34, 157, 184–85, 219–20, 290, 297–98, 301, 303, 356, 363, 382–83, 387–88, 523

Marvin, Frederic Rowland, 582 n. 16; letter, 354

Marvin, Walter Taylor, 580 n. 11; letters, 314–15, 376–77

Matteucci, Carlo, 79, 565 n. 9

May, Joseph, 107, 567 n. 5

Mead, Edwin Doak, 57, 563–64 n. 25

Mead, George Herbert, 316, 580 n. 12

Meinong, Alexius, 467, 589 n. 6

Merriman, Daniel, 177–78, 384, 572 n. 6

Merriman, Helen Bigelow, 561 n. 2, 572 n. 6; letters, 28, 175–78

Merriman, Roger B., 188, 573 n. 15

Meyer, Adolf, 573 n. 10; letters, 181, 269–70

Mezes, Sidney Edward, 60, 311, 564 n. 28

Miller, Dickenson Sergeant, 95, 120, 125, 181, 184, 187, 193, 199, 208, 214, 229, 235, 252, 334, 338–40, 340, 341–42, 345, 362, 370, 377, 389, 429, 459, 486, 549, 566 n. 22, 569 n. 23, 573 n. 13, 581 n. 5, 587 n. 1

Minot, Charles Sedgwick, 495, 590 n. 27

Montague, William Pepperell, 171, 182, 234, 572 n. 3

Moore, Addison Webster, 310, 364, 580 n. 8

Moore, George Edward, 345, 451, 466, 472, 513–14, 581–82 n. 7, 588 n. 16, 589 n. 6

Morgan, C. Lloyd, 354, 582 n. 15

Morrell, Ottoline Lady, 589 n. 15; letters, 478–79. 491–92

Moutier, Alexandre, 551, 554

Mulford, Prentice, 478, 589 n. 15

Müller, F. Max, 196, 573 n. 19

Müller, Georg Elias, 82, 565 n. 11

Münsterberg, Hugo, 87, 98, 105, 112, 116, 120, 127, 133, 135, 140, 142, 143, 146, 149, 151, 154, 159, 161, 163, 179, 186, 190, 192, 198, 200, 204, 205, 208, 218, 222, 235, 239, 242, 243, 275, 308, 312, 336, 339, 340, 341, 344, 365, 385, 388, 474, 487, 529, 539, 545, 547, 565 n. 12, 568 n. 17, 569 n. 31, 570 n. 7, 571 nn. 12, 19, 573 n. 15, 574 nn. 31, 28, 575 n. 17, 581 n. 4, 592 n. 25, 593 n. 6; letters, 83–85, 206–7

Murray, David Leslie, 454, 588 n. 17

Myers, Frederic William Henry, 87, 219, 220, 221, 246, 247, 250, 255, 276, 292, 309, 335, 364, 369, 565 n. 13, 579 n. 16

Nelson, Leonard, 590 n. 23

Nevius, John L., 569 n. 28

Newcomb, Simon, 562 n. 10; letters, 36–37, 40–41, 70

Nichols, Herbert, 85, 105, 119, 120, 134, 135, 149, 565 n. 12, 569 n. 33, 570 n. 10

Nietzsche, Friedrich Wilhelm, 507, 591 n. 8

Noiré, Ludwig, 196

Norton, Charles Eliot, 242, 540, 593 n. 7

Norton, Grace, 121, 568 n. 19, 576 n. 20; letter, 240–42

Norton, Rupert, 374, 375, 583–84 n. 11
Nunn, Sir T. Percy, 556, 594 n. 16
Nutt, Arthur Chase, 192, 573 n. 17

Ochorowicz, Jules, 49, 563 n. 18
Olney, Richard, 136, 569–70 n. 34
Ormond, Alexander Thomas, 370, 583 n. 7
Osler, William, 335, 581 n. 3
Osten-Sacken, Baron Carl Romanovich, 239, 576 n. 19
Ostwald, Wilhelm, 292, 353, 368, 377, 437, 579 n. 16, 583 n. 5
Otis, Maj. Gen. Elwell Stephen, 324, 581 n. 20

Palladino, Eusapia, 529, 539, 592 n. 25
Palmer, George Herbert, 27, 46, 60, 153, 160, 164, 171, 182, 204, 208, 230, 274, 311, 389, 409, 561 n. 1; letter, 307–8
Papini, Giovanni, 425, 447, 449, 454, 507, 587 n. 12
Parker, George Howard, 146, 570 n. 7
Patten, Simon Nelson, 492, 590 n. 25
Patton, Francis Landey, 60, 564 n. 28
Paulhan, Frédéric, 108, 109, 568 n. 7
Paulsen, Friedrich, 163, 358, 401, 418, 571 n. 22, 585 n. 6
Peabody, Francis Greenwood, 52, 563 n. 20
Peirce, Charles Sanders, 51, 256, 287, 289, 301, 305, 438, 452, 454, 563 n. 19, 572 n. 5, 576 n. 8, 580 n. 4, 584 n. 13, 588 n. 17
Peirce, Herbert Henry Davis, 201
Perkins, C. H., 323, 581 n. 19
Perry, Ralph Barton, 208, 224, 311, 370, 390, 445, 571–72 n. 23, 573 n. 18, 575 n. 12, 576 n. 3, 578 n. 2, 582 n. 11, 585 n. 25, 586 n. 10, 591 n. 13; letters, 193, 213–15, 218, 226, 228–30, 230–31, 249, 251–52, 257–58, 270, 274–75, 348, 402–4, 404–6, 407, 409–10, 418, 490, 516–17, 528–29, 536, 553, 554–55
Perry, Thomas Sergeant, 565 n. 8; letter, 78
Peterson, James B., 161–62, 178, 571 n. 20, 572 n. 7
Pflüger, Eduard, 45, 562 n. 16
Phillips, Wendell, 51, 563 n. 20
Picot, Georges, letter, 170
Piddington, John George (née Smith), 255, 292, 483, 557, 576 n. 7
Pierce, Arthur Henry, 127, 231, 569 n. 25, 575 n. 13

Pillon, Francois, 96, 566 n. 23
Pillsbury, Walter Bowers, 469, 545, 546, 589 n. 8
Piper, Leonore E., 179, 189, 198, 276, 415, 572 n. 8, 591–92 n. 16
Pitkin, Walter Boughton, 552, 558, 593–94 n. 13
Plato, 78, 147, 174, 261, 291, 400, 401, 415
Plutarch, 543
Podmore, Frank, 335
Poincaré, Henri, 394, 585 n. 2
Preyer, Wilhelm Thierry, 37, 562 n. 10
Prince, Katharine James, 561 n. 6; letters, 32–33, 33–34, 35–36, 42–44
Prince, Morton, 322, 588 n. 17
Prince, William Henry, 561 n. 6
Pringle-Pattison, A. Seth, 524, 592 n. 19
Pritchett, Henry Smith, 444, 587 n. 11
Putnam, James J., 35, 213, 257, 295, 464, 561 n. 8

Rashdall, Hastings, 333, 581 n. 3
Read, Carveth, 384, 584 n. 19
Reid, George Archdall O'Brien, 578 n. 10; letter, 285–86
Remsen, Ira, 39, 408, 562 n. 11
Renouvier, Charles Bernard, 97, 228, 336, 566 n. 23
Rhodes, Cecil John, 278, 578 n. 5
Richardson, Leon Joseph, 61, 564 n. 28
Richet, Charles, 220, 574–75 n. 5
Rickert, Heinrich, 518, 591 n. 14
Rieber, Charles Henry, 340, 366, 367, 581 n. 6, 583 n. 3
Robertson, George Croom, 51, 563 n. 19
Rodgers, Katherine and Henrietta, 371, 417, 566 n. 17, 586 n. 18; letters, 90–91, 193–94, 197, 215–16, 227, 253, 258, 263–64, 329–30, 350–51, 374, 374–75, 421–22, 430–32, 511–12
Rogers, David Camp, 311, 580 n. 9
Roosevelt, Pres. Theodore, 550, 593 n. 12
Ross, Dorothy, 562 n. 16
Ross, George W., 59, 60, 564 n. 26; letter, 58
Rowland, Henry Augustus, 227, 575 n. 11
Royce, Josiah, 60, 84, 104, 132, 140, 151, 160, 169, 172, 190, 201, 208, 214, 217, 226, 252, 270, 274, 287, 303, 312, 332, 335, 336, 345, 370, 401, 442, 446, 447, 466, 495, 510, 537, 564 n. 28,

· 601 ·

Strong, Charles Augustus, 39, 47, 295, 321, 341, 369, 371, 382, 425, 451, 459, 466, 489, 515, 551, 562 n. 11, 579 n. 20, 581 n. 6, 588 n. 1
Strouse, Jean, 564 n. 2
Stumpf, Carl, 121, 127, 568 n. 19
Sturt, Henry Cecil, 346, 414, 415, 537, 578 n. 6, 593 n. 4
Sully, James, 204, 574 n. 26
Swedenborg, Emanuel, 522

Tanner, Amy E., 592 n. 25
Taylor, Alfred Edward, 344, 362, 382, 394, 397, 414, 444, 460, 506, 547, 581–82 n. 7, 585 n. 4
Thaw, Alexander Blair, 467, 589 n. 6
Thilly, Frank, 571 n. 22, 589 n. 7; letters, 163–64, 468
Thomas, Martha Carey, 563–64 n. 25; letters, 57, 125, 128–29, 282
Thompson, Mrs. (printer), letter, 274
Thompson, Mrs. R., 255, 576 n. 7
Thorndike, Edward Lee, 312, 429, 580 n. 10
Thorne, Bezly, 208
Tiffany, Louis Comfort, 117, 568 n. 14
Titchener, Edward Bradford, 122–23, 136, 152, 179, 312, 545, 547, 568 n. 20, 569 n. 34, 572 n. 8, 573 nn. 16, 17; letters, 131, 185–86, 188–90, 191–92, 546
Todd, David Peck, 570 n. 5; letter, 144
Towianski, Andrzej, 212, 574 n. 1
Tweedy, Edmund, 36, 561 n. 9

Van Hise, Charles Richard, 408, 586 n. 9
Van Winkle, Edgar B., 579 n. 3; letter, 304
Veblen, Thorstein Bunde, 241, 576 n. 20
Villari, Pasquale, letter, 316–17

Walters, Henry Guy, 464, 587 n. 3, 588 n. 4; letter, 433
Ward, James, 89, 199, 280, 371, 489, 541, 566 n. 16, 574 n. 21
Ward, Thomas W., 99
Warren, Mrs. Fiske, 479, 535, 589 n. 16, 593 n. 2

Warren, Howard C., 570 n. 34
Warren, T. Herbert, 593 n. 8; letter, 541–42
Washburn, Margaret Floy, 313, 362, 580 n. 10
Waterlow, Sidney Philip, 549, 593 n. 12
Watson, John B., 546, 593 n. 11
Welby, Victoria Lady, 583 n. 10; letter, 373
Wells, Herbert George, 285, 425, 434, 478 n. 10, 587 n. 21, 589 n. 12, 590 n. 18; letters, 426, 475–76, 483–84, 484–85
Wendell, Barrett, 374, 583 n. 8
West, Andrew Fleming, 408, 586 n. 9
Wheeler, Benjamin Ide, 234, 352, 408, 575 n. 15, 582 n. 12
Whipple, L. E., 567 n. 2
Whitehead, John, 592 n. 17; letter, 522
Whitman, Sarah Helen, 576 n. 2; letter 247–48
Wicksteed, Joseph Hartley, 476, 589 n. 13
Wiener, Leo, 164, 571 n. 22
Wilmarth, Mary J., 584 n. 15; letter, 378
Wister, Owen, 247, 540, 576 n. 2, 588 n. 4, 593 n. 7; letters, 317–18, 464
Witmer, Lightner, 152, 312, 508, 571 n. 12, 591 n. 9
Wood, Robert Williams, 530, 592 n. 25
Woodbridge, Frederick James Eugene, 362, 366, 383, 384, 401, 406, 463, 509–10, 548, 583 n. 1
Woods, James Houghton, 339, 581 n. 5
Woodworth, Robert Sessions, 492, 590 n. 25
Woolsey, Theodore S., 408, 586 n. 9
Worcester, W. L., 115, 568 n. 13
Wormeley, Katherine Prescott, 350, 582 n. 13
Wundt, Wilhelm, 123, 227, 568 n. 20
Wyatt, Edith Franklin, 267, 577 n. 16

Young, George Paxton, 59, 60, 564 n. 27

Zeuthen, Hieronymus Georg, 580 n. 7; letter, 308